Convergences

Inventories of the Present

Edward W. Said, General Editor

Frontispiece: Canaletto, *Campo S. Vidal and Santa Maria della Carita* ('The Stonemason's Yard'). An unusal picture in that it shows Venetian labour as well as Venetian spectacle – Venice as 'quarry' as well as Venice as 'palace'. (Reproduced by courtesy of the Trustees of The National Gallery, London)

AMHL

Venice Desired

Tony Tanner

Harvard University Press
Cambridge, Massachusetts
1992

Printed in Great Britain
10 9 8 7 6 5 4 3 2 1

This book is printed on acid-free paper, and its binding materials have been chosen for strength and durability.

Library of Congress Cataloging-in-Publication Data

Tanner, Tony.
Venice desired/Tony Tanner
p. cm. – (Convergences)
Includes bibliographical references and index.
ISBN 0-647-93312-5 (acid-free paper)
1. Venice (Italy) in literature. 2. Literature, Modern – 19th century – History and criticism. 3. Literature, Modern – 20th century – History and criticism. I. Title. II. Series: Convergences (Cambridge, Mass.)
PN56.3. V4T36 1992b
809'. 93324531 – dc20 91-37758
CIP

Contents

Preface

In the Preface he wrote for the New York edition for the volume containing *Portrait of a Lady*, Henry James recalled writing much of it in Venice.

> I had rooms on Riva Schiavoni, at the top of a house near the passage leading off to San Zaccaria; the waterside life, the wondrous lagoon spread before me, and the ceaseless human chatter of Venice came in at my windows, to which I seem to myself to have been constantly driven, in the fruitless fidget of composition, as if to see whether, out in the blue channel, the ship of some right suggestion, of some better phrase, of the next happy twist of my subject, the next true touch for my canvas, mightn't come into sight. But I recall vividly enough that the response most elicited, in general, to these restless appeals was the rather grim admonition that romantic and historic sites, such as the land of Italy abounds in, offer the artist a questionable aid to concentration when they themselves are not to be the subject of it. They are too rich in their own life and too charged with their own meanings merely to help him out with a lame phrase; they draw him away from his small question to their own greater ones; so that, after a little, he feels, while thus yearning toward them in his difficulty, as if he were asking an army of glorious veterans to help him arrest a peddler who has given him the wrong change.[1]

This is a book about Venice and writing, and their interaction in the work of a number of writers ranging from Byron to Jean-Paul Sartre. It primarily concerns the works in which, in one way or another, for one reason or another, they seek to address the great romantic and historic site of Venice directly – attempt, using James's image, to arrest the 'army of glorious veterans' itself. The extent to which the city sent them 'ships of some right suggestion' or confronted them with 'grim admonitions' will be a matter for recurring consideration.

My choice of writers – intended to cover the period of, roughly, late Romanticism to late modernism – must justify itself, or simply fail to do so. I am aware of how much and how many I have left out. What about – might come a legitimate voice – Wordsworth's sonnets; Shelley's poems and letters; Samuel Rogers; Goethe's Venetian Epigrams; Stendhal's Journals; Schiller's 'Ghost Seer'; Balzac's *Facino Cane* ('Venise est une belle ville, j'ai toujours eu la fantasie d'y aller' – Proust must have read *that*); Clough's *Dipsychus*; Wilkie Collins's 'That Haunted Hotel'; Nietzsche's Venetian lyric (in *Ecce Homo*: 'When I seek another word for music, I always find only the word Venice'); come to that, Wagner and Liszt's Venetian music; Baron Corvo's 'Desire and Pursuit of the Whole'; d'Annunzio, and Marinetti's Futurist Manifesto ('forget Venice'); Simone Weil's 'Venise Salvagé'; Ernest Hemingway's *Across the River and into the Trees*; Italo Calvino's *Invisible Cities* ('Every time I describe a city I am saying something about Venice'); Robert Duncan's long 'Venice' poem; Mary McCarthy's 'Venice Observed'; or even Ian MacEwan's *Comfort of Strangers*, or Robert Coover's *Pinocchio in Venice*; etc.? To which I can only reply: I know, I know. To the extent that it is felt this book is defaced by its omissions, I stand condemned. My only defence is that, such is the wealth and range of literary material concerning Venice, any book addressing the topic of Venice and writing runs the risk of producing an anthology with a lame interlinking commentary – a hazard which some may feel I have myself but imperfectly avoided. Nevertheless, I must stand by my conviction that the works I have considered constitute, in sum, the most interesting writing to have been, in one way or another, generated by the incomparable city.

All quotations from languages other than English I have given in translation, except where it seemed helpful to have the original word or phrase included. In the case of quotations from Dante which were particularly important to Ruskin and Pound, I have included the original Italian as well as a translation.

I must start by thanking my old friend, Sergio Perosa, who invited me to a conference on 'Henry James and Venice' in 1985 and thus, indirectly, helped to initiate the present work. In addition to him I must thank other Venetian friends who have all been helpful in different ways and who all help to make my too rare visits to their city such a rich pleasure – among others, then, Sergio and Alberta Persoa, Gilberto Sacerdoti, Enrica Villari, Rosella Zorzi, Alide Cagidemetrio. Barbara Lanati in Turin gave me some timely help as well as unstinting hospitality. Bernard Schlurick from Geneva engaged me in some particularly stimulating and helpful conversations and communications concerning Proust and, among other things, gave me my third epigraph. I have enjoyed, and profited from, regular discussions with Clive Wilmer for some time now, and he has been exceptionally generous with his immense knowledge of both primary and secondary material concerning Ruskin and Pound. My title, I seem to remember, came out of a conversation with Keith Hopkins – in any case, it is a pleasure here to acknowledge how much I enjoy our regular exchanges, as I do those with Iain Fenlon, another valued colleague. I owe special thanks to Diego Gambetta who has been a good and helpful friend throughout the writing of this book, and has benignly helped me through my exceptionally maladroit entry into the mysteries – for me – of the word-processor. Special thanks also to Pascal Boyer who instantly and uncomplainingly filled the same role when Diego was unavailable. I should add that my debt to both these last-named concerns more than the merely technical and mechanical, since they furnish me with some of my most constantly congenial company here at King's College. Daniel Pick has made helpful suggestions from time to time and is always stimulating company, and I have enjoyed and profited from the discussions of Venice and Ruskin I have had with my research student, Robert MacIntosh. Special thanks to that princely polymath Richard Macksey, both for his own work on Ruskin and Proust and his generosity to my own efforts. Thanks, also, to Paddy O'Donovan for courteous textual help and good conversation. I owe a more diffuse debt to Frank Kermode simply for the ongoing pleasure of his company in Cambridge, a company which is, among other things, a constant education and enrichment. Special thanks to my copy-editor, Linden Stafford, who caught my solecisms, banished my hyphens, shrank my capitals and in general cleaned me up with a vigilant meticulousness for which I am very grateful. All remaining errors are my own. Special thanks, also, to my editor Andrew McNeillie who was not only exceptionally helpful but also manifested an encouraging enthusiasm such as warms an author's heart. Thanks, too, to the editors at Blackwell – Philip Carpenter, who most encouragingly started me off; and Stephan Chambers, who so expeditiously saw me through. Many thanks also to the librarian and staff at King's College who with unfailing courtesy and promptness have brought me the books I wanted (no small matter when it involves the complete works of Ruskin).

Since Nadia Fusini, who has been a constant encouragement and help, was the inspirer of this book, so she is the recipient.

Acknowledgements

The author and publisher wish to acknowledge the following: Faber & Faber Ltd and New Directions Publishing Corporation for extracts from *The Cantos of Ezra Pound* by Ezra Pound. Copyright © 1934, 1937, 1948, 1962 by Ezra Pound; and 'Night Litany' from *Collected Early Poems* by Ezra Pound, Faber and Faber, and *Personae* by Ezra Pound, New Directions, Copyright © 1926 by Ezra Pound; Random Century Group for extracts from *Remembrance of Things Past Vol. III* by Marcel Proust, trans. C. K. S. Moncrieff and T. Kilmartin, Chatto and Windus, 1981; The University of Arkansas Press for an extract from *The Autobiography of John Gould Fletcher.* Copyright © 1988 by The University of Arkansas Press.

Every effort has been made to trace all the copyright holders, but if any have been inadvertently overlooked the publishers will be pleased to make the necessary arrangement at the first opportunity.

List of Illustrations

Plates between pages (240–241)

The publishers apologize for any errors or omissions in the above list and would be grateful to be notified of any corrections that should be incorporated in the next edition or reprint of this book.

This book is for Nadia – absolutely.

You know I promised them no Romance, I promised them stones. Not even bread. I do not *feel* any Romance in Venice. It is simply a heap of ruins.

John Ruskin, letter to his father

this amphibious city – this Phocaea, or sea-dog of towns, – looking with soft human eyes at you from the sand, Proteus himself latent in the salt-smelling skin of her

John Ruskin, *St Mark's Rest*

je ne dis pas Venise par hasard

Marcel Proust, *A la recherche du temps perdu*

1

Introduction: Some Exquisite Sea-Thing

THE concluding lines of W. H. Auden's poem, 'In Memory of Sigmund Freud', read:

> One rational voice is dumb: over a grave
> The household of impulse mourns one dearly loved.
>   Sad is Eros, builder of cities,
>   And weeping anarchic Aphrodite.[1]

Auden probably has in mind such passages as the following from Freud's *Civilization and its Discontents*: the 'peculiar process' of culture 'proves to be in the service of Eros, which aims at binding together single human individuals, then families, then tribes, races, nations, into one great unit, that of humanity. Why this has to be done we do not know; it is simply the work of Eros.'[2] As against, and opposed to, the 'instincts of destruction', Eros is constructive, and both urges and promotes the building and extending of the containing structures and edifices of civilization. There is the possibility of a paradox, not to say contradiction, in such a proposition, as Auden recognizes by giving 'impulse' a 'household', and making the anarchic Aphrodite mourn alongside Eros the 'builder'. And this of course is recognized by Freud as well. The 'core' of Eros's being is 'his aim of making one out of many; but when he has achieved it in the proverbial way through the love of two human beings, he is not willing to go further.'[3] Again: 'the interrelations between love and culture lost their simplicity as development proceeds. On the one hand, love opposes the interests of culture; on the other, culture menaces love with grievous restrictions.'[4] Eros, it would seem, is not originally a 'builder of cities'; he has, as it were, to be co-opted. In pursuit of its larger communal 'bindings', culture has to 'levy energy from sexuality'. Clearly, to operate with such vast and vague abstractions and personifications as 'culture' and 'Eros' can yield little in the way of precise thinking. But the always possibly paradoxical relationship between desire and the city is one which I simply want to state at the outset: desire as the force that engenders, maintains and extends the city, and as the drive which may oppose and subvert it; conversely, the city as a site which engenders, maintains and extends desire, and as a complex of contingencies, constraints and compulsions which may thwart or pervert it.

Let us consider a rather different version of the origin of the city. This is from Plutarch's life of Theseus, the legendary founder of Athens:

> After Aegeus's death Theseus conceived a wonderful and far-reaching plan, which was nothing less than to concentrate the inhabitants of Attica into a capital. In this way he transformed them into one people belonging to one city, whereas until then they had lived in widely scatter-ed comunities, so that it was difficult to bring them together for the common interest, and indeed at times they even quarrelled and fought one another. So he now travelled around Attica and strove to convince them town by town and clan by clan. The common people and the poor responded at once to his appeal, while to the more influential classes he proposed a constitution without a king: there was to be a democracy, in which he would be no more than the commander of the army and guardian of the laws, while in other respects everyone would be on an equal footing.
>
> . . . He then proceeded to banish the town halls, council chambers, and magistracies in the various districts. To replace them he built a single town hall and senate house for the whole community on the site of the present acropolis, and he named the city Athens and created a Pan-Athenaic festival as a ceremony for the whole of Attica.[5]

Here, indeed, is the 'binding together' in a 'greater unity' the previously scattered, dispersed and latently hostile units or atoms which precede the city; only the agent in this version is not Eros, but a reasoning, persuading human author and authority who centralizes and organizes and names. This mythological version of the origin of Athens – for of course it has nothing to do with history – has much in common with the Socratic, ideal construction of the city in *The Republic*. And it is notable that this ideally conceived city attempts to *occlude* – or exclude, or abstract from – Eros. Here let me quote from *The City and Man* by Leo Strauss:

> The parallel of the city and the soul is based on a deliberate abstraction from *eros*, an abstraction characteristic of the *Republic*. This abstraction shows itself most strikingly in two facts: when Socrates mentions the fundamental human needs which give rise to human society, he is

> silent about the need for procreation, and when he describes the tyrant, he presents him as *Eros* incarnate. This is to say nothing of the fact that the *Republic* almost opens with a curse on *eros*. In the thematic discussion of the respective rank of spiritedness and desire, Socrates is silent about *eros*. It seems there is a tension between *eros* and the city and hence between *eros* and justice: only through the depreciation of *eros* can the city come into its own. *Eros* obeys its own laws, not the laws of the city however good: lovers are not necessarily fellow citizens (or fellow party-members); in the good city *eros* is simply subjected to the requirements of the city: only those are permitted to join each other for procreation who promise to bring forth the right kind of offspring. The abolition of privacy is a blow struck at *eros*. The city is not an erotic association although in a way it presupposed erotic associations. There is not an erotic class of the city as there are classes of rulers, warriors, and money-makers. The city does not procreate as it deliberates, wages war, and owns property. As far as possible, patriotism, dedication to the common good, justice must take the place of *eros*, and patriotism has a closer kinship to spiritedness, eagerness to fight, 'waspishness', indignation, and anger than to eros. Both the erotic association and the political association are exclusive, but they are exclusive in different ways: the lovers exclude themselves from the others (from 'the world') without opposition to the other or hate of the others, but the city cannot be said to seclude itself from 'the world': it separates itself from others by opposing or resisting them; the opposition of 'We and They' is essential to the political association.[6]

This is indeed the Platonic polis; but over against the abstract, reasoned, reasonable city (or city of reason) of Theseus and Socrates we may suggest, or fantasize, the concrete, desirable, desired city (or city of desire) of Eros – and Cain. For it is Cain, of course, who builds the first city in the Bible, and it could hardly be more intimately related and connected to procreation: 'Cain knew his wife, and she conceived and bore Enoch; and he built a city, and called the city after the name of his son, Enoch.' And Cain, as we know, is a cursed and banished murderer, a marked man condemned to be a 'vagrant' and a 'vagabond'. It seems strange that the fugitive, transgressive nomad should be the first builder of the city, though, if we think of the latent nomadism and transgressiveness of desire, Cain is perhaps as apt a builder as Eros. We are dealing here with metaphors, and, as Gerald Bruns suggests in an excellent article covering some of this ground, the Cain and Abel story is 'an allegory of desire against reason that figures the city explicitly in terms of nomads, transgressors, and the need to be nameless and invisible'.[7]

I quote Bruns again: 'over against the polis theory there is a metaphorics of the city which stresses wandering, vagrancy, anonymity, randomness, the underground, the outlaw, the fugitive, the slave, the alien, the streetwalker, the beggar, the trader, and the exile. Here the basic opposition would not be between the city and the country but between the polis and the labyrinth.'[8] We might say that reasoning man dreams the polis, while desiring man lives the labyrinth – but that, perhaps, is to succumb to an extreme of diagrammatic facility. Nevertheless, if there is one city, at once a magnificent polis *and* a literal labyrinth, which might fairly be said to demonstrate and embody and image forth the constructive consummation of reason *and* desire – Theseus and Eros working gloriously together – it would be Venice: a thousand-year triumph of rational legislation *and* aesthetic and sensual self-expression, self-creation – powerful, lovely, serene. *Serenissima.*

My interest, here, is in writing and the city; or, more concisely, writing the city. Unique in so many ways, Venice also seems unique in her relationship to writing. London has Dickens; Paris has Balzac; Petersburg has Dostoevsky; Vienna has Musil; Dublin has Joyce; Berlin has Döblin – and so one might go on. There simply is no comparable writer for – of, out of – Venice. (Goldoni was a Venetian, but his plays tell us very little of the city *qua* city.) The one great writer produced by Venice in the very period of its final dissolution and decline was – it is astonishingly appropriate – Casanova, who did not 'write' Venice so much as embody it. From one point of view, this is quite explicable: the genre of the city is, supremely, the novel, and Venice was fading out of history during the period in which the novel was evolving its mongrel identity. It effectively disappeared from history altogether in 1797 when the thousand-year republic was defeated by Napoleon, and later handed over to the Austrians. After that, it seems to exist as a curiously marooned spectacle. Literally marooned, of course – the city mysteriously growing out of the sea, the beautiful stones impossibly floating on water; but temporally marooned as well – stagnating outside of history (apart from a brief recrudescence of its old republican virtues and energies in 1848, when it held out longer than any of the other revolutions of that insurrectionary year).[9] But *as* spectacle – the beautiful city *par excellence*, the city of art, the city *as* art – and as spectacular example, as the greatest and richest and most splendid republic in the history of the world, now declined and fallen, Venice became an important, I would say central, site (a topos, a topic) for the European imagination. And more than any other city it is inextricably associated with desire. Desire of Venice, desire for Venice, desire in Venice – this is a crucial force and feature in European literature from Byron to Sartre, as this book will seek to show.

Venice is cited and variously described and deployed in literature at least from the fourteenth century. The earliest reference to Venice in English writing seems to occur in Sir John Mandeville's *Travels* (1356–7), in which it is likened to Cathay and invoked thus as a fabulous and exotic place. It was indeed the main point of embarkation for pilgrims and Crusaders, and many of these wrote of the magnificence of Venice and the richness of its trade and merchandise. Sir Roger Ascham is perhaps the first writer to identify Venice as a place, *the* place, of love, lechery, sensuality, prostitution, *as well as* a place of wise rulers and just laws (1570). Its citizens were notably free and, perhaps hence, notably licentious. This is an image – a perception, a projection – which has endured. There was a brothel in Elizabethan London called simply 'Venice'.

The fact that, in addition to being a powerful and enormously rich republic, Venice was effectively a police state with its notorious secret tribunals (the Council of Ten, the Council of Three); the fact of its famous masquerades and carnivals (six months of the year were carnival time by the eighteenth century); the fact of its labyrinthine little streets and canals and endless bridges; the uncanny silence of its gliding traffic; the supposed 'supersubtlety' of its agents and citizens – all these attributes composed an easily available scenario or imaginary topography for writers from afar. Watery, dark, silent; a place of sensuality and secrecy; masks and masquerading; duplicity and desire; an always possibly treacherous beauty; Othello and Shylock (and why *did* Shakespeare set his two plays with figures from marginalized groups – a black, a Jew – as protagonists, in Venice?); Volpone and greed; conspiracy and courtesans in Otway's *Venice Preserved* – all these associations made Venice an obvious setting for Gothic novels such as *The Mysteries of Udolpho* (Ann Radcliffe never visited Venice, but that is just the point – there is a 'Venice' compounded of just such reiterated association always to hand) and 'Monk' Lewis's *The Bravo of Venice.* But it also attracted much greater and more serious writers who broke the clichés and opened up entirely new possibilities in the process of writing Venice. The general point here is that Venice is not really ever written from the inside, but variously appropriated from without. And as it slips or falls out of history, Venice – the place, the name, the dream – seems to lend itself to, to attract a new variety of, appreciations, recuperations and dazzled hallucinations. In decay and decline (*particularly* in decay and decline), falling or sinking to ruins and fragments, yet saturated with secretive sexuality – thus emanating or suggesting a heady compound of death and desire – Venice becomes for many writers what it was, in anticipation, for Byron: 'the greenest island of my imagination'. When Byron left Venice two years later, it had become a 'sea Sodom'. Venice has a way of turning on her writerly admirers as no other city does.

In 1833, Emerson was in Venice and he wrote in his journal for 3 June:

> I am speedily satisfied with Venice. It is a great oddity, a city for beavers, but, to my thought, a most disagreeable residence. You feel always in prison, and solitary. Two persons may live months in adjoining streets and never meet, for you go about in gondolas, and all the gondolas are precisely alike, and the persons within commonly concealed; then there are no news rooms; except St Mark's Piazza, no place of public resort. It is as if you were always at sea. And though, for a short time, it is very luxurious to lie on the eider-down cushions of your gondola and read or talk or smoke, drawing to, now the cloth-lined shutter, now the Venetian blind, now the glass window, as you please, yet there is always a slight smell of bilgewater about the thing, and houses in the water remind one of a freshet and of desolation, anything but comfort. I soon had enough of it.[10]

One might call this the zero-sum response to Venice. And there is something more than comical in the spectacle of the sublimely non-social and serenely self-sequestering Emerson – draw the shutter, the blind, the window, as you please, indeed! – complaining about the obstacles to meeting people and lack of places for public mingling and congregating. It is a response which consists of a refusal to respond, and it is part of that defensive carapace sometimes worn by Americans when faced by the supreme product of European art and civilization. 'Because there is safety in derision' – Yeats's words apply perfectly to this syndrome which fights shy of being impressed, and takes shrinking refuge in gestures of deflation rather than opening up to the possibilities of delight. You can find it in Mark Twain, too. It is, one might say, one way of coping with the almost unhandleable amount of beauty with which Venice confronts pilgrim and tourist, and any 'innocent abroad', alike.

Somewhere near the opposite end of the spectrum, we might locate the response of another American, William Dean Howells. He – rather guiltily – spent the years of the American Civil War in Venice in the sinecure post of American Consul. With a lot of time on his hands, he familiarized himself thoroughly with the city and in addition to writing a novel with a Venetian setting, *A Foregone Conclusion*, he produced two volumes describing ***Venetian Life***. These consist of a series of low-keyed, slow-pulsed annotations of daily life in Venice – meals, clothes, shops, theatres, baptisms, marriages, funerals, holidays, and, yes, churches and pictures, the lagoon, and so on. As so often with Howells, the writing is honest, scrupulous and a little laboured – a sort of respectful itemizing. Lacking imagination himself, he was suspicious of its transforming, embellishing, amplifying (he would have said potentially mendacious) powers. For Howells, what you see is what you get, and what you get is what you write. The result is a mixture. Howells has a good eye for the prose of a place, and he certainly gives us what few other writers do – some sense of everyday life in nineteenth-century Venice. But in his decent, resolute way he manages to turn the poetry of the place into prose as well, and the result, it has to be said, is at times prosaic in the slightly pejorative sense. This is Venice with the magic left (or kept) out. It is a work which neither takes you there nor pulls you back. One has a slight sense of an opportunity missed. The place was perfect – a Venice entirely unwritten about; the time was right enough – just approaching the final years of the Austrian occupation; but it wasn't quite the right writer. It is an inside report but from an outside eye. At times you get the feeling that, mentally, Howells has not left small-town America. Yet, as he comes to leave, it does seem as though the place has reached and stirred him.

> Never had the city seemed so dream-like and unreal as in this light of farewell, – this tearful glimmer which our love and regret cast upon it. As in a maze, we haunted once more and for the last time the scenes we had known so long, and spent our final phantasmal evening in the Piazza; looked, through the moonlight, our mute adieu to islands and lagoons, to church and tower; and then returned to our own palace, and stood long upon the balconies that overhung the Grand Canal. There the future became as incredible and improbable as the past; and if we had often felt the incongruity of our coming to live in such a place, now, with ten-fold force, we felt the cruel absurdity of proposing to live anywhere else. We had become part of Venice; and how could such atoms of her fantastic personality ever mingle with the alien and unsympathetic world?[11]

But his very final worry is whether his landlord will 'embrace and kiss me, after the Italian manner'. Here is a worry indeed! But he is relieved – 'by a final inspiration they spared me the ordeal.' With his Anglo-Saxon-Puritan sensibility intact and, mercifully, unembraced, he will, in fact, be more at ease in that 'alien and unsympathetic world'. It is where he lives.

But it is the reaction of a third American, who neither takes the Emerson option nor has recourse to the Howells stratagem, which is imaginatively of most interest. In April 1857, Herman Melville spent a few days in Venice. His journal for the visit simply records his hurried itinerary, with one or two impressions briefly noted.

> Mirage-like effect of fine day – floating in air of ships in the Malamocco Passage, & the islands. To the church of Santa Maria Salute. . . . Walked in the Piazza of St Mark. Crowds of people promenading. Pigeons. Walked to Rialto. Looked up and down the G. Canal. Wandered

further on. Numbers of beautiful women. The rich brown complexions of Titian's women drawn from nature, after all. The clear, rich, golden brown. The clear cut features, like a cameo – The vision from a window at the end of a long, narrow passage. . . . You at first think it a freshet, it will subside, not permanent – only a temporary condition of things. – St Mark's at sunset. Gilt mosaics, pinnacles, looks like a holiday affair. As if the Grand Turk had pitched his pavilion here for a summers day. 800 years![12]

Unlike Emerson, Melville positively appreciates the fact that it reminds him of a 'freshet' (i.e. a rush of fresh water flowing into the sea; or the flooding of a river from heavy rain or melting snow). It adds to the sense of a bewitching mixture of watery impermanence and actual long-lastingness which Venice uniquely generates. A mirage. Yet – 800 years! And Melville, while he may not have remarked on the Austrians, has certainly noticed the women, which Emerson, busy drawing his blinds, as certainly did not. Melville is clearly having a better time than Emerson!

He wrote two poems concerning Venice, and it is interesting to see what his imagination takes, hold of and how he pursues and shapes his material. 'Venice' is an impersonal meditation and salutation, something of an ode.

> With Pantheist energy of will
> The little craftsman of the Coral Sea
> Strenuous in the blue abyss
> Up-builds his marvellous gallery
>   And long arcade,
> Erections freaked with many a fringe
>   Of marble garlandry,
> Evincing what a worm can do.
>
> Laborious in a shallower wave,
>   Advanced in kindred art,
> A prouder agent proved Pan's might
> When Venice rose in reefs of palaces.[13]

The conceit is clinched by the final words, 'reefs of palaces'. Venice is culture's answer to nature; or, rather, Venice is nature's response to the cultivated craftsmanship evinced by the coral reef. Characteristically, Melville seeks to confound and link even to merging the two realms of nature and culture, suggesting, as he increasingly did, that many of our cherished oppositions and binary divisions begin to show signs of reversibility and interchangeability, when submitted to a little imaginative scrutiny and pressure. So here the Coral Sea is peopled by craftsmen, and architectured with galleries, arcades and garlands, and the worm has a 'Pantheist energy of will'. Venice, on the other hand, is not crafted and built, but simply 'rises' as if in some wondrous surge – an emanation and demonstration, not of some pan*theist* energy, but of 'Pan's might' itself. Nature is a laborious pantheist: Venice is an epiphany of Pan. The repetition of the syllable-name 'Pan' in both stanzas is undoubtedly meant to reinforce the suggestion that the arts which build coral reefs and Venetian palaces are 'kindred'. But Pan's agent, and agency, is 'prouder', and, we are allowed to feel, in the last analysis his power is greater. In offering a vision of Venice as the triumphant manifestation of Pan, Melville is indeed suggesting that it is a special testimony to the constructive genius of Eros, a unique site where the distinctions between nature and art are dazzlingly dissolved in the reefy palaces engendered by the art of Eros, the erotics of art. One way and another, this is a vision of Venice which we will find being constantly rehearsed.

The erotic aspect of Venice appears in another mode in the second poem, which is, by contrast, personal, narrative, even confessional. It takes place, and is entitled, 'In a Bye-Canal', which suggests a more secretive, even furtive, part of Venice – and, we might add, of Melville too. The opening line – 'A swoon of noon, a trance of tide' – sets the atmosphere: it is also 'Dumb noon, and haunted like the night / When Jael the wiled one slew'. Just why a Venetian noon should suggest a murderous Old Testament woman to Melville soon becomes clear, for the apparent incongruity is premonitory:

> A languid impulse from the oar
> Plied by my indolent gondolier
> Tinkles against a palace hoar,
>   And, hark, response I hear!
> A lattice clicks; and lo, I see
> Between the slats, mute summoning me,
> What loveliest eyes of scintillation,
> What basilisk glance of conjuration![14]

Venice has turned her sexual eye on the impressionable American; or, rather, Melville has opened his desire, and perhaps his sexual fantasies and fears, in and to Venice. This glimpse of a glance of a mute and latticed eye, leaves – permits, provokes – everything to be imagined. 'Basilisk', the mythical reptile with a look that killed, compounds the sense of latent apprehension or terror adumbrated by 'Jael', fearless slayer of Sisera with a tent-peg; and, if the poet may be arguably presumptuous in imagining that the barely discernible eyes are 'summoning' him, there is little doubt about the sexual dread with which he flees from them. The next part of the poem says, in effect – I have encountered most of what is dangerous in nature and man: I have swum between whales and sharks; I have wandered in enemy deserts;

I have turned on the leprous figures of Envy and Slander which have noiselessly dogged me:

All this. But at the latticed eye –
'Hey! Gondolier, you sleep, my man;
Wake up!' And, shooting by, we ran;
The while I mused, This, surely now,
Confutes the Naturalists, allow!
Sirens, true sirens verily be,
Sirens, waylayers in the sea.

Well, wooed by these same deadly misses,
Is it shame to run?
No! flee them did divine Ulysses,
  Brave, wise, and Venus' son.[15]

This rationalization and defence of the somewhat panic-stricken flight from some fantasized sense of the possibility of sirenic seduction is hard to judge tonally. Is the invocation of sirens and Ulysses a deliberate exaggeration – mock-heroic burlesque? Or is Melville, with characteristic ambiguity of tone, articulating some real sense of dread – an intimation of the possible deadly-ness, death-bringingness, of a kind of mute and appallingly enticing mode of sexuality, 'summoning' the male tourist-visitor to who knows what form of oceanic or lacustrine ecstatic extinction associated with Venice? It is an intimation most famously to be explored by Thomas Mann, but it is a far from uncommon one in connection with 'tranced' Venetian reveries. It is also worth just noting that Melville is, deliberately or not, messing up or confusing his mythology. Ulysses' mother was Anticleia, daughter of Autolycus; while the son of Venus is, traditionally, Cupid or Eros. Perhaps he wants Venus' son to be fleeing the very city of Venus, as Venice surely is – at the same time as he wants to be Ulysses fleeing the sirens, though even that is wrong, since Ulysses had himself tied to the mast so that he could hear their siren-song without succumbing to it. It would not do to make too much of this, but the merging and crossing of figures does suggest the awakening of troubled feelings and apprehensions concerning the writer's relation to female sexuality. Certainly, the sorts of feelings – desires, anxieties, dreads – which may be awakened by the 'latticed eye' in some unfamiliar part of Venice, some literal or metaphoric 'bye canal' stumbled or glided into, by chance or otherwise, often recur as writers' imaginations turn to Venice, and Melville is neither the first nor the last writer to suggest that the city's Venus eye may turn out to be a 'basilisk glance'. For Ruskin, it was Medusa. Neither is Melville the first or last writer to flee.

His two poems comprise a doubleness of response to the city which could fairly be called paradigmatic.

But Venice can be used more panoramically, so to speak – even, to talk of first and last things. My example here is Browning's *Fifine at the Fair* (1872) in which, taking his cue from Molière's *Don Juan*, Browning imagines Don Juan seeking to explain to his now wife Elvire why it is licit and necessary to pursue his attraction for the gypsy strolling-player girl, Fifine, while remaining at the same time loyal to Elvire. Elvire, understandably enough, asks him to clear up this 'fine mysteriousness'. The scene set for the dialogue – though it is mainly his monologue – is a fair at which the itinerant entertainers are putting on their show. Don Juan wonders why it is that these self-marginalizing people, 'Misguided ones who gave society the slip', even though disgraced, 'seem to relish life the more'(VII).[16] 'What compensating joy . . . Turns lawlessness to law?' (XIII). His wife is already 'in trouble', but Don Juan explains his attraction to the beautiful and alluring Fifine – dancer, tambourine player, probably prostitute – by saying that she will 'make my thoughts be surer what they mean' (XV). Fifine seems to embody a principle which would radically challenge and disturb all sorts of orthodox Victorian precepts, namely 'self-sustainment made morality' (XVI). Don Juan/Browning maintains that 'by demonstrating the value of Fifine' he can show that 'sparks from heaven transpierce earth's coarsest covertures' (XXVIII). The 'sparks' are important: Don Juan believes in, and supremely values, the 'self-vindicating flash' which he believes is potentially present in everybody. 'Howe'er produced', he says, 'flame is flame' – and *that* for him is the 'fine mysteriousness' 'Whereof solution is to seek'. And he seeks the solution in, or through, Fifine, and the desire she arouses.

Elvire is less than impressed by what she regards as a shamelessly specious line of argument. As far as she is concerned, Don Juan is simply drawn to shining filth: 'my husband hankers ever / After putridity that's phosphorescent'. For all his talk of 'soul, in search of soul', she regards his explanation as a piece of deceptive – self-deceptive? – rationalization which simply allows him to 'review the sex . . . of womankind', rather like a bee sampling whatever flower he comes across and taking his 'Matter-of-course snatched snack' – a telling-enough formulation! Undismayed, Don Juan maintains that he is always seeking the True, even if that means enmiring himself in the False, and Elvire, fairly enough, asks him to explain how one might 'rise into the true out of the false?' (LXIV). He replies with an example. I went bathing this morning, he says, and if I put my head under the water it promised 'dark and death at once'. But raise the head back into the air, and you are reassured that 'light and life' can still be reached. This is so attractive that there comes an instinct to try to climb out of the dark and deathly water altogether:

> Try to ascend breast-high? wave arms wide free of tether?
> Be in the air and leave the water altogether?
> Under went all again until I resigned myself
> To only breathe the air, that's footed by an elf,
> And only swim the water, that's native to a fish.
> (LXIV)

I will note here that these sentiments – or this realization – are echoed almost exactly in one of the most famous passages that Conrad wrote. The philosophic, if enigmatic, Stein is explaining his view of man's ontological condition to Marlow as they discuss the case of Jim:

> Yes! Very funny this terrible thing is. A man that is born falls into a dream like a man who falls into the sea. If he tries to climb out into the air as inexperienced people endeavour to do, he drowns – *nicht war*? . . . No! I tell you! The way is to the destructive element submit yourself, and with the exertions of your hands and feet in the water make the deep, deep sea keep you up.[17]

The background to both passages is, of course, Darwinism and evolution, and the Victorian rediscovery in new terms of an old truth – namely, that man is in every sense amphibious, physically, philosophically, metaphysically, and must learn to negotiate both elements, from watery origins to aerial (call them transcendent) aspirations. It is to my purpose to note that Venice is exactly a city that crosses, or merges or binds, the elements – both, and always, in and out of the water at once. I hope the relevance of this will emerge.

As far as Don Juan is concerned, 'our business' is 'with the sea' –'not with the air, but just o' the water, watery'. We have, and are bound, to 'keep immersed' in 'this wash o' the world, wherein we life-long drift' (LXVI). The water is, at once, the realm of the real, and 'the false'. We must move in it, through it, even while trying to emerge upwards out of it – hence those moments when 'we taste aether, scorn the wave' (LXVIII). But, most importantly, water is the realm of Woman. It is she – this is very Victorian – who, as it were, helps man, Man, in his upward aspirations. 'Woman does the work' (LXIX). Just so, for Don Juan, it is Fifine who has given 'the lucky lift' (LXVII). It is not entirely clear what the 'lucky lift' is *to* – truth? purity? a soul of blue air? – or *from* – the wash of sexual appetites? the foul rag and bone shop of the heart? the liquid uncertainty of temporal knowledge? But it has to be a woman who helps you up – 'still some Thalassia saves' (LXIX). This idea of the saving sea-goddess is important for Browning, and will be very important for Ezra Pound. Browning has already imagined a Michelangelo statue – like those inchoate slaves struggling to emerge from the rock of which they are made – of a woman, 'partly blent / With stuff she needs must quit' (LII). I do not know the statue (perhaps he invented it), but he thinks that Michelangelo meant it to depict 'the daughter of the old man o' the sea / Emerging from her wave, goddess Eidothée' (LII). It is just this image of a saving, sensual beauty rising from the water which I want to focus on, since I think it prepares for the denouement of the poem in which Venice so extraordinarily figures. From sea-goddesses emerging from the waves, it is no very great imaginative leap to dolphins – 'dolphins, my instance just' (LXXVIII). Byron sees Venice as a dolphin-city – magically rising, poignantly falling – and the general moral which Don Juan draws from his long meditation on sea-born(e) saviours, from goddesses to dolphins, which 'Fifine' or elevate us out of our hapless flounderings, is a faith, or a hope, which is central to this whole book:

> Whatever roughness rage, some exquisite sea-thing
> Will surely rise to save.
>
> (LXXVIII)

The lines suit equally well whether you believe in Venus, or Venice. Or, of course, both.

Much of Don Juan's argument has to do with Browning's belief that man cannot attain directly to the single white light of Truth but instead must, as it were, traverse the spectrum of partial, multi-coloured reality, following the Fifines of the world as and when they alluringly occur – to learn, I suppose, what fragment of the truth of this destructive element, in which we are perforce immersed, they may embody. It is a convenient, not to say self-serving, doctrine, and one can understand Elvire's scepticism. But the safe, the known, the domestic, the land-locked, offer no scope for discovery – it is in this poem that the famous line 'My hunger both to be and know the thing I am' (CII) occurs – and in pursuit of 'fire and life and truth' (XCI) Don Juan feels he must, as it were, go down to the ships and trust in 'sea-tracklessness' (LXXXII).

Yet it is not the sea which provides Don Juan with his final image for the wide realm of the real. He describes how, after a smoke, he fell into a reverie and played Schumann's *Carnival*. So: 'the Fair expands into the Carnival, / And Carnival again to . . . ah, but that's my dream' (XCI). As he drifts into a dream – 'gone off in company with Music' (XCIII) – his destination is predictable: 'Whither bound / Except for Venice? She it was, by instinct found / carnival-country proper' (XCIV). In St Mark's Square he sees:

a prodigious Fair
Concourse immense of men and women, crowned or casqued,
Turbaned or tiar'd, wreathed, plumed, hatted or wigged,
but masked –
Always masked, – only, how?
(XCV)

What the crowd collectively displays for him is the 'infinitude of passions, loves and hates' (XCVI) which move, and mar, humanity. It is a vision simply, comprehensively, of 'life', in all its 'variant quality' (CI). Venice equals carnival equals 'Life' might not seem a particularly arresting, or original, equation – though it was crucial for Byron, as will emerge in a later chapter. But Browning, or Don Juan, goes on to ask a more interesting question.

Experience, I am glad to master soon or late,
Here, there and everywhere i' the world, without debate!
Only, in Venice why? What reason for Mark's Square
Rather then Timbuctoo?

It is a pertinent question. As Proust will later write, 'I do not say Venice by chance', and that is one of the mottoes of this book. Browning effectively gives two answers. One might be thought to be unremarkable:

what I took of late
For Venice was the world; its Carnival – the state
Of mankind, masquerade in life-long permanence
For all time, and no one particular feast-day.
(CVIII)

The other answer is more interesting. It takes the form of a vision in which the proud buildings of Venice start to merge, like clouds at sunset:

heights and depths, beneath the leaden stress
– Crumble and melt and mix together, coalesce.
Re-form, but sadder still, subdued yet more and more
By every fresh defeat, till wearied eyes need pore
No longer on the dull impoverished decadence
Of all that pomp of pile in towering evidence.
So lately:-
(CVI)

Even thus nor otherwise, meseemed
That if I fixed my gaze awhile on what I dreamed

Was Venice' Square, Mark's church, the scheme was straight
unschemed,
A subtle something had its way within the heart
Of each and every house I watched, with counterpart
Of tremor through the front and outward face, until
Mutation was at end; impassive and stock-still
Stood now the ancient house, grown – new, is scarce the phrase,
Since older, in a sense, – altered to . . .

(CVII)

Altered to – what? For a while, Don Juan meditates on change and permanence in a way which need not detain us, then he starts to imagine, rather apocalyptically, 'the close of things' – before he returns to the matter of what the edifices of Venice have been altered to.

Just so, in Venice' Square, that things were at the close
Was signalled to my sense; for I perceived arrest
O' the change all round about. As if some impulse pressed
Each gently into each, what was distinctness, late,
Grew vague, and line from line no longer separate,
No matter what its style, edificed . . . shall I say,
Died into edifice? I find no simpler way
Of saying how, without or dash or shock or trace
Of violence, I found unity in the place
Of temple, tower, – nay hall and house and hut, – one blank
Severity of peace in death; to which they sank
Resigned enough till . . . ah, conjecture, I beseech,
What special blank did they agree to, all and each
What common shape was that wherein they mutely merged
Likes and dislikes of form, so plain before?

(CXX)

What is this 'special blank' and 'common shape' into which the buildings of Venice resignedly die? The short answer – Browning, it need hardly be said, is long about it – is a 'Druid monument'. This is, presumably, the earliest human erection (I use the word advisedly) Browning can think of. Last things turn out to be first things. Browning clearly thinks the 'piled stones' were phallic (I think there is no evidence for this, but that hardly matters). He explains how the Christians tried to efface or overlay the pagan meaning of the pile of stones – but the 'folk' were not mocked.

Hence, when the earth began its life afresh in May,
And fruit-trees bloomed, and waves would wanton, and the bay
Ruffle its wealth of weed, and stranger-birds arrive,

And beasts take each a mate, – folk, too, found sensitive,
Surmised the old grey stone upright there, through such tracts
Of solitariness and silence, kept the facts
Entrusted it, could deal out doctrine, did it please:
No fresh and frothy draught, but liquor on the lees,
Strong, savage and sincere: first bleedings from a vine
Whereof the product now do Curés so refine
To insipidity, that, when heart sinks, we strive
And strike from the old stone the old restorative.

(CXXIII)

Not much doubt what 'the old restorative' is, nor what 'the old stone' signifies. What *is* remarkable is Don Juan's dream-vision of Venice resolving itself into a phallic monument.

To this it was, this same primeval monument,
That, in my dream, I saw building with building blent
Fall: each on each they fast and founderingly went
Confusion-ward; but thence again subsided fast,
Became the mound you see. Magnificently massed
Indeed, those mammoth-stones, piled by the Protoplast
Temple-wise in my dream!

(CXXIV)

Never mind about the Protoplast, whoever or whatever He might be, for Browning this is clearly the erection behind *all* the other erections of mankind – 'strong, savage and sincere' – even, no, *particularly*, the magnificent creation which is Venice. Venice 'unschemed' is no more, and no *less*, than an amazing memorial to, and manifestation of, the most primordial generative drives. Venice 'schemed' is about as far from a Druid column as man can travel, yet through the one Browning sees the other. Eros, builder of cities – first and last things, indeed. This is the reverse of reductive. 'Whatever roughness rage, some exquisite sea-thing / Will surely rise to save': the words now take on an added resonance. And Venice – rising – is simply the most 'exquisite sea- thing' there is.

2

Lord Byron: A Sea Cybele

My Venice, like Turner's, had been chiefly created for us by Byron.
(Ruskin)

BYRON arrived in Venice in 1816 but he had visited it long before in the pages of *The Mysteries of Udolpho.* Mrs Radcliffe had herself never been to Venice but had experienced it in the writing of Mrs Piozzi. It is absolutely appropriate that the image of Venice which came to dominate the nineteenth-century imagination – Ruskin's and thus Turner's – should be at least grounded in an image (Byron's) which in turn was nourished by a textually based text. Venice is always the already written as well as the already seen, the already read. The Venice Mrs Radcliffe would have found through the clear eighteenth-century eyes and in the sensible, annotative prose of Mrs Piozzi is one in which St Mark's Place is both beautiful and liable to 'stink one to death, as nobody, I believe, thinks of changing their baskets'. Carnival and masquerading are noted almost in passing as a sort of temporary madness – her tone is one of amiable tolerance – while the range of shops and products and the available foods are carefully itemized (the fresh sturgeon is 'incomparable', the fried liver 'sad stuff'). She finds the inhabitants of the Venetian republic 'less savage and more happy' than the Italians of the mainland but she deplores 'the heaps of dirt and crowds of beggars, who infest the streets and poison the pleasures of society'. She is more interested in the people than the overall spectacle of the place. She finds them 'devout and decorous' on sacred occasions, and is impressed that 'they have preserved their laws inviolate, their city unattempted, and their republic respectable, through all the concussions that have shaken the rest of Europe.' It is strange to read the following: 'The patriotism inherent in the breasts of individuals makes another strong cause of this State's exemption from decay; they say themselves that the soul of old Rome has transmigrated to Venice' – this, eight years before the definitive collapse of the thousand-year republic. Whether this argues an impercipience or gullibility on the part of Mrs Piozzi – or whether, as is more likely, it is another example of the ability of the Venetians of the late eighteenth century to mask-masquerade the true state of affairs, their blindness or indifference, to the realities of history which were accelerating their imminent demise – we can hardly ascertain. Mrs Piozzi was aware of the 'licentious dissoluteness' to be found in the city but maintained that 'with all this appearance of levity, however, there is an unremitted attention to the affairs of state.'[1] This is still Venice as an enviably successful republic, despite the dirt and the beggars.

Of course she does also respond to the beauties of Venice:

> Whoever sees St Mark's place lighted up of an evening, adorned with every excellence of human art and pregnant pleasure, expressed by intelligent countenances sparkling with every grace of nature, the sea washing its walls, the moonbeams dancing on its subjugated waves, sport and laughter resounding from the coffee-houses, girls with guitars skipping about the square, masks and merry-makers singing as they pass you, unless a barge with a band of music is heard at some distance upon the water, and calls attention to sounds made sweeter by the element over which they are brought – whoever is led suddenly, I say to this scene of seemingly perennial gaiety, will be apt to cry out in Venice, as Eve says to Adam in Milton:
>
> 'With three conversing I forget all time
> All seasons and their change – all please alike.'[2]

This is the Venice of poetry – a pastoral, Watteau-like site – as opposed to the Venice of politics. To be sure, Mrs Piozzi immediately follows this literary ecphrasis with the prosaic comment that you never see a horse or cow in Venice and that it is said that 'numberless inhabitants live and die in this great capital, nor ever find out or think of inquiring how the milk brought from *terra firma* is originally produced.' Mrs Radcliffe would take the Miltonics and ignore the widespread Venetian ignorance of the udder. But Mrs Piozzi introduces a word into her evocations of Venice which was to have a quite disproportionate influence on subsequent representations of the city. When she first see St Mark's Place it is at night under a full moon and she is entranced. 'The general effect produced by such architecture, such painting, such pillars, illuminated as I saw them last night by the moon at full, rising out of the sea, produced an effect like enchantment.' And when she leaves Venice, this gay, 'this gallant city, so often described, so certainly admired – seen with rapture, quitted with regret', her words are: 'Seat of enchantment! head-quarters of pleasure, farewell!'[3] From all that I have read, I think Milton Wilson is correct in saying that 'It seems to have been the sensible Mrs Thrale, in 1787, who introduced the "enchantment" of Venice to English readers', and his eloquent amplification of the implications of this observation seems to me exactly right: 'certainly Venice became more magical as she became less real; and, when the republic died, the ghost of a city became more enchanted than ever.'[4] Venice has been many things to many observers and visitors during its spectacular history – sumptuous, glorious, fabulous, exotic, dazzlingly rich and opulent in materials, wealth, costume, buildings, ceremony and ritual, but, even when dreamlike from a distance, always wondrously material – or materially wonderful. The notion or impression that it is 'enchanted' – both enchanting and the product of enchantment – shifts Venice decisively towards the apparitional. And magic always involves mystification.

It was Mrs Thrale's 'seat of enchantment' that Mrs Radcliffe would appropriate and amplify for her descriptions of Emily's visit to Venice:

> Nothing could exceed Emily's admiration of her first view of Venice with islets, palaces, and towers rising out of the sea, whose clear surface reflected the tremulous picture of all its colour. The sun, sinking in the west, tinted the waves and the lofty mountains of Friuli, which skirt the northern shores of the Adriatic, with a saffron glow, while on the marble porticos and colonnades of St Mark were thrown the rich lights and shades of evening. As they glided on, the grander features of this city appeared more distinctly: its terraces, crowned with airy yet majestic fabrics, touched, as they now were, with the splendour of the setting sun, appeared as if they had been called up from the ocean by the wand of an enchanter, rather than by mortal hands.[5]

Mrs Radcliffe has turned Venice into a 'fairy city' – or, rather, she has written a fairy city and named it 'Venice'. Mrs Piozzi had described how, when viewed from the top of the campanile, the islets of Venice 'started up in the midst of the sea, so as to excite amazement', so for Emily to see Venice 'rising out of the sea' was, in itself, not new. But when Mrs Thrale wrote of St Mark's Place at night it was *the moon* which was 'rising out of the sea', while, as Milton Wilson has pointed out, in Mrs Radcliffe it is the whole city which 'rises' out of the sea – not as a phenomenological description of the city as seen from a certain vantage point (the top of a tower), but as the work of the 'wand of an enchanter'. And Byron is, of course, both quoting and acknowledging Mrs Radcliffe when in the first stanza of canto IV of *Childe Harold's Pilgrimage* he wrote:

> I saw from out the wave her structures rise
> As from the stroke of the Enchanter's wand!

What Byron also makes clear is that this was part of a literary image of Venice acquired long before he actually went there:

> I loved her from my boyhood; she to me
> Was as a fairy city of the heart,
> Rising like water columns from the sea,
> Of joy the sojourn, and of wealth the mart;
> And Otway, Radcliffe, Schiller, Shakespeare's art,
> Had stamp'd her image in me, and even so,
> Although I found her thus, we did not part;
> Perchance even dearer in her days of woe,
> Than when she was a boast, a marvel, and a show.
> (canto IV, 18)

To see Venice as a 'fairy city' conjured into existence by the wand of some unidentified 'Enchanter' is at once to forget the 'mortal hands' that 'reared' her, and occlude or overlook the contemporary inhabitants who are having somehow to eke out a non-magical existence there: to dematerialize it thus is also to dehistoricize and un-people it. To have (to see, conceive) Venice in any way autonomously, magically, 'rising' from the sea is, supremely, to 'naturalize' it and thus to beg (elude/elide) every political, historical, cultural question. And just such a vaporized and de-substantiated 'Venice' has been purveyed by thousands of empty texts and pictures from the end of the eighteenth century to the present day.

But Byron recognizes that there is a necessary difference between the enchanted and enchanting literarily received and literarily bequeathed image, and the experienced reality, no matter to what extent the former will inform and predetermine the latter: indeed, he will write some of his best poetry out of just this felt difference. Ruskin, too, writes of an anticipatory 'enchanted' image having to give way to something more complex and melancholy as when in *Praeterita* he recalls his excitement attendant on his first approach to Venice as an adult:

> the enchanted world of Venice enlarging in front of me. . . . I had only once yet seen her, and that six years ago, when still a child. That the fairy tale should come true now seemed wholly incredible, and the start from the gate of Padua in the morning – Venice, asserted by people whom we could not but believe to be really over there, on the horizon, in the sea! How to tell the feeling of it!

Venice – *really over there*! The eager desire and the anticipatory wonder which can be aroused and brought into play by the 'stamped image' of Venice are crucial to Ruskin's own work, not to mention the writer most influenced in turn by *his* textual Venice – Proust. For Ruskin there were, autobiographically speaking, two Venices – the one he anticipated and still enjoyed as a wondering child, and the one which revealed itself to the uncompromising, searching eye of the cultural critic.

> The two chapters closing the first, and beginning the second volume of the 'Stones of Venice' were written, I see on re-reading, in the melancholy experience of 1852, with honest effort to tell every traveller what was really to be seen. They do not attempt to recall my own joys of 1835 and 1841, when there was not even the beginning of a railway bridge; when everything, muddy, muddy Brenta, vulgar villa, dusty causeway, sandy beach, was equally rich in rapture, on the morning that brought us in sight of Venice: and the black knot of gondolas in the canal of Mestre, more beautiful to me than a sunrise full of clouds of scarlet and gold.[6]

The Venice 'really over there' can also be the Venice 'really back then' and Ruskin projects his own experience of two Venices into his massive historical-mythical version of Venetian history in which a Venice of perpetual rapture (and to that extent enchanted) gives way to a fallen Venice which is dark indeed. The more general point is that, once Venice is inscribed – 'stamped' – as 'enchanted' in the perpetual over-there of previous writing, any encounter with the actual city, even if it is impossible to disentangle the image from the reality, or, as James will say, the model from the painting, is bound to involve, ensure, some sort of dis-enchantment, or, it may be, re-enchantment in a different mode.

Byron did not come to Venice with the intention of writing.

> Of Venice I shall say little. You must have seen many descriptions; and they are most of them like. It is a poetical place; and classical, to us, from Shakespeare and Otway. I have not yet sinned against it in verse, nor do I know that I shall do so, having been tuneless since I crossed the Alps, and feeling, as yet, no renewal of the estro.[7]

That last word is a favourite one of Byron's – 'Venice is in the *estro* of her carnival'[8] – and it is peculiarly apt, since in no writer is the identity – or inseparable continuity or contiguity – of sexuality and writing more marked than in Byron, particularly Byron in Venice when long nights of sexual indulgence would give way to bouts of writing with out a break. (Sometimes the contiguity seems to have been literal, as when he writes to John Murray: 'There's a whore on my right / For I rhyme best at Night / When a C—t is tied close to *my* Inkstand'.[9] It is notable that, in addition to having no intention to write, Byron intimates that he intended to 'give up gallivanting altogether'.[10] In the event he was to embark on the most sexually promiscuous period of his life – ***and*** his most fertile time of literary creation. One cannot draw lines of simple cause and determination, but Venice, writing and sexuality come together in Byron in a uniquely interrelated way. Yet it is remarkable that just four months before he was to start writing Canto IV of *Childe Harold* he wrote to Thomas Moore: 'If I live ten years longer, you will see, however that it is not over with me – I don't mean in literature, for that is nothing; and it may seem odd enough to say, I do not think it my vocation.'[11] He did not have his ten years; but, although he made a name by his death in Greece, it was his greatest literary achievements which were, at this moment, all before him.

Just what Byron's vocation was when he arrived in Venice, he would undoubtedly candidly have found it impossible to say ('I have not the least idea where I am going, nor what I can do. . . . I stayed at Venice chiefly because it is not one of their "dens of thieves"; and here they but pause and pass'[12] – 'their' referring to the 'tribe of wretches' or the 'staring boobies, who go about gaping and wishing to be at once cheap and magnificent': in Byron's time Venice was not a serious tourist resort). He was a man without a home, a party, a country; he had given up on politics as he had given up on family and England (he specifically asks not to have any political news from England, adding that he reads neither English nor Italian newspapers). He does dash off his Luddite hymn to Thomas Moore,[13] but this is only because in his mood of disgust with England he clearly relishes the idea of all and any 'breakers of frames'; of the Austrian occupation of Venice he says very little – he refers to the 'Definitive Treaty of Peace (and tyranny)' of 1814[14] and once refers to 'the Veneto-Lombard public, who are, perhaps, the most oppressed in Europe',[15] but this is as nothing to the long accounts he gives of his amorous adventures. Concerning his expenditures in Venice he wrote to James Wedderburn Webster: 'more than half was laid out on the Sex – to be sure I have had plenty for the money – that's certain – I think at least two hundred of one sort or another – perhaps more – for I have not lately kept the recount.'[16] And again: 'I have been f——g incessantly for the last three months.'[17] As he said, Italy 'disfranchises the thoughts'.[18] He shows flickers of interest when his friends Douglas Kincaird and Hobhouse are elected to Parliament, and he is always ready with abuse and anger for certain pet English political hates, but the disengagement is really total. 'I love a row,' he tells Augusta Leigh when the prospect of political violence in England seems temporarily to tempt him to think of returning, but it was the violence, not the politics, which attracted him.[19] He does maintain that *Beppo* 'has politics and ferocity',[20] but just what 'politics' might have meant to Byron in Venice is something to be considered below; certainly nothing that would furnish him with anything recognizably like a 'vocation'. For the most part Byron would seem to have identified with the mood and condition he envisaged in 'The Lament of Tasso':

> Long years of outrage, calumny, and wrong;
> Imputed madness, prison'd solitude,
> And the mind's canker in its savage mood.

As he wrote to Douglas Kincaird: 'you might consider me as *posthumous*.'[21] Such is Byron's mood in Venice.

Vocation or none, there were days and nights to be occupied and for a while Byron filled them in two ways. He immersed himself in the available sexuality of the city – and he started to learn Armenian. His sexual adventures in Venice were legion and he filled his letters with accounts of them and the jealousies, fights, scenes, accidents and varying tempestuousnesses precipitated by them. The long account of his relatonship with Margarita Cogni in a letter to John Murray on 1 August 1819 may be taken as representative.[22] She was from the 'lower orders', could 'neither read nor write', was poor and married to a baker. She was 'a very fine Animal . . . wild as a witch and fierce as a demon'. In her jealousy ('I, being at that time somewhat promiscuous') she tried to take a knife to him, and then threw herself in the canal – whence she was rescued. When Byron called her '*Vacca*' (cow) she turned and curtsied and answered, '"Vacca tua, Celenza"' ('"Your cow, please your excellency"'). She was one of many 'animals'. This is the Byron who wrote of *Don Juan*, the new poem he had started in Venice: 'It may be profligate but is it not *life*, is it not *the thing*, Could any man have written it who has not lived in the world? and tooled in a post-chaise? – in a hackney coach? – in a gondola? – on a table? – and under it?'[23] Three months before leaving Venice for good he wrote: 'I like women- God he knows – but the more their system here develops upon me, the worse it seems . . . here the *polygamy* is all on the female side. I have been an intriguer, a husband, a whoremonger, and now I am a Cavalier Servente – by the holy! It is a strange sensation.'[24] The woman was Teresa Guiccioli, and Byron did not like the sensation at all. (He had written of an earlier affair: 'I told my fair one – at setting out – that as to the love and the Cavaliership – I was quite of accord – but as to the *servitude* – it would not suit me at all so I begged to hear no more about it'.) This is the woman he nearly hands into the canal, and he comments: 'so much for love and all that.'[25]

When he writes at the end of his Venetian stay that 'There is no freedom in Europe – that's certain; it is besides a worn out portion of the globe;[26] one might fairly wonder if it is not Byron who is worn out. Early on he had described how the carnival 'had knocked me up a little' and added, 'though

I did not dissipate much upon the whole, yet I find "the sword wearing out the scabbard", though I have but just turned the corner of twenty-nine',[27] going on in the same letter to inscribe the lyric which starts 'So we'll go nor more a roving / So late into the night' – which is lovely and untrue, since at this point in time (February 1817) Byron had many roving nights ahead of him. There is little reason to doubt that in Venice Byron pushed himself to an extreme of sexual dissipation. We have Shelley's account of him in a letter of December 1818. He

> hardens himself in a kind of obstinate and self-willed folly. . . . He associates with wretches who seem almost to have lost the gait and physiognomy of man, and who do not scruple to avow practices which are not only not named but I believe seldom even conceived in England. He says he disapproves, but he endures. . . . I do not doubt, and for his sake I ought to hope, that his present career must end up soon by some violent circumstances which must reduce our situation with respect to Alba into its ancient tie.[28]

Certainly Shelley was upset at having to leave Allegra (Alba – Byron's daughter) in Venice, having become so attached to her, and the letter is unbalanced; but even so, as John Buxton points out, it is rather extreme to hope for Byron's murder – in his own best interests![29]

Shelley had been greatly stimulated by his 1818 visit to Byron in Venice – indeed, the meeting seems to have been mutually enriching, since within a few days of meeting and conversing together at length each of them was at work on might fairly be regarded as their greatest works, *Don Juan* and *Prometheus Unbound*; but, even allowing for his worry over Alba, Shelley leaves us in little doubt that Byron had taken sexual excess to a physically debilitating extreme. When Byron was approaching Venice it was 'the greenest island of my imagination';[30] while he was there he became deeply attached to what he called its 'marine melancholy'. Just before he leaves he writes to Richard Hoppner; 'we will make the Adriatic roar with our hatred for that now empty Oyster shell without its pearl – the city of Venice',[31] and shortly after he has left he refers to it simply as 'the sea-Sodom'[32] I am not trying to cast Byron as some sort of real-life de Sade – he is of course much closer to Casanova – but he clearly took sexual experimentation to some length in the city which, he said, had every vice except perhaps a vice-consul.[33] There is experimentation in the writing as well and a new kind of tolerance for kinds of doubleness; doubleness of the sort he read out of and wrote into a Venice which was both an island of the imagination and a Sodom of the body. 'I've taught me other tongues – and in strange eyes / Have made me not a stranger' (Childe Harold, IV, 8).

I was not being frivolous when I suggested that Byron, in search of an occupation in Venice, took up sex and Armenian. He links the two often in his early letters from the city – 'I should have gone too, but I fell in love, and must stay that over. I should think that and the Armenian alphabet will last the winter'[34] He was clear about his motive for taking up the language: 'By way of divertisement, I am studying daily, at an Armenian monastery, the Armenian language. I found that my mind wanted something craggy to break upon; and this – as the most difficult thing I could discover here for an amusement – I have chosen, to torture me into attention.'[35] Again: 'I find the language (which is *twin*, the literal and the *vulgar*) difficult, but not invincible (at least I hope not). I shall go on. I found it necessary to twist my mind round some severer study; and this, being the hardest I could devise here, will be a file for the serpent.'[36] I am not sure of the exact implications of 'literal' here, but it is at least interesting that Byron took up studying a 'twin' language in the city he had made into a sort of quintessence of doubleness. And I think there is a connection between his choice of women and his choice of Armenian, even allowing for the part played by what circumstances happened to make available. The women, like Margarita Cogni, were often working class, illiterate, wild, 'animal' and a tax on the body – and Armenian was the craggiest and most difficult thing he could find for his mind ('my daily course of life being much the same – studious in the day and dissolute in the evening'.[37] Self-exiled from everything, and every woman, English, Byron it seems to me was seeking some form of extreme otherness, both sexual and linguistic. Of course he kept to the English language for his writing, but I think that he wrote from a new position of detachment, a new site of disengagement; indeed, I would say he established a new sort of relationship with English and thus a new way of writing poetry (particularly in *Beppo* and *Don Juan*), and this must in part be due to the 'other tongues' and 'strange eyes' which he deliberately courted and, as it were, embraced in all their physically turbulent and mentally craggy difference and difficulty. Files for the serpent in every sense.

Less than three months before he started canto IV of *Childe Harold* he wrote: 'I hate things *all fiction*; and therefore the *Merchant* and *Othello* have no great associations to me: but *Pierre* has. There should always be some foundation of fact for the most airy fabric, and pure invention is but the talent of a liar.'[38] How Byron turned fact into fabric – or, as we might say, *fabric-ated* fact – in his Venetian writings is the concern of this chapter and I will just note here that the Venice he describes in canto IV is indeed Venice seen from an 'airy distance', as though the city itself was always already a miraculous 'airy fabric/fabrication'. It is a place of rising, soaring, dilation; but also confinement, contraction, decline. It is worth looking at the letter in which he first announces that he is working on canto IV. It is to John Murray, 1 July 1817.

> Mr Lewis is at Venice, and I am going up to stay the week with him there as it is one of his enthusiasms also to like the city.
>
> I stood in Venice, on the 'Bridge of Sighs';
> A palace and a prison on each hand:
> I saw from out the wave her structures rise
> As from the stroke of (the) Enchanter's wand:
> A thousand years their cloudy wings expand
> Around me, and a dying Glory smiles
> O'er the far times when many a subject land
> Looked to the winged Lion's marble piles,
> Where Venice sate in state, throned on her Seventy Isles.
>
> The 'Bridge of Sighs' (i.e. *Ponte dei sospiri*) is that which divides, or rather joins, the palace of the Doge to the prison of the state.[39]

Apart from changing seventy to a round hundred, this is as the stanza was published. He wants the palace close to the prison, and he wants them *joined.* A sense of dismal confinement must be linked – linked, not merged – with intimations of expansionary magnificence; more generally, contraction with dilation. The second line occasioned some rather patronizing strictures – not least from Wordsworth – with the suggestion that what Byron really meant to say was a prison on one hand and a palace on the other. But, as Milton Wilson quite rightly observes, 'what Byron really "meant to say" is not so easy to be sure of as Wordsworth and Rogers thought, nor are prisons and palaces that easy to keep apart, in Byron and a host of other writers . . . and maybe at Venice in particular.' Wilson produces evidence that there were visitors in the seventeenth and eighteenth century who found the state prison fair and the Doges' Palace ugly.[40] And of course in any literal terms you cannot see anything but water from the Bridge of Sighs. Byron's Venice is generalized, conceptualized and imagined from an 'airy distance'. In *The Two Foscari* Venice is described as 'a crowd of palaces and prisons' and is indeed partly set in a ducal palace which is also a prison. In Byron's visionary Venice the palatial is shadowed by the carceral; as with other opposites in the canto, they are 'mellowed and mingling, yet distinctly seen' (to adapt his description of dusk at Lake Leman in canto III, 86). (It is quite possibly due to Byron that, when the Dorrits set up house in Venice, 'It appeared on the whole, to Little Dorrit herself, that this same society in which they lived, greatly resembled a superior sort of Marshalsea.'[41])

In the letter in which he referred to Venice as 'the greenest island of my imagination' Byron went on to write: 'It has not disappointed me; though its evident decay would, perhaps, have that effect upon others. But I have been familiar with ruins too long to dislike desolation.'[42] A week later he wrote to John Murray: 'Venice pleases me as much as I expected – and I expected much – it is one of those places which I know before I see them – and has always haunted me the most – after the East. – I like the gloomy gaiety of their gondolas – and the silence of their canals – I do not even dislike the evident decay of the city.'[43] Canto IV is centrally concerned with ruin and decay: or, rather, in the absence of a centre it hovers restlessly and obsessively around ruins and ruination. There are of course glimpses of ruins in the earlier cantos: 'ruin'd splendour' lingers around Lisbon (canto I, 22); there are the 'mouldering shrines' of Greece (canto II, 15), where 'Thy fanes, they temples to thy surface bow, / Commingling slowly with heroic earth' (canto II, 85); and of course there is the French Revolution and the Terror which witnessed what Macbeth calls 'ruin's wasteful entrance' with a vengeance:

> But good with ill they also overthrew,
> Leaving but ruins, wherewith to rebuild
> Upon the same foundation, and renew
> Dungeons and thrones.
>
> (canto III, 82)

Or, as one might say, prisons and palaces, and it's the same damned and bloody thing all over again. The restoration of the *ancien régime* proved to Byron, if he needed any proof, that 'History', 'with all her volumes vast, / Hath but *one* page' (canto IV, 108).

Ruins are, of course, a recurrent feature of the romantic landscape as of the Gothic novel, and it is possible to surmise a direct connection with the French Revolution. In a very interesting essay, Geoffrey Ward suggests this:

> The taste of ruins . . . is contemporary with the emergence of republicanism, a connexion drawn at the time by the Marquis de Sade who saw in the tale of terror an indirect reaction to political upheaval. It is improbably probable, therefore, that the Gothic ruin has become the most continuously attractive and popular icon of the last two hundred years, because it unites in a vivid way the power of the old and the newly interesting condition of fragmentation. Once Bastille and Palace had fallen, the smashed architecture of feudalism and the aristocratic order . . . began through broken windows to emit mysterious and multiple significations, being charmingly picturesque in decay, a focus for nostalgia and conservative resentment, hauntings, but also new order and the promise of material change.[44]

Much of this is certainly relevant to Byron, ('there is a power / And magic in the ruined battlement'; canto IV, 129), but I would like to add some remarkable speculations or meditations on 'The Ruin' by Georg Simmel.

> The ruin of a building, however, means that where the work of art is dying, other forces and forms, those of nature, have grown; and that out of what of art still lives in the ruin and what of nature already lives in it, there has emerged a new whole, a characteristic unit . . . a unity which is no longer grounded in human purposiveness but in that depth where human purposiveness and the working of non-conscious natural forces grow from their common root . . . what strikes us is not, to be sure, that human beings destroy the work of man – this indeed is achieved by nature – but that men let it decay. From the standpoint of the idea of man, such indifference is, so to speak, a positive passivity, whereby man makes himself the accomplice of nature and of that one of its inherent tendencies which is dramatically opposed to his own essential interests. . . . reversal of the typical order, is felt as a return to the 'good mother', as Goethe calls nature . . . the ruin often strikes us as so often tragic . . . because destruction here is not something coming senselessly from the outside but rather the realization of a tendency inherent in the deepest layer of existence of the destroyed . . . in the case of the ruin, with its extreme intensification and fulfilment of the present form of the past, such profound and comprehensive energies of our soul are brought into play that there is no longer any sharp division between perception and thought.[45]

Of no other city could it more truly be said that 'men *let it decay*', and, faced with the spectacle of Venice, 'with its extreme intensification and fulfilment of the present form of the past,' Byron wrote poetry pondering the intimation and significance of ruin and decay in which, indeed, 'there is no longer any sharp division between perception and thought'.

> But my soul wanders; I demand it back
> To meditate amongst decay, and stand
> A ruin amongst ruins.
>
> (canto IV, 25)

Topographically non-specific, vague, allusive as Byron characteristically is – he indeed writes as a man without a place, unpositioned, and only rarely situates himself in the writing – the ruins here might be Venetian, Roman, or simply and inclusively Italian, but the specific identification, 'a ruin amongst ruins', albeit perhaps a little posturing, affords some insight into the powerful *attraction* of ruins for Byron during this Venetian sojourn, and, perhaps only superficially paradoxically, they can engender and nourish a sumptuous and potent writing:

> Statues of glass – all shiver'd – the long file
> Of her dead Doges are declin'd to dust;
> But where they dwelt, the vast and sumptuous pile
> Bespeaks the pageant of their splendid trust;
> Their sceptre broken, and their sword in rust,
> Have yielded to the stranger; empty halls,
> Thin street, and foreign aspects, such as must
> Too oft remind her who and what enthrals,
> Have flung a desolate cloud o'er Venice's lovely walls
> (canto IV, 15)

What Byron asserts more generally about 'fair Italy' is particularly relevant to his poetic evocation of a Venice in some ways even lovelier in her desolation:

> Thou art the garden of the world, the home
> Of all Art yields, and Nature can decree;
> Even in thy desart, what is like to thee?
> Thy very weeds are beautiful, thy waste
> More rich than other climes' fertility;
> Thy wreck a glory, and thy ruin graced
> With an immaculate charm which can not be defaced.
> (canto IV, 26)

Notice that Art 'yields', which is what the earth more usually does, while Nature 'decrees' a civic art: as Simmel said of ruins, 'where the work of art is dying other forces and forms, those of nature, have grown.' A garden which is a 'desart', a fertile waste, weeds which are beautiful, and ruin which cannot be defaced – out of the apparent oxymorons Byron is coaxing value from the positive beauty of manifest decline. And Nature and Art are exchanging provinces and powers.

The first twenty-nine stanzas of canto IV comprise the specifically Venetian part of the canto – of which sixteen stanzas variously evoke images of Venice past and present – though this section initiates and touches on themes and preoccupations which will be developed and pursued throughout the canto until Byron ends by returning to the ocean, which echoes the start of the canto. In these stanzas, Byron's image of Venice 'fresh from ocean' – part imagination, part history, part fantasy, part dream, part observation, part memory, part self-projection, part literature – is dazzlingly constituted. It is these opening twenty-nine stanzas, so crucial and generative for Turner and Ruskin and countless others, that I wish to look at in some detail.

After the palace/prison opening and the 'structures' of Venice – an abstract collective word – rising from the sea at the stroke of the enchanter's wand, Byron brings in two words which anticipate some of the primary tugging oscillations which inform the canto:

> A thousand years their cloudy wings expand
> Around me, and a *dying* Glory smiles
> O'er the far times.
>
> (canto IV, 1; my italics)

Byron everywhere meets with things dying – palaces, cities, civilizations – memorably summed up and crystallized in the figure of the dying gladiator in Rome, vividly brought back into the present in the powerful stanzas 140 and 141. At the same time he constantly seeks something, some energy, some belief, some capacity which can counteract and survive this deathward, downward, drive and drift; which can 'expand' amidst the tendency of everything human and man-made to wither and contract. His own imagination expands in the second stanza, which he added later, perhaps to counteract the emphasis on the decay of contemporary Venice. (That emphasis is underlined by Hobhouse's notes which prosaically and unambiguously tend to stress that Venice is 'dying daily', that it 'must fall to pieces at once, and sink more rapidly than it rose', and which seem even to relish the prospect of the time when 'Venice shall have sunk into the slime of her choked canals'.[46] There is nothing expansionary in such notes – Venice without vision.)

> She looks a sea Cybele, fresh from ocean,
> Rising with her tiara of proud towers
> At airy distance, with majestic motion,
> A ruler of the water and their powers:
> And such she was; – her daughters had their dowers
> From spoils of nations, and the exhaustless East
> Pour'd in her lap all gems in sparkling showers.
> In purple was she robed, and of her feast
> Monarchs partook, and deem'd their dignity increas'd.
>
> (canto IV, 2)

Definitively feminized and regalized and mythologized into another manifestation of the ancient mother goddess, this Venice is not so much the immensely successful trading republic but a fantasized compound of divinity and majesty and maternity receiving homage for herself and her 'daughters' in the form of an eroticized mercantilism which 'pour'd' 'sparkling showers' of gems into her lap. This is Byron's most opulent evocation of a figural

Venice which rises triumphantly from his dreaming imagination. Venice has now twice been described as 'rising' in the first stanzas, first magically, then divinely, and this simple-seeming word turns out to be crucial as the canto progresses.

I want to trace this out, but first we should look at the following stanzas, in which the expanding, the rising and the sparkling are reversed in a composite prospect of contemporary Venice where the gondoliers are 'silent' and 'songless', and the palaces are 'crumbling'; 'States fall, arts fade'. This is evidence of the downward, emptying, diminishing movement which the poet and poem have to struggle against. And note where he here locates the saving, retrieving resource:

> but Nature doth not die,
> Nor yet forget how Venice once was dear,
> The pleasant place of all festivity
> The revel of the earth, the masque of Italy!
> (canto IV, 3)

You could read 'forget' as an imperative addressed to the reader, but the movement of the lines suggests irresistibly that it is *Nature* which will not forget Venice at its most festive and masqued. It is a bold stroke given that elsewhere Nature is seen as an obliterating force, and suggests mysterious modes of preservation in the midst of processes of decline. Vanishing Venice *cannot* be allowed to just vanish; the forces of nature will find a way to retain the memory of the city that was the triumph of art. Again, Nature and Art are envisaged as doing each other's work.

But there is another course and form of preservation, as the next stanza insists:

> But unto us she hath a spell beyond
> Her name in story, and her long array
> Of mighty shadows, whose dim forms despond
> Above the dogeless city's vanish'd sway;
> Ours is a trophy which will not decay
> With the Rialto; Shylock and the Moor,
> And Pierre, can not be swept or worn away –
> The keystones of the arch! though all were o'er,
> For us repeopled were the solitary shore.
> (canto IV, 4)

There are three Venices here. A present one, now entirely insubstantial and dematerialized, composed of 'shadows . . . dim forms' desponding with intransitive loss of heart over the vacancy of the 'vanish'd sway'; the Venice which has 'her name in story' – that compound of history and legend which may be in Nature's keeping; and the Venice which has been written into literature, notably by Shakespeare and Otway, from which the vacant aftermath following the final disappearance of the actual and historical Venice could be 'repeopled'. Venice Preserved – entirely in and by writing. The question of what writing might do with and for Venice, and the larger questions adumbrated by that concern, are very much to the fore of this canto.

One thing it could do was to make Venice rise and rise again, as he has already demonstrated. She 'rises' again in stanza 18 – 'a fairy of the heart, rising like water-columns from the sea' – where she is thus seen as a particularly spectacular surge or eruption or indeed emission of Nature. But always there is the recurring presence of the movement in the contrary direction:

Venice, lost and won,
Her thirteen hundred years of freedom done,
Sinks, like sea-weed, into whence she rose!
(canto IV, 13)

While Venice is rising in poetry she is sinking in history.

Let me run together some passages to indicate what I think Byron is trying to do in his writing, what he thinks or hopes that writing is capable of:

Redemption rose in the Attic Muse,
Her voice their only ransom from afar
(canto IV, 16)

(this refers to the story of the Greek prisoners who were set free because they were singing words of Euripides)

He arose
To raise a language, and his land reclaim
From the dull yoke of her barbaric foes.
His mansion and his sepulchre; both plain
And venerably simple, such as raise
A feeling more accordant with his strain
(canto IV, 30–1)

(this refers to Petrarch)

Europe . . .
Shall yet redeem thee, and all backward driven,

Rolls the barbarian tide, and sue to be forgiven
(canto IV, 47)

(this is addressed to Italy as a whole)

These are four minds, which, like the elements,
Might furnish forth creation: – Italy!
Time, which hath wrong'd thee with a thousand rents
Of thine imperial garment, shall deny,
And hath denied, to every other sky,
Spirits which soar from ruin: – thy decay
Is still impregnate with divinity,
Which gilds it with revivifying ray;
Such as the great of yore, Canova is today.
(canto IV, 55)

(the four minds are Angelo, Alfieri, Galileo, Machiavelli)

Alas! the lofty city! . . .
Alas, for Tully's voice, and Virgil's lay,
And Livy's pictured page! – but these shall be
Her resurrection; all beside – decay.
(canto IV, 82)

(this is addressed to Rome)

Ransom, redeem, reclaim, revivify, resurrect – these are all aspects and forms of the 'raising' or reraising power which Byron at once asserts, honours, celebrates and seeks to emulate, and which he attributes to Muses, minds, voices, pages and poetic language. It is this he sets against the inexorable tendency of all man-made 'structures' – like, and primarily, Venice – to 'sink'. The canto does indeed 'track Fall'n states and buried greatness' as the poet resolves amid the Venetian ruins, until it confronts the 'Chaos of ruins' which is the vacant and vacated heart of Rome:

where we steer
Stumbling o'er recollections; now we clap
Our hands, and cry 'Eureka!' it is clear –
When but some false mirage of ruin rises near.
(canto IV, 81)

In such a dizzy, directionless disorientation amid ruins, he must assert and affirm the possibility of 'Spirits which soar from ruin' and cannot accept the idea of 'Rome and her Ruin past Redemption's skill'.

It should be noted that no specifically political or revolutionary 'soaring' is envisaged. One can see certain stanzas as gesturing in the direction of some sort of *risorgimento*, and at times Byron exorts Europe, particularly England (in *some* respects a modern Venice), to come to the aid of the occupied city:

> thy lot
> Is shameful to the narrations – most of all,
> Albion! to thee: the Ocean queen should not
> Abandon Ocean's children; in the fall
> Of Venice, think of thine, despite thy water wall.
> (canto IV, 17)

Jerome McGann, in his important work on the canto, rightly points out: 'It is, in fact, curious that so notorious a revolutionary poem should be so lacking in visions of a transformed political order in Italy (or anywhere else). The climactic statement of human creative capabilities set forth at St Peter's and the Vatican Galley is totally without political references. Rather, it is the dramatization of an act of an individual consciousness.' McGann also rightly stresses Byron's insistence on man's unconquerable mind and its power and need to arrive at, entertain and formulate 'great conceptions'.[47] Too often the mind is restricted, restrained, conditioned into constraint:

> 'tis a base
> Abandonment of reason to resign
> Our right of thought – our last and only place
> Of refuge; this, at least, shall still be mine:
> Though from our birth the faculty divine
> Is chain'd and tortured – cabin'd, cribb'd, confined,
> And bred in darkness, lest the truth should shine
> Too brightly on the unprepared mind,
> The beam pours in, for time and skill will couch the blind.
> (canto IV, 127)

The mind, then, can be another of those prisons adumbrated in the opening stanza. But it is possible for it to experience palatial expansion. As in St Peter's:

> thy mind,
> Expanded by the genius of the spot,
> Has grown colossal. . . .

this
Outshining and o'erwhelming edifice
Fools our fond gaze, the greatest of the great
Defies at first our Nature's littleness,
Till, growing with its growth, we thus dilate
Our spirits to the size of what they contemplate.
(canto IV, 155, 158)

As Venice rises from the sea, so can the spirit soar and the mind dilate, and writing revivify, reclaim and redeem. This is a central claim – or hope – in the poem.

But can Venice be reclaimed as opposed, say, to redreamed?

The spouseless Adriatic mourns her Lord;
And, annual marriage now no more renewed,
The Bucentaur lies rotting unrestored,
Neglected garment of her widowhood!
St Mark yet sees his lion where he stood
Stand, but in mockery of his withered power,
Over the proud Place where an Emperor sued,
And monarchs gazed and envied in the hour
When Venice was a queen with an unequalled dower.
(canto IV, 31)

The Bucentaur was, of course, the Doge's magnificent state barge which was left to rot in the Arsenal after he fall of the republic. It was an obvious and often cited emblem of Venice's lost greatness and current decay. It was also the barge from which was celebrated the marriage of Venice to the Adriatic on Ascension Day each year – the Doge casting a ring into the water. The original ceremony intended to celebrate Venice's ongoing dominion of the sea so that it was both lord and queen of the Adriatic, which was no less than appropriate for such a rare phenomenon as a sea-city. Byron keeps this double-gendered aspect by making Venice 'lord' in the first line and 'queen' in the last. But the lord is lost and the queen is past; the power is withered, and the rot is unrestored. Looking at Venice Byron must see the neglected mourning window as well as the surgingly triumphant Cybele.

The final three stanzas of the Venice sequence were added after the first draft of the poem and although they do not name Venice they effectively cast light on all he has written about the city. I shall quote them in full, partly because they are among the most magical in the sequence – the 'enchanter's wand' revealing itself to be Byron's pen – and for another reason that I shall return to:

The moon is up, and yet it is not night –
Sunset divided the sky with her – a sea
Of glory streams along the Alpine height
Of blue Friuli's mountains; Heaven is free
From clouds, but of all colours seems to be,
Melted to one vast Iris of the West,
Where the Day joins the past Eternity;
While, on the other hand, meek Dian's crest
Floats through the azure air – an island of the blest!

A single star is at her side and reigns
With her o'er half the lovely heavens; but still
Yon sunny sea heaves brightly, and remains
Roll'd o'er the peak of the far Rhaetian hill,
As Day and Night contending were, until
Nature reclaim'd her order; – gently flows
The deep-dyed Brenta, where their hues instil
The odorous purple of a new-born rose,
Which streams upon her stream, and glass'd within it, glows,

Fill'd with the face of heaven, which from afar,
Comes down upon the waters; all its hues,
From the rich sunset to the rising star magical variety diffuse:
And now they change; a paler shadow strews
It's mantle o'er the mountains; parting day
Dies like a dolphin, whom each pang imbues
With a new colour as it gasps away,
The last still loveliest, till – 'tis gone – and all is gray
(canto IV, 27–9)

The material Venice is not addressed: this is Venice by implication, as it were. There are no 'structures' – everything is in terms of, reduced or dilated to, light, colour, water, reflections, atmospherics. The characteristic nouns are 'moon', 'sunset', 'sea', 'clouds', 'colours', 'Iris', 'air', 'hues', 'purple', 'rose', 'stream', 'waters', 'dolphin', 'shadow'; the adjectives are 'blue', 'azure', 'lovely', 'sunny', 'far', 'odorous', 'deep-dyed', 'magical', 'paler', 'parting', 'last', 'loveliest', 'gray'; the verbs (and participles) 'divides', 'joins', 'melted', 'floats', 'heaves', 'contending', 'reclaim'd', 'flows', 'streams', 'glass'd', 'glows', 'filled', 'diffuse', 'strews', 'dies', 'gasps', 'gone'. It is that time of day when everything is indeterminate, indeterminable, in a bright, crepuscular liminality of evening. Like Venice's palaces and prisons, things are divided, as between sun and moon, or rather joined, as the present is now joined to the past. There is contention – between Day and Night – but things, or rather not things but lights, colours, the elements, are floating, heaving, melting together. As in Venice itself, the reflections are becoming indistinguishable from the reflected, as with 'the odorous purple of a new-born rose, Which streams upon her stream, and glass'd within it, glows', where the almost indistinguishable shift from verb to noun – 'streams . . . stream' – suggests the almost-identity. The subsequent clause reminds us that glowing Venice is, too, 'glass'd' within the waters. It is 'not night' – not yet – while the contending/coming together of sun and moon, Day and Night, 'heaven' and 'waters', creates a kind of apocalypse of colours out of air, light and water, which yields to 'one vast Iris of the West'. This suggests not just the day dissolving in a last summation of colour, but also the final flower and flowering of the glory of Western civilization – such as, seen in a certain light, Venice was for Byron. Like the day, Venice too was dying 'like a dolphin', that most beautiful and lovable of animals which, again like Venice, amphibiously rises from and returns to the sea with such heart-thrilling, heart-breaking beauty and grace, arousing a quite peculiar joy and sadness. As the day yields to night there are of course hints and portents of greater decline, more sombre conclusions, more apocalyptic terminations. Venice too, Venice as aesthetic spectacle seen from 'airy distance', was a distillation of 'magical variety' bringing together, as it were, all the colours and hues that the best Western art had conjured up. It was a sort of ultimate efflorescence, in some senses a summation and climax of 'the West'. And it was gasping away – not least under the Austrians; it was parting; it was dying. And, as with day, the final flush of mortality made it even more beautiful than it had ever been – loveliest in its lastness. The conclusion, it has to be noted, says and intimates nothing about resurrection or *risorgimento* – 'tis gone – and all is gray'. It seems to anticipate and adumbrate an irreversible loss, a time indeed when Nature will have 'reclaim'd her order', which was of course the ultimate message of the ruin. And, for Byron, Venice was simply the loveliest ruin of them all. The Venice of these stanzas is of course Turner's Venice, which is the other reason I have quoted them in full. He too saw and painted a Venice dissolving and disappearing into a glorious cataclysm of light and looked less and less at any 'structures'. The wand which was the pen in Byron's hands becomes the brush.

'Yet once more let us look upon the sea': appropriately Byron ends the whole canto by the ocean – but this time there is only ocean, no Venice or 'structure' of any kind.

> Man marks the earth with ruin – this control
> Stops by thy shore . . .
>
> Unchangeable save to thy wild waves' play –
> Time writes no wrinkle on thine azure brow –
> (canto IV, 179, 182)

It is still a 'mirror' but what it 'glasses' now is 'the Almighty's form'. Byron here has done with history and civilization and is thinking only of ultimate, eternal-seeming forces. The caresser and lover of many women and cities now stretches out a hand to the original, all-originating sea, as he reaches back to his own childhood. It is explicitly that return to the 'good mother' which Simmel said ruins both portend and suggest.

And I have loved thee, Ocean
Of youthful sports was on thy breast to be
Borne, like thy bubbles, onward: from a boy
I wantoned with thy breakers – they to me
Were a delight; and if the freshening sea
Made them a terror – 'twas a pleasing fear,
For I was as it were a child of thee.
And trusted to thy billows far and near,
And laid my hand upon thy mane – as I do here.
(canto IV, 184)

'Mane' has occasioned some comment, but, if we remember that Byron used to ride his horses along the sands of the Lido in between writing and womanizing, this last 'stroke' – of the pen (he is finishing), and of the 'mane' of woman/horse consummated in and subsumed and superseded by a last stroking of the sea – will seem a fitting enough gesture. He then stops, with the intimation that, like so much that he has written about, he too is going down, going out – the dream which was the writing is over:

My task is done – my song hath ceased – my theme
Has died into an echo; it is fit
The spell should break of this protracted dream.
The torch shall be extinguished which has lit
My midnight lamp – and what is writ, is writ,
Would it were worthier! but I am not now
That which I have been – and my visions flit
Less palpably before me – and the glow
Which in my spirit dwelt, is fluttering, faint, and low.
(canto IV, 185)

In the very last stanza he simply leaves the 'moral' of the writing with the reader – and disappears. Almost, one is tempted to say, thinking of the opening Venetian sequence of the stanza, he sinks back into the elements from which he and his writing rose.

For Byron his identity was confirmed, if not constituted, by writing:

'Tis to create, and in creating live
A being more intense, that we endow
With form our fancy, gaining as we give
The life we image, even as I do now.
What am I? Nothing; but not so art thou,
Soul of my thought!
(canto III, 6)

Or, as he says in the Venetian sequence, 'the beings of the mind' can come into *being* only if they are materialized, in Byron's case written. It is this drive to create which 'First exiles, then replaces what we hate'. Primarily and crucially it is effective on two fronts – 'watering the heart . . . and . . . replenishing the void' (canto IV, 5). As is often noted, there is no teleology in his writing, no sense of purpose or direction in the poem. He roams, he wanders, he sits, he sees, he meditates; but underneath it all there is always the question, 'where should I steer? / There woos no home, nor hope, nor life, save what is here' (canto IV, 105) – and 'here' is just wherever he happens to be. One senses that he wrote as eagerly, as casually, as joyously, as easily, as frequently – and at times as desperately, as well as with the acquired ease – as he made love. It is as if he is writing to keep a sense of permanent displacement, or non-placement, at bay. It really does seem to be a case of: I write, therefore I am. Vincent Newey is quite right to say of the latter cantos of *Childe Harold* that they are 'pervaded by this sense of the self which is constantly brought into existence in the mind and through language – and which is therefore also always provisional and on the point of dissolution'.[48] Identity becomes a matter of continuous improvisation amid ongoing contingency and – particularly in Italy, ***particularly*** in Venice – vacancy and ruin. In his own – not Hobhouse's – note to the lines on Madame de Staël he says:

> Corinna has ceased to be woman, she is only an author. . . . She will enter into that existence in which the great writers of all ages and nations are, as it were, associated in a world of their own, and, from that superior sphere, shed their eternal influence for the control and consolation of mankind. But the individual will gradually disappear as the author is more distinctly seen.[49]

It was through writing that Byron, homeless and astray in an intensely felt transience, transforms the too-provisional individual into the enduring author. Byron the individual was constantly giving up writing as a marginal activity compared to the part he sought to play in world-historical events, but Byron the author was writing literally to the end.

> I sent you Beppo – . . . it has politics & ferocity. . . . It is the height of the Carnival – and I am in the strum & agonies of a new intrigue – with I don't know exactly whom or what – except that she is insatiate of love – & wont take money . . . & that I met her at the Masque – & that when her mask is off I am as wise as ever.[50]

> And after all, what is a lie? 'Tis but
> The truth in masquerade.
> (*Don Juan*, XI, 37)

> I will answer your friend C.V. who objects to the quick succession of fun and gravity – as if in that case the gravity did not (in intention at least) heighten the fun. – His metaphor is that 'we are never scorched and drenched at the same time!' – Blessings on his experience! – Did he never play at Cricket or walk a mile in hot weather? – did he never spill a dish of tea over his testicles in handing a cup to his charmer to the great shame of his nankeen breeches? . . . was he ever in a Turkish bath – that marble of sherbert and sodomy . . . did he never tumble into a river or lake fishing – and sit in his wet clothes in the boat – or on the bank afterwards 'scorched and drenched' like a true sportsman?[51]

Byron finished canto IV of Childe Harold 29 July 1817 and by 12 October of the same year he was informing Murray that *Beppo* was finished; and he was f——g, incessantly. It is very appropriate that when on 27 January 1818 he wrote to tell Murray that he had sent him the new poem he should, in the same letter, announce that he is writing from amid the 'height of the Carnival', involved with an indeterminate and insatiable someone, as inscrutable and unknowable with the mask on or off. For *Beppo* is indeed a carnival-masquerade poem, written at a time of carnival, about a story set in an earlier carnival, and itself – it might be said – carnivalizing poetry, masquerading as a poem. Since the pioneer work of Bakhtin and the supplementary work of such writers as Terry Castle we have come to appreciate the ramifying significance of these socially licensed periods of misrule, disorder and release. Terry Castle on masquerade in general writes:

> However comically conceived the inversions of the masquerade, they had serious implications. Donning a costume brought into being a symbolic scandal. The costumed body posed a mysterious relationship between antinomies, connection where before there had been only separation. On the inividual level the conventional alienation between self and other was phantasmagorically overcome. . . . Like the 'carnivalised' body of ancient festive tradition described by Bakhtin,

> the double body of masquerade 'is not a closed, complete unit; it is unfinished, outgrows itself, transgresses its own limits.'[52]

Terry Castle is addressing herself specifically to the masquerades which were popular in eighteenth-century London. These masquerades ceased with what she describes as a mysterious abruptness in the later years of the century, when what Bakhtin describes as the 'carnival fires' of European culture were going out all over Europe.

The sort of carnival that lingered on in Venice was perhaps more rococo and self-consciously theatrical than the earlier forms described by Terry Castle. Bakhtin wrote:

> Carnival serves a different role in rococo literature. Here the gay positive tone of laughter is preserved. But everything is reduced to 'chamber' lightness and intimacy. The frankness of the marketplace is transformed into erotic frivolity and gay relativity becomes skepticism and wantonness. And yet, in the 'hedonistic boudoir' atmosphere a few sparks of the carnival fires which burn up 'hell' have been preserved. In the setting of gloomy seriousness so widespread in the eighteenth century, rococo perpetuated after a fashion the traditional carnivalesque spirit.[53]

This is perhaps closer to the lightness of touch and the apparent frivolity of tone of Byron's poem. In general we may say of carnival and masquerade that to some degree or other (and we may be dealing with vestigial traces or the slightest of hints) they involve intimations of the inversion or collapse of hierarchy; the destabilization of genre and perhaps gender; a promiscuous mingling of both classes and sexes; a suspension or failure of habitual taxonomies; an experience of the provisionality and fictionality of customary classificatory systems; possibilities of metamorphosis; a liberation from conventions; an undermining of the dualities and binary oppositions on which culture is founded; category collapse, and perhaps just the faintest glimpse of Chaos and old Night. Masking – which can release inhibition while concealing intention, intimate unknowable secrets or depthless enigmas and indicate what Bakhtin calls the rejection of 'conformity to oneself' – necessarily raises questions of identity on all levels. Who are you? *What* are you? Come to that, what am I? Masks generate what Terry Castle calls 'the central enigma of masquerade phenomenology, the mysterious nature of the other'. Who is that mysterious, dark Muslim at the carnival in *Beppo*? Laura's Christian husband? 'And are you *really*, *truly*, now a Turk?' Metamorphosis, reversal, a possible dissolution of category differences – the apparently most alien turns out to be the most intimately familiar, the far the near, the other the same. Can we '*really*, *truly*' know who or what another person is – even if we share the same bed? Does it matter? Such are some of the questions which flicker over the ending of Byron's poem. Masquerade, suggests Terry Castle, sets up a relentless structural interplay 'between self and other, the natural and the artificial, the familiar and the alien'.[54] Even though masquerade was socially licensed (though strongly opposed) and may therefore be seen as offering some sort of ritual containment of its implicit anarchization of reality, it could be (and was) seen as having a worrying disruptive power. 'The way the masquerade rendered a dialectical fluidity between opposites, magic unities instead of differences, was a symbolic revocation of cosmos itself. At its worst the masquerade resembled a convulsive, unstoppable ripple through the core of things, a metaphysical shock wave.'[55] The Lisbon earthquake, Terry Castle reminds us, was blamed on masquerades.

Byron's Venetian letters contain many references to contemporary carnivals, masquerades and masks and, though these things are necessarily not demonstrable, it seems to me that the style, the tone, the touch, the timbre, of *Beppo* – and thence of *Don Juan* ('I have finished the First Canto . . . of a poem in the style and manner of "Beppo". . . . It is called "Don Juan", and is meant to be a little quietly facetious upon every thing'[56]) – owe more to Venice and her carnivals than to Whistleforth or Italian models. One can sense Byron's incredulous glee at the criticism of the 'quick succession of fun and gravity' in *Beppo* on the grounds that 'we are never scorched or drenched at the same time'. You are never, perhaps, if you insist on trying to keep your experience in rigid, unitary compartments; if you put your stress on well-policed boundaries; if you refuse ambiguity and deny ambivalence; if you set your face against the flowing inter-mixedness of life; if you dread what Castle calls 'ontological promiscuity' and campaign at once to simplify and to mystify 'the real'. But Byron knew that of course we can and do think two things at effectively the same time, feel two things in such rapid succession that they are inseparable, and you simply cannot draw a line between the levity and the gravity, the gladness and the sadness; indeed, that we can even feel ourselves to be more than one person or identity at the same time. Scorched *and* drenched at the same time? Certainly, and – if the truth be told – all the time and in all sorts and conditions of life. And this we may say is the carnival-masquerade effect: the experienced co-presence of only apparent mutual exclusivities. The pagan turns out to be a Christian; the stranger only a delayed intimate; and the husband can borrow the lover's underclothes. And why not?

In a letter of 6 November 1816 Byron wrote: 'There was a famous improvvisatore who held forth while I was there. His fluency astonished me.'[57] In *Beppo* Byron clearly aims for an improvised, improvising air, to the point where at times it seems trivializing, almost flippant. But to see it so would be to betray a ponderously heavy sort of expectation of what is proper and requisite for a narrative mode. Notoriously, only about half the stanzas deal with and advance the narrative, while the other half are various digressions. Indeed, the poem starts as digression and only fitfully recalls itself to the story. But, as it is a matter of half and half, you could as well say that the narrative interrupts the digression as the other way about, and see the story as a digression from the digression. (In the eighteenth century the carnival was sometimes six months long, in which case would you say that carnival was a temporary secession from 'normal real' life, or vice versa?) Byron's poem is neither definitively – *really, truly* – one thing or the other. It could be this and it could be that. Don't try to fix, determine and arrest.

> Of all the places where the Carnival
> Was most facetious in the days of yore,
> For dance, and song, and serenade, and ball.
> And Masque, and mime, and mystery, and more
> Than I have time to tell you now, or at all,
> Venice the bell from every city bore, –
> And at the moment when I fix my story,
> That sea-born city was in all her glory.
>
> (*Beppo*, X)[58]

'Fixing' his story is hardly what Byron contrives or even attempts to do; as he writes when he returns to it for the fourth time after a digression on fashion, Napoleon and Fortune, 'the devil take it! This story slips for ever through my fingers', but a slippery story is right for the sea-born city, and this is emphatically a Venetian story. Venice here is the place where the carnival was 'most facetious', a word which had a richer and more positive resonance for Byron than, perhaps, for us. According to the *OED* it once meant 'polished, agreeable, urbane', applied to style or manners, and it also means 'characterized by or addicted to pleasantry, jocose, waggish, formerly often with a laudatory sense; witty, humorous, amusing'. Byron, who, as we have noted, also used the word to describe the tone and mood of *Don Juan*, seems to have found qualities in Venetian carnival which he would emulate in his writing, and that surely included the urbanity as well as the wit and waggishness.

For this Venice is not only the place of 'masque, and mime, and mystery' but the place of *more* – 'more / Than I have time to tell you now, or at all'. It exceeds telling, and ultimately slips through the fingers that seek to hold, or write, it. And it is just that sense of the *more* – the more of life than we can ever finally contain in writing, never mind constrain by moral systems – that Byron's poem, with all its digressions, qualifications, hesitations, parenthetic self-interruptions, interpolated expansions and self-reflexive comments, is continually gesturing to. More, literally, than time can tell.

And it is in recognition of this that Byron keeps the touch as light, and the tone as urbane and humorous – as 'facetious' – as possible.

Lists also help to convey the sense of unorganized over-abundance which the poem seeks to recognize, and there are many – not least in the opening stanzas, which evoke the swarming heterogeneity and rich commingling multiplicity of the carnival. The first stanza ends:

> With fiddling, feasting, dancing, drinking, masking,
> And other things which may be had for asking.

And the second:

> And here are songs and quavers, roaring, strumming,
> Guitars, and every other sort of strumming.

Sex is the 'other thing', the 'other sort' which must conclude, or originate, every list. One way or another, and the ways are rich and various indeed, it all and always comes back to, comes from, that. No matter how it is masked, mimed or mystified; no matter if it be euphemized, ignored or denied, the 'other thing' is, somewhere, always there. The other thing is *the thing*. Byron's recognition of this in the poem is 'facetious' but not at all, to my mind, reductive. In the most urbane way imaginable, this is what his slippery Venetian story is all about.

After his evocation of the carnival atmosphere and his paean to Venice, Byron approaches his story with three steps which seem random and discontinuous – fostering the air of unpremeditation and improvisation – but which possess an associative logic which is crucial to the poem. The first involves a eulogy to Venetian women, comparing them to works of art, at the same time emphasizing, and extolling, their physicality and transience.

> They've pretty faces yet, those same Venetians,
>   Black eyes, arch'd brows, and sweet expressions still;
> Such as of old were copied from the Grecians,
>   In ancient arts by moderns mimick'd ill;
> And like so many Venuses of Titian's
>   (The best's at Florence – see it, if ye will).
> They look when leaning over the balcony,
> Or stepp'd from out a picture by Giorgione.
>
> Whose tints are truth and beauty at their best;
>   And when you to Manfrini's palace go,
> That picture (howsoever fine the rest)
>   Is loveliest to my mind of all the show;

It may perhaps be also to *your* zest,
  And that's the cause I rhyme upon it so:
'Tis but a portrait of his son, and wife,
And self; but *such* a woman! love in life!

Love in full life and length, not love ideal,
  No, nor ideal beauty, that fine name,
But something better still, so very real,
  That the sweet model must have been the same;
A thing that you would purchase, beg or steal,
  Were't not possible, besides a shame:
The face recalls some face, as 'twere with pain,
You once have seen, but ne'er will see again,

One of those forms that flit by us, when we
  Are young, and fix our eyes on every face;
And, oh! the loveliness at times we see
  In momentary gliding, the soft grace,
The youth, the bloom, the beauty which agree,
  In many a nameless being we retrace,
Whose course and home we knew not, nor shall know,
Like the last Pleid seen no more below.

(XI–XIV)

The intention here is to subvert the notion of 'ideal beauty', or to relocate the ideal in the 'real'. So the Venetian women have the beauty of both ancient and Renaissance art, which suggests a kind of commemorative fixity and permanence; but – better – they have stepped out of the pictures and have the reality and movement, and the pathos of transience, of life; the 'loveliness' which we can sometimes see in, and only in, 'momentary gliding'. For Byron art is at its best when, impossibly, it seems to fix the fleetingness of beauty, of 'love *in life*' (my emphasis). Such a beauty is 'a thing' which it is forever impossible to appropriate in any way (it cannot be purchased, begged or stolen); which in its fugitivity cannot even be caught in name; whose origin and destination (destiny) and ultimate home are forever unknowable. In all this it is better than anything transcendent or ideal because, precisely, 'so very real'. Venetian women, like the city itself, incorporate and body forth a beauty to be found, and only to be found, in transience; a beauty in which art and life – the picture and the model – are indistinguishable, identical in being 'so very real'. 'Love in life' – and *only* in life. In that sense as slippery – ungraspable – as the story which Byron will, in his own way, go on to tell. It is a beauty which comes to birth and is perceived only in the moment of its vanishing and so can never be had or held but only 'retraced' and remembered – experienced as absence, appreciated as loss.

In the next step Byron moves from the general timelessness of art to contemporaneity, and from the beauty of woman as aesthetically distanced to the close and often violent actualities of sexuality. From stillness to action.

> I said that like a picture by Giorgione
>   Venetian women were, and so they *are*,
> Particularly seen from a balcony
>   (For beauty's sometimes best set off afar),
> And there, just like a heroine of Goldoni,
>   They peep from out the blind, or o'er the bar;
> And truth to say, they're mostly very pretty,
> And rather like to show it, more's the pity!
>
> For glances beget ogles, ogles sighs,
>   Sighs wishes, wishes words, and words a letter,
> Which flies on wings of light-heel'd Mercuries,
>   Who do such things because they know no better;
> And then, God knows what mischief may arise,
>   When love links two young people in one fetter,
> Vile assignations and adulterous beds,
> Elopements, broken vows, and hearts, and heads.
>
> (XV–XVI)

The shift from painting (Giorgione) to drama (Goldoni) heralds the shift to dramatic action when, as it were, female beauty is moved and gets on the move. It may be a pity, says Byron with something of a mock sigh of resignation, that pretty women like to show themselves, but there it is – they quite naturally do. And then, immediately, 'the other thing' is involved and by an unstoppably rapid sequence of acts and events, which almost blur into each other in the inevitability of their progression or succession, all sorts of 'mischief' (there is no vocabulary of evil in this poem) rise, involving perhaps 'Vile assignations and adulterous beds' and who knows what assorted breakages, including the unmentioned hymenal one. All this, suggests the tone, is as true as it is inevitable and the main question – it is, if you like, the question of the whole poem – is what should be the mode and manner of our response? Our response, that is, to two phenomena inseparable from sexuality – infidelity and jealousy.

Byron then shifts into another key as he moves from Goldoni and his comedies about Venetian intrigues to Shakespeare's *Othello*, perhaps the greatest Western tragedy to study, among other things, the pathology of jealousy. (In a letter of 20 February 1818, that is just after the completion and dispatch of *Beppo*, Byron wrote to Murray: 'Tomorrow night I am going to see "Othello" an opera from our "Othello" – and one of Rossini's best, it is said, it will be curious to see in Venice – the Venetian story itself represented – beside to discover what they will make of Shakespeare in Music.'[59] Byron the poet watching a musical version of the dramatic representation of the Venetian story – a series of recessions which suggests that in Venice it is hard to determine where art leaves off and 'life' begins, to tell the picture from the model.)

Shakespeare described the sex in Desdemona
  As very fair, but yet suspect in fame,
And to this day from Venice to Verona
  Such matters will probably be the same,
Except that since those times was never known a
  Husband whom mere suspicion could inflame
To suffocate a wife no more than twenty,
Because she had a 'cavalier servente'.

Their jealousy (if they are ever jealous)
  Is of a fair complexion altogether,
Not like that sooty devil of Othello's,
  Which smothers women in a bed of feather.
But worthier of these much more jolly fellows,
  When weary of the matrimonial tether
His head for such a wife no mortal bothers,
But takes on at once another, or another's.

(XVII–XVIII)

The suggestion is that the great English drama has, as it were, got it wrong; or, at least, shows how wrongly, and with what lethal stupidity, jealousy may be handled. It is wrong, diabolical (this much of evil *is* allowed into the poem, only to be ridiculed and dismissed), to take jealousy to the point of tragedy – indeed, to take jealousy to any point at all. The 'worthier' response is exemplified by the behaviour of the 'jolly fellows' of Venice and its environs. There is no point in trying to minimize the extent of Byron's contestatory devaluing of the rigid moral rules customarily associated with the 'matrimonial tether'. Nor will it do to dismiss it as the trivializing flippancy of a Regency dandy. The suggestion in the last quoted line that the difference between taking 'another' wife and 'another's' wife is so barely perceptible as to be unimportant is indeed a direct challenge to any notion of the sacredness of so-called legitimized love, with its fiercely guarded exclusivities. To the charge that to take this attitude is effectively to degrade and dissolve the sanctities which supposedly surround and uphold the state of marriage, Byron might reply that it it better to be 'facetious' than murderous. Better, certainly, to be 'jolly' than dead. No 'mortal' should 'bother' too much about a slippery wife, or husband come to that – and we are all, more or less, like Shakespeare's Barnardine, 'desperately mortal'.

The importance of death, and living in, and with, an awareness of mortality, is taken up in the next step when Byron suddenly starts to talk, with only apparent irrelevance, about gondolas.

> Didst ever see a Gondola? For fear
>   You should not, I'll describe it you exactly:
> 'Tis a long cover'd boat that's common here
>   Carved at the prow, built lightly, but compactly,
> Row'd by two rowers, each call'd 'Gondolier',
>   It glides along the water looking blackly.
> Just like a coffin clapt in a canoe,
> Where none can make out what you say or do.
>
> And up and down the long canals they go,
>   And under the Rialto shoot along,
> By night and day, all paces, swift and slow,
>   And round the theatres, a sable throng,
> They wait in their dusky livery of woe, –
>   But not to them do woeful things belong,
> For sometimes they contain a deal of fun,
> Like mourning coaches when the funeral's done.
>
> (XIX–XX)

The gondola is, of course, indissociably associated with Venice; indeed was, or became, a virtual synecdoche of the city itself. According to Milton Wilson, it was only travel writing of the 1740s which started to 'turn gondolas into hearses', though the canopy and hull had always been black, a blackness 'prescribed by a series of sumptuary laws to restrict private extravagance'. In his Venetian epigrams Goethe compares the gondola to a cradle carrying a coffin, but, according to Wilson, Byron's version of the gondola owes most to Madame de Staël's *Corinne*, in which, in the words of a translation of 1807, the black gondolas which glide along the canals resemble 'coffins or cradles, the first and last receptacles of man'.[60] Be the debt as it may, Byron's sudden veering into a description of the gondola at this moment in his poem clearly has a special, locally pertinent, point. Certainly it suggests death: it looks 'blackly', 'like a coffin'; many of them together, a 'sable throng' in 'their dusky livery of woe'. But 'not to them do woeful things belong'; from another point of view, given Venice and given Byron, they are undoubtedly phallic – 'up and down the long canals they go' – and no matter what they look like they can often 'contain a deal of fun'. They look like death and yet may be enabling vehicles of the compulsive sexual activity their very movement seems to imitate. They represent and facilitate an exemplary obscurity and impenetrability – 'none can make out what you say or do'. They make it hard to tell the 'woe' from the 'fun', and impossible to separate and distinguish them. In the Venetian gondola, as in the gondola which is sea-born(e) Venice, you may indeed be 'scorched and drenched' at the same time, and nobody can precisely tell when the fun becomes fun-ereal or, indeed, when the funeral becomes fun. Confronting the heavy matters of jealousy and murder, Byron suggests it may be better to take and travel life like a gondola which 'glides along the water'. To that end he writes a gliding, gondola sort of poem which may, to some eyes, look 'blackly' and yet turn out to contain 'a deal of fun'; and of course, by the same token, may simply look like fun and turn out to contain a deal of blackness. Don't make the mistake of trying to separate the scorching from the drenching, the woe from the fun. And don't kill young women.

And *now*, at last, Byron is ready to attempt to narrativize.

> But to my story. – 'Twas some years ago,
> It may be thirty, forty, more or less,
> The Carnival was at its height, and so
> Were all kinds of buffoonery and dress;
> A certain lady went to see the show,
> Her real name I know not, nor can guess,
> And so we'll call her Laura, if you please,
> Because it slips into my verse with ease.
>
> (XXI)

The name slips into the versification of the slippery story with ease . . . it would be wilfully and perversely blind not to recognize that Byron is deliberately foregrounding the lubricity of writing in his always half-foundering attempt to write about the problems posed and the felicities produced – the woe and the fun – by our inescapable sexuality. Of, if you prefer, call it simply our gendered condition. And we notice that, from the start, Byron foregrounds the apparent arbitrariness and inexactness of his story, and both the improvisatory casualness of the teller and the indeterminability if not unknowability of the tale. He will keep up this foregrounding to the end – or rather cessation – of the poem:

> My pen is at the bottom of a page,
> Which being finished, here the story ends;

'Tis to be wish'd it had been sooner done,
But stories somehow lengthen when begun.
(XCIX)

'*A* page' not 'the page', as Drummond Bone noted in an excellent article on the poem:[61] the breaking off is as arbitrary as the beginning seemed to be constantly interrupted and deferred. This, together with the desultory, informal and colloquial tone of the whole poem, gives the impression of the writing gliding and slipping around all over the place, only imperfectly under Byron's control. For this is as much a poem about Byron writing as a narrative about Laura loving.

The tale that Byron manages, just, to get told, is seemingly of great simplicity. Laura – call her Laura – was happily and faithfully married to a merchant trader named Giuseppe (Beppo). Beppo failed to return from one of his travels and after waiting for 'several years' Laura 'thought it prudent to connect her / With a vice-husband *chiefly to protect her*' (XXIX). She chooses a wealthy count – 'a perfect cavaliero', an urbane and gifted man not without some Byronic characteristics ('He patronised the Improvisatori, / Nay, could himself extemporise some stanzas,' writes Byron extemporizingly). Of course, they occasionally have their differences –

But, on the whole, they were a happy pair,
As happy as unlawful love could make them.
(LIV)

This is not *merely* witty: one of the thrusts of the whole poem is to call into question the uncritical (Byron would say hypocritical) privileging of so-called '*lawful*' love and the attendant condemnation of any other kind. There are obvious biographical reasons for Byron to have England in mind as the object of his attack, but he is doing more than satisfying a personal grudge when he sets the flexible and tactfully permissive Venetian *mores* against the abrasive legalism which results from England's chilly codes of respectability:

But Heaven preserve Old England from such courses!
Or what becomes of damage and divorces?
(XXXVII)

Instead of 'damage and divorces' when Laura's husband finally returns, disguised as a Turk, and confronts Laura and her count at the carnival, there is amity and accommodation. The count is all courtesy, while Laura deluges Beppo with an uninterruptible scattering of unrelated questions which effectively prevents reproach and disarms any possibility of recrimination, or distongues it, rather; for Beppo is to all intents rendered speechless

('What answer Beppo made to these demands / Is more than I know'), and indeed he never speaks a word in the poem bearing his name. All possibility of discord is deflected; indeed, one could say that potentially oppositional differences are dissolved as together they drink coffee which is, notes Byron in one of those apparently casual asides that felicitously touch on weighty matters in the lightest way:

> A beverage for Turks and Christians both,
> Although the way they make it's not the same.
> (XCI)

Why fight over only apparent – procedural – differences, when the essence is the same? When Beppo throws off his Turkish garments he 'borrow'd the Count's smallclothes for a day' and 'I've heard the Count and he were always friends'. (XCIV) And so the poem stops and the tale concludes. No jealousy, no murder; no damage, no divorce. If to English eyes it does not seem a very moral tale, it is, nevertheless, certainly a tale with a moral.

For Byron has taken Venice – 'the seat of all dissoluteness', as the cryptically initialled S. A. quoted in the epigraph to *Beppo* defines it (Samuel Ayscough (1745–1804), an editor of Shakespeare; his note on Venice actually said 'licentiousness', not 'dissoluteness') – and his quintessentially Venetian tale has shown it as a realm of alternative, positive values, a place where art and artifice *conjoin* with the 'so very real', and where 'the other thing' is recognized and accepted – and celebrated – in a way which, in its triumph over destructive violence and factitious difference, is not merely 'jolly' nor just pragmatically urbane, but which deserves to be called truly civilized. So-called 'decadence' is turned into a higher humaneness as Byron, in Venice, turns on England.

And that, of course, is part of the point of the poem – how it all isn't 'English'. After extolling Venice and Venetian women, – particularly married women 'Because they know the world, and are at ease, / And being natural, naturally please' (XXXVIII) – Byron enlarges his commendation to Italy, and 'things' and arts Italian, and contrasts it with his homeland.

> With all its sinful doings, I must say,
> That Italy's a pleasant place to me,
> Who love to see the sun shine every day,
> And vines (not nail'd to walls) from tree to tree
> Festoon'd much like the back scene of a play,
> Or melodrame, which people flock to see,
> When the first act is ended by a dance
> In vineyards copied from the south of France.

I like on Autumn evenings to ride out,
  Without being forced to bid my groom be sure
My cloak is round his middle strapp'd about,
  Because the skies are not the most secure;
I know too that, if stopp'd upon my route,
  Where the green alleys windingly allure,
Reeling with grapes red waggons choke the way –
In England 'twould be dung, or dust, or a dray.

I also like to dine on becaficas,
  To see the sun set, sure he'll rise tomorrow,
Not through a misty morning twinkling weak as
  A drunken man's dead eye in maudlin sorrow,
But with all heaven t'himself; the day will break as
  Beauteous as cloudless, nor be forced to borrow
That sort of farthing candlelight which glimmers
Where reeking London's smoky cauldron simmers.

I love the language, that soft bastard Latin,
  Which melts like kisses from a female mouth,
And sounds as if it should be writ on satin,
  With syllables which breathe on the sweet South,
And gentle liquids gliding all so pat in,
  That not a single accent seems uncouth,
Like our harsh northern whistling, grunting guttural,
Which we're obliged to hiss, and spit, and sputter all.

I like women too (forgive my folly),
  From the rich peasant cheek of ruddy bronze,
And large black eyes that flash on you a volley
  Of rays that say a thousand things at once,
To the high dame's brow, more melancholy,
  But clear, and with a wild and liquid glance,
Heart on her lips, and soul within her eyes,
Soft as her clime, and sunny as her skies.

Eve of the land which still is Paradise!
  Italian beauty! didst thou not inspire
Raphael, who dies in thy embrace, and vies
  With all we know of Heaven, or can desire,
In what he hath bequeath'd us? – in what guise,
  Though flashing from the fervour of the lyre,

Would *words* describe thy past and present glow
While yet Canova can create below?

(XLI–XLVI)

Italy is here constituted as a paradisal land of light which continually, effortlessly, aspires to the condition of art; and, through its artists, women and beauty, offers and affords us 'all we know of Heaven, or can desire'. Everything is made to seem to contribute to the unashamed arousal and satisfaction of desire, including the language, indeed particularly the language, with its 'gentle liquids gliding all so pat in' – which could hardly be more frankly lubricious. By contrast England – and English – is all darkness and dissonance, associated with dung, dust and, indeed, death. Where in Italy the erotic and the aesthetic are at one with life, England is a place of rank uncouthness, where sunlight struggles to penetrate the gloom and smoke, just as the voice loses itself in grunting and spitting. Where Italy offers constant consummation, this England is a place of negation and repression, and, where all in Italy seems to 'glow', in England you have to borrow 'farthing candlelight'.

England is indeed directly addressed in the following three stanzas which begin: '"England! with all thy faults I love thee still" / I said at Calais, and have not forgot it' (XLVII). After his own personal praise for Italy it is manifestly a belittling irony to have recourse to a quotation – from Cowper – to articulate an affection for England. It is as though Byron recognizes that such a sentiment exists but he himself holds it at arm's length, as if to test its plausibility. He then goes on to list, with increasing inconsequentiality, the things about England he 'likes', and in each case every positive quality or phenomenon is immediately qualified, undermined or retracted, as in: 'I like the weather, when it is not rainy, / That is, I like two months of every year'. (XLVIII) – so that at the end of the list he arrives at the ironic conclusion 'Which means that I like all and everything', having shown how little he likes anything. Another list follows, including such items as 'Our cloudy climate, and our chilly women', which in turn concludes, 'All these I can forgive, and can forget' (XLIX), thus demonstrating that he has certainly not forgotten, and perhaps not forgiven, anything. But again the touch is light: this is no vicious, resentful invective; indeed, the satire is, as Drummond Bone nicely suggests, 'dissipated' by comic inconsequentiality and 'the increasingly tangential relevancy of the list'.[62] From Byron's Venetian perspective the chilly women and the cloudy skies seem very far away and are no longer able to impose their darkness or inflict their *froideur*. The triumph of the poem – which is in part a triumph of tone – depends on not allowing anything too cloudy or chilly to settle on the poem and lower its spirits. In the established lexicon and moral geography of the poem, it is the triumph of Venice over England.

There is still, in the Doge's palace the black veil painted over Falieri's picture & the staircase whereon he was first crowned Doge, and subsequently decapitated. – This was the thing that most struck my imagination in Venice.[63]

The veil which blackens o'er this blighted name,
And hides, or seems to hide, these lineaments,
Shall draw more gazers than the thousand portraits
Which glitter round it in their pictured trappings.[64]

What letters are these which
Are scrawl'd along the inexorable wall?
Will the gleam let me trace them? Ah! the names
Of my sad predecessors in this place,
The dates of their despair, the brief words of
A grief too great for many. This stone page
Holds like an epitaph their history. . . .
Alas!
I recognise some names familiar to me,
And blighted like to mine, which I will add,
Fittest for such a chronicle as this,
Which only can be read, as writ, by wretches. . . .
These walls have been my study,
More faithful pictures of Venetian history,
With all their blank, or dismal stains, than is
The hall not far from hence, which bears on high
Hundreds of doges, and their deeds and dates.[65]

Byron's two Venetian dramas contain 'writing on the wall' which figures crucially, and in crucially different ways. In *Marino Faliero, Doge of Venice*, what arouses the Doge's anger to the point of conspiring against his own state and planning the murder of his own class is a gratuitous and mendacious obscenity scrawled by a young libertine on the Doge's own palace wall:

A wretch like this may leave upon the wall
The blighting venom of his sweltering heart,
And this shall spread itself in general poison
(*MF* II. i. 1426–8)

Byron does not repeat the words in his play, but historically, or perhaps apocryphally, they were:

Marin Falier
Has a wife that is fair,
He has to keep her while other men lay 'er.

Because the perpetrator, Steno, was a member of 'the Forty' he received what Faliero saw as not only a derisively but an insultingly light sentence (a month in gaol). Hence his resolve to attempt to extirpate the whole patrician class in Venice. This writing both alludes to the prevalent sexuality supposedly rife in Venice, and is also a lie. In *The Two Foscari* the writing which Jacopo Foscari traces out is on the prison wall and testifies to the hidden miseries of the buried and incarcerated victims of Venice's ruthless and secret state apparatus. These miserable inscriptions, and inscriptions of misery – simply names – must be true. Near the end of the play when the old Doge, Francis Foscari, having been dispossessed of his rand and title, prepares to leave the Ducal Palace, he refers to it in these terms:

Its *old* walls, ten times
As *old* as I am, and I'm very old,
Have served you, as have I, and I and they
Could tell a tale.
(*TF* V. i. 214–17)

What is the real tale that Venetian walls have to tell? That the truth of the palace is to be found in the prison? We have seen this conjunction before in Byron's Venetian writing – one might say it is the start and ground of it – and here again Marina, Jacopo's wife, when trying to persuade her husband out of his (to us, insane) insisted preference for torture and imprisonment in Venice rather than exile, succinctly states:

This crowd of palaces and prisons is not
A paradise; its first inhabitants
Were wretched exiles.
(*TF* III. i. 148–50)

This is the prosaic, realistic, disabused perspective on Venice; not only built on water and rooted in exile, but also, compounding the paradox of its existence, a mixture of palaces and prisons in which it can be difficult to tell the palatial from the carceral. What Byron suggests in both plays is that in this city, so conspicuously endowed with sumptuous public commemorations of historical personages and events, the *more* real history is the history behind, below: the veil tells more than the portrait; the 'blanks' on the prison wall give 'more faithful pictures of Venetian story' than the names and dates in the hall. Look for the truth in the erasures; in the writing under the writing.

This is a different Venice from the one evoked in *Beppo*, and, if that can be seen as a 'carnival' poem, Byron is emphatic that in his plays he is concerned – exclusively as he would, implausibly, have it – with Venetian history: 'The Venetian play too is rigidly historical.'[66] The plays were written after he had moved from Venice to Ravenna and during a time when he was involved with a secret revolutionary society of the Carbonari and a planned uprising against the Austrians which very quickly failed. As he completed *Marino Faliero* in July 1820 he wrote, 'we are here upon the eve of evolutions and revolutions.'[67] He admitted that the play 'is full of republicanism'[68] and was well aware of turbulent political events in England – Peterloo (August 1819), the Cato Street conspiracy (February 1820), the extraordinary row surrounding the Queen Caroline affair (after she was acquitted of the trumped-up adultery charges Byron wrote that the acquittal 'will prevent a revolution'[69] – feelings ran very high indeed), and even the prosecution of his friends Cartwright and Hobhouse. Nevertheless he insisted:

> I suspect that in Marino Faliero you and yours won't like the politics which are perilous to you in these times – but recollect that it is *not* political play – & that I was obliged to put into the mouths of the Characters the sentiments upon which they acted. – I hate all things written like Pizarro to represent France England & so forth – all I have done is meant to be purely Venetian – even to the very prophecy of it's present state.[70]

(*Pizarro* is a play by Sheridan in which 'Peru' is a thin mask for considerations of contemporary tensions between England and France.) Byron claims he has one advantage over Shakespeare and Otway – 'that – of having been at Venice – and entered into the local Spirit of it – I claim no more'.[71] This disclaiming of all possible contemporary relevance is of a piece with his insistence that the plays were *not* written to be performed; or, one might say, written to be not performed. 'I wrote for the *Closet*,' he insists;[72] and again, he asserts that the stage 'is not my object – but a *mental theatre*'.[73] This last claim has been challenged and it is likewise impossible not to discern *some* possible contemporary relevance in the plays. But it is worth considering just what kind of closet drama, or 'mental theatre', Byron created out of his immersion in Venice and Venetian history.

His two chosen protagonists are Doges who have done the state some – considerable – service, but who are finally rejected (executed or deposed) by that state. They are, or become, intensely aware of their impotence. This is no less than the historical truth, since the intricate rules of decision-making within the republic ensured that the figure of the Doge combined a maximum of pomp with a minimum of power. At the start of *Marino Faliero* he is depicted thus:

Placed at the ducal table, cover'd o'er
With all the apparel of the state; petitions,
Despatches, judgments, acts, reprieves, reports,
He sits rapt in duty.
(*MF* I. i. 7–10)

What follows is his violent awakening from that 'rapt' state. Upon hearing of the light sentence meted out to Steno which he takes as a personal insult, he 'dashes down the Ducal bonnet' and when addressed as the 'Duke of Venice' replies: 'There is no such thing – / It is a word – nay worse – a worthless word' (I. i. 99–100). Just which words are worthless and which are worthful is a matter at issue in the play, and near the end Faliero says, 'true *words* are *things*' (V. i. 289), going on to utter a prophetic curse on Venice which Byron, given his position in history, can make sure is a true thing. When he is persuaded to reassume the ducal cap he refers to it as a 'hollow bauble' and a 'degraded toy' and complains that the senate makes the 'people nothing, and the prince a pageant' (I. i. 270). He refers to himself as a 'poor puppet', 'A thing of robes and trinkets, dizen'd put / To sit in state as for a sovereign's picture' (II. ii. 187–8), and it is against this condition that he rebels, aligning himself fatally with the 'nothing' of the people, finding that prince and plebeians are alike ultimately powerless and that he only becomes another kind of puppet. Foscari, impotent to save his son, refers to his ceremonial diadem and ring as 'geegaws', and, when the Ten resolve to try to cover the fact that they are rudely deposing him by insisting on a ritualized formal departure, he rejects these 'vain insults' which 'only ulcerate the heart'. After his death the Ten resolve that the obsequies and funeral rites shall be 'princely', but the spirited Marina (widow of the dead Jacopo) denounces the intention as 'mockery':

you, signors,
Purpose, with idle and superfluous pomp,
To make a pageant over what you trampled.
A princely funeral will be your reproach,
And not his honour.
(*TF* V. i. 327–31)

What all this points up is at once the emptiness and concealing falseness of all the ceremonials and rituals of Venetian public life, the vacuity of the appurtenances and trappings of apparent power. The real power is elsewhere – hidden, devious and lethal.

One power which is abroad is 'hate', which effectively motivates the actions of both plays. Byron was clearly fascinated by Faliero's legendary quickness of temper and liability to ungovernable outbursts of anger – he was said to have boxed the ears of a bishop who was slow in offering him the sacraments! – and in the play his wife, Angiolina, reproaches him for his 'restless hate', the hate which makes him want to destroy the Venetian patriciate because of what he takes to be a slight on his honour. His nephew Bertuccio says to him that 'This fury doth exceed the provocation, / Or any provocation' (*MF* I. ii. 6–7), and his 'Fury', says Israel, one of the conspirators, 'Grows capable of all things for revenge' (II. ii. 173). Similarly it is the 'hereditary hate' of Loredano, who believes that Foscari poisoned his father and uncle, which makes him work remorselessly for the destruction of the two Foscari. Utterly implacable, he is said to be 'a very Ovid in the art of *hating*' (*TF* V. i. 136), and the words of the milder senator Barbarigo have a pertinence which extends to both plays:

There is no passion
More spectral or fantastical than Hate;
Not even its opposite, Love, so peoples air
With phantoms, as this madness of the heart.
(*TF* IV. i. 334–7)

Faliero's hate discharges itself in intemperate images of toxicity aimed at his own class, referring often to the 'aristocratic hydra' as an 'envenom'd pestilence' which has made Venice a 'lazar-house of tyranny' (*MF* III. i. 9) and leading him to decide and declare that *all* the patricians must be slaughtered, because it is 'The spirit of this aristocracy / Which must be rooted out' (II. ii. 40–1). But since he himself is from this aristocratic class his generalizations about 'patrician pestilence' necessarily implicate himself – 'And I am tainted' (III. i. 14). Worse than that, he begins to confront the irresolvable and intolerable paradox that if injustice must be countered with slaughter – poison by poison – then the cause is self-polluting. 'Murder most foul, as in the best it is.' Hamlet's paralysed ambivalence is relevant here, for if tyrants can only be eradicated by tyrannous acts then history indeed has only one page. Must we 'work by crime to punish crime? . . . I must not ponder this' (IV. ii. 168–70). It is a truth which indeed must not be scanned.

As soon as he has agreed to join the planned plebeian uprising, Faliero experiences the onset of intense ambivalence about the proposed slaughter of his class.

And it is then decided. Must they die? . . .
My own friends by blood and courtesy,
And many deeds and days – the senators?
(*MF* III. ii. 448–50)

Understandably, Israel, the leader of the proposed plebeian uprising who has conscripted Faliero for their cause, is less than reassured by this hesitation: 'this vacillation is unworthy.' He fairly points out to the discontented Doge, 'You acted, and you act, on your free will', and this precipitates a key speech of the play. Faliero replies:

> You *feel* not – *you* go to this butcher-work
> As if these high-born men were steers for shambles:
> When all this is over, you'll be free and merry,
> And calmly wash those hands incarnadine;
>
> But I, outgoing thee and all thy fellows
> In this surpassing massacre, shall be,
> Shall see and feel – Oh God! Oh God! 'tis true,
> And thou dost well to answer that it was
> 'My own free will and act', and yet you err,
> For I *will* do this! Doubt not – fear not; I
> Will be your most unmerciful accomplice!
> And yet I will act no more on my free will,
> Nor my own feelings – both compel me back;
> But there is *hell* within me and around,
> And like the demon who believes and trembles
> Must I abhor and do.
>
> (*MF* III. ii. 506–21)

We may immediately compare with this outburst Foscari's response when Marina upbraids him for allowing his role of Doge (which forces him to approve the torture and punishment of his guilty son) to suppress his feelings as father. She calls him simply a 'mystery' and he replies:

> All things are so to mortals; who can read them
> Save he who made? Or, if they can, the few
> And gifted spirits, who have studied long
> That loathsome volume – man, and pored upon
> Those black and bloody leaves, his heart and brain,
> But learn a magic which recoils upon
> The adept who pursues it: all the sins
> We find in others, nature made our own. . . .
> All is low,
> And false, and hollow – clay from first to last,
> The prince's urn no less than potter's vessel.
> Our fame is in men's breath; our durance upon days,
> Our days on seasons; our whole being on

Something which is not *us*! – so, we are slaves,
The greatest as the meanest – nothing rests
Upon our will; the straw itself no less
Depends upon a straw than on a storm;
And when we think we lead we most are led,
And still towards death, a thing which comes as much
Without our act or choice as birth, so that
Methinks we must have sinn'd in some old world,
And *this* is hell: the best is, that it is not
Eternal.

(*TF* II. i. 333–66)

Faliero denies his free will in the act of asserting it – 'I quiver to behold what I must be' (*MF* III. ii. 498), where 'must' recognizes or perceives at once an obligation and a fate, a determination and an inevitability. For Foscari it is a coming-to-see that 'when we think we lead we are most led'. Puppets all: a condition perceived most sharply in the moments when, like the two Doges, we find that we 'abhor and do', do and abhor. And both Doges ascribe this intolerable doubleness of our condition – most actually passive when most seemingly active – to forces or phenomena which are more metaphysical than historical or political: the hell within and the hell without. 'Why this is hell, nor am I out of it' – nor is it out of me. In revulsion against politics, Byron has turned Elizabethan.

The moment that Faliero has resolved to kill the members of his own class, he begins to feel – re-feel – solidarity with them. By the same token, the moment he agrees to join the conspiracy of plebeians, he feels revulsion from the 'loose mechanicals', as he has no hesitation in calling them to their faces. Before he makes the acquaintance of Israel he regards the plebeians as 'mere machines / To serve the nobles' most patrician pleasure' (*MF* I. ii. 302–3), and after he has agreed to join their planned uprising he immediately wonders what he is doing – 'With common ruffians leagued to ruin states' (I. iii. 582). When he goes to his meeting with Israel, which clinches his commitment to the plebeians, he shows himself singularly unapt in the discourse of revolution and does not mince his aristocratic words:

the die was thrown
When I first listen'd to your treason. – Start not.
That is the word; I cannot shape my tongue
To syllable black deeds into smooth names.

(III. i. 54–7)

Nor, we might add, to syllable personal resentment into legitimate popular grievance. He is instinctively offended when Israel complains that 'we' are not 'traitors': '*WE* – *we*! – no matter – you have earn'd the right / To talk to *us*' (III. i. 66–7) – never was a concession to assumed commonality with 'the people' more grudgingly given. Seen from a distance they are a 'groaning people'; seen with a patrician eye they are 'discontented ruffians'. Faliero is caught between the proud equestrian statue of his dead ancestor and the 'stung plebians' whose plot he joins. And we might note at this point that Byron admits he has altered the historical facts – so far as they are known – in a very significant way. As he says in his preface, he represents 'the conspiracy as already formed, and the Doge acceding to it; whereas, in fact, it was of his own preparation'. This major shift exonerates the discontented Doge from originating and initiating the idea of revolution, and shifts the dirty responsibility to the 'stung plebians', who can be thought of as a groaning people or discontented ruffians, it doesn't much matter which. The Doge is thus always a reluctant complier with a rebellious movement already in place and which he disdains even as he joins. He thus acts only and purely out of his (patrician) anger and not at all from any revolutionary convictions or genuine sympathy with the plebeians. In this, it must be said, he looks very like Byron himself, who was, always, oppositional, you might say insurrectionary, but never truly revolutionary. It is an appropriate touch that for the final scene, of Faliero's execution, Byron's stage-direction stresses that 'the outer gates are shut against the people', and while Faliero utters his last prophetic curse on the city (another Byronic change – the historical Faliero died with a confession of guilt and an apology) he is literally out of earshot of the people:

FIRST CITIZEN: Curse upon the distance!
His words are inarticulate, but the voice
Swells up like mutter'd thunder; would we could
But gather a sole sentence!
SECOND CIT.: Hush! we perhaps may catch the sound.
FIRST CIT.: 'Tis vain,
I cannot hear him.

(*MF* V. iv. 11–16)

Comparably, the deposed Foscari is prevented from making a public exit:

CHIEF OF THE TEN: It must not be – the people will perceive it.
DOGE: The people! – There's no people, you well know it,
Else you dare not deal thus by them or me.
There is a *populace*, perhaps, whose looks
May shame you.

(*TF* V. i. 257–61)

The 'people' occasionally 'murmur', as indeed they do in the Bible. But they are never allowed, or given, or conceived as having, a proper voice.

And although the Doges speak out passionately against their own class, with whom they are deeply at odds, they can never really 'hear' the people, nor be heard by them – in this again, like Byron. Curse upon the distance!

'Everything about Venice is, or was, extraordinary – her aspect is like a dream, and her history is like a romance.' Thus Byron in his preface to *Marino Faliero*. And Doge Foscari says at one point to the relentlessly and passionately sensible Marina:

> That answer only shows you know not Venice
> Alas! How should you? she knows not herself
> In all her mystery.
>
> (*TF* II. i. 84–6)

Faliero refers to 'this monster of a state' (*MF* III. ii. 165). Dream, romance, mystery, monster: Byron's dramatic Venice (or rather the Venice of his 'mental theatre') is composed of the dreamlike, the romantic, the mysterious and the monstrous. Though indisputably grounded in historical facts, these are not historical plays; and, though full of political discussion, if anything they demonstrate the futility and hopelessness of politics – generating a nowhere-to-go, nothing-to-do sort of feeling. Hence the stress on impotence, on an anger which produces the class-bound and self-defeating hatred of Faliero, and on a law-bound frustration which produces the paralysing passivity of Foscari. When Faliero desperately hopes that perhaps the rebellion he has joined will produce 'a fair free commonwealth' he immediately qualifies this: 'Not rash equality but equal rights' (*MF* III. ii. 170), which is something of a distinction without a difference and certainly not a proposition on which you could base a political programme. In his good book on *Byron's Politics*, Malcolm Kensall persuasively argues that the Venetian plays reflect or project Byron's feelings of hopelessness about the contemporary situation and his own role or non-role – as a disaffected Whig and irredeemable aristocrat – in that situation.

> The two Venetian tragedies show one of the great republican states famous to history, and traditionally likened to Britain, locked in a constitutional impasse. Good order is corrupted; decline seems inevitable leading to the euthanasia of the Constitution, corruption and extinction. . . . But it is not possible to see the Venetian plays as advancing contemporary nationalism or liberalism. . . . Byron's heroes are not builders of nations. The issue they face is the resistance against the corruption of their own class . . . the family of the Foscari honourably and legalistically follow the constitutional authorities of Venice, and in so doing expressly draw a series of contrasts with Doge Faliero. But the outcome is equally tragic. Neither resistance, nor obedience,

> offer a way forward. Taken together the two plays are indicative of a total impasse producing, in Venice, decline and eventual extinction. . . . Byron's political education, therefore, is not in revolution but in disenchantment.[74]

Byron's Venice becomes a place where not the kissing but the politics had to stop – discovering their own inefficacy, if not their impossibility.

But there is a yield of poetry. It is not just a celebration of the achievements of the founders of Venice; in Marina's words (sea-borne words we might call them, noting her name):

> And yet you see how, from their banishment
> Before the Tartar into these salt isles,
> Their antique energy of mind, all that
> Remain'd of Rome for their inheritance,
> Created by degrees an ocean Rome.
>
> (*TF* III. i. 151–5)

And it is not just the standard encomium to its unique history:

> a just and free state, known to all
> The earth as being the Christian bulwark 'gainst
> The Saracen and the schismatic Greek,
> The savage Hun, and not less barbarous Frank;
> A city which has open'd India's wealth
> To Europe; the last Roman refuge from
> O'erwhelming Attila; the ocean's queen;
> Proud Genoa's prouder rival!
>
> (*MF* V. i. 10–17)

(This might be called the official version, pronounced by the Chief of the Ten, Benintende, in *Marino Faliero.*) There is also a poetry which seeks to capture or constitute the ambiguous, the conflicting feelings aroused by the spectacle, the phenomenon, the experience and the thought of 'Venice'. Here I want to quote at length from a remarkable soliloquy by Lioni in *Marino Faliero.* Lioni is a loyal patrician and senator. At the beginning of Act IV, and immediately before he is apprised of the plotted insurrection by the too tender-hearted Bertram, he is depicted as returning to his palazzo from a ball.

> The music, and the banquet, and the wine,
> The garlands, the rose odours, and the flowers,
> The sparkling eyes, and flashing ornaments,
> The white arms and the raven hair, the braids

And bracelets; swanlike bosoms, and the necklace,
An India in itself, yet dazzling not
The eye like what it circled; the thin robes,
Floating like light clouds' twixt our gaze and heaven;
The many-twinkling feet so small and sylph-like,
Suggesting the more secret symmetry
Of the fair forms which terminate so well –
All the delusion of the dizzy scene,
Its false and true enchantments – art and nature,
Which swam before my giddy eyes, that drank
The sight of beauty as the parched pilgrim's
On Arab sands the false mirage, which offers
A lucid lake to his eluded thirst,
Are gone. Around me are the stars and waters –
Worlds mirror'd in the ocean, goodlier sight
Than torches glared back by a gaudy glass;
And the great element, which is to space
What ocean is to earth, spreads its blue depths,
Soften'd with the first breathings of the spring;
The high moon sails upon her beauteous way,
Serenely smoothing o'er the lofty walls
Of those tall piles and sea-girt palaces,
Whose porphyry pillars, and whose costly fronts,
Fraught with the orient spoil of many marbles,
Like altars range along the broad canal,
Seem each a trophy of some mighty deed
Rear'd up from out the waters, scarce less strangely
Than those more mossy and mysterious giants
Of architecture, those Titanian fabrics,
Which point in Egypt's plains to times that have
No other record. All is gentle: nought
Stirs rudely; but, congenial with the night,
Whatever walks is gliding like a spirit.
The tinklings of some vigilant guitars
Of sleepless lovers to a wakeful mistress.
And cautious opening of the casement, showing
That he is not unheard; while her young hand,
Fair as the moonlight of which it seems part,
So delicately white, it trembles in
The act of opening the forbidden lattice,
To let in love through music, makes his heart
Thrill like his lyre-strings at the slight; the dash
Phosphoric of the oar, or rapid twinkle

Of the far lights of skimming gondolas,
And the responsive voices of the choir
Of boatmen answering back with verse for verse;
Some dusky shadow checkering the Rialto;
Some glimmering palace roof, or tapering spire,
Are all the sights and sounds which here pervade
The ocean-born and earth-commanding city –
How sweet and soothing is this hour of calm.
(*MF* IV. i. 51–105)

This may be called an aesthetic version of Venice with an elegiac atmosphere of sadness and disenchantment, diffusing over the scene a slightly weary feeling for the emptiness and fleeting meretriciousness of the ball with dazzling artificial light 'Which show'd all things, but nothing as they were'. There is a Watteau-like quality with the 'false and true enchantments – art and nature' swimming together in a haze of beauty and transience, of a class dancing into decline. (This will be Browning's Venice.) The view from the window is another Venice of uncanny, mysterious beauty where the palaces 'rear up from out the waters', where the light is 'smoothing' and the only movement is 'gliding', and the one defining act is the white hand of the girl trembling in 'The act of opening the forbidden lattice', for even in its awesome greatness 'The ocean-born and earth-commanding city', is inseparable from the notion of illicit love. Taken together these two Venetian aspects would serve to constitute an image – or a dream – of Venice which would become increasingly familiar down the century.

Yet, as so often happens, a revulsion from the city follows. Byron's task was easy here, for he could allow Faliero in his death speech to foretell the decline of Venice and its eventual humiliating capitulation to Napoleon ('Shall yield, and bloodlessly and basely yield, / Unto a bastard Attila'). But the vituperation is surprising and, since Byron knew full well that Faliero actually died confessing his guilt and asking forgiveness, it can only be some powerful personal accumulation of feeling which is discharging itself. The very long speech is full of lines such as:

Despised by cowards for greater cowardice,
And scorn'd even by the vicious for such vices.
As in the monstrous grasp of their conception
Defy all codes to image or to name them. . . .
Vice without splendour, sin without relief
Even from the gloss of love to smooth it o'er,
But in its stead, course lusts of habitude,
Prurient yet passionless, cold studied lewdness,
Depraving nature's frailty to an art.
(*MF* V. iii. 76–89)

It concludes:

> Thou den of drunkards with the blood of princes!
> Gehenna of the waters! thou sea-Sodom!
>
> (V. iii. 98–9)

This is effectively Byron's farewell to Venice, and no doubt his feelings of frustration, his troubled personal relations, the failure of the wretched Carbonari and his own ill-health all contributed to this intemperate flow of nausea. But he is not the last writer to find the 'ocean-born and earth-commanding city' can turn a very different face; or, we might say, can provoke the projection of a entirely different scenario – comminatory, negative, doomed! Where the writing is all too graphically on the wall.

3

John Ruskin: This Sea-Dog of Towns

In the chapter on 'Castel-Franco' which Ruskin added to the 1877 Traveller's Edition of *The Stones of Venice*, he laments, as usual, the 'non-acceptance of the book's teaching' and then makes the extraordinary statement that the obvious reason for this non-acceptance is 'the entire concealment of my personal feelings throughout', as if the reader cannot feel the heat of his passions and prejudices, his ecstasies and horrors, in every line – even if he is only telling you how to build a wall, or why we mend a roof. He is sure that if, like an 'egoistic person', he had simply given his 'impressions' and 'not the history of Venice' his book would have found more favour with the equally egoistic reader. For instance, he says in his note on the Bridge of Sighs, the reader will find that he attributes the influence of it on the public mind to the 'ignorant sentimentalism of Byron'. I must quote his following comment at length:

> Now, these words are precisely true; and I knew them to be true when I wrote them, and thought it good for the reader to be informed of the truth, namely, that Byron did not know the date of the Bridge of Sighs, nor of the Colleone statue; and that his feelings about Venice had been founded on an extremely narrow acquaintance with its history. I did not think it at all necessary for the public to know that, in spite of all my carefully collected knowledge, I still feel as Byron did, in every particular; or that I had formed my own precious 'style' by perpetual reading of him, and imitation of him in various alliterative and despairing poems, of which the best, the beginning of a Venetian tragedy written when I was sixteen, has by luck never seen the light. . . . Nor, again, did I think it would at all advance the acquaintance of my readers with the principles of Venetian Gothic or Venetian

> policy, to be told that for love of Byron, I had run the risk of fever in drawing the under-canal vaults, and the desolate and mud-buried portico of the ruined Casa Foscari.[1]

It may seem remarkable that Ruskin identifies himself so closely with Byron in his feelings about Venice, the vehement Victorial moralist seeming so different from the nonchalant Regency aristocrat (we may find a comparable strangeness in Proust's idolization of Ruskin), though, as we shall see, in his oscillating evaluations and evocations of the city he repeats the 'greenest garden/sea-Sodom' ambivalence of the poet, albeit on a much more massively projected and intricately detailed scale. The difference that Ruskin insists upon is his superior mastery of the 'history' of the city, his 'carefully collected knowledge'. Despite his claims to have achieved an impossible impersonality and objectivity, and without going into the debate concerning the very recuperability of the past anyway, we can say that Ruskin created a highly particular kind of 'history' of Venice. The uses and abuses of that history – how, to what end? – will be one of the concerns of this chapter, for what Ruskin magically concocted from his 'carefully collected knowledge' was a personal myth of Venice (called 'Venice') of quite extraordinary power and utterly incalculable influence.

In the concluding lines of the passage just quoted, Ruskin reveals, if indirectly, the care that indeed went into the collecting of his knowledge. But more, Byron lived in Venice. He made use of it and satisfied his social and sexual appetites there. He studied some of its history and indeed drew the sort of possible similarity between Venice then and England (or London) now which became part of Ruskin's scenario. But Byron's evocations of the city are invariably general, generic. In his letters the city is a backdrop to his sexual adventures – gondolas for secrecy, canals fallen into, and so on. How different Ruskin. In Venice with his young wife Effie, their marriage unconsummated, his abstinence could hardly be further from Byron's dissipation. Whereas Effie enjoyed the available social life, Ruskin preferred to avoid it and attended on sufferance, suffering. His business was with those under-canal vaults and mud-buried porticos. I might have said his assignation – for Ruskin seems to have literally crawled and climbed over the whole ruined body of a city; peering with his incomparable eye into every darkened and neglected nook and cranny, high and low; gently picking over the abandoned stones of decaying palaces; gliding into and down the darkest and dingiest canals. It would be too easy and not particularly illuminating to talk of a massive displacement of the activities of the marriage bed into the exploration of the city. But, if the word means anything at all, there can be no doubt that Ruskin's most intense love-affair was with Venice, and his writings about her from first to last manifest, at their extreme, the positive and negative efflorescences of the unresting desire which the very idea, image, memory of the city aroused in him. At the very end, as we shall see, he effectively bracketed the whole affair out of his life, just as he literally wrote his actual wife out of his final accountings. But that was just before the final madness and long silence – by which time he had felt too much and almost all passion was spent.

The Byronic fragment he referred to is *Marcolini* and is little more than a pastiche, but he left another uncompleted work from that time (1835–6) which contains a passage worth noting. The fragment is called *Chronicles of St Martin* and starts with the familiar device of the narrator being given an old manuscript to read and then giving his own version of what he read, which was called 'Velasquez, the Novice'. The story does not matter but the start involves an approach to Venice; I shall quote it in full, since the whole question of approaching Venice, entering, getting into, being in, the city – literally, metaphorically – is a constitutive part of his obsession. He ends the first chapter with the single word 'Venezia' (as in a different mode he will do in *The Stones of Venice*), then chapter 2 starts with some lines quoted (and misquoted) from Shelley's 'Lines Written among the Euganean Hills' and then:

> And, as if summoned out of the deep at the word, the city palaces rose into their view, her towers and cupolas running along the line of the blue sea, which was seen stretching away to the southward into the glow of the distant heaven, while here and there the line of its horizon was broken by an island of sculptured marble, or dotted with the sails of innumerable shipping. The city itself was at a distance of about two miles, but not the slightest haze diminished the clearness with which its buildings were defined upon the eye; the column of St Mark's rose high and distinguished towards its centre, and the noble domes of the churches of San Giorgione and della Salute glittered in the brightness of the noonday sun, like the chief gems of the diadem which the Adritis wears so royally.
>
> Nevertheless, as the forest of towers and cupolas which belong to the principal parts of the city are seen, on the approach from Mestre, rising from behind a comparatively low and confused line of buildings, which consist chiefly of suburbs and habitations of the lower classes, there might be perhaps a slight feeling of disappointment in the silence with which our travellers first regarded the prospect which lay before them. But, as the swift gondola passed rapidly in its invisible path, as it advanced along the frequented thoroughfare of waters, which, distinguished only by a line of low piers from the trackless infinity of the Adriatic, leads from the last land to the gates of Venice, as they shot past that low shrine, which, washed for ever by the surrounding surges, is so appropriately named the Madonna del Aqua, and to which the

> gondolier breathes his low, short prayer as he darts by . . . and when they beheld the noble city gradually extending its line, and, as it were, stretching its arms wider and wider around them, and could distinguish the entrances of her streets, paved by the sea, and the haughty lines of marble palaces by which they were bordered, all feeling of disappointment gave way to one of reverence, admiration, and delight. (*CW* 1, 543)

It is notable that the growing 'delight' is, or seems to be, contingent upon somehow occluding, looking over or overlooking, no longer seeing, those 'habitants of the lower classes' and moving into the embrace of the palatial Venice in all its hauteur. Visions of Venice do not have much space for the manifestations of the 'lower classes' – or if they do appear they threaten to contaminate the visionariness – and usually they are, indeed, put under erasure. But Ruskin is noting, in a small enough way, a possible problem in writing about Venice, or being drawn into the vortex of the 'Venice' constituted by Byron, by Rogers, by Shakespeare, and so on. What are you actually writing about? Writing at the expense of what? Of whom? Is there perhaps 'Venice' and Venice? There is certainly Venice then and Venice now, and even in this early fragment Ruskin inscribes the sense of a possible ending:

> I have said that the crowds of travellers of different nations, who have lately inundated Italy, have not yet deprived the city of Venice of much of its original character, although its change of government and withering state of prosperity had brought the shade of melancholy upon its beauty which is rapidly increasing, and will increase, until the waves which have been the ministers of majesty become her sepulchre. (*CW* 1, 544)

So, from the start, delight – certain; disappointment – possible; doom – inevitable.

In 1836 Turner exhibited a strange and magnificent painting, *Juliet and her Nurse*. Strange because it is set in Venice and, while Juliet certainly had a nurse, equally certainly Shakespeare did not bring them to that city. Magnificent because of the majestic magic of the scene. From reproductions (the original is now in Argentina) one can only guess at the impact of the painting in which St Mark's seems to be dematerializing into dreamy gold; the Watteau-like assembly in the great square move from corporeal clusters to what seems like a combustible fusion; the dark blue of the lagoon sets off the incandescence of the city; Juliet in light and the nurse in shadow form an enigmatic corner as we look down from a dizzy height over the whole wondrous panorama; and the blue-yellow-white of the sky bathes or burns the whole with a light as timeless and magic as the city it is so equivocally illuminating, seemingly terminating in explosions on the right – festive fireworks or fires of apocalypse. However, the *Blackwood's Edinburgh Magazine* critic certainly did not like it, writing in October 1836:

> 'Juliet and her Nurse' – That is indeed a strange jumble – 'confusion worse confounded.' It is neither sunlight, moonlight, nor starlight nor firelight, though there is an attempt at a display of fireworks in one corner, and we conjecture that these are meant to be stars in the heavens. . . . Amidst so many absurdities we scarcely stop to ask why Juliet and her nurse should be at Venice. For the scene is a composition as from models of different parts of Venice, thrown higgledy-piggledy together, streaked blue and pink, and thrown into a flour tub.

Ruskin, who already idolized Turner, though still just seventeen composed a reply. He answered the criticisms point by point. Among other things he maintained that it was a perfectly accurate view from a locatable point on the roofs at the south-west angle of St Mark's Place, and to the accusation that Turner is 'out of nature' Ruskin replied that Turner is 'not so stark mad as to profess to paint nature. He paints *from* nature, and pretty far from it, too; and he would be sadly disappointed who looked in his pictures for a possible scene.' This combination of claims is particularly worth remembering in the case of Ruskin – for whom the 'truth' of painting became a supremely important consideration – since for his own writing he claimed absolute accuracy and yet it would have to be said that he writes *from* nature and, at times, pretty far from it too. Ruskin then moves on to one of those coruscating passages which triumph through an irresistible excess.

> His imagination is Shakesperian in its mightiness. Had the scene of 'Juliet and her Nurse' risen up before the mind of a poet, and been described in 'words that burn', it had been the admiration of the world: but, placed before us on the canvass, it becomes – what critics of the brush and pallett may show their wit upon at the expense of their judgement; and what real artists and men of feeling and taste *must* admire, but dare not attempt to imitate. Many-coloured mists are floating above the distant city, but such mists as you might imagine to be aetherial spirits, souls of the mighty dead breathed out of the tombs of Italy into the blue of her bright heaven, and wandering in vague and infinite glory around the earth that they have loved. Instinct with the beauty of uncertain light, they move and mingle among the pale stars, and rise up into the brightness of the illimitable

> heaven, whose soft, sad blue eye gazes down into the deep waters of the sea forever – that sea whose motionless and silent transparency is beaming with phosphor light, that emanates out of its sapphire serenity like bright dreams breathed into the spirit of a deep sleep. And the spires of the glorious city rise indistinctly bright into those living mists, like pyramids of pale fire from some vast altar; and amidst the glory of the dream, there is as it were the voice of a multitude entering by the eye, – arising from the stillness of the city like the summer wind passing over the leaves of the forest, when a murmur is heard amidst their multitude.
>
> This, oh Maga, is the picture which your critic has pronounced to be like 'models of different parts of Venice, streaked in blue and white, and thrown into a flour tub'! That the picture is not seen by either starlight, sunlight, moonlight, or firelight, is perfectly true; it is a light of his own, which no other artist can produce, – a light which seems owing to some phosphorescent property in the air. The picture can be, and ought only to be viewed as embodied enchantment, delineated magic. (*CW* 3, 639)

The notoriously taciturn (or reticent) Turner persuaded Ruskin not to send the letter and it was not published. It is conceivable that he was even a little embarrassed by the unblushing rhapsodic flights of Ruskin's prose. He might even have felt that in a curious way he was being displaced. Had this scene, said Ruskin, been described in 'words that burn' . . . well, now watch me and I'll do just that. The unfettered soaring of half-free association, the self-renewing, self-amplifying, proliferating embellishment, these form a commentary which both aspires to emulate the original text and threatens to replace it – a supplement which begins to crowd out the original as in his own later works some of Ruskin's unstoppable footnotes impede or heft aside the would-be main body of his text. Though he surely appreciated Ruskin's support and admiration, Turner, thank you, would just get on with his painting and let the critics rattle on as they might. But Ruskin has discovered something. With Turner you can be at once accurate and out of nature. Venice as a work of art, Venice painted, Venice Turner-ized, can serve as a site of excess, of writing released and pushed to the limit of *jouissance*.

Ruskin refers to the painting again in the first volume of *Modern Painters*, part II, 'Of Truth'. In chapter 7, 'General Application of the Foregoing Principles', towards the end Ruskin enumerates some of Turner's virtues. He notes, incidentally, that one Italian city afforded Turner special release: – 'At Venice he found freedom of space, brilliancy of light, variety of colour, massy simplicity of general form; and to Venice we owe many of the motives in which his highest powers of colour have been displayed' (*CW* 3,

244) – words which are curiously self-applicable. Having concluded his exposition of some of Turner's unique virtues, Ruskin offers to illustrate his meaning 'by a comparison of the kind of truths impressed upon us in the painting of Venice by Canaletti, Prout, Stanfield and Turner'. It is a long peroration working slowly towards its powerful climax, so I will have to be selective:

> The effect of a fine Canaletti is, in its first impression, dioramic. We fancy we are in our beloved Venice again, with one foot, by mistake, in the clear, invisible film of water lapping over the marble steps of the foregound. . . . Presently, however, we begin to feel that it is lurid and gloomy, and that the painter, compelled by the lowness of the utmost light at his disposal to deepen the shadows, in order to get the right relation, has lost the flashing, dazzling, exulting light, which was one of our chief sources of Venetian happiness. . . . It is, indeed, painting nature – as she appears to the most unfeeling and untaught of mankind. The bargeman and the bricklayer probably see no more in Venice than Canaletti gives – and are just as capable of appreciating the facts of sunligt and shadow, by which he deceives us, as the most educated of us all. But what more there is in Venice than brick and stone – what there is of mystery and death, and memory and beauty – what there is to be learned or lamented, to be loved or wept – we look for to Canaletti in vain.
>
> Let us pass to Prout. The imitation is lost at once. The buildings have nothing like their real relief against the sky; there are multitudes of false distances; the shadows in many places have a great deal more Vandyke-brown than darkness in them; and the lights very often more yellow-ochre than sunshine. But yet the effect on our eye is that very brilliancy and cheerfulness which delighted us in Venice itself, and there is none of that oppressive and lurid gloom which was cast upon our feelings by Canaletti. . . . Now we begin to feel that we are in Venice; this is what we think we could not get elsewhere; it is worth seeing, and drawing, and talking and thinking of – not an exhibition of common daylight or brick walls. But let us look a little closer; we know those capitals very well; their design was most original and perfect, and so delicate that it seemed to be cut in ivory; what have we got for them here? Five straight strokes of a reed pen! No, Mr. Prout, it is not quite Venice yet.
>
> Let us take Stanfield then. Now we are farther still from anything like Venetian tone; all is cold and comfortless, but there is air and good daylight, and we will not complain. And now let us look into the buildings, and all is perfection and fidelity. . . . But it is all drawn hard and sharp, there is nothing to hope for or find out, nothing to

dream of or discover; we can measure and see it from base to battlement, there is nothing too fine for us to follow, nothing too full for us to fathom. This cannot be nature, for it is not infinity. No, Mr. Stanfield, it is scarcely Venice yet.

But let us take, with Turner, the last and greatest step of all. Thank heaven we are in sunshine again – and what sunshine! Not the lurid gloomy, plague-like oppression of Canaletti, but white flashing fulness of dazzling light, which the waves drink and the clouds breathe, bounding and burning in intensity of joy. The sky, – it is a visible infinity – liquid, measureless, unfathomable, panting and melting through the chasms in the long fields of snow-white, flaked, slow-moving vapour, that guide the eye along the multitudinous waves down to the islanded rest of the Euganean hills. Do we dream, or does the white forked sail drift nearer, and nearer yet, diminishing the blue sea between us with the fulness of its wings? It pauses now; but the quivering of its bright reflection troubles the shadows of the sea. Those azure, fathomless depths of crystal mystery, on which the swiftness of the poised gondola floats double, its back beak lifted like the crest of a dark ocean bird, its scarlet draperies flashed from the kindling surface, and its bent oar breaking the radiant water into a dust of gold. Dreamlike and dim, but glorious, the unnumbered palaces lift their shafts out of the hollow sea, – pale ranks of motionless flame, – their mighty towers sent up to heaven like tongues of more eager fire – their grey domes looming vast and dark, like eclipsed worlds – their scupltured arabesques and purple marble fading farther and fainter, league beyond league, lost in the light of distance. Detail after detail, thought beyond thought, you find and feel them through the radiant mystery, inexhaustible as indistinct, beautiful, but never all revealed; secret in fulness, confused in symmetry, as nature herself is to the bewildered and foiled glance, giving out of that indistinctness, and through that confusion, the perpetual newness of the infinite and the beautiful.

Yes, Mr. Turner, we are in Venice now. (*CW* 3, 255–7)

It is by any standards an amazing passage. Here, indeed, is a way to 'approach' Venice – via Canaletto's flatness, Prout's thinness and Stanfield's sharpness. In their various way these painters fail to give us the 'more' of Venice; they close it off in their various finitudes or impoverish it with their tenous approximations. Ruskin wants something – somewhere – which is inexhaustible, immeasurable, with unfathomable plenitudes and unfollowable finenesses; a realm in which one can dream and discover for ever, a space of endlessly gratified and endessly re-aroused desire – an artefact which doubles nature's infinitude. And he finds it in Turner's painting of Venice. This is a

Venice all of light and water and crystal mystery and colour and fire. It is not the gondola but its 'swiftness' that floats, and the palaces turn into flame. We have nothing to do, here, with Venice the historical-political entity – the city state. All that disappears or merges into the whole 'radiant mystery'. As Ruskin starts to write Turner's canvas, verbs start to come in and do what paint never does – 'bounding . . . burning . . . panting and melting' – and the quickening self-excitation of the passage is little short of orgasmic. The last line can be read as a climactic cry of exultation, or a deep sigh of ease after consummation. Either way, Ruskin has found a way of getting into Venice – and a Venice to be in – which permits or stimulates him to a tremendous release of ecstatic verbal energy. This is Turner's Venice, and for a second time the writing takes off from – into – the painting.

Ruskin does not do this again, and in the third edition of *Modern Painters*, volume I (1846), he completely excised the long comparison of the four paintings of Venice. Whether or not this was simply because his older self deprecated what he felt to be a piece of too ostentatiously fine writing, mere rhapsodic verbiage as he would say, does not matter. The letter was not published and now Ruskin deletes his second appropriation of Turner's Venice. For whatever rich mixture of motives – the ones he gives and the ones he doesn't – Ruskin was to set out to build a Venice of his own. Stone, as it were, by stone.

Between Byron's time and Ruskin's, Venice had become a tourist city – as opposed to a possible stopping-off point on the Grand Tour, which was rather different. I suppose that with tourism it is a matter of quantitative increase finally precipitating qualitative change, as in the famous example of boiled water turning into steam. The change may be most conveniently marked by the publication of the first tourist guide to Venice – *Murray's Handbook of Northern Italy*, published in 1842 (Ruskin used the third edition). Without embarking on an analysis of the discursive layout of the guidebook we may simply observe that it treats the city as frozen spectacle and turns it into a list of separate consumable items – complete with a starring system. History is reduced to an inert series of notes, while more dynamic attention is paid to advice to the traveller to ensure maximum comfort while consuming the spectacle. What Denis Cosgrove calls the 'Disneyfication of Venice'[2] certainly and above all served to strip the city and its myth of contemporary political relevance. Arbitrarily this process may be said to start, or receive crucial impetus, from the poetry of Samuel Rogers, which effectively transformed Venice into a dehistoricized, indeed detemporalized, 'dream' (as we have seen, Byron could do this but he was well aware that Venice had a history, which moreover contained parallels with, and carried possible warnings to, contemporary England). Ruskin was initially drawn to this ahistorical 'dream' Venice through the paintings of Turner, as described (although Turner's paintings of Venice have much more of a historical and even political charge than is commonly realized[3]). But on his visit to Venice in 1845 he was shocked to find the railway built to Mestre and the city illuminated by gaslight – 'All the romance of it is gone, and nothing that I see ever makes me forget that I am in the 19th century,' he wrote to his father.[4] The romance of Venice never, quite, went for Ruskin, but certainly his major work on it was written by someone who was intensely aware of being in the nineteenth century, and of Venice as having had a history or at least a past. Aware in his own way, however. Few readers of *The Stones of Venice*, indeed *no* reader of *just* that work, would realize that it was written immediately after, and in the very manifest wake of, the longest and initially most successful of the republican risings of 1848 – the republic declared by Daniel Manin in March 1848 which only succumbed (more to famine and cholera than the Austrians) in August 1849. As far as one can gather, Ruskin's only concern was whether the 'blockheads', by holding out too long, would cause more of the buildings to be destroyed. Ruskin was to call himself a communist, but he was certainly never a republican.

Yet what was Venice but the greatest and longest-lasting republic the world had ever seen? Cromwell's Parliament sought advice from it on the survival of republics, and Locke and Voltaire regarded Venice as 'a living demonstration of fundamental truths about society'. Denis Cosgrove points out that the myth of Venice as the perfect society, indeed an achieved utopia because of the perfect rational balance of its fixed government, was developed and elaborated during the sixteenth century, which was a period of 'vulnerability change and uncertainty' for Venice, and indeed could be said to see the beginning of its long slow decline. Ruskin, of course, was to create a very different myth of Venice and her history. He made himself intensely aware of the past of Venice but in a highly selective, indeed distortive manner which was entirely his own, and for his own nineteenth-century purposes. He read some history (he struggled for years with Sismondi's *History of the Italian Republics*, at one point asking his wife to take over for him and scour out the bits about Venice) but he was no historian. He made himself intimate with the materials of the city, but had no interest in material history. Cosgrove remarks: 'He failed to mention Venetian navigation, mercantile relations, the political consequences of its trading hegemony, the *stato de mar* or the *terraferma* and the shift to rentier activity in early modern Venice.[5] Of his account of the founding of Venice, Clegg rightly observes that Ruskin has effectively 'demilitarized, decommercialized and desecularized the greatness of Venice'.[6] What he *did* do was to moralize the history of Venice, partly in order to mount a critique of, and utter dire warnings to, contemporary England, with just a faint, intermittent and soon-to-be-extinguished hope that he might correctively turn it in the right direction so that it might avoid the dismal fate of its great precursor. But this extraordinary work deserves more than just a word. And as we approach it we might bear in mind a contention, a conviction, which he articulated in a later book on Venice, that 'a nation's art is its only reliable biography,' (*CW* 24, 203). To find the story (which is as much the lesson as the history) of Venice, it is necessary to read its architecture (plus painting), so Ruskin starts with the buildings, or rather the stones, the stones of which they were composed and the disassembled stones into which too many of them had declined.

On his preparatory visit to Venice in 1849, Ruskin found a city which seemed to be losing its historical memory. 'Every date in question was determinable only by internal evidence; and it became necessary for me to examine not only every one of the older palaces, stone by stone, but every fragment throughout the city which afforded any clue to the formation of its style' (*CW* 9, 4). Indeed, this is a search, not so much for lost time, but for an identity which if it is not yet lost is fast fading and becoming overlaid or diffused. For where should he find a real 'Venice' as he set about reading buildings which were palimpsests – writing over writing over writing over writing?

> By far the greater number present examples of three or four different styles, it may be successive, it may be accidentally associated; and, in many instances, the restorations or additions have gradually replaced the entire structure of the ancient fabric, of which nothing but the name remains, together with a kind of identity, exhibited in the anomalous association of the modernised portions: the Will of the old building asserted through them all, stubbornly, though vainly, expressive; yet animating what would otherwise be a mere group of fantastic masque. (*CW* 9, 5)

What *kind* of a 'kind of identity' can you find when you have nothing to go on but replacements? How get at 'the Will of the old building' through those codicils and falsifications? And suppose it was, after all, merely a 'fantastic masque'? We should read *The Stones of Venice* as an attempt to reconstitute that identity, trace and transcribe that will and animate the masque – of course, in and on Ruskin's own terms. As he looked round at the palaces of Venice, Ruskin saw that they all had 'sustained interpolations', sometimes of an extremely 'intricate' kind (*CW* 9, 6). Later he asserts:

> The whole architecture of Venice is architecture of incrustation . . . the Venetian habitually incrusted his work with nacre: he built his houses, even the meanest, as if he had been a shell-fish, – roughly inside, mother-of-pearl on the surface: he was content, perforce, to gather

> the clay of the Brenta banks, and take it into brick for his substance of wall; but he overlaid it with the wealth of the ocean, with the most precious of foreign marbles. You might fancy early Venice as one wilderness of brick, which a petrifying sea had beaten upon till it coated it with marble: at first a dark city – washed white by the sea foam. (*CW* 9, 323)

These words strike me as entirely applicable to Ruskin's own writing, if you look at it in a certain way – grounded in the brick of fact, overlaid with the wealth of the widths and depths of the language, sometimes indeed even to foaming. His own work could certainly be said to be marked by 'interpolation' and 'incrustation'. I do not wish to advance the foolish proposition that in writing about Venice Ruskin was writing about his own writing – he is the least reflexive of writers, having too much else to do. But between his Venice, as it emerges, and his writing, as it proceeds, the relationship is of the intensest, the intimacy of the closest – in ways which I hope will become clear.

That he had set himself quite a task Ruskin would seem to make clear by the title of his first chapter, 'The Quarry'. No man more apt with a suggestive – or cryptic or eccentric or inscrutable – title, Ruskin clearly points to something to be pursued as well as the source of the stones he must scrutinize. Indeed, he begins with the end – the end he has in view and the end of his story. The opening points the way for what is to follow.

> Since the first dominion of men was asserted over the ocean, three thrones, of mark beyond all others, have been set upon its sands: the thrones of Tyre, Venice and England. Of the First of these great powers only the memory remains; of the Second, the ruin; the Third, which inherits their greatness, if it forget their example, may be led through prouder eminence to less pitied destruction. (*CW* 9, 17)

This sets the agenda. Venice is a ruin turning into a memory – 'left for our beholding in the final period of her decline: a ghost upon the sands of the sea, so weak – so quiet, – so bereft of all but her loveliness, that we might well doubt, as we watched her faint reflection in the mirage of the lagoon, which was the City, and which the Shadow' (*CW* 9, 17). As in some Turners, Ruskin makes us feel that the city is all but disappearing before our eyes, desubstantiating and dissolving into the water which reflects it. Why does the solidity – the body – of 'greatness' attenuate into ruin and disappear into memory? But it does, and England take note!

This opening also sets up a pattern which Ruskin will deploy to organize his material – thinking in threes. There will be three periods of Venetian history: from its fifth-century foundation to 1297, the date of the *serrata*, when the class of the nobility was juridically defined and its powers and privileges statutorily determined, which, as far as Ruskin was concerned, formed the basis for the city's constitutional perfection by creating a benevolent elite; from 1297 to the death of Doge Carlo in 1418; and a final period from 1423, when Doge Mocenigo died, to whenever, since Ruskin does not have much to say about political events after 1500. This is a curious kind of history, to be sure, since the decline of Venice hardly started before the sixteenth century and it still had some three hundred years life in her. But this is not the point for Ruskin. He schematizes his three periods (he can be inconsistent and contradictory about dating the start of the Fall, as Clegg has pointed out) to coincide with what he projects as the three stages of healthy energetic beginnings; a mature, prosperous and civilized middle; and a decadent decline. To match this political and moral triad there are of course three styles of architecture – Byzantine, Gothic and Renaissance. And there is a 'triple question' posed by these interlocking phenomena: whether the oligarchy caused the 'Fall of Venice'; or whether the establishing of an oligarchy was rather the 'sign' and not the cause of 'national enervation'; or (lastly) whether, 'as I rather think, the history of Venice might not be written almost without reference to the construction of her senate or the prerogatives of her Doge. It is the history of a people eminently at unity in itself, descendants of a Roman race, long disciplined by adversity, and compelled by its position either to live nobly or to perish: – for a thousand years they fought for life; for three hundred years they invited death: – their battle was rewarded, and their call heard' (*CW* 9, 22–3). One could say that they were exterminated by Ruskin's compulsion to think in threes. Not, like so many nineteenth-century figures fond of historical triadism (Hegel, Arnold, Marx, Ibsen, etc. etc.), past, present and future; but beginning, middle and *end*. ('Venice reaped the fruits of her former energies, consumed them, – and expired'; *CW* 9, 19.) The doom is in the thought pattern, though of course the contemporary abject condition of Venice made it particularly amenable to this mapping.

More interesting to notice, however, is that Ruskin all but says that the 'history' can be written without reference to politics, politicians, institutions, power-struggles, and so on. There is just the spectacle of '*a* people' – making life and then marring it. After this it should come as no surprise if we find nothing resembling orthodox history. He mentions cases of 'individual heroism' (though his real heroes are likely to be artists, like Tintoretto, the very writers of the national biography), but his main aim is to throw light 'upon the private tendencies of the Venetian character'. And he wishes to concentrate on this – generic and generalized – 'private character' for the following revealing reason:

> the most curious phenomenon in all Venetian history is the vitality of religion in private life, and its deadness in public policy. Amidst the enthusiasm, chivalry, or fanaticism of the other states of Europe, Venice stands, from first to last, like a masked statue; her coldness impenetrable; her exertion only aroused by the touch of a secret spring. That spring was her commercial interest. (*CW* 9, 24)

This of course is a travesty (and needless to say subsequently contradicted by many amendments and 'interpolations'), since the interconnections between religion, public policy and commercial interest – not to mention art – must be deemed to be of all but undisentanglable intricacy and complexity in medieval Venice – as, no doubt, in medieval almost anywhere. But Ruskin was still a fervent believer and he wanted to marginalize the (to him) distasteful commercial, public, political part of Venice (which constituted much of its glory and achievement), and go direct from some hypothetical or imagined private religious vitality to the artistic construction and embellishment of the city – or read off the former from the latter. He notes, as evidence of Venice's inversion of priorities, that it is the only important city in which 'its cathedral was not the principal feature'. But as so often Ruskin is almost immediately at war with himself, since the principle feature was the ducal palace – and he certainly did not want to marginalize that. Quite absolutely the contrary.

In the past Venice had been regarded as a sacred centre, an *axis mundi*, and Ruskin reanimates the notion with a difference. Venice was particularly regarded as a central point between the Christian West and the Islamic East. Ruskin makes it the meeting-point of the Lombard North and the Arab South:

> Opposite in their character and mission, alike in their magnificence of energy, they came from the North and from the South, the glacier torrent and the lava stream: they met and contended over the wreck of the Roman Empire; and the very centre of the struggle, the point of pause of both, the dead water of the opposite eddies, charged with the embalmed fragments of the Roman wreck, is VENICE. (*CW* 9, 38)

The Ducal Palace of Venice contains the three elements in exactly equal proportions – the Roman, Lombard and Arab. It is the central building of the world. Central not because of its religious significance but because it is a triumph – for Ruskin *the* triumph – of art. He makes it the central building in his work too, and here I think we can detect some 'reciprocal interference' (Ruskin's phase, and I shall come back to it) of the sense of the city as a book (which Ruskin has throughout) and the making of a book somehow like the city. In the one possible self-reflexive sentence I have noticed, Ruskin declares, right at the start, that he wants to try somehow to catch Venice before it disappears: 'I would endeavour to trace the lines of this image before it be for ever lost, and to record, as far as I may, the warning which seems to me to be uttered by every one of the fast-gaining waves, that beat like passing bells, against the STONES OF VENICE' (*CW* 9, 17). Admittedly the 'the' is not capitalized but the rest is, as nowhere else. Page one, and Ruskin plants just the seed of a suggestion that there is to be some kind of connection or resemblance between the city which has almost gone and the book which is to come – and will reconstitute it. Accurately, but not out of history; out of imagination. Or – out of *nature* and *out* of nature.

It is from the beginning a city of extremes. 'Now Venice, as she was once the most religious, was in her fall the most corrupt, of European states . . . and the dying city, magnificent in her dissipation, and graceful in her follies, obtained wider worship in her decrepitude than in her youth, and sank from the midst of her admirers into her grave' (*CW* 9, 46–7). It is not quite clear which Venice, and indeed which death, Ruskin is referring to here. 'Magnificent in her dissipation' is an uncharacteristic concession for Ruskin at this time, and later he has extremely vituperative, even venomous, words for what he portrays as the foul dissoluteness of the dying city. But the extremes: most religious, most corrupt. And this connects with a remarkable feature of Ruskin's writing about changes in art movements or cities or, indeed, civilizations, which I can only call the notion of absolute abruptness. Writing of the signs of the change from Gothic to early Renaissance, he says: 'This change appears first in a loss of truth and vitality in existing architecture all over the world. . . . All the Gothics in existence, southern or northern, were corrupted at once' (*CW* 9, 44). When the Renaissance adopted rationalism and cast aside religion,

> *Instant* degradation followed in every direction – a flood of folly and hypocrisy. . . . Gods without power, satyrs without rusticity, nymphs without innocence, men without humanity, gather into idiot groups upon the polluted canvas, and scenic affectations encumbered the street with preposterous marble. And thus, Christianity and morality, courage, and intellect, and art *all* crumbling *together*, we are hurried on to the fall of Italy, the revolution in France, and the condition of art . . . in the time of George II. (*CW* 9, 45; my italics)

We are indeed 'hurried on', and hurried over and hurried through as well. This is a history with the history left out. It is remarkable that the man who above all others could note and trace and describe the subtle gradations and almost imperceptible but manifestly accruing changes in the formation of a cloud, the seamless unarrestable motion of a wave, the movement of snow into drifts, the growth of plants and trees, has no time for, perhaps no sense of, the infinitely complex transformations through time of human societies and the varying rates of change of different parts and activities of those societies. It is matter of all-at-onceness and all-together. 'I date the commencement of the Fall of Venice from the death of Carlo Zeno, 8th of May, 1418' (*CW* 9, 21). You feel he could give you the hour. On 7 May – most religious; 9 May – most corrupt. Of course it does not work out like that once he starts to go into details, but there is a marked historical – anti-historical – tendency in his imagination which will reveal itself spectacularly as he goes on to compose a Venice which seems to be almost entirely composed of, and always tending to, extremes.

At the end of 'The Quarry' he explains why entrance into Venice will be deferred by a whole volume.

> Come, then . . . and let us know, before we enter the streets of the Sea city, whether we are indeed to submit ourselves to their undistinguished enchantment, and to look upon the last changes which were wrought on the lifted forms of her palaces, as we should on the capricious towering of summer clouds in the sunset, where they sank into the deep of night; or whether, rather, we shall not behold in the brightness of their accumulated marble, pages on which the sentence of her luxury was to be written until the waves should efface it, as they fulfilled – 'God has numbered thy kingdom, and finished it.' (*CW* 9, 59)

Before we try to read the stones of Venice – and *The Stones of Venice* – Ruskin wants to prepare us, educate us, train us. He wants to establish 'canons of judgement' and hopes 'in making the Stones of Venice [capital letters but not capitalized words – neither and both city and book] touchstones, and detecting, by the mouldering of her marble, poison more subtle than ever was betrayed by the rending of her crystal' (CW 9, 57). Canons and touchstones – very Arnoldian and high Victorian: the overt and announced polemical intent is to show up the 'baseness' of the last three centuries (no less) of European architecture. But his real urge is to look into how you build a temple, a cathedral, a palace, and to this end he feels he has to go, indeed, right back to the quarry. The first volume is accurately and comprehensively entitled *The Foundations.*

'All European architecture . . . is derived from Greece through Rome, and coloured and perfected from the East' (*CW* 9, 34). The apodictic, universalizing, generalizing which brooks no possibility of denial or question is characteristic of Ruskin and is part of a strategy and a need. Somehow he wants to hold everything – *everything* – together; contain it, control it, relate it. This opening generalization is, he says, a 'great connecting clue, you may string all the types of successive architectural invention upon it like so may beads'. Immediately after, he informs us that the Greeks probably received their 'shaft system' – the original pillar of all architecture – from Egypt; but the possibly earlier derivation does not matter to the reader. 'It is only necessary that he should be able to refer to a fixed point of origin.' The search for such a point of origin is indeed the 'quarry' of many Victorian thinkers – be it of species, societies, religions, words. And the need for some 'connecting clue' goes along with this. To the extent that things are disoriginated, there is the danger that they may reveal themselves to be unrelated – and that things and people should be properly and significantly and harmoniously related is very important to Ruskin: 'we may also permit men or cities, to gather themselves into companies, or constellate themselves into clusters, but not to fuse themselves into mere masses of nebulous aggregation' (*CW* 9, 134). This permission or prescription informs both his politics (no democratic masses) and his writing, which constantly seeks to resist aggregation and produce constellation.

But from the start he has admitted that the 'point of origin' is not in fact finally determinable, so he establishes it by his own fiat, which means that all the subsequent connections and constellations which are directly or indirectly based on it are of his own making. Which in turn means that his prose has to have tremendous constructive and carrying power: to raise his own Venice he must build slowly and firmly and make his foundations sure.

> Do not think that Nature rusticates her foundations. Smooth sheets of rock, glistening like sea waves, and that ring under the hammer like a brazen bell, – that is her preparation for her first *stories.* She does rusticate sometimes: crumbly sandstones, with their ripple marks filled with red mud; dusty limestones, which the rains wash into labyrinthine cavities; spongy lavas, which the volcano blast drags hither and thither into ropy coils and bubbling hollows; – these she rusticates, indeed, when she wants to make oyster-shells and magnesia of them; but not when she needs to lay *foundations* with them. Then she seeks the polished surface and iron heart, not rough looks and incoherent substance. (*CW* 9, 350–1)

Volume II will be called *The Sea Stories,* but before that Ruskin has to write his *Foundations.* For that, there must be no crumbly, dusty, spongy writing, but, like nature, something firm and glistening which will ring under the hammer like a bell – polished, iron-like, coherent. And that is what we get. Though, as always with Ruskin, we get something more as well: that unconfinable surplus which – it is part of his greatness as a writer – he is helpless to exclude and compelled to inscribe.

Since he has to start from the beginning – or a beginning – he is resolved to take us with him on what he announces will be a long journey: 'I shall endeavour so to lead the reader from the foundation upwards, as that he may find out for himself the best way of doing everything, and having so discovered it, never forgot it' (*CW* 9, 73). And so we go right back to basics, down in the etymology of building as it were (Ruskin is very keen on etymology): the wall (and what is a wall? 'an even and united fence, whether of wood, earth, stone or metal') and, from the wall, the pier, then the shaft; the capital, the arch, the arch load, the roof, the buttress, and then on to ornamentation – he is trying to reconstruct the reader as apprentice medieval craftsman. 'Now as I gave the reader the ground and the stones, that he might for himself find out how to build his wall, I shall give him the block of marble, and the chisel, that he may himself find out how to shape the column'; 'The reader is now master of all he need know respecting construction of capitals'; 'The reader has now some knowledge of every feature of all possible architecture.' As a reward we move on to ornament: 'We have no more to do with heavy stones and hard lines; we are going to be happy' (*CW* 9, 253) – and enjoy ourselves in decorating architecture in ways derived from whatever gives us pleasure in the forms and movements in the natural world. For the most part he keeps fairly methodically to his task of tutoring master craftsman who occasionally, as he admits, has to 'speak dictatorially' – particularly when it comes to value judgements. He *knows* what is bad and ugly. Just occasionally he gets ahead of his subject as it were; when discussing roofs he mentions cupolas: 'I enjoy them in St Mark's chiefly because they increase the fantastic and unreal characters of St Mark's Place; and because they appear to sympathise with an expression, common, I think, to all the buildings of that group, of a natural buoyancy, as if they floated in the air or on the surface of the sea' (*CW* 9, 184). But he soon brings himself back to the consideration of essentials: 'We are, however, beginning to lose sight of our roof structure in its spirit, and must return to our text' (*CW* 9, 188).

A crucial feature of that text is the ongoing attempt to reduce all the relevant material to an itemizable order, an enumerable coherence, to produce 'a great coherent system', to use his own term for the Gothic. There are numbers and lists and definitive statements throughout: six divisions of architecture, twelve possible permutations of shaft arrangements, five orders of capital, four subjects of ornament, perhaps most ambitiously 'the whole range of systematised inorganic and organic forms' reduced to twelve, running from 'Abstract lines' to 'Mammalian animals and man'. There are 'three conditions of humanity' and simply 'two great influences which must for ever divide the heart of man: the one of Lawful Discipline, with its perfection and order, but its danger and degeneracy into Formalism; the other of Lawful Freedom, with its vigour and variety, but its danger of degenerating into Licentiousness' (*CW* 9, 383). The urge to taxonomize and classify extends to illustrations, so we are given sheets of 'cornice profiles' and 'Profiles of Bases' and so on – and there is a geometric diagram purporting to show the possible 'Varieties of Chamfer' which at first glance looks more like one of Stevie's drawings in *The Secret Agent*, a classification or 'rendering of cosmic chaos . . . a mad art attempting the inconceivable'. And that may be the point. You get the feeling at times that he wants – or needs? – to systematize and classify everything. Certainly he wants things circumscribed, under control. 'This is the form of all good doors, without exception, over the whole world and in all ages, and no other can ever be invented' (*CW* 9, 222). So there's doors at least definitively in their place. (I cannot resist quoting his comments on the 'paltry' doors of English cathedrals 'which look as if they were made, not for the open egress, but for the surreptitious drainage of a stagnant congregation'; (*CW* 9, 214).) Somewhere behind all this will to number, order, and thus in a sense subdue, is a kind of mixture of nineteenth-century taxonomizing scientism and the Ten Commandments, yielding a sense that phenomena, as it were, contain and constrain themselves by laws at once natural and religious, as may be illustrated by the following remarkable passage concerning a floral ornament within a geometric frame:

> Observe, however, and this is of the utmost importance, that the value of this type does not consist in the mere shutting of the ornament into a certain space, but in the acknowledgement *by* the ornament of the fitness of the limitation; – of its own perfect willingness to submit to it; nay, of a predisposition in itself to fall into the ordained form, without any direct expression of the command to do so; an anticipation of the authority, and an instant and willing submission to it, in every fibre and spray; not merely *willing*, but *happy* submission, as being pleased rather than vexed to have so beautiful a law suggested to it, and one which to follow is so justly in accordance with its own nature. You must not cut out a branch of hawthorn as it grows, and rule a triangle round it, and suppose that it is then submitted to a law. Not a bit of it. It is only put in a cage, and will look as if it must get out, for its life, or wither in the confinement. But the spirit of triangle must be put into the hawthorn. It must suck in isoscelesism with its sap. Thorn and blossom, leaf and spray, must grow with an awful sense of triangular necessity upon them, for the guidance of which they are to be thankful, and to grow all the stronger and more gloriously. And though there may be a transgression here and there, and an adaptation to some other need, or a reaching forth to some other end, greater even than triangle, yet this liberty is to be always accepted under a solemn sense of special permission, and when the full form is reached and the entire submission expressed and every blossom has a thrilling sense of its responsibility down into its tiniest stamen, you may take your terminal line away if you will. No need of it any more. The commandment is written on the heart of the thing. (*CW* 9, 305–6)

All of Ruskin's politics are in that passage – or one should say his political and indeed his cosmological most fervent hopes. Things, with obedient joy and joyous obedience, ordered themselves. You didn't really need the externally imposed triangles: they sucked in isoscelesism as they grew. That would be a withering away of the state indeed. And a withering away of the statement too, for in such a world things would speak themselves and arrange themselves by their own syntax, with no need for the connecting and constellating scribe.

But at times an imposed geometry is necessary and beneficial. Of the designs in St Michele of Lucca, Ruskin writes:

> Geometry seems to have acted as a febrifuge, for beautiful geometrical designs are introduced among the tumult of the hunt; and there is no more seeing double, nor ghastly monstrosity of conception; no more ending of everything in something else; no more disputing for spare legs among bewildered bodies; no more setting on of heads wrong side foremost. *The fragments have come together*: we are out of the Inferno with its weeping down the spine; we are in the fair hunting fields of the Lucchese mountains. (*CW* 9, 430)

The italicized words point to an ongoing need and search for Ruskin, until at the end on the verge of his last madness he found that 'things bind and blend themselves together': how do you make the fragments come together? How avoid the Inferno and keep yourself in the fair hunting fields? (This was to be Ezra Pound's – one might even say modernism's – problem.) It might be argued that this Inferno is a cultural nightmare and that, for Ruskin, Nature is still to be perceived as sweetly and serenely self-administering. Usually so indeed, and he often turns to Nature to see 'with what imagery she will fill our thoughts'. Yet it is not always the desired or needed model. 'But we want no cold and careful imitation of catastrophe; no calculated mockery or convulsion; no delicate recommendation of ruin. We are to follow the labour of nature, but not her disturbance; to imitate what she has deliberately ordained, not what she has violently suffered, or strangely permitted' (*CW* 9, 270). But how can you tell the labour from the disturbance, the difference between the permitted and the ordained? Ruskin needs his confident lists and classifications, his almost obessive systematizations, at the same time as he reveals that they depend on arbitrary, if impetuous exclusions, just as his work is based on an origin which is deemed rather than discovered. While 'proving four laws' governing the ways in which capitals may change according to changes in proportion, he admits, or marvels, 'infinity of infinities in the sum of possible change' (*CW* 9, 142). Infinity is always seeping into Ruskin's writing, as his writing everywhere acknowledges; constantly, arborescently reaching out for the not-yet-included, even while numbering, listing and generally seeking to bring to rule. 'This infinite universe is unfathomable, inconceivable, in its whole.' It is matched by 'the infinity of the written word (*CW* 9, 410). Ruskin wrote in and between, and in the fullest possible knowledge of, these two infinities. For the purposes of perception and description, a key strategy is finding the appropriate distance. As an example, he cites the case of looking at a mountain. If you want to see 'its great harmonies of form' you 'don't climb up it where, seen close to, all is disorder and accident.' Rather, you draw away and, as you see more and more, 'dim sympathies begin to busy themselves in the disjointed mass; line binds itself into stealthy fellowship with line; group by group, the helpless fragments gather themselves into ordered companies . . . until the powerless chaos is seen risen up with girded loins, and not one piece of all the unregarded heap could now be spared from the mystic whole' (*CW* 9, 294–5). This is a kind of polity of vision whereby you retire to the point at which reality begins to form groups, fellowships, companies, with sympathies and bindings and gatherings gradually becoming visible. It is a form of perspectivism. It is a matter of finding the right way of looking, the right standpoint from which to look (and seeing is everything in Ruskin), which can transform the 'powerless' (or perhaps potentially all too powerful) 'chaos' into a 'mystic whole'. For Ruskin's immediate purpose it will be a matter of retiring from the contemporary stones of Venice, lying indeed in 'disorder and accident', until, deploying his civics of vision, he can see it as some part of a 'mystic whole'.

Eliding the mediations of history allows Ruskin to posit – to insist on – not just the close connection between, but effectively the identity of, morality and materiality. It 'is equally true in morals and mathematics, that the strength of materials or of men, or of minds, is always most available when it is applied as closely as possible to a single point' (*CW* 9, 101). Materials, men, minds and morality – these are constantly run together; 'this, in arch morality and in man morality, is a very simple and easily to be understood principle – that if either arch or man expose themselves to their special temptations or adverse forces, *outside* of their voussoirs or proper and appointed armour, both will fall' (*CW* 9, 157). As Venice fell; and, if Venice fell, so, by that easily to be understood principle, must have the Venetians. By this principle of intimate interconnection – or identity – Ruskin can apply his moral discourse to the hapless materials. Of a certain base on the Piazzetta side of the Ducal Palace he writes that it 'already shows the loose, sensual, ungoverned character of fifteenth century ornament in the dissoluteness of its rolling'. (*CW* 9, 343) The dissoluteness of its rolling – it is as if the very stones had been caught out in a Cleopatra-like wantonness! It is indeed notable that Ruskin's terms of disapprobation, when they are not deriding and deprecating 'lifelessness', are usually rather over-excitedly condemning some manifestation of 'lasciviousness', the terms themselves often being of a 'sensual, ungoverned character', as when he refers to the 'utter licentiousness' of certain Renaissance cornices. More elegantly, he sometimes finds that the latencies of the language do his work for him by operating at once on the two planes he wants to merge. 'For instance, whether in archivolts, jambs, or buttresses, or in square piers, or at the extremity of the entire building, we necessarily have the awkward (moral or architectural) feature, the *corner*. How to turn a corner gracefully becomes, therefore, a perfectly general question' (*CW* 9, 311). This is what Ruskin wants to make it – a perfectly general question, so that you cannot, really, tell the work from the workman, nor moral deportment from material enactment.

Since *earlier* means *better*, more moral, an important question begins to loom for Ruskin which will dominate much the rest of his writing and indeed life. He wants to arrive at 'some perception of the kind of enfantillage or archaicism to which it may be possible, even in days of advanced science, legitimately to return' (*CW* 9, 289). 'But how far it may be possible to recur to such archaicism, or to make up for it by any voluntary abandonment of power, I cannot as yet venture in any wise to determine' (*CW* 9, 285). He was to become a good deal more certain that such a return was not only possible but absolutely essential if England was to save itself, but we may note that Ruskin is formulating here a desire and a problem which produce that streak of primitivism that is a constitutive part of modernism. Can you, by an act of the enlightened will, *will* yourself to return to (what is imagined to be) an earlier state of a happier, healthier, more unified, more reverent, less self-reflexive, undissociated, more integrated state of consciousness – whether it is to be found among the Aztec religions of Mexico, the natives of Tahiti, the seamen of Malaya, the Buddhist serenities of India, early seventeenth-century England, the wheelwright's shop – or Gothic Europe? Can a too complex, self-tormenting consciousness consciously return to a simpler state of consciousness. The answers, as it now seems, can only be a variety of more or less rueful negatives, though of course there have been any number of self-deceiving (and sometimes self-torturing – this of D. H. Lawrence) *willed* affirmatives. This is not my immediate concern here but it is important to see Ruskin's attempt to re-create and reconstitute an earlier, purer Venice, as, in a sense, a form of primitivism, or – to adopt his suggestive word – of 'enfantillage'.

Finally, then, Ruskin is ready for another approach to Venice. 'And now come with me, for I have kept you too long from your gondola: come with me, on an autumnal morning, through the dark gates of Padua, and let us take the broad road leading towards the East.' And this time it is all disappointment – or worse. Everything in both nature and culture augurs ill. It is a protracted journey through a modern wasteland. The vines are 'hectic', their clusters 'gloomy blue'. The Brenta is a 'muddy volume of yellowish-grey water' which 'glides heavily between its monotonous banks, with here and there a short, babbling eddy twisting for an instant into its opaque surface, and vanishing, as if something has been dragged into it and gone down' (presaging the final sinking of Venice?). The road is 'dusty and shadeless', the sunshine is 'feverish', a villa is 'spectral', windows are fictitious, an architrave is in 'bad perspective', a wall is 'dead'.

> Another dreary stage . . . half-stagnant canals . . . villas sinking fast into utter ruin, black, and rent, and lonely . . . blighted fragments of gnarled hedges and broken stakes for their fencing . . . a few fragments of marble steps . . . now setting into the mud in broken joints, all a slope and slippery with green weeds . . . the view from the balcony is not cheerful: a narrow street . . . a ditch with slow current in it . . . a close smell of garlic and crabs . . . much vociferation . . . down to the water, which latter we fancy for an instant has become black with stagnation; another glance undeceives us, – it is covered with the black boats of Venice. We enter one of them . . . and glide away; at first feeling as if the water were yielding continually beneath the boat and letting her sink into soft vacancy . . . we lose patience, and extricate ourselves from the cushions. . . . Forward still: the endless canal bends at last, now torn to pieces and staggering in ugly rents towards the water. . . . Now we can see nothing but what seems a low and monotonous dockyard wall, with flat arches to let the tide through it; – this is the railroad bridge, conspicuous above all things. But at the end of those dismal arches there rises, out of a wider water, a straggling line of low and confused black buildings, which but for the many towers which are mingled among them, might be the suburbs of an English manufacturing town. Four or five domes, pale, and apparently at a greater distance, rise above the centre of the line; but the object which first catches the eye is a sullen cloud of black smoke brooding over the northern half of it, and which issues from the belfry of a church.
>
> It is Venice. (*CW* 9, 413–15)

End of volume I. Ruskin leaves us with a Venice constituted *entirely* of negation and signs of ill-omen, drawing repeatedly on a vocabulary of blight, stagnation, death, darkness, dreariness, ruin and decay. All the vestigial, lingering beauty of the city is deliberately occluded so there is no tempering or relieving the gloom. Ruskin is being absolute. *This* is modern Venice. As much as to say, this is what modernity has done to the most beautiful city the world has ever seen.

He reveals the reason for this 'approach' (to his city, to his subject) at the start of volume II. He concedes that it has induced 'disappointment' but then he draws the reader nearer and nearer and into the city, deliberately re-creating a mounting excitement with a series of 'when first's' – when first you saw this, saw that – culminating thus:

> and when at last that boat darted forth upon the breadth of the river sea, across which the front of the Ducal palace, flushed with its sanguine veins, looks to the snowy dome of our Lady of Salvation, it was no marvel that the mind should be so deeply entranced by the visionary charm of a scene so beautiful and so strange, as to forget the darker truths of its history and its being. Well might it seem that such a city had owed her existence rather to the rod of the enchanter, than the fear of the fugitive; that the waters which encircled her had been chosen for a mirror of her-state, rather than the shelter of her nakedness; and that all which in nature was wild and merciless, – Time and Decay, as well as the waves and tempests, had been won to adorn her instead of to destroy, and might still spare, for ages to come, that beauty which seemed to have fixed for its throne the sands of the hour-glass as well as of the sea. (*CW* 10, 6–7)

This first chapter is entitled 'The Throne', and this is the first time the word is used in it. Ruskin is going right back to establish just what it is that the regality of Venice 'sits' upon – apart from sand and time that is forever running out. His nod to Byron makes it clear that he wants to focus on – as the source for the original city – not the magic wand but fugitive fear; and his attempt will clearly be to disperse the 'visionary charm' and bring out the 'darker truths'. He admits, readily, that modern Venice, though (particularly thanks to recent history) it is full of defaced palaces and 'desecrated ruins', still has its 'magic'. There then follows a long passage which in a later note he declared to be one of 'my best finished passages'. It does indeed reveal a great deal about his project as he saw it.

> They, at least, are little to be envied in whose hearts the great charities of the imagination lie dead, and for whom the fancy has no power to repress the importunity of painful impressions, or to raise what is ignoble and disguise what is discordant, in a scene so rich in its remembrances, so surpassing in its beauty. But for this work of the imagination there must be no permission for the task which is before us. The impotent feelings of romance, so singularly characteristic of this century, may indeed gild, but never save, the remains of those mightier ages to which they are attached like climbing flowers; and they must be torn away from the magnificent fragments, if we would see them as they stood in their own strength. Those feelings, always as fruitless as they are fond, are in Venice not only incapable of

> protecting, but even of discerning, the objects to which they ought to have been attached. The Venice of modern fiction and drama is a thing of yesterday, a mere efflorescence of decay, a stage dream which the first ray of daylight must dissipate into dust. (*CW* 1, 7–8)

The temptations of Venice for the imagination are conceded but robustly renounced. Ruskin has an unseducible eye for things as they are: romantic accretions will be 'torn away' as he discerns, and in discerning protects, what is truly there of value. But while he banishes the Venice of fiction and drama and dream from his pages, he will in fact *replace* it with his own dreamed and dramatized Venice, in which the historicism and literary accuracy of his facts cannot conceal the modernity of *his* fiction, and where the 'efflorescence of decay' will occasionally flare up with unparalleled brilliance. Once again he announces that he is seeking a Venice which no longer exists. The mighty Doges of the past, he affirms, would today simply not know where they were – 'would literally not recognise one stone of the great city'.

> The remains of *their* Venice lie hidden in many a grass-grown court, and silent pathway, and lightless canal, where the slow waves have sapped their foundations for five hundred years, and must soon prevail over them forever. It must be our task to glean and gather them forth, and restore out of them some faint image of the lost city; more gorgeous a thousandfold than that which now exists, yet not created in the day-dream of the prince, nor by the ostentation of the noble, but built by iron hands and patient hearts, contending against the adversity of nature and the fury of man, so that its wonderfulness cannot be grasped by the indolence of imagination, but only after frank inquiry into the true nature of that wild and solitary scene, whose restless tides and trembling sands did indeed shelter the birth of the city, but long denied her dominion. (*CW* 10, 9)

Ruskin's imagination was never 'indolent', and we may rephrase what he brings to his task as 'frank inquiry' motivated, informed and animated by an intense energy of the imagination, so that the Venice he will re-create will not, indeed, be the 'day-dream of a prince' but rather the work-dream of a passionate nineteenth-century writer. We must note that he is seeking to constitute an 'image of the *lost* city' – Ruskin is one of the great writers of loss, and his writing has, correspondingly, incomparable regaining powers. 'I do not wonder at what men suffer, but I wonder often at what they Lose' (*CW* 10, 178). Ruskin writes always to rescue, to preserve, to bring things back. It is no wonder – and a matter for wonder – that he inspired Proust to set out to retrieve lost time. Ruskin, for the moment, is after the Venice which lost itself.

His first task, then, is to take us back to the 'wild and solitary scene' which saw the 'birth of the city', and this takes him into geology – the primal sediment, the bank of sand, the calcerous mud, the marshy islets, the crowded cluster of islands on which Venice could be built. To get some sense of the scene confronting the original settlers, Ruskin advises the traveller to take a boat: 'let him remove, in his imagination' – note that imagination is indispensable from the start –

> the brightness of the great city that still extends itself in the distance, and the walls and towers from the islands that are near; and so wait, until the bright investiture and sweet warmth of the sunset are withdrawn from the waters, and the black desert of their shore lines in the nakedness beneath the night, pathless, comfortless, infirm, lost in dark languor and fearful silence, except where the salt runlets splash into the tideless pools, or the sea-birds flit from their margins with a questioning cry; and he will be enabled to enter in some sort into the horror of heart with which this solitude was anciently chosen by man for his habitation.

A primal scene indeed, and as far as possible from the magic-wand fancies of origin. Even before reminding us of the *work* involved in building the city, Ruskin stresses that, at bottom, it was initially a matter of the tides being just right. No tide would have meant a 'pestiferous' marsh. 'Eighteen inches more of difference between the level of the flood and the ebb . . . the streets of the city would have been widened, its network of canals filled up, and all the peculiar character of the place and people destroyed.' Again, he has his reason for thus pushing the reader's nose, as it were, in the original mud. 'The reader may perhaps have felt some pain in the contrast between this faithful view of the site of the Venetian Throne, and the romantic conception of it which we ordinarily form.' But instead of that pain, he says, we should wonder at the 'inscrutableness and the wisdom of the ways of God.'

Had we been present two thousand years ago, watching these waters, how little we could have 'imagined' that

> in the laws which are stretching forth the gloomy margins of those fruitless banks, and feeding the bitter grass among their shallows, there was indeed a preparation, and *the only preparation possible*, for the founding of a city which was to be set like a golden clasp on the girdle of the earth, to write her history on the white scrolls of the sea-surges, and to word it in their thunder, and to gather and give forth, in world-wide pulsation, the glory of the West and of the East, from the burning heart of her Fortitude and Splendour! (*CW* 10, 13–15)

This is Ruskin's providentialism – Venice was not magically conjured but divinely ordained, enthroned alike in mud and sea, and in God's inscrutable purposes. And note that in Ruskin's terms she will 'write her history on the white scrolls of the sea-surges'. In entitling this second volume *The Sea Stories*, Ruskin is again coupling two phenomena. The actual phrase occurs in the chapter on 'Byzantine Palaces', where he laments the fact that 'in the only two cases in which the second stories are left the ground floors are modernised, and in the others where the sea stories are left the second stories are modernised'. (*CW* 10, 146). It is inevitable that the sea-city will have sea stories to tell, and Ruskin finds much of the 'writing' on the first level of the buildings above the foundations where the city rests on the sea. The story of this 'storey' is thus vital to his work. This is a crucial part of what Venice 'wrote' on the sea. How much else of Venice is conceived in terms of writing will become clearer later.

The two focal point of this volume are the two buildings of St Mark's and the Ducal Palace, but, as Jean Clegg noted, Ruskin starts at the peripheries. First at Torcello, now in a stage of utter 'desolation' but with the duomo of Santa Fosca still having a story to tell, or for Ruskin to interpret. He reads it as a 'hurried erection . . . built by men in flight and distress' – which takes all the historic time out of its slow construction and makes it into a mythological event. This is to Ruskin's overall purpose, and he concludes the chapter:

> And if the stranger would yet learn in what spirit it was the dominion of Venice was begun, and in what strength she went forth conquering and to conquer, let him not seek the wealth of her arsenals or number of her armies, nor look upon the pageantry of her palaces, nor enter into the secrets of her councils; but let him ascend the highest tier of the stern ledges that sweep round the altar of Torcello, and then, looking as the pilot did of old along the marble ribs of the goodly temple-ship, let him repeople its veined deck with the shadows of its dead mariners, and strive to feel in himself the strength of heart that was kindled within them, when first, after the pillars of it had settled in the sand, and the roof of it had been closed against the angry sky that was still reddened by the fires of their homesteads – first, within the shelter of its knitted walls amidst the murmur of the waste of waves and the beating of the wings of the sea-birds round the rock that was strange to them, – rose that ancient hymn, in the power of their gathered voices:
>
> THE SEA IS HIS, AND HE MADE IT:
> AND HIS HANDS PREPARED THE DAY LAND
>
> (*CW* 10, 34–5)

Out with the armies and palaces and councils goes the whole secular history of the making of Venice (even if the palaces do reappear as artefacts). The ship which inaugurates this Venice is not one of their ships of commerce, but a 'temple-ship', and its sea story will take place, not so much on the sea which enables trade and imperial expansion, as from the sea created and owned by God.

Contemporary Murano is evidence that Venice, like the human body, shows its first signs of decrepitude 'at the extremities', and once again Ruskin evokes scenes of desolation including – rather unusually, for Ruskin's Venice is not very populated – what we might call symptomatic inhabitants: 'woeful groups of aged men and women, wasted and fever-struck, fixed in paralytic supplication, half-kneeling, half-crouched upon the pavement. . . . Fit inhabitants, these, for what was once the garden of Venice' (*CW* 10, 65). The cathedral of San Donato still stands, although the 'original plan' can only be partially recuperated. 'The whole impression and effect of the building are irretrievably lost, but the fragments of it are still precious' (*CW* 10, 42). As ever, Ruskin is keen to recapture something 'lost', trace back to an 'original' from precious fragments. Having done what he can of meticulous annotation and reconstruction, Ruskin concludes that 'the whole edifice is, therefore, simply a temple of the Virgin' (*CW* 10, 66). As in many ways a fiercely intransigent Protestant at the time, Ruskin was constantly having trouble with Mariolatry (indeed the female altogether) and more generally the undeniable fact that it was Catholicism which had inspired or informed much of the art and architecture he most admired (while Protestantism seemed to nourish little or none). And here Ruskin takes a very important step – one which will conclude by his abandoning orthodox Christianity entirely – by, as it were, generalizing the notion of reverence. 'For there is a wider division of men than that into Christian and Pagan: before we ask what a man worships, we have to ask *whether he worships at all*' (*CW* 10, 67). It is arresting that Proust makes an almost identical issue of comparable moment, only his word is not 'worship' but 'desire'. Their closeness on this issue leads them to tangle over a key topic – idols, idolizing, 'idolatry'; or rather it leads Proust to question the stand Ruskin took on the matter. But more of that in time. Here Ruskin has identified a crucial clue to differentiate the old Venetians and the new Victorians, 'the calculating, smiling, self-governed man, and the believing, weeping, wondering, struggling, Heaven-governed man', 'for that is indeed the difference which we shall find, in the end, between the builders of this day and the builders on that sand island long ago. They *did* honour something out of themselves; they did believe in spiritual presence judging, animating redeeming them; they built to its honour and for its habitation' (*CW* 10, 67–8). Many Victorian writers were worried by what they took to be an alarming increase of ego, egoism, 'egotist', in everyday life. If I may collapse almost as much history into one sentence as Ruskin himself sometimes does, I would say that what concerned many of these writers was not so much the desacralization of the world as what we might call the egotizing of Victorian society. For Ruskin, of course, the latter followed on from the former as surely as night follows day. But his conviction that people should, must, 'honour something out of themselves' comes from a growing dread he shared with other Victorian observers that increasingly people were honouring only the self.

Ruskin is now ready to approach St Mark's, characteristically first asking the reader to 'imagine' 'its aspect in that early time, when it was a green field, cloister-like and quiet'. Then, because he likes to work by dramatic contrasts and abrupt shifts, he asks the reader to 'imagine', again, that he is in a 'quiet English cathedral town' and to think of 'that scene, and the meaning of all its small formalisms, mixed with its serene sublimity'. Estimate its secluded, continuous, drowsy felicities and then just as we *are* beginning to drowse – 'let us quickly recollect we are in Venice' (*CW* 10, 71, 78, 80). Taking us through the confused and noisy alleys as kinaesthetically as only Ruskin can, things getting darker and closer and more claustrophobic until we almost have to push through the prose, suddenly we are out into air and space:

> there rises a vision out of the earth, and all the great square seems to have opened from it in a kind of awe, that we may see it far away; – a multitude of pillars and white domes, clustered into a long low pyramid of coloured light; a treasure heap, it seems, partly of gold, and partly of opal and mother-of-pearl, followed beneath into five great vaulted porches, ceiled with air mosaic, and beset with sculpture of alabaster, clear as amber and delicate as ivory – sculpture fantastic and involved, of palm leaves and lifes, and grapes and pomegranates, and birds clinging and fluttering among the branches, all twined together into an endless network of buds and plumes . . .

and so on up and up, for at times Ruskin's prose is almost vertiginously ascensual, until:

> and above them, in the broad archevolts, a continuous chain of language and of life – angels, and the signs of heaven, and the labours of men, each in its appointed season upon the earth; and above these, another range of glittering pinnacles, mixed with white arches edged with scarlet flowers – a confusion of delight, amidst which the breasts of the Greek horses are seen blazing in their breadth of golden strength, and the St Mark's lion, lifted on a blue field covered with stars, until at last, as if in ecstasy, the crests of the arches break into a marble foam, and toss themselves far into the blue sky in flashes and wreaths

> of sculptured spray, as if the breakers on the Lido had been frost-bound before they fell, and the sea-nymphs had inlaid them with coral and amethyst.
>
> Between that grim cathedral of England and this, what an interval! (*CW* 10, 82–4)

And between Ruskin's avowed Protestantism and the unconfessed paganism and aestheticism of writing such as this, what an interval too! What he wants, and what he makes *this* Venice into, is exactly 'a continuous chain of language and of life' where the signs and labours, the sacred and the secular, meet and merge. Continuity is of the essence: 'what we now regard with doubt and wonder, as well as with delight, was then the natural continuation, into the principal edifice of the city, of a style which was familiar to every one throughout all its lanes and streets' (*CW* 10 118–19). Churches then 'were never built in any separate, mystical, and religious style; they were built in the manner that was common and familir to everybody at the time . . . they were merely more finished and full examples of a universal style' (*CW* 10, 120–1). The accuracy of this may be questioned, but the intention behind the assertion is clear – to posit the possibility of a seamlessness of life and style, unmarked by the kind of discontinuities and disjunctions which make, in modern times, such a cathedral a thing apart, at once a wonder and a relic, unrelated to contemporaneity. It is to show up such disjunction that Ruskin repeatedly stresses the utter obliviousness of contemporary Venetians to their great cathedral – as though they were suffering from some collective amnesia and spiritual lobotomy. 'You may walk from sunrise to sunset, to and fro, before the gateway of St Mark's, and you will not see an eye lifted to it, nor a countenance brightened by it. Priest and layman, soldier and civilian, rich and poor, pass by it alike regardlessly' (*CW* 10, 84). Again we may doubt the literal accuracy of so sweeping a generalization, but Ruskin wants to depict a modern Venice which can no longer see, let alone read, that 'continuous chain of language and of life' still inscribed on this miraculous piece of old Venice. He is writing in discontinuous times. Ruskin's Venice was wholly and continuously meaningful, but now 'we have destroyed the goodly architecture of our cities; we have substituted one wholly devoid of beauty and meaning' (*CW* 10, 119). Instead of the city beautiful, Ruskin saw his contemporaries busily engaged in constructing what James Thomson would soon call 'the city of dreadful night'.

That St Mark's is to be *read* is a constant and reiterated theme: 'the whole edifice is to be regarded less as a temple wherein to pray, than as itself a Book of Common Prayer, a vast illuminated missal, bound with alabaster instead of parchment, studded with porphyry pillars instead of jewels, and written within and without in letters of enamel and gold' (*CW* 10, 112).

Having succumbed to a book which described a cathedral as a book, Proust would in turn write a book which described itself as a cathedral. But there was an even more important corollary for Ruskin of the cathedral as book and one which became of critical importance for Proust. That story must await a subsequent chapter, but the passage in question is necessary here since it is the climax and conclusion of Ruskin's evocation of St Mark's.

> Never had a city a more glorious Bible. Among the nations of the North, a rude and shadowy sculpture filled their temples with confused and hardly legible imagery; but, for her, the skill and the treasures of the East had gilded every letter, and illuminated every page, till the Book-Temple shone from afar off like the star of the Magi. In other cities, the meetings of the people were often in places withdrawn from religious association, subject to violence and to change; and on the grass of the dangerous rampart, and in the dust of the troubled street, there were deeds done and counsels taken, which, if we cannot justify, we may sometimes forgive. But the sins of Venice, whether in her palace or in her piazza, were done with the Bible at her right hand. The walls on which its testimony were written were separated but by a few inches of marble from those which guarded the secrets of her councils, or confined the victims of her policy. And when in her last hours she threw off all shame and all restraint, and the great square of the city became filled with the madness of the whole earth, be it remembered how much her sin was greater, because it was done in the face of the House of God, burning with the letter of His Law. Mountebank and masquer laughed their laugh and went their way; and a silence followed them, not unforetold; for amidst them all, through century after century of gathering vanity and festering guilt, that white dome of St Mark's had uttered in the dead ear of Venice, 'know thou, for all these things God will bring thee into judgment.' (*CW* 10, 141–2)

Thus Ruskin ends the chapter, as he does on several occasions, with an intimation, anticipation, even evocation of the final death of Venice, which like its Fall seems to happen over and over again. Venice is a long time Falling and a long time Dying. But, more immediately: sin, if you believe in sin, is presumably the same sin wherever you commit it. There is no cultural, geographic or situational relativity in the Ten Commandments. To maintain that the sins of Venice were 'greater' *because* they were done in the proximity of such an incomparably beautiful Book-Temple is arguably – and Proust would so argue – to be guilty of an over-valuation of artefacts. And this would be a form of idolatry.

The word and the issue indeed appear, crucially in this chapter, in connection with Ruskin's discussion and impassioned defence of the great mosaics of St Mark's. He justifies them primarily as offering a 'stone manuscript' to those who would only read pictures – texts for the illiterate, an idea with a very long pedigree. But more importantly he sees them as the best, most 'effective' works of 'religious art' – that phrase being itself a somewhat unstable compound, always liable to decompose and reveal itself as an oxymoron; and certainly Ruskin, like many others, clearly had something more than a sneaking suspicion that the more something was 'art' the less it was 'religious', while the more it stressed religion the less it succeeded as art. Mosaics, for Ruskin, have the mixture just right.

> They stand exactly midway between the debased manufacture of wooden and waxen images which is the support of Romanist idolatry all over the world, and the great art *which leads the mind away from the religious subject to the art itself.* The manufacture of puppets, however influential on the Romanist mind of Europe, is certainly not deserving of consideration as one of the fine arts. It matters literally nothing to a Romanist what the image he worships is like. . . . Idolatry, it cannot be too often repeated, is no encourager of the fine arts. But, on the other hand, the highest branches of the fine arts are no encouragers either of idolatry or religion. No picture of Leonardo's or Raphael's, no statue of Michael Angelo's, has ever been worshipped, except by accident. Carelessly regarded, and by ignorant persons, there is less to attract in them than in commoner works. Carefully regarded, and by intelligent persons, *they instantly divert the mind from their subject to their art*, so that admiration takes the place of devotion. . . . Effective religious art, therefore, has always laid, and I believe must always lie, between the two extremes – of barbarous idol-fashioning on one side, and magnificent craftmanship on the other. (*CW* 10, 130–1)

This is an extremely important matter, not only for Ruskin, since it raises the whole question of what we are doing, what we are getting, when we derive pleasure (but what kind of pleasure?) from, and pay some kind of focused attention (but what kind?) to, images and representations. Ruskin returned to the matter in an appendix titled 'proper Sense of the Word Idolatry'.

> The Church of Rome does indeed distinctively violate the *second* commandment; but the true force and weight of the sin of idolatry are in the violation of the first, of which we are all guilty, in probably a very equal degree. . . . Idolatry is, both literally and verily, not the mere bowing down before sculptures, but the serving or becoming

> the slaves of any images or imaginations which stand between us and God, and it is otherwise expressed as 'walking after the *Imagination*' of our own hearts. (*CW* 10, 451)

The first and second commandments, just to have the exact words before us, are 'Thou shalt have no other gods before me. Thou shalt not make unto thee any graven image, or any likeness of any thing that is in heaven above, or that is in earth beneath, or that is in the water beneath.' Ruskin certainly had other gods – Turner and Tintoretto, to name but two – and their 'images' and 'likenesses' aroused in him an 'admiration' which in its intensity of appreciation and apprehension, almost appropriation, is hard to tell from a kind of 'devotion'. And while it is all very well for Ruskin to italicize '*Imagination*', and while he debarred it as it were on page one of his book, from page two he finds it indispensable and appeals to it continually – imagine you are here, imagine you were there, imagine it was like this, might have been like that. Indeed, imagine *this* Venice I am evoking before you. Ruskin is constantly, and usually irresistibly, asking us to walk after the Imagination of his own heart.

The point of this scrutiny is not to show up Ruskin as, in spite of himself, a kind of idolater. For one thing, he would hardly try to elude the charge: 'which of us is not an idolater?' Which of us has the right to speak scornfully of our fellow men just because 'they have been accustomed to bow their knees before a statue? Which of us shall say that there may not be a spiritual idolatry in our own apparent worship?' (*CW* 10, 451). This is not just a matter of a Protestant art critic being fair to Catholics, who, as it happens and perhaps not coincidentally, have all the best art. What Ruskin is pointing towards (apart from what one would take to be the indisputable observation that there can be idolatrous Protestants and worshipful Catholics) – and this is the larger matter I wish to bring forward – is the absolute indeterminability of one's, of anyone's, relation to the 'image'.

> For indeed it is utterly impossible for one man to judge of the feeling with which another bows before an image. From that pure reverence in which Sir Thomas Browne wrote, 'I can dispense with my hat at the sight of a cross, but not with a thought to my redeemer', to the worst superstition of the most ignorant Romanist, there is an infinite series of subtle transitions; and the point where simple reverence and the use of the image to render conception more vivid, and feeling more intense, change into definite idolatry by the attribution of Power to the image itself, is so difficultly determinable that we cannot be too cautious in asserting that such a change has actually taken place in the case of the individual. (*CW* 10, 451)

This is wisely observed, and let us see what follows from all this. There is, say, a spectrum. At one extreme there is a form of worship or devotion which makes no distinction between the image and that Power (or conception) which it is supposed to image *forth* or be an image *of*, but sees them as one and the same thing. Somewhere around the middle there is a reverence (say) which can keep the two things separate and appreciate the intensifying power of the image without mistaking it for what it images. At the other extreme there is an admiration which is no longer interested in what is imaged – 'the subject' – but is wholly concentrated on the art which went into the making of the image. By this scheme, Ruskin is a man of reverence who was constantly drawn to worship and admiration. What this did for his orthodox Christianity we know, but one can see that what is more generally at risk is not orthodoxy but referentiality. By the same token the distinction between worship and admiration seems insecure. 'Admiration' sounds cool and connoisseur-ish; 'worship' or 'devotion' sounds both more passionate and more mindless. Yet what they have in common is that they both see nothing beyond the given artefact; and to the extent that they respond to it at all, both worshipper and admirer are responding to a Power which is immanent in the artefact itself and not in anything to which it may seemingly refer or which it might be thought to represent. When Ruskin describes a painting by Turner or Tintoretto, or the front of St Mark's, or the image of a lost Venice which he, and he alone, can evoke, it becomes impossible to tell the admiration from the devotion: reverence is drowned in worship. And then the art *is* – ultimately – for the sake of the art. When Ruskin wrote of the 'many Protestants who idolise nothing but their own opinions or their own interests' (*CW* 10, 452), he must have had, or certainly should have had, himself in mind, but what he serves to expose is something more encompassing: that there is something idolatrous (some would now say fetishistic) in *all* our relationships and traffic with images and representations. It would be too glib to say that Ruskin went to Venice for the 'subject' (the religious moral rise and fall of a great republic) and stayed for the art – since he would doubtlessly have said he was doing justice to both, and that anyway the one was inextricably bound up with the other. But the danger is that the latter will subsume the former or replace it. In later years Ruskin complained that, although *The Stones of Venice* was his most influential work on contemporary art, all the 'medicine' – by which he presumably meant the moral and religious lessons and warnings he is constantly pointing – was simply thrown out of the window. His readers may or may not have come for the matter, but certainly most of them stayed mainly for the art. As Ruskin himself said, great works 'instantly divert the mind from their subject to their art'. It might be argued that he was referring to paintings and, what is certainly true, that written works are inescapably semantic in a way that painted ones are not. Nevertheless it does seem to me that, in writing about Venice, Ruskin is constantly addressing a subject, in a work whose Power as constantly 'diverts' us to its art. Right against the grain of his avowed intentions, Ruskin is implicitly engendering, and at times enacting, an aesthetic of art for art's sake. To say that we 'admire' the art that goes into his artefactual 'Venice' is, for me, a considerable understatement, though quite what we do with the pleasure we derive from it I am not sure. It no longer has a taste of the medicinal, and even his apocalypses are glorious. Indeed, they particularly.

After a survey of Byzantine palaces – 'all are either ruins, or fragments disguised by restoration' – Ruskin draws together his general evocation of that 'ancient city of Venice, altogether different in aspect from that which now exists' (*CW* 10, 143). It is his work of imaginative reconstruction.

> Such, then, was that first and fairest Venice which rose out of the barrenness of the lagoon, and the sorrow of her people; a city of graceful arcades and gleaming walls, veined with azure and warm with gold, and fretted with white sculpture like frost upon forest branches turned to marble. And yet, in this beauty of her youth, she was no city of thoughtless pleasure. There was still a sadness of heart upon her, and a depth of devotion, in which lay all her strength. (*CW* 10, 171)

There is an unresistant pure and pensive placidity about this picture of the first, lost Venice which is distinctly Pre-Raphaelite. Apart from the places where the writing starts to fret itself into ravished excitement, and where the very naming of the precious stones and rare metals and coloured materials makes the prose start to pulsate – as it invariably does, this Venice seems curiously quiet, and still, and solemn. 'She became in after times the revel of the earth, the masque of Italy; and *therefore* is she now desolate: but her glorious robe of gold and purple was given her when first she rose a vestal from the sea, not when she became drunk with the wine of fornication' (*CW* 10, 177).

This vanished Venice is conceived of as still having a unique 'power': 'And it is true that the power with which this Venice had been entrusted was perverted, when at its highest, in a thousand miserable ways: still, it was possessed by her alone; to her all hearts have turned which could be moved by its manifestation, and none without being made stronger and nobler by what her hand had wrought' (*CW* 10, 178). Thus invoked, it still has an inspirational potency, in terms of both 'Landscape' and 'Mythology':

> measure the compass of that field of creation, weigh the value of the inheritance that Venice thus left to the nations of Europe, and then judge if so vast, so beneficent a power could indeed have been rooted in dissipation or decay. It was when she wore the ephod of the priest,

> not the motley of the masquer, that the fire fell upon her from heaven; and she saw the first rays of it through the rain of her own tears, when, as the barbaric deluge ebbed from the hills of Italy, the circuit of her palaces, and the orb of her fortunes, rose together, like the Iris, painted upon the Cloud. (*CW* 10, 179)

But his main 'quarry', and the climax of his 'story', is the DUCAL PALACE, writ large to indicate its pre-eminence, since it is 'the building which at once consummates and embodies the entire system of the Gothic architecture in Venice' (*CW* 10, 327). Before embarking on his account of that edifice Ruskin feels it necessary, as usual, to go back – back to first principles and basics, and establish 'The Nature of Gothic'. He is in pursuit of '*Gothicness*'. It is a justly famous chapter, and the sustained passage in which he imagines what a bird sees as it flies over the changing landscape from south to north is one of his most impressive imaginative *tours de force*. From this passage one would sense that his sympathies were drawn northward. The south is seen as serene (later as 'languid', even 'listless') – 'a great peacefulness of light, Syria and Greece, Italy and Spain, laid like pieces of a golden pavement into the sea-blue'. But Ruskin's prose is more energized – galvanized – as the landscape gets rougher: 'and then, farther north still to see the earth heave into mighty masses of leaden rock and heathy moor, bordering with a broad waste of gloomy purple that belt of field and wood, and splintering into irregular and grisly islands midst the northern seas, beaten by storm, and chilled by ice-drift, and tormented by furious pulse of contending tide' (*CW* 10, 186–7). Ruskin's prose heaves and splinters with the land. Similarly when he imagines the generic or ur-craftsman in each sphere:

> Let us watch him with reverence as he sets side by side the burning gems, and smooths with soft sculpture the jasper pillars, that are to reflect a ceaseless sunshine, and rise into a cloudless sky: but not with less reverence let us stand by him, when, with rough strength and hurried stroke, he smites an uncouth animation out of the rocks which he has torn from among the moss of the moorland, and heaves into the darkened air the pile of iron buttress and rugged wall, instinct with a work of an imagination as wild and wayward as the northern sea; creations of ungainly shape and rigid limb, but full of wolfish life; fierce as the winds that beat, and changeful as the clouds that shade them. (*CW* 10, 187–8)

Not with less reverence indeed, and, it would seem, with a good deal more excitement, and attracting more of Ruskin's prose by a factor of three to one.

Ruskin's moralized or aestheticized geography is all his own, and we should not be concerned with cartographic accuracy or consistency. Venice as the midway, intersecting or meeting point of all directions, tendencies, forces, energies, styles must be the place where the Gothic touches and pauses on a moment of perfection. But one can feel Ruskin's imagination pulling northward. Here is one of his most striking formulations of the nature of Gothic, which he rather oddly calls 'the *only rational* architecture': 'it can shrink into a turret, expand into a hall, coil into a staircase, or spring into a spire, with undegraded grace and unexhausted energy' (*CW* 10, 212). This is what draws him, and his own expanding, coiling, springing writing; and rationality is, really, little to the point. His prose does not much like to 'bask in dreamy benignity of sunshine' (the south) but tends more to 'wilderness of thought, and roughness of work' (the north) (*CW* 10, 188). Two of the features of Gothic which seem most important for him are excess and unfinishedness, unfinishableness. His list of the six 'moral elements' of Gothic commences with 'Savageness' and concludes with 'Redundance', which he will amplify as 'the uncalculating bestowal of the wealth of its labour'. One can everywhere detect Ruskin's impatience and dissatisfaction with any art, or work, which seems to aim for and be content with 'finish', closure, perfection – 'to banish imperfection is to destroy expression, to check exertion, to paralyse vitality'. He likes the 'perpetual change both in design and execution' that he finds in Gothic work ('the workman must have been altogether set free'); he esteems 'the infringement of every servile principle'; he cherishes forms which were '*capable of perpetual novelty*' and celebrates the proportions of the pointed arch because they are 'changeable to infinity'. You can feel his prose warming to Gothic ornament which 'stands out in prickly independence, and frosty fortitude, jutting into crockets and freezing into pinnacles; here starting up into a monster, there germinating into a blossom, anon knitting itself into a branch, alternately thorny, bossy, and bristly, or writhed into every form of nervous entanglement' (*CW* 10, 203–4, 208, 240). Whatever else it is describing, this is writing that is describing itself. For clearly this is where Ruskin is at home, is indeed making his home:

> It is that strange *disquietude* of the Gothic spirit that is its greatness; that restlessness of the dreaming mind, that wanders hither and thither among the niches, and flickers feverishly around the pinnacles, and frets and fades in labyrinthine knots and shadows along wall and roof, and yet is not satisfied, nor shall be satisfied. The Greek could stay in his triglyph furrow, and be at peace; but the work of the Gothic art is fretwork still, and it can neither rest in, nor from, its labour, but must pass on, sleeplessly, until its love of change shall be pacified for ever in the change that must come alike on them that wake and them that sleep. (*CW* 10, 214)

At such moments Ruskin lays the heart of his own writing bare. The nature of Gothic turns out to be, whatever else, the nature of Ruskin. One begins to wonder how he will get back to Venice.

And he never does seem to get back in quite the same way in what follows. He now moves towards the planned climax and central point of the work, the Ducal Palace – because it 'stands comparatively alone, and fully expresses the Gothic power'; because 'the majesty of this single building was able to give pause to the Gothic imagination in its full career; stayed the restlessness of innovation in an instant, and forbade the powers which had created it thenceforth to exert themselves in new directions, or endeavours to summon an image more attractive.' The consummation was also the conclusion; the miraculous 'pause' becomes a terminal arrest. Here again we see Ruskin plucking the building out of the gradualisms of historical time. It was 'the great and sudden invention of one man . . . there is literally *no* transitional form between them [earlier palaces] and the perfection of the Ducal Palace.' 'The Ducal Palace is the Parthenon of Venice, and Gradenigo its Pericles'. It was this sudden appearance of perfection (which, in Ruskin's terms, at the same time acted as a blockage of all possible further development) that dominated the whole work: 'it was the determination of this one fact which occupied the greater part of the time I spent in Venice' (*CW* 10, 312). Yet in his descriptions of the Ducal Palace there is none of the exfoliating ecstasy with which he evokes the front of St Mark's, none of the savagery and redundancy, the disquietude and unsatisfiability which he found at the heart of 'Gothicness'. The Gothic seems to become something simpler, more peaceful, and associated with, of all things, 'domesticity'. Ruskin admits he has not been able to do the research into the daily domestic life of the Venetians he had hoped to do, so he contents himself with 'merely noting this assured fact, that *the root of all that is greatest in Christian art is struck in the thirteenth century*; that the temper of that century is the life-blood of all manly work thenceforward in Europe; and I suppose that one of its peculiar characteristics was . . . a singular simplicity in domestic life' (*CW* 10, 306–7). I think that this shift of tone in Ruskin's characterization of the Gothic is deliberate and, as it were, political. He has clearly become convinced that a Gothic revival is not only possible but desirable, even indispensable, with no lingering anxiety about self-conscious archaicism or 'enfantillage'. As he notes and describes the general form, and then the windows, doors, balconies and parapets of the main Gothic palaces of Venice, it becomes clear that Ruskin has in mind their possible suitability and relevance for contemporary England.

> And they are especially to be noted for us at this day, because these refined and richly ornamented forms were used in the habitations of a nation as laborious, as practical, as brave and as prudent as

> ourselves. . . . And, farther, they are interesting because perfectly applicable to modern habitation. The refinement of domestic life appears to have been far advanced in Venice from her earliest days, and the remains of her Gothic palaces are, at this day, the most delightful residences in the City. . . . the traveller may ascertain, by actual experience, the effect which would be produced upon the comfort or luxury of daily life by the revival of the Gothic school of architecture. He can still stand upon the marble balcony in the soft summer air, and feel its smooth surface warm from the noontide as he leans on it in the twilight; he can still see the strong sweep of the unruined traceries drawn on the deep serenity of the starry sky, and watch the fantastic shadows of the clustered arches shorten in the moonlight on the chequered floor; or he may close the casements fitted to their unshaken shafts against such wintry winds as would have made an English house vibrate to its foundations, and, in either case, compare their influence on his daily home feeling with that of the square openings in his English wall. (*CW* 10, 312)

This is not a lost Venice, irretrievable and 'other' for the modern world, but a Venice which may yet serve as a model for English architecture and thus, of course, English life. For here again there are indissociable factors involved. Gothic building is not only more beautiful, it is 'more to be trusted'. It is the sheer untrustworthiness of modern building which is a sign for Ruskin that there is something rotten in the state.

> There is hardly a week passes without some catastrophe brought about by the base principles of modern building: some vaultless floor that drops the staggering crowd through the jagged rents of its rotten timbers; some baseless bridge that is washed away by the first wave of a summer flood; some fungous wall of nascent rottenness that a thunder-shower soaks down with its workmen into a heap of slime and death. (*CW* 10, 313)

This is why, says Ruskin, 'I plead for the introduction of the Gothic form into our domestic architecture, not merely because it is lovely, but because it is the only form of faithful, strong, enduring, and honourable building' (*CW* 10, 312). It is perhaps partly for that reason that Ruskin approaches the Ducal Palace – 'which at once consummates and embodies the entire system of the Gothic architecture in Venice' – in a cooler and as it were more professional manner: 'it remains for us, therefore, at present, only to review the history, fix the date, and note the most important particulars in the structure of the building' (*CW* 10, 327). St Mark's was simply a marvel: the Ducal Palace might yet serve as a model.

The history – of course – falls into three phases. There is the Byzantine palace, the Gothic palace, the Renaissance palace. By his own idiosyncratic computations, Ruskin dates the Gothic palace from 1301 to 1423. He has, of course, his reasons. 'Three generations at least had been accustomed to witness the gradual advancement of the form of the Ducal Palace into more stately symmetry, and to contrast the works of sculpture and painting with which it was decorated, – full of the life, knowledge, and hope of the fourteenth century, – with the rude Byzantine chiselling of the palace of the Doge Ziani' (*CW* 10, 347). He had already committed himself to the terminating date of 1423 – the death of Mocenigo – and he here connects it with the decision taken to rebuild the palace which started to be put into action in 1424 when 'the first hammer was lifted up against the old palace of Ziani'.

> The hammer stroke was the first act of the period properly called the 'renaissance'. It was the knell of the architecture of Venice – and of Venice herself. The central epoch of her life was past; the decay had already begun. . . . A thousand palaces might be built upon her hundred islands, but none of them could take the place, or recall the memory, of that which was the first built upon her unfrequented shore. It fell; and, as if it had been the talisman of her fortunes, the city never flourished again. (*CW* 10, 352)

The Renaissance decided to erase or destroy the traces of its Byzantine foundations – thus, for Ruskin, it wilfully disoriginated itself, ensuring its decline and fall. This has little or nothing to do with history, and everything to do with Ruskin's horror of loss, obliteration, and all forms of perverse self-deracination. The feeling is closer to that Shakespearean moment when Albany says to Goneril:

> That nature which contemns its origin
> Cannot be bordered certain in itself,
> She that will sliver and disbranch
> From her material sap, perforce must wither
> And come to deadly use.
> (*King Lear*, IV. ii. 32–6)

Venice has contemned its origin and must *perforce* wither and come to deadly use.

Aside from these general characterizations of types of architecture, there is not a great deal about the actual building. Ruskin spends most of his time examining the thirty-six pillars of the Ducal Palace. At the conclusion of his chapter on 'The Nature of Gothic' Ruskin's last piece of advice was: '*Read* the scuplture. Preparatory to reading it, you will have to discover whether it is legible (and, if legible, it is almost certain to be worth reading).... Thence forward the criticism of the building is to be conducted precisely on the same principles as that of a book' (*CW* 10, 269). Ruskin certainly spends most of his time 'reading' the sculptures on the pillars, quoting Dante freely and Spenser copiously as if to show that there is no difference between the textuality of the Gothic stone and that of the Gothic script. This tends to take him away from Venice into a generalized realm of medieval Vices and Virtues – though there is one moment when he addresses 'the much disputed question of the character of the later government of Venice' which legend and romantic fictions (such as Fenimore Cooper's *The Bravo*, which Ruskin read and greatly disliked) represented as a compound of secrecy, treachery, hypocrisy and cruelty. Ruskin spiritedly – and plausibly – attacks these fictions, and affirms his belief (mainly from studying the portraits) that 'these Venetian nobles of the fifteenth century did, in the main, desire to do judgment and justice to all men'. For Ruskin it is clear that 'the final degradation of the Venetian power appears owing not so much to the principles of its government, as to their being forgotten in the pursuit of pleasure' (*CW* 10, 428). On the basis of his plays (to say nothing of his pleasures), one has to speculate that Byron would have disagreed.

If he drifts away from the palace proper into the world of medieval allegory, however, he returns sharply enough at the end of the chapter to the contemporary state of dilapidation and neglect of the building and its treasure, 'which at this moment, as I write, is piece by piece being destroyed for ever.' This applies particularly to the paintings – which Ruskin had announced would not be considered in this chapter. But they cannot be wholly kept out, as Ruskin animadverts on their contemporary plight, not only in the palace but throughout Venice.

> They are . . . almost universally neglected, whitewashed by custodes, shot at by soldiers, suffered to drop from the walls piecemeal in powder and rags by society in general; but, which is an advantage, more than counterbalancing all this evil, they are not often 'restored'. Whatever is left of them, however ruinous, however obscured and defiled, is almost always *the real thing*; there are no fresh readings: and therefore the greatest treasures of art which Europe at this moment possesses are pieces of old plaster on ruinous brick walls, where the lizards burrow and bask, and which few other living creatures ever approach: and torn sheets of dim canvas in waste corners of churches; and mildewed stains, in the shape of human figures on the wall of dark chambers, which now and then an exploring traveller causes to be unlocked by their tottering custode, looks hastily round, and retreats from in a weary satisfaction at his accomplished duty. (*CW* 10, 436–7)

'Venice'. And Venice now. Ruskin works by strong contrasts and not subtle gradations. Some form of contemporary desolation is always implicitly or explicitly in the foreground of his work – rather as he always discerned some litter or rubbish in the foreground of Turner's. In 1851–3 Ruskin was working and writing from some very actual litter of a Venice everywhere seemingly returning to its constituent stones. To the extent that this process was arrested and reversed, much of the credit must go to Ruskin himself, his reconstitutive imaginative genius, and his incomparable eye for '*the real thing*'.

It is the painters – particularly Tintoretto and Veronese – that he has pre-eminently in mind at the end of the volume, when he draws away from the Ducal Palace and meditates on it from a distance, thinking on how their paintings had made the walls of the palace 'as precious as so many kingdoms':

> so precious, indeed, and so full of majesty, that sometimes when walking at evening on the Lido, whence the great chain of the Alps, crested with silver clouds, might be seen rising in front of the Ducal Palace, I used to feel as much awe in gazing on the buildings as on the hills, and could believe that God had done a greater work in breathing into the narrowness of dust the mighty spirits by whom its haughty walls had been raised, and its burning legends written, than in lifting the rocks of granite higher than the clouds of heaven, and veiling them with their various mantle of purple flower and shadowy pine. (*CW* 10, 438–9)

Here the Ducal Palace – the central building of the central city – becomes *the* supreme work of art; culture's answer to nature indeed, and – given Ruskin's feeling for the godliness of mountains – it is an almost unprecedented concession; perhaps something more.

The Fall, the title of volume III, points unambiguously to a decline and disintegration which is at once and inseparably moral and material, the deterioration, in Ruskin's eyes, as usual telling all. He starts by conjuring up once more a memory of Venice and how it might have looked at its period of 'greatest energy and prosperity' – 'its street inwrought with rich sculpture, and even . . . glowing with colour and gold'. He then asks the reader, 'keeping this gorgeous image before him', to go out into a street in contemporary London and simply ask himself what – given the great discrepancy between the 'gorgeous image' and modern spectacle – can have 'induced so vast a change in the European mind' (*CW* 11, 4). As we know, Ruskin will not be attempting any kind of plausible historical explanation. The perfection achieved in phase two *inevitably* ushers in phase three, which must, as inevitably, chart irreversible degeneration and declension all the way to a repeatedly and vigorously imagined end (with an enclave of exceptionality allowed for the great painters – Tintoretto, Veronese, Titian – who rather vexingly happen to work during phase three). The Fall in turn breaks down into three stages, with Ruskin trying to do something of the same sort of thing for the nature of Renaissance as he had done for the nature of Gothic, but seeming to be far less sure of his direction and less in command of his material. He suffers from not having two superb edifices on which to focus and round which to build his own work. He is looking at and writing about works which he increasingly dislikes, until we find him refusing to 'pollute' his pages with illustrations of the artefacts he is referring to. Ruskin can write as powerfully out of distress as he can out of admiration, but balance is threatened and the prose shows a tendency to distract itself away from the matter in hand. Trying to compress and comprehend the Fall of Venice into a coherent and sustained volume, Ruskin digresses strangely, though, being Ruskin, invariably into something rich and rare. Yet, by allowing the idea of the 'Fall of Venice' to be the (suitably littered) site for his meditations on what had happened to the European mind during the last four hundred years or so, Ruskin found himself having thoughts and ideas which, presumably, he could or would not have arrived at in any other way.

His explanations for the beginning of the rot in the 'Early Renaissance' are by now predictable – over-luxuriance, over-refinement, jaded faculties, intemperance in moral habits, satiety, search for morbid excitement, voluptuousness, feebleness and want of soul (as evidenced in architecture) and ornament, which one might be tempted to say exist more in the eye of the beholder, though with so formidable a beholder as Ruskin one instinctively treads with care. He is on surer ground when he points to the importance of the 'sudden enthusiasm for classical literature', though he does not enlarge on the results of this enthusiasm until the next chapter, for which, one feels, he is rather keeping his powder dry. But he does pause to point out that 'at this point of our inquiry . . . we must bid farewell to colour . . . as '*The Renaissance frosts came.*' Ruskin responded *passionately* to colour, particularly the colours he finds in medieval chivalric costume and heraldic devices, and in Gothic illustrations and miniatures. Describing these colours, Ruskin isolates one particular attribute which he says he never found before or after (basically 1250–1350) – 'namely, the union of one colour with another by reciprocal interference' (*CW* 11, 22–3). He explains by saying that 'if a mass of red is to be set beside a mass of blue, a piece of red will be carried into the blue and a piece of blue carried into the red.' I am not sure whether he means that adjacent colours 'carry over' into each other by a little apparent bleeding into each other, or more mosaically as in a shield, when (his own example) a colour in the top right quarter will reappear in the bottom left. What is remarkable is the importance he derives from this perceived principle of 'reciprocal interference'.

> And I call it a magnificent principle, for it is an eternal and universal one, not in art only, but in human life. It is the great principle of Brotherhood, not by quality, nor by likeness, but by giving and receiving; the souls that are unlike, and the nations that are unlike, and the natures that are unlike, being bound into one noble whole by each receiving something from and of the others' gifts and the others' glory. I have not space to follow out this thought – it is of infinite extent and application . . . in whatever has been made by the Deity externally delightful to the human sense of beauty, there is some type of God's nature or of God's law; nor are any of His laws, in one sense, greater than the appointment that the most lovely and perfect unity shall be obtained by the taking of one nature into another, I trespass upon too high ground. (*CW* 11, 24)

He mentions souls and nations and natures 'giving and receiving' – but not bodies; yet his 'magnificient' and 'universal' principle of 'reciprocal interference', which involves 'the taking of one nature into another', surely applies even more certainly to sexual intercourse than the possible (feudal) Brotherhood of Man. He may have been trespassing not upon 'too high ground' but upon too dangerous ground. In outlining, with evident excitement ('no space to follow . . . of infinite extent and application'), a politics and a metaphysics of colour, Ruskin, I suggest, has in fact most powerfully described an *erotics* of colour. Venice, as he conceived it, was for him the *supreme* city of colour, and aroused in him extremes of ecstasy and revulsion which seem at times to be, indeed, little short of sexual.

Before finally leaving Gothic Venice for his full attack on the Renaissance, Ruskin says 'let us take with us one more lesson, the last which we shall receive from the Stones of Venice, except in the form of warning' (*CW* 11, 35). The note is ominous – *only* warnings ahead! And the lesson at first seems a relatively slight one. These Venetians knew how to use inlaid marble as a means of colour. That art has been lost until in modern times we find modes of decoration which actually use painted imitations of marble (or wood). A regrettable descent into spuriousness, no doubt, but see what Ruskin makes of it. Among other things, it gives some sense of his quite extraordinary feeling for the given materialities of the natural world. Of course, he goes right back to the beginning. 'Consider, then, first,' – the three commas marking steps back to the essential – 'what marble seems to have been made for.' A paragraph follows of lyrical geology which wonderfully conveys the unique marbleness of marble: 'This rock, then, is prepared by Nature for the sculptor and architect, just as paper is prepared by the manufacturer for the artist' (*CW* 11, 26–7). Providentialism again, and this is all very satisfactory on the part of God and Nature. And since Nature has taken 'so much care to provide for us . . . this precious paper' we should 'take Nature at her word' and 'use it as Nature would have us'. Nature *has* a word – the artist's job is to let her speak it. And it is not just that the colours in marble offer a 'prepared palette':

> There is history in them. By the manner in which they are arranged in every piece of marble, they record the means by which that marble has been produced and the successive changes through which it has passed. And in all their veins and zones, and flame-like stainings, or broken and disconnected lines, they write various legends, never untrue, of the former political state of the mountain kingdom to which they belonged, of its infirmities and fortitudes, convulsions and consolidations, from the beginning of time.
>
> Now, if we were never in the habit of seeing anything but real marbles this language of theirs would soon begin to be understood; that is to say, even the least observant of us would recognise such and such stones as forming a peculiar class, and would begin to inquire where they came from, and, at last, take some feeble interest in the main question, Why they were only to be found in that or the other place, and how they came to make a part of this mountain, and not of that? And in a little while, it would not be possible to stand for a moment at a shop door, leaning against the pillars of it, without remembering or questioning of something well worth the memory or the inquiry, touching the hills of Italy, or Greece, or Africa, or Spain; and we should be led on from knowledge to knowledge, until even the unsculptored walls of our streets became to us volumes as precious as those of our libraries.
>
> But the moment we admit imitation of marble, this source of knowledge is destroyed. None of us can be at the pains to go through the work of verification. If we knew that every coloured stone we saw was natural, certain questions, conclusions, interests, would force themselves upon us without any effort of our own; but we have none of us time to stop in the midst of our daily business, to touch, and pore over, and decide with painful minuteness of investigation, whether such and such a pillar be stucco or stone. And the whole field of this knowledge, which Nature intended us to possess when we were children, is hopelessly shut out from us. Worse than shut out, for the mass of coarse imitations confuses our knowledge acquired from other sources; and our memory of the marbles we have perhaps once or twice carefully examined, is disturbed or distorted by the inaccuracy of the imitations which are brought before us continually. (*CW* 11, 37–9)

Ruskin here offers a vision of a totally legible world which would be totally transparent as to its origins and ontology. The condition for the existence of this world is absolute authenticity of materials by which everything is what it seems to be. In such a world you could, while leaning against the pillar of a shop door, 'be led on from knowledge to knowledge' until you would be reading the political history of mountains, the cultural history of the world. It is a paradisal vision of effortless access to total knowledge. But there was a Fall: a fall into imitation. And suddenly we are 'shut out' from that immediately knowable world and left to grope confusedly around with never enough time for sufficient verifications. The very condition for 'imitation' is that some material or substance is made to look like something else, and, taken to an extreme, Ruskin's ideal world would be one without any re-presentations. But clearly he is more concerned with the increase of the ersatz, the encroachment of the pseudo, the proliferation of the fake. It is as if he had a prophetic glimpse of a possible future world entirely domiciled in inauthenticity, contentedly cocooned in the substitute, the replica, the simulacrum – to its own ultimate and utter confusion. Jean Baudrillard purports to detect intimations or even actualization of just such a world in contemporary America. We can discount his Gallic generalizations without dimissing Ruskin's Victorian dread or desire. It is not as if he is against synthesized materials (at least not always). If he could accept paper, he could have accepted plastic. Rather, he wants materials to be allowed, enabled, to tell the truth, their truth. Such a crusade against substitutability and fungibility is one that, like most of his other crusades, he could only lose. But his resistance to material duplicity and his vision of an undeceiving world are curiously telling, and it is just such a world that he has sought to conjure up in his version, his 'gorgeous image', of Venice – before, that is, the Fall.

As he moves into his attack on the 'Roman Renaissance' in Venice, he asserts that one of the main mistakes of the Renaissance schools 'lay in supposing that science and art were the same things'. This immediately leads him into an articulation of the basic difference between their ways of dealing with the world, between the motivations of their gaze. It is remarkable to what extent Ruskin stresses the necessary passivity, even the blankness, of the artist: 'the artist is bound to receive all things on the broad, white, lucid field of his soul, not to grasp at one.' 'And all the breadth to which he can expand himself, and all the white emptiness into which he can blench himself, will not be enough to receive what God has to give him.' This notion of the artist 'blenching' himself into a 'white field' or rather a 'white emptiness' – becoming a sort of entirely sensitized invisible paper – is far more extreme than, for example, T. S. Eliot's highly personal theories of the 'Impersonality' of art, in the intensity of its imagined self-effacement. The existentialist corollary for this is that the artist 'should be fit for the best society, *and should keep out of it*', to which is added the poignant footnote that 'Of course a painter of men must be *among* men; but it ought to be

1 J. M. W. Turner, 'Looking East from the Giudecca'. This and the following plate were painted in 1819 and thus offer us images of Byron's Venice at the time he completed 'Childe Harold' canto iv. See p. 37. (Tate Gallery, London)

2 J. M. W. Turner, 'Campanile of St Mark's'. (Tate Gallery, London)

3 J. M. W. Turner, 'Juliet and her Nurse'. See p. 70. (Private Collection)

4 J. M. W. Turner, 'Campo Santo, Venice', 1842. This is almost certainly the painting Ruskin had in mind in the long description quoted on p. 74. (The Toledo Museum of Art; purchased with funds from the Libbey Endowment, Gift of Edward Drummond Libbey)

5 John Ruskin, 'Riva degli Schiavoni, the Ducal Palace and the Tower of St Mark's', 1870 – 'really the best colour study I made in Venice' – John Ruskin. (© Fitzwilliam Museum, Cambridge)

6 John Ruskin, 'Palazzo Dario'. Brantwood 1590. This illustrates Ruskin's intensely appreciative sense of the beauty of architectural surface decoration in Venice. (The Brantwood Trust, Coniston)

7 John Ruskin, 'Stilted Archivolts, from a Ruin in the Rio di Ca'Foscari'. 'It was a beautifully picturesque fragment; the archivolt sculptures being executed in marble, which seemed, in some parts, rather to have gained than lost in whiteness by its age, and set off by the dark and delicate leaves of the Erba della Madonna, the only pure piece of modern addition to the old design, all else being foul plaster and withering wood.' (*Examples of the Architecture of Venice* Works 11.336). (The Ruskin Galleries, Bembridge School. Photo: Frank Taylor)

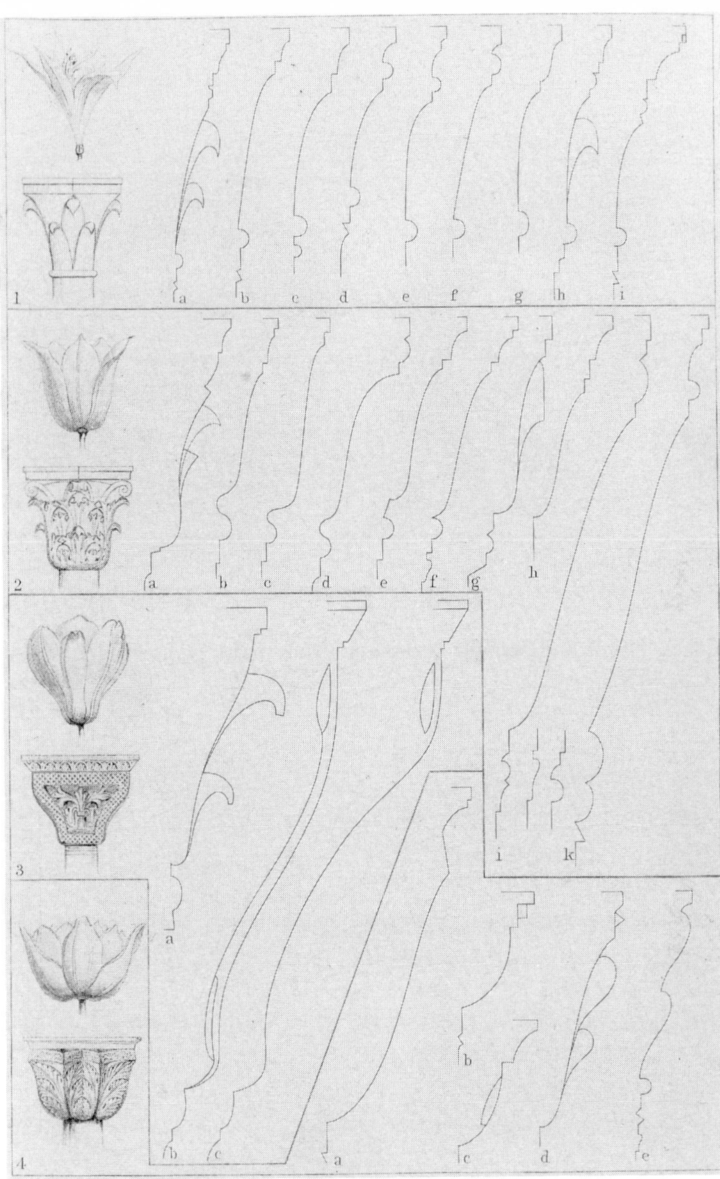

8 John Ruskin, 'The Four Venetian Flower Orders' from *Stones of Venice II*, plate 31. 'Upon these profoundly studied outlines, as remarkable for their grace and complexity as the general mass of the capital is for solid strength and proportion to its necessary service, the braided work is wrought with more than usual care . . . ' – an example of the minute care and attention with which Ruskin anatomised 'the stones'.

9 John Ruskin, 'Noble and Ignoble Grotesque' from *Stones of Venice III*, plate 44. See p. 118.

10 John Ruskin, 'Venga Medusa' from *Modern Painters V*, plate LXXI. See note on p. 119.

11 'Solomon and the Queen of Sheba'. This was the painting which Ruskin said effected, or completed, his conversion from orthodox Protestantism (see p. 128). At that time it was attributed to Veronese but I gather this attribution is no longer regarded as certain. (Author)

12 Giorgione, 'Standing Nude: Fragment of a Fresco'. *Giorgione* by Pignatti, Phaidon 1971, plate 56. See p. 129. (The Bodleian Library, Oxford)

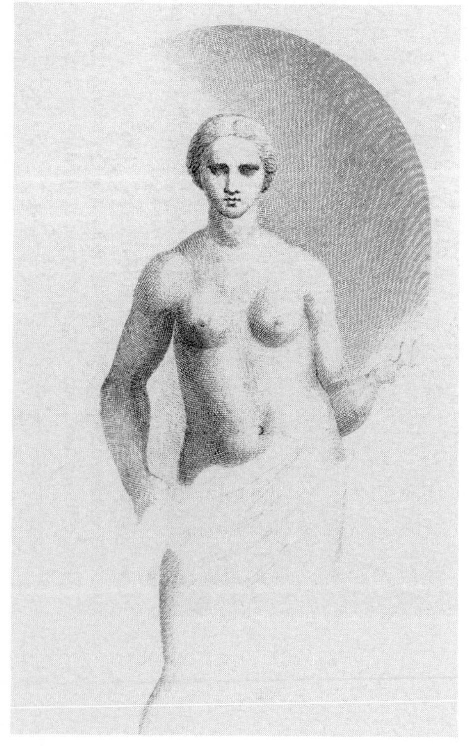

13 John Ruskin, 'Hesperid Ægle' from *Modern Painters V*, plate LXXIX. See p. 129.

as a watcher, not as a companion' (*CW* 11, 47, 51–3) – poignant when you recall Ruskin's own situation at the time in Venice, when Effie was having a high social life, particularly with the Austrians, and as a companion not as a watcher, while Ruskin himself was trying to disappear under darkened porticos and up distant canals. The idea of the artist as spectator grew throughout the century – Henry James is a particularly felicitous incarnation. And there was no greater 'spectator' in the nineteenth century – in his chosen fields – than Ruskin. The fact, as it seems, that the greatest eye of the century belonged to a man who was, if not impotent, then sexually dormant and inactive has not only a poignancy but even perhaps a parabolic aptness. The possibility that impotence, conceived in one way or another, might be a *condition* of art, or the *cost* of it, keeps recurring in art itself, and the writing and thinking about art, throughout the later nineteenth century and all through modernism – arguably, beyond.

Ruskin has another way of conceiving of the artist or rather what art *does* – as opposed to how the artist receives.

> But what we want art to do for us is to stay what is fleeting, and to enlighten what is incomprehensible, to incorporate the things that have no measure, and immortalize the things that have no duration. The dimly seen, momentary glance, the flitting shadow of faint emotion, the imperfect lines of fading thought, and all that by and through such things as these is recorded on the features of man, and all that in man's person and actions and in the great natural world, is infinite and wonderful . . . (*CW* 11, 62)

I will leave Ruskin here where, as so often, he himself seems to be becoming 'infinite'. But an aesthetic which concentrates on the momentary; the dim and the faint; the fleeting, the flitting, the fading – an aesthetic which sees the main purpose of art as to 'stay' things, continually vanishing things, and, we might add, to act *as* a stay among things, imminently confusing things – this is an aesthetic which I think is central to, if not constitutive of, whatever we like to think of as modernism: it is Conrad's aesthetic as much as it is Proust's. And I would be surprised if you could find it so formulated before Ruskin. With his eye fixed firmly on art of the past (with the exception of Turner), Ruskin deploys a vocabulary which will in fact be more, or even more, suitable and fitting for the aspirations – and consolations – of much art that was yet to come. When he goes on to write that men (and we must suppose women) are 'not dead walls encompassing dead heaps of things known and numbered, but running waters in the sweet wilderness of things unnumbered and unknown' (*CW* 11, 66), we are no distance at all from the last volume of *A la recherche du temps perdu*, or the last section of *Ulysses*, or any of those other works which conceive of people more as rivers than walls – little enough, it has to be admitted, that Ruskin would have liked them.

Ruskin has moved some way away from his initial attack on what he saw as the Renaissance schools' misplaced and erroneous pride in their scientific 'knowledge', but he brings himself back to his subject by moving on to 'PRIDE OF STATE', and here he reveals the social nature, as it were, of his animus against the Renaissance. What he reads in every line of this architecture is 'an expression of aristocracy in its worst characters' just as his Gothic Venice everywhere gave evidence of aristocracy in its *best* characters (if it isn't the one, it has to be the other: nothing in between). This is what he reads: 'coldness, perfectness of training, incapability of emotion, want of sympathy with the weakness of lower men, blank, hopeless, haughty self-sufficiency. . . . It is rigid, cold, inhuman; incapable of glowing, of stooping, of conceding for an instant.' Self-incriminating sermons in stones indeed – Ruskin is a formidable reader. He is, I think, projecting here and, being Ruskin, attempting to fasten to a specific moment of time, his more general sense that the aristocracy of Europe had betrayed its trust and been guilty of some gross and almost certainly irreparable dereliction of duty. It has somehow – somewhen, somewhy – withdrawn from the warm, integrated communality and solidarity which Ruskin reads in Gothic, and abdicated its true paternalistic responsibilities. 'The dead Renaissance drew back . . . into its stateliness, out of all that was impulsive, reverent, and gay.' It was cold, cold, cold – except in one domain: 'But it understood the luxury of the body' (*CW* 11, 74–6). The scented gardens, trickling fountains, the shady grottoes, the warm rooms, the painted walls and roofs 'covered with the last lasciviousness of Paganism': all these Renaissance features, for Ruskin bespoke – one might say boasted, flaunted, perhaps taunted him with – a released and relished sexuality which causes him, his prose, manifest anguish and unease. Since 'Venetian piety' had 'once truly distinguished the city from all others' (*CW* 11, 114), when Venice falls its shameless sexuality must disgrace it beneath all others. As we shall see, it once again becomes a sea-Sodom. It is, one might say, the same old sea story – though never before or since so graphically and passionately told.

Since Ruskin is after the 'dead Renaissance' in all its deadness, it is doubtless deliberate, and certainly appropriate, that he should spend most of the chapter discussing tomb scuplture. This work, asserts Ruskin, in Venice presents 'more remarkable extremes . . . than in any other city'. But this is hardly surprising, since Ruskin has constituted his 'Venice' precisely *as* a city of extremes in which it would seem there *is* only the best and the worst. Just so, Gothic tombs are seen 'confessing the power, and accepting the peace, of death, openly and joyfully', while later tombs are 'a ghastly struggle of mean pride and miserable terror' (*CW* 11, 82–3). Ruskin duly takes us on a tour of tombs, tracing 'the pride of state in its gradual intrusion upon the sepulchre; and the consequent and correlative vanishing of the expression of religious feeling, and heavenly hope' (*CW* 11, 103) – we note that when Ruskin gets down among actual objects there are 'gradualisms' which have no place in his larger panorama. It is a convincing tour with a plausible thesis and a comprehensible drift. But Ruskin has, I think, a larger 'quarry' in view, and he won't find it among the tombs. Near the end of the chapter, he turns to consider the lasting adverse effects of the Reformation and the ensuing and ongoing struggle between Protestantism and Romanism. Yet more insidious than this was the growing interest in paganism which seemed to flourish in this dissentious soil. It starts with that 'enthusiasm for classical writers' mentioned earlier and now Ruskin elaborates on the effects of that 'renewal of the study of Pagan writers'. Oddly, and interestingly, he first asserts that it turned 'the attention of all men to words instead of things'. It did this because 'it was discovered that the language of the Middle Ages had been corrupt, and the primal object of every scholar became now to purify his style. . . . Of the debasing tendency of philology, no proof is needed beyond once reading a grammarian's notes on a great poet' (*CW* 11, 127). Ruskin is less imaginative about grammarians than Browning, though perhaps had a comparable sense of the 'funereality' of their work. But there was something far worse than men becoming word-locked:

> the systems of Pagan mythology began gradually to assume the places in the human mind from which the unwatched Christianity was wasting. Men did not indeed openly sacrifice to Jupiter, or build silver shrines for Diana, but the ideas of Paganism nevertheless became thoroughly vital and present with them at all times; and it did not matter in the least, as far as respected the power of true religion, whether the Pagan image was believed in or not, so long as it entirely occupied the thoughts. (*CW* 11, 129)

This was something infinitely more dangerous.

To the extent that the mind was occupied, and satisfied, with the image *as* image, and not as vehicle or reminder of some higher truth, there is a danger that the imagination will approach a state of terminal confusion – or indifference. It is worth following the steps in Ruskin's argument. 'It would have been better to have worshipped Diana at once, than to have gone on through the whole of life naming one God, imagining another, and dreading none. Better, a thousandfold, to have been "a Pagan suckled in some creed outworn", than to have stood by the great sea of Eternity, and seen no God walking on the waves, no heavenly world on its horizon.' This is the familiar Victorian position that any firmly held belief was better than none. Nothing was more dreadful than the loss of dread. But Ruskin sees the mischief spreading further and deeper. 'The imagination of the age was actively set to realise these objects of Pagan belief; and all the most exalted faculties of man, which, up to that period, had been employed in the service of Faith, were now transferred to the service of Fiction . . . the imagination which formerly had helped men to apprehend the truth, now tempted them to believe a falsehood' (*CW* 11, 129–30). It is as though he sees the whole allegiance and direction of European art switching to the production of fictions, the promotion of fictionality. And this in turn ushers in what he sees as the last 'evil' resulting from this prolonged dalliance with pagan images, which might be called the homogenization of value.

> Exactly in the proportion in which Jupiters and Mercuries were embodied and believed, in that proportion Virgins and Angels were disembodied and disbelieved. The *images summoned by art began gradually to assume one average value in the spectator's mind;* and incidents from the Illiad and from the Exodus to come within the same degree of credibility. And, farther, while the powers of the imagination were becoming daily more and more languid, because unsupported by faith, the manual skill and science of the artist were continually on the increase. When these had reached a certain point, they began to be the principal things considered in the picture, and its story or scene to be thought of only as a theme for their manifestation. Observe the difference. In old times, men used their powers of painting to show the objects of faith; in later times, they used the objects of faith that they might show their powers of painting. The distinction is enormous, the difference incalculable as irreconcilable. And thus, the more skilful the artist, the less his subject was regarded; and the hearts of men hardened as their handling softened, until they reached a point when sacred, profane, or sensual subjects were employed, with absolute indifference, for the display of colour and execution; and gradually the mind of Europe congealed into that state of utter apathy – inconceivable, unless it had been witnessed, and unpardonable, unless by us, who have been infected by it – which permits us to place the Madonna and the Aphrodite side by side in our galleries, and to pass, with the same unmoved inquiry into the manner of their handling, from a Bacchanal to a Nativity. (*CW* 11, 130–1; my italics)

By Ruskin's own account in the previous volume, great art 'leads the mind away from the religious subject to the art itself', and we have seen him moving very close to an aesthetic which would indeed value a work of art primarily, perhaps exclusively, for its felt power of 'colour and execution'. Clearly, when he looked at some of the possible implications of this in another light, he shied away from them. But I think what most disturbs him here is the possible confusion of the sacred and the profane, or rather, as he recognizes, the sacred and the sensual. What happens when, as you certainly can in the museum world of relocated and uncoordinated images, you pass from a Madonna to an Aphrodite? Suppose you prefer – enjoy – the latter more than the former. Suppose you like them equally well. Suppose you can't tell the difference. Suppose you don't care about the difference, or even feel that, in some obscure way, there *isn't* really any difference that matters. Ruskin has caught a glimpse of this slippery slope to apparent indifferentism and it clearly appals him. Once the iconic quarantining of the sacred and the sensual is imperilled, is lifted, by this 'averaging' of the value of the image; then art, unconstrained, may indeed as easily take its material from the *Iliad* or Exodus, or *The Golden Ass*, come to that. Then old hierarchies of value and certainties of significance and priorities of devotion are indeed threatened with dissolution, and a possibly rampant eclecticism may seem about to transform our cultural heritage – sacred and pagan – into a vast image-bazaar in which whoever pleases may shop around. The very possibility of such a state of degree-zero orientation would be a nightmare for Ruskin. But what I think touched him with a particularly troubling vertigo is a possible confusion of modern consciousness whereby you go to a Madonna and find an Aphrodite; you see Nativities and dream Bacchanals. Suppose you see the sacred turning uncontrollably into the sensual before – no, *in* – your very eyes; that would be perhaps the most unbearable loss of difference and collapse or convulsion of value of them all. And this is what Ruskin makes happen to Venice.

So pagan did Ruskin think Europe had become that he judged it to be, at heart, about 'as Pagan as it was in the second century', only rather worse since nominally proclaiming itself Christian. Curiously enough, he seems to think – at this moment of time – that things are going to get much better fairly soon, at least in England. Not, of course, ever, in Venice.

> I believe that in a few years we shall wake from all these errors in astonishment, as from evil dreams [the sort, perhaps, in which Madonnas turn into Aphrodites], having been preserved, in the midst of their madness, by those hidden roots of active and earnest Christianity which God's grace has bound in the English nation with iron and brass. But in the Venetian those roots themselves had withered; and, from the palace of their ancient religion, their pride cast them forth hopelessly to the pasture of the brute. From pride to infidelity to the unscrupulous and *insatiable pursuit of pleasure*, and from this to irremediable degradation, the transitions were swift, like the falling of a star. The great palaces of the haughtiest nobles of Venice were stayed, before they had risen from above their foundations, by the blast of a penal poverty; and the wild grass, on the unfinished frag-

> ments of their mighty shafts, waves at the tide-mark where the power of the godless people first heard the 'Hitherto shalt thou come.' And the regeneration in which they had so vainly trusted, – the new birth and clear dawning as they thought it, of all art, all knowledge, and all hope, – became to them as that dawn which Ezekiel saw on the hills of Israel; 'Behold the Day; behold it is come. The rod hath blossomed, pride hath budded, violence is risen up into a rod of wickedness. None of them remain, nor of their multitude; let not the buyer rejoice, nor the seller mourn, for wrath is upon all the multitude of there. (*CW* 11, 133–4; my italics)

Not for the first, nor for the last time, Ruskin buries Venice under the Bible, drawing on scriptural wrath and prophecy to inscribe at once its damnation and annihilation. Ruskin cannot sufficiently desecrate and deface the 'gorgeous image' of his own creation: he seems to be stamping on it and despoiling it in disgusted fury. The transition from gorgeousness to garbage is swift indeed. In matters such as these, transitions are always swift in Ruskin, indeed often non-existent. Matters, I mean, which bring him anywhere near to thoughts or fancies of the 'insatiable pursuit of pleasure'. Just as Ruskin had made Venice the supreme abode of piety, he imagines it as the most abandoned site of pleasure, the insatiable pursuit of pleasure, the nightmare thought – say it, Ruskin – of insatiable sexuality. As quick as a falling star – or falling city – the Madonna has turned into an Aphrodite. *Damn* Venice!

I might have said from gorgeousness to grotesqueness, since Ruskin effectively concludes his work on Venice with a chapter on 'Grotesque Renaissance' in which he attempts to describe the final degradation and degeneration – as he sees it – of his city beautiful. But in attempting to explore the domain of the 'grotesque' Ruskin finds himself in some very troubling, not easily negotiable, territory. He starts with his usual assertive confidence. Since Venice is no longer the realm of the best, it must be exactly the opposite. 'The architecture raised at Venice during this period is among the worst and basest ever built by the hands of men, being especially distinguished by a spirit of brutal mockery and insolent jest, which, exhausting itself in deformed and monstrous scuplture, can sometimes be hardly otherwise defined than as the perpetuation in stone of the ribaldries of drunkenness'. Ruskin's problems will arise from his attempts at once to define and control the deformed and the monstrous, to keep it in (contained) and keep it out (dismissed). His starting-point is a site where a past Venice has been entirely obliterated, the spot where once stood the church dedicated to St Mary the Beautiful, associated with the 'true legend of the Brides of Venice' – the Brides who were miraculously rescued from pirates, at a time when all the marriages of the year took place on one day 'so that all might rejoice together'. Such a sign of communality could only be immensely attractive to Ruskin: 'imagine the strong bond of brotherhood thus sanctified among them'. Of this church there is not 'one stone left upon another'. But the spot can still yield a lesson, 'though a painful one'. Again, Ruskin first asks the reader to imagine that earlier, erased Venice: 'let him first fill his mind with the fair images of the ancient festival' (*CW* 11, 135–6, 139, 144). Then he sets before the reader a description of a head carved on the base of a tower of the church which now stands there:

> A head – huge, inhuman, and monstrous, – leering in bestial degradation, too foul to be either pictured or described or to be beheld for more than an instant: yet let it be endured for that instant; for in that head is embodied the type of the evil spirit to which Venice was abandoned in the fourth period of her decline; and it is well that we should see and feel the full horror of it on this spot, and know what pestilence it was that came and breathed upon her beauty, until it melted away like the white cloud from the ancient field of Santa Maria Formosa. (*CW* 11, 145)

This is the Medusa face of Venice. I invoke the name advisedly, since Ruskin himself did. As opposed to the producers of the true and noble grotesque, the person who could fashion this face is effectively damned:

> the other workman never felt any Divine fear; he never shuddered when he heard the cry from the burning towers of the earth,
>
> 'Venga Medusa; sì lo faremdi smalto.
>
> He is stone already, and needs no gentle hand laid upon his eyes to save him. (*CW* 11, 169)

The quotation is from canto IX of Dante's *Inferno* and it is worth having the passage before our – protected – eyes. Dante and Virgil have encountered the Furies, who cry out:

> 'Venga Medusa, sì il farem di smalto,'
> dicevan tutte riguardando in giuso;
> 'mal noi vengiammo in Teseo l'assalto.'
>
> 'Volgiti indietro, e tien lo viso chiuso:
> chè, se il Gorgon si mostra, e tu il vedessi,
> nulla sarebbe del tornar mai suso.'

Così disse il maestro; ed egli stessi
mi volse, e non si tenne alle mie mani,
che con le sue ancor non mi chiudessi.

('Let Medusa come, that we may change him
into stone,' they all said, looking downwards;
'badly did we avenge the assault of Theseus.'

'Turn thee backwards, and keep thy eyes closed:
for if the Gorgon shew herself, and thou shouldst
see her, there would be no returning up again.'

Thus said the Master, and he himself turned me,
and trusted not to my hands, but closed me also with his own.[7]

Ruskin can cover our eyes, but there was no one to protect him, and it is clear that at such moments – confronted by such bestial heads – Venice turned her Gorgon face to him. *Venga Medusa*. And, for Ruskin, come she did.[8]

There are, continues Ruskin, *hundreds* of these bestial heads, all over the city. It is as if he is constructing a nightmare for himself – as if the world of Bellini had suddenly become the world of Bosch. Ruskin is confronting at last something which he has hitherto avoided, or at least hardly touched on – the grotesque, the monstrous. In art: in mind. And he sees that it confronts him with an 'immediate task . . . to *distinguish* between this base grotesqueness, and that magnificent condition of fantastic imagination which was . . . one of the chief elements of the Northern Gothic mind' (*CW* 11, 145). He must establish 'the *distinction* between the true and false grotesque'. This urgent need to distinguish, insist on a distinction, between kinds and types of 'grotesque' – 'sportive . . . terrible', 'noble . . . ignoble', and so on – dominates the chapter and is crucial for Ruskin, since, in his view, nearly all great architectures of the world (he admits the possibility of a few exceptions, and by an extrapolation I would maintain he implies all great art) 'depend for their power on some development of the grotesque spirit'. And this because man is a playing animal – *homo ludens* indeed – who is bound to play even in the most sacred art, and this play can be wise, and is certainly necessary: 'It is impossible to exaggerate its importance, whether in polity, or in art.' But 'the jest may crawl too far', in Emily Dickinson's words, and 'inordinate play' can produce nightmares of grossness – 'exaggerations, incoherences and monstrosities' (*CW* 11, 151, 166, 158, 154, 161).

It is almost impossible to believe the depth to which the human mind can be debased in following this species of grotesque. . . . Grossness,

> of one kind or another, is, indeed, an unfailing characteristic of this style; either latent, or in the refined sensuality of the more graceful arabesque, or, in the worst examples, manifested in every species of obscene conception and abominable detail. In the head, described in the opening of this chapter, at Santa Maria Formosa, the *teeth* are represented as *decayed*. (*CW* 11, 162)

Man is also and necessarily a fearful creature. Partly because he is constantly made aware of 'the destructive phenomena of the universe', and more generally because he is everywhere surrounded by dying, death: 'the blasted trunk, the barren rock, the moaning of the bleak winds, the roar of the black, perilous, merciless whirlpools of the mountain streams, the solemn solitudes of moors and seas, the continual fading of all beauty into darkness, and of all strength into dust, have these no language for us?' A man truly living in the world, and particularly an artist, will acknowledge that fearfulness. 'It is the world's work he is doing, and world's work is not to be done without fear' (*CW* 11, 164–5). In a remarkable passage, Ruskin imagines such an artist, aware of 'the dreadfulness of the world around him', returning to his (Gothic) work. He is no longer thinking consciously about all the darkness and discordance and danger in the world, but

> there is a shadow of them still present with him: and as the bright colours mingle beneath his touch, and the fair leaves and flowers grow at his bidding, strange horrors and phantasms rise by their side; grisly beasts and venomous serpents, and spectral fiends and nameless inconsistencies of ghastly life, rising out of things most beautiful, and fading back into them again, as the harm and the horror of life do out of its happiness. He has seen these things; he wars with them daily; he cannot but give them their part in his work. (*CW* 11, 163)

This is, if you like, a wise and necessary fearfulness;[9] just as there was a wise and necessary playfulness, there is the corollary of incontinent and inordinate play in his designation of a 'diseased and ungoverned imaginativeness' which can produce 'a manufactured terribleness'. There is a possible problem in all this from the start. At what point can we say that 'necessary play' overplays itself into inordinateness? When the horrors and phantasms start to rise, who can say if the generating dread is healthy or sick? Is it really possible to 'distinguish'? Ruskin is well aware of the problem: 'The reader will have some difficulty, I fear, in keeping clear the various divisions of our subject' (CW 11, 169, 160).

> For observe, the difficulty which . . . exists in distinguishing the playful from the terrible grotesque arises out of this cause: that the mind,

> under certain phases of excitement, *plays* with *terror*, and summons images which, if it were in another temper, would be awful, but of which, either in weariness or in irony, it refrains from the time to acknowledge the true terribleness. And the mode in which this refusal takes place distinguishes the noble from the ignoble grotesque. (*CW* 11, 166)

But Ruskin can hardly stabilize the distinction by asserting that the noble grotesque really appreciates what it mocks while the ignoble does not. The difficulty is evident on a larger scale. Ruskin recognizes and honours the products of the great civilizations of the past – Egyptian, Arabian, Assyrian, Persian, Greek, Gothic, and so on – and asserts that when they were in their 'utmost nobleness' then 'the grotesque is developed in its utmost energy' (*CW* 11, 184).

But he immediately has to try to draw some limits and distinctions.

> The reader . . . may, however, at first have some difficulty in distinguishing between the noble grotesque of these great nations, and the barbarous grotesque of mere savageness, as seen in the work of the Hindoo and other Indian nations; or, more grossly still, in that of the complete savage of the Pacific islands; or if, as is to be hoped, he instinctively feel the difference, he may yet find difficulty in determining wherein that difference consists. (*CW* 11, 189)

We are hovering around the start of comparative anthropology here (chronologically too), for the 'mere savageness' of those Pacific islanders may be easy to assert but prove rather harder to define, and, if the Assyrian grotesque is a sign of noble energy, how is the Indian not? When Ruskin, to assist the reader who may be having difficulty with the 'difference', insists that 'he will discover, on consideration, that the noble grotesque *involves the true appreciation of beauty*, though the mind may wilfully turn to other images, or the hand resolutely stop short of the perfection, which it must fail, if it endeavoured, to reach; while the grotesque of the Sandwich islander involves no perception or imagination or anything above itself' (*CW* 11, 189) – one could reply that, on consideration, that difference was far from clear. And if 'in the exact proportion in which the grotesque results from an incapability of perceiving beauty, it becomes savage or barbarous,' it might become difficult, by Ruskin's own terms, to tell Venice from Tahiti. To which he might, I suppose, have said that between Venice in decline and a Pacific island there was no important difference to tell.

The most interesting moment in his analysis of the grotesque comes when he considers one of the sources and causes of ignoble grotesque – 'ungovernableness of the imagination . . . the error and wildness of the mental impressions, caused by fear operating upon strong powers of imagination, or the failure of the human faculties in the endeavour to grasp the highest truths'. But how governable *is* the imagination?

> The grotesque which comes to all men in a disturbed dream is the most intelligible example of this kind, but also the most ignoble; the imagination, in this instance, being entirely deprived of all aid from reason, and incapable of self-government. I believe, however, that the noblest forms of imaginative power are also in some sort ungovernable, and have in them something of the character of dreams; so that the vision, of whatever kind, comes uncalled, and will not submit itself to the seer, but conquers him, and forces him to speak as a prophet, having no power over his words or thoughts. Only, if the whole man be trained perfectly, and his mind calm, consistent, and powerful, the vision which comes to him is seen as in a perfect mirror, serenely, and in consistence with the rational powers; but if the mind be imperfect and ill trained, the vision is seen as in a broken mirror, with strange distortions and discrepancies, all the passions of the heart breathing upon it in cross ripples, till hardly a trace remains unbroken. So that, strictly speaking, the imagination is never governed. (*CW* 11, 178–80)

A footnote acknowledges that the idea of inspiration as a form of madness is as old as Plato, but more important here is Ruskin's recognition that the greatest art might have something crucial in common with the lowest (most ignoble-seeming) dreams. And we do not have to adduce the tragic fact that the mind which wrote these words would itself be 'deprived of all aid from reason' for long years, to make the point that all minds are more or less broken mirrors. (That all the mind-mirrors were more or less broken would seem to be borne out then, returning to the metaphor in *Modern Painters*' volume V, he writes: 'the soul of man is a mirror of the mind of God. A mirror dark, distorted, broken, use what blameful words you please of its state' (*CW* 7, 260).) Similarly Ruskin had maintained that virtually all art contained inevitable and *essential* imperfections – or, to put it another way permitted by his own terms, *some* element of the grotesque had to be present in art as it is in dreams, not excrescentially but constitutively. Not only could you not keep it out; you had to have it in ('it would seem to be rare that any very exalted truth should be impressed on the imagination without some grotesqueness'; *CW* 11, 181). And although Ruskin tries any number of ways to establish and maintain some clear differentiating distinctions between 'the two extremes of great and base' when confronting this phenomenon of the grotesque, I think he is aware – indeed I think he reveals – that the distinctions will not hold, the lines cannot be drawn. By another kind of 'reciprocal interference' the apparently higher and the deputedly lower will never leave each other alone – 'impurity and malice stealing gradually into nobler forms, and invention and wit elevating the lower, according to the countless minglings of the elements of the human soul' (*CW* 11, 178). But this suggests or threatens an erosion of difference, a condition in which you begin to see things in a Madonna-Aphrodite blur and you cannot keep the Bacchanal out of the Nativity. Ruskin is pushing – heroically one might think, recklessly another – towards conclusions which he would find intolerable, and indeed unacceptable.

This, I think, is why he has recourse to such an extreme dichotomizing in his reconstruction of Venice which occludes the 'countless minglings' of the movements of history. The condition of maintaining a dream vision of an entirely beautiful, pure and pious city was the creation of a counter-city which took into itself everything in Ruskin's imagination which might contaminate or pollute it, and if the first city is almost unbelievably chaste, the other is quite uncontrollably concupiscent. It is tempting to say that, at times, it is hard to be entirely sure which attracts him more; though, to suggest that, we would have to be ready to detect a kind of perverse pleasure in his returning again and again to the thought of Venice fallen, Venice falling – as he does again at what is to all intents and purposes the end of the work. He returns to his hinge date of 1423 and notes that on the accession of Mocenigo's successor (Foscari), '"The city kept festival for a whole year"'. This 'sign' is all Ruskin needs for his conclusion:

> Venice had in her childhood sown, in tears, the harvest she was to reap in rejoicing. She now sowed in laughter the seeds of death. Thenceforward, year after year, the nation drank with deeper thirst from the fountains of forbidden pleasure, and dug springs, hitherto unknown, in the dark places of the earth. In the ingenuity of indulgence, in the varieties of vanity, Venice surpassed the cities of Christendom as of old she has surpassed them in fortitude and devotion; and as once the powers of Europe stood before her judgment-seat, to receive the decisions of her justice, so now the youth of Europe assembled in the halls of her luxury, to learn from her the arts of delight.
>
> It is as needless as it is painful to trace the steps of her final ruin. That ancient curse was upon her, the curse of the Cities of the Plain, 'Pride, fulness of bread, and abundance of idleness'. By the inner burning of her own passions, as fatal as the fiery rain of Gomorrah, she was consumed from her place among the nations; and her ashes are choking the channels of the dead, salt sea. (*CW* 11, 194–5)

How estimate what possible 'forbidden pleasure' might be enjoyed by this imagining of a Venice finally drowning in its own lubricity and burning from the utterly unfettered indulgence of its most perverse desires?

This was effectively the conclusive conclusion of *The Stones of Venice*. Ruskin did in fact add a 'Conclusion', which he admits will be 'rambling', and which is written in a very different key from most of what preceded it. It has a note of exhaustion, as if Ruskin has tired himself out in charting what he regarded as the final end of 'the career of the architecture of Europe'. In this 'spent' mood as he contemplates the possibilities for post-Venetian Europe; Ruskin allows himself a rather shallow optimism which would prove to be very short-lived.

> That modern science, with all its additions to the comforts of life, and to the fields of rational contemplation, has placed the existing races of mankind on a higher platform than any that preceded them, none can doubt for an instant; and I believe the position in which we find ourselves is somewhat analogous to that of thoughtful and laborious youth succeeding a restless and heedless infancy. (*CW* 11, 196)

He may have wanted to believe this, but as a gesture of faith in the positive potentialities of nineteenth-century science and technology it is – by Ruskin's rhetorical standards – weak, and proved to be transient. I think it is there mainly because Ruskin has by this time persuaded himself that a Gothic revival in architecture might do the trick and turn the tide – if I may deliberately somewhat trivialize what now seems like, and soon came to seem to Ruskin, a very foredoomed hope indeed. Looking round, he sees evidence of the 'destruction of beauty' in all walks of life: in dress ('the splendour of chivalry has faded into the paltriness of colour') as in architecture. Indeed, just about the only place where he can find some contemporary beauty is in the paintings of the English school of landscape which, 'culminating in Turner, is in reality nothing else than a healthy effort to fill the void which the destruction of Gothic architecture has left'. But the land needs more even than Turner and, if we can get rid of – 'cast out utterly' – everything whatever 'connected with the Greek, Roman, or Renaissance architecture, in principle or in form', then, the dust duly shaken from our feet, it will be 'easy' to 'turn our prison into a palace'. The relative tallness of this demolition order seems, here, to dismay Ruskin not one bit. Gothic is there, Gothic is ready – 'Gothic is animated, serviceable, and faithful': Gothic will fill the void. He manages to persuade himself into a degree of enthusiasm by the close, though it lacks the true hypnotic excess:

> It is hardly possible at present to imagine what may be the splendour of buildings designed in the forms of English and French thirteenth century *surface*, wrought out with the refinement of Italian art in the details. . . . Let this be the object of our ambition, and let us begin to approach it, not ambitiously, but in all humility, accepting help from

> the feeblest hands; and the London of the nineteenth century may yet become as Venice without her despotism, and as Florence without her dispeace. (*CW* 11, 225–30)

When Ruskin next seriously considers medieval Venice and contemporary England together, in the same breath as it were, the optimism has entirely gone. Another Venice rises again, and it is England that has fallen.

Ruskin did not visit Venice again for seventeen years (not until 1869), but he returned to visions of Venice in the last part of the concluding (fifth) volume of *Modern Painters*, which appeared in 1860. If one wants to detect a point at which the emphasis in Ruskin's work shifted definitively from art criticism to various forms of social criticism it would perhaps be just here. Immediately after completing and publishing volume V, Ruskin wrote *Unto this Last*, perhaps the most powerful of all of his many attacks on English capitalism. And in this concluding volume Venice plays a rather different role. To appreciate the mood which dominates or informs this last part it might help to know that it was written in a new realization of 'the absolute darkness which has covered the national mind' – 'the form which the infidelity of England, especially, has taken, is one hitherto unheard of in human history' (*CW* 7, 445). The terminal point of declension is no longer eighteenth-century Venice but nineteenth-century England, and from the beginning he stresses darkness. His broad artistic topic here, as indeed throughout, is landscape and landscape painting. Right away he explains that he will not be including 'Christian' art 'because its first assumption is false, namely, that the natural world can be represented without the element of death' (*CW* 7, 265). Death, pain, decay, grief – they are always somewhere there in the landscape (Ruskin tells a piteous tale to demonstrate the fact): the prettiest scene has its shadows to the eye which can see them, and grace them (Ruskin traces the evidence of rapine, starvation and death in a generic lovely Highland landscape). The human mind derives its power from 'the resolution to see fearlessly, pitifully', and so 'all great and beautiful work has come from first gazing without shrinking into the darkness'. He continues: 'If, having done so, the human spirit can, by its courage and faith, conquer the evil, it rises into conceptions of victorious and consummated beauty. It is then the spirit of the highest Greek and Venetian art.' The Greeks could face up to the fact that the beautiful given world was none the less 'highly ambiguous' – as the spear in Hector's throat exemplifies. The Greeks confronted, accepted, even defied the ambiguity, and made of this present life what they could. This in itself was a form of 'conquest'. 'So defied, the betraying and accusing shadows shrank back; the mysterious horror subdued itself to majestic sorrow. Death was swallowed up in Victory' (*CW* 7, 271, 275, 277). It is this 'heroic spirit of Greek religion and art' which relates the Greek to the Venetian artists.

And it is with the Venetian painters that Ruskin is now exclusively concerned. In 'The Wings of the Lion' they are celebrated by their 'sincerity' and 'power' – 'this heroic landscape of theirs was peopled by spiritual beings of the highest order. And in this rested the dominion of the Venetians over later schools. They were the *last believing* school of Italy' (*CW* 7, 286). The argument sustaining this assertion is both passionate and precarious, and it centres on Ruskin's intense feeling for, and attraction to, colour. I have spoken of an erotics of colour in his writing, and in this volume, in one of the longest of his many long footnotes – for when Ruskin starts talking about colour he finds it unusually difficult to stop – we may say he makes the connection explicit.

> As colour is the type of Love, it resembles it in all its modes of operation; and in practical work of human hands, it sustains changes of worthiness precisely like those of sexual love . . . so it is with the type of Love – colour. Followed rashly, coursely, untruly, for the mere pleasure of it, with no reverence, it becomes a temptation, and leads to corruption. Followed faithfully, with intense but reverent passion, it is the holiest of all aspects of material things. (*CW* 7, 417)

Once again, Ruskin is attempting to establish a critical distinction which in practice it is difficult to securely maintain. For how can you tell if colour was applied with rashness or with faith; as opposed, say, to rash faithfulness, or even a faithful rashness. These things come mixed, and one can sense the strain as Ruskin strives to keep them separate. But there is no doubt or uncertainty in the corner-stone of his argument: 'The Venetians began, I repeat, with asceticism; always, however, delighting in more massive and deep colour than other religious painters' (*CW* 7, 279–80). What that massive and deep colour could be used to depict might, however, cause problems.

Given his esteem for its spiritual power it might seem somewhat contradictory that Ruskin should insist that 'the worst point we have to note respecting the spirit of Venetian landsape is its pride.' He attributes this partly to the fact that they had 'no gardens', though he admires what they gained from what they had, as it were, instead – namely the 'wave-training' enforced by the sea to which he thinks they owe both their bodily health and their religious liberty. But it is still a lack that 'the Venetians possessed, and cared for, neither fields nor pastures.' Thus the backgrounds of the paintings are 'without sign of laborious rural life' and thus without the Wordsworthian 'simple joy' which may be found in that life. Instead: 'Only stateliness and power; high intercourse with kingly and beautiful humanity, proud thoughts, or splendid pleasures; throned sensualities, and ennobled appetites.' This is a thrilling and surely volatile range of resources and stimuli, for who can be sure that all the appetites will be ennobled, and, while the throne may dignify the sensuality, may not the sensuality at times degrade the throne? Ruskin addresses the possible difficulty: 'Perhaps when you see one of Titian's splendidly passionate subjects and find Veronese making the Marriage in Cana one blaze of worldly pomp, you imagine that Titian must have been a sensualist, and Veronese an unbeliever.' Perhaps you might, if you thought it important to decide one way or another. Ruskin pins his faith on another plausible, but still precarious, assertion – 'of an evil tree, men never gather good fruit'. As much as to say, if it is good art, it must needs be grounded in and spring from goodness or something good. If it is good art and manifestly sensual then we have, yes, 'good sensualism' (*CW* 7, 284, 280, 286–7). This is certainly tenable but equally it is dangerous for Ruskin.

Dangerous ground and possibly irreligious ground, for Ruskin is approaching what was in effect for him his Road to Damascus. Only for Ruskin it was a reverse road, for he was travelling the other way. Or, rather, the religion which his eyes were finally fully opened to was not the might of Christianity but the power of art. He was later to describe the moment when he finally lost his faith after moving from the Turin art gallery, where he had been looking at Veronese's *Presentation of the Queen of Sheba*, to a Nonconformist chapel with its pathetically drab congregation and ludicrously self-aggrandizing priest.[10] Here he simply describes the painting as 'of quite inestimable value' and evokes, as only he can, its 'tragic power', along with its concomitant nobility, grace and occasional playfulness. The power is the point. Whatever it is, whatever it comes from, whatever it is doing, Ruskin can sense it and he cannot, and will not, resist it. On the contrary, *that*, whatever it is, is what is truly religious. Ruskin confesses that he used to consider Titian to be an unreligious painter (particularly compared with Tintoretto), 'But in this I was mistaken; – the religion of Titian is like that of Shakespeare – occult behind his magnificent equity' (*CW* 7, 293, 295). It is a magnificent formulation. The only possible difficulty is that it may not always be possible to be sure when the 'religion' is there but 'occult', and when it has been finally occluded. It will all depend on the power of the power.

The problem, to call it that, comes to a head at the close of the chapter, when Ruskin, yet again, has to condemn Venice to a sudden, precipitous, irreversible fall. He faces the problem head on – bravely, as one might think. What about Titian's *manifestly* sensual paintings? He asks and answers, the question in his own terms.

> It may perhaps appear more difficult to account for the alternation of Titian's great religious pictures with others devoted wholly to the

> expression of sensual qualities, or to exulting and bright representation of heathen deities. The Venetian mind, we have said, and Titian's especially, as the central type of it, was wholly realist, universal, and manly. In this breadth and realism the painter saw that sensual passion in man was, not only a fact, but a Divine fact; the human creature, though the highest of the animals, was, nevertheless, a perfect animal.

A *perfect* animal, or a perfect *animal* – the slightest tilt of emphasis could make all the difference. And at this point Ruskin confronts, as he rarely does, the female nude.

> I do not stay to trace the reasons why, at Venice, the female body could be found in more perfect beauty than the male; but so it was, and it becomes he principal subject, therefore, both with Giorgione and Titian. They painted it fearlessly, with all right and natural qualities; never, however, representing it as exercising any overpowering attractive influence on man; but only on the Faun and Satyr.

He approaches; and avoids. Or rather distances. The painters are fearless; only the fauns and satyrs are sexually aroused. Desire is displaced into a mythical world elsewhere and elsewhen. And, we might say, he does not stay to trace the reasons. The female body in Venetian art is rendered statuesque: 'in the greatest studies of the female body by the Venetians, all other characters are overborne by majesty, and the form becomes as pure as that of a Greek statue' (*CW* 7, 297). Later he cites a fresco of a nude by Giorgione as 'as fair a type as I am able to give in any single figure, of the central Venetian art' (*CW* 7, 372). By Ruskin's time all that was left of this fresco was indeed the 'last traces', and the fading, crumbling magnificence of this work will coalesce with Turner's paintings and the fading of Venice in one of his most powerful passages. But he also includes an engraving of what was left of the fresco. The figure is, appropriately enough, almost totally erased from the waist down. The upper part – which, of course, the gods inherit – seems indeed Greekly remote and coldly calm in its 'majesty', and marmoreally de-eroticized. This was the *perfect* animal, and little anough of the animal at that. This, presumably, is 'good sensualism'. Nevertheless by invoking the image of a naked woman as the very 'type' of Venetian art, Ruskin is confronting and admitting the central and indispensable role of the sexual in the productive power, and the powerful productions, of the city. Later he will replace this splendid, outward-looking, proud, naked woman with a little girl asleep in bed.

'In all its roots of power, and modes of work; – in its belief, its breadth, and its judgment, I find the Venetian mind perfect. How, then, did its art so swiftly pass away? How become, what it became unquestionably, one of the chief causes of the corruption of the mind of Italy, and of her subsequent decline in moral and political power?' (*CW* 7, 298). However it was, we can be sure that it was indeed swift – having created his cherished image of Venetian perfection, of mind, of art, Ruskin really *cannot* stay to trace the reasons of its vanishing. He adduces 'one fatal fault' to explain the passing away – 'recklessness in aim. Wholly noble in its source, it was wholly unworthy in its purposes.' If man could never gather good fruit of an evil tree, it might be expected that to follow a noble source could not nourish an unworthy purpose. Indeed, in expanding on this fault of 'recklessness', Ruskin as if in spite of himself transforms it into the distinguishing mark of greatness. Venetian art, like the young Samson, 'wantoned in untimely pleasure', and this surely should be bad. But Ruskin cannot rein in his argument, and it takes on a powerful direction of its own.

> No Venetian painter ever worked with any aim beyond that of delighting the eye, or expressing fancies agreeable to himself or flattering to his nation. They could not be either, unless they were religious. But he did not desire the religion. He desired the delight.
>
> The Assumption is a noble picture, because Titian believed in the Madonna. But he did not paint it to make any one else believe in her. He painted it, because he enjoyed rich masses of red and blue, and faces flushed with sunshine. . . . Other men used their effete faiths and mean faculties with a high moral purpose. The Venetian gave the most earnest faith, and the lordliest faculty, to gild the shadows of an antechamber, or heighten the splendours of a holiday.
>
> Strange and lamentable as this carelessness may appear, I find it to be almost the law with the great workers. Weak and vain men have acute consciences, and labour under a profound sense of responsibility. The strong men, sternly disdainful of themselves, do what they can, too often merely as it pleases them at the moment, reckless what comes of it. (*CW* 7, 298–9)

Surely the reverse of lamentable. For who, in these terms, would wish to be effete and mean and moral; or weak and vain and responsible – as opposed to being strong, disdainful and reckless? Better, surely, a great carelessness than an acute conscience-fulness. Ruskin, by his own terms, has become Venetian. There is nothing *he* enjoys more than 'rich masses of red and blue, and faces flushed with sunlight'. And now when *he* went to a painting he too did not desire the religion. He desired the delight.

All of which means that this concluding account – again – of the Fall of Venice, is quite different in tone from the previous ones. There is no biblical wrath, no excoriating denunciation, no stamping on the gorgeous face. The mood is now wistful, elegiac.

> I know not how far in humility, or how far in bitter and hopeless levity, the great Venetians gave their art to be blasted by the sea winds or wasted by the worm. I know not whether in sorrowful obedience, or in wanton compliance, they fostered the folly, and enriched the luxury of their age. This only I know, that in proportion to the greatness of their power was the shame of its desecration and the suddenness of its fall. The enchanter's spell, woven by centuries of toil, was broken in the weakness of a moment; and swiftly, and utterly, as a rainbow vanishes, the radiance and the strength faded from the wings of the Lion. (*CW* 7, 299)

Venice and its history have become a matter of magic again – and to vanish like a rainbow is a finer and fairer fate than being scattered like the Cities of the Plain. The truth is that Ruskin no longer has any reason to condemn Venice; he can only lament her somehow ceasing to be what he imagines she was. Her biography was her art, and that art was quite as sensual as it was spiritual, and quite possibly even more reckless than it was religious. *Whatever* its sources, it has incontestable, incomparable power. And it is that power which makes it great.

Moving through a series of comparisons – Dürer and Salvator, Claude and Poussin, Rubens and Cuyp, Wouvermans and Angelico – Ruskin arrives at the two painters who represented for him, effectively, the beginning and end of Venetian art, Giorgione and Turner (for Ruskin often refers to Turner in ways that make him seem like the last of the great Venetians). It is particularly interesting that he chooses to imagine, and imaginatively recreate, 'The Two Boyhoods' of the artists. Around the mid-nineteenth century a new sub-genre of painting seems to have emerged. From the later part of the eighteenth century there appeared a very large number of paintings devoted to the lives and works of other artists, but 'in the 1830s a new theme begins to appear; suddenly artists are discovered to have had childhoods.' In Francis Haskell's words, 'Young Masaccios and Rembrandts, Carraccis, Murillos and Poussins – even a baby Thomas Lawrence – these began to outnumber the deathbed scenes.'[11] Haskell sees this an indicative of the climax of the idea of the 'innocent eye', and clearly it derives from more general Romantic, Wordsworthian ideas that in important ways the child is father to the man. Certainly, when Ruskin turns to the theme to show up the difference between Venice then and London, and England, now, his opening emphasis is on the infant eye. 'Have you ever thought what a world his eyes opened on – fair, searching eyes of youth?' (*CW* 7, 374). There follows one of his most poetic evocations of Venice – one that particularly took possession of Proust's memory and imagination – in which Ruskin dreams again a Venice composed entirely of beauty, strength and purity', 'unsullied', 'no foulness nor tumult', certainly no 'insatiable pursuit of pleasure', indeed no living individual inhabitants at all, since even the 'mothers and maidens' have been turned into 'pillars of alabaster'. Explicitly, 'all the common and poor elements of life' have been 'banished' from the world, and what we have left is one of the most vivid pieces of medieval fantasizing to be found in nineteenth-century writing. This is Ruskin's dream:

> A city of marble did I say? nay, rather a golden city, paved with emerald. For truly, every pinnacle and turret glanced or glowed, overlaid with gold, or bossed with jasper. Beneath, the unsullied sea drew in deep breathing, to and fro, its eddies of green wave. Deep-hearted, majestic, terrible as the sea, – the men of Venice moved in sway of power and war; pure as her pillars of alabaster, stood her mothers and maidens; from foot to brow, all noble, walked her knights; the low bronzed gleaming of sea-rusted armour shot angrily under their blood-red mantle-folds. Fearless, faithful, patient, impenetrable, implacable, – every word a fate – sate her senate. In hope and honour, lulled by flowing of wave around their isles of sacred sand, each with his name written and cross graved on his side, lay her dead. A wonderful piece of world. Rather, itself a world. . . . A world from which all ignoble care and petty thought were banished, with all the common and poor elements of life. No foulness, nor tumult, in those tremulous streets, that filled, or fell, beneath the moon; but rippled music of majestic change, or thrilling silence. . . . And around them, far as the eye could reach, still the soft moving of stainless waters, proudly pure. . . . Ethereal strength of Alps, dream-like, vanishing in high procession beyond the Torcellan shore; blue islands of Paduan hills, poised in the golden west. Above, free winds and fiery clouds ranging at their will; – brightness out of the north, and balm from the south, and the stars of the evening and morning clear in the limitless light of arched heaven and circling sea.
>
> Such was Giorgione's school – such Titian's home. (*CW* 7, 374–5)

This dazzling and hypnotic dream is exactly that, so that when Ruskin abruptly shifts to contemporary Covent Garden he can secure a maximum of contrast. No gold and emerald, no knights and few beautiful ladies, no majesty of dress or anything else, and 'furrowed cabbage leaves' for jasper – the only gold to be seen 'magnificence of oranges in wheelbarrows' ('Enchanted oranges gleam in Covent Gardens of the Hesperides' – these gleaming oranges will become very important). Given these 'circumstances', Ruskin asks what would be the 'necessary effects . . . upon the boy' (*CW* 7, 376). He assumes that Turner is Giorgione's equal if not superior when it comes to 'sensibility', so the question is what would the young Turner's

Venetian sensibility fasten on in the absence of Venetian beauty. Since, asserts Ruskin, 'child love' will necessarily attach itself to images of its birthplace, Turner's sensibility inevitably went out to ugliness.

> Hence, to the very close of life, Turner could endure ugliness which no one else, of the same sensibility, would have borne with for an instant. Dead brick walls, blank square windows, old clothes, market-womanly types of humanity – anything fishy and muddy, like Billingsgate or Hungerford Market had great attraction for him; black barges, patched sails, and every possible condition of fog. You will find these tolerations and affections guiding or sustaining him to the last hour of his life; the notablest of all such endurances being that of dirt. No Venetian ever draws anything foul; but Turner devoted picture after picture to the illustration of effects of dinginess, smoke, dust, and dusty texture; old sides of boats, weedy roadside vegetation, dung-hills, straw-yards, and all the soilings and stains of every common labour. And more than this, he not only could endure, but enjoyed and looked for *litter*, like Covent Garden wreck after the market. His pictures are often full of it, from side to side; their foregrounds differ from all others in the natural way that things have of lying about in them. (*CW* 7, 377)

Instead of 'limitless light' we are now confronted with unlimited litter; instead of a boy looking out on a world of unsullied purity we are shown an artist immersed in a world entirely constituted by varieties of 'dirt', be it smoke, dust, fog or mud; instead of 'stainless waters' and 'sacred sand', just 'soilings and stains'. Turner's London is exactly the negative of Ruskin's Venice, as Ruskin indicates when, after evoking Giorgione's Venice, he writes, 'Turner saw the *exact reverse* of this' (*CW* 7, 385; my italics). It is indeed the ultimate opposition and reversal: 'For St Mark ruled over life; the Saint of London over death; St Mark over St Mark's Place, but St Paul over St Paul's Churchyard' (*CW* 7, 383). From the actual cemetery, Ruskin extends and expands the panorama of mortality until it takes in the whole continent. Other cultures had faced Death, and other artists had painted it: 'But the English death – the European death of the nineteenth century – was of another range of power; more terrible a thousand-fold in its merely physical grasp and grief; more terrible, incalculably, in its mystery and shame.' And since this London–England–Europe was – exactly and totally – the reverse of the Venetian dream, it must be degradation, darkness and horror devoid of redeeming grace or dignity:

> the life trampled out in the slime in the street, crushed to dust amidst the roaring of the wheel, tossed countlessly away into howling winter

> wind along five hundred leagues of rock-fanged shore. Or, worst of all, rotted down to forgotten graves through years of ignorant patience, and vain seeking for help from man, for hope in God – infirm, imperfect yearning, as of motherless infants starving at the dawn; oppressed royalties of captive thought, vague ague-fits of bleak, amazed despair.

When Ruskin becomes obsessed and extreme – and anguished and angry – at this, one might feel that the 'oppressed royalties of captive thought' are primarily his own. For now it is death everywhere, death of everything – 'death, not of myriads of poor bodies only, but of will, and mercy, and conscience; death, not once inflicted on the flesh, but daily fastening upon the spirit; death, not silent and patient, waiting his appointed hour, but voiceful, venomous; death with the taunting word, and burning grasp, and infixed sting. This was the sight which opened on the young eyes . . . of Turner in his youth' (*CW* 7, 386–8). Turner is Giorgione in a charnel-house, and Death has become a monster. Dragonish. Pythonish. Ruskin is preparing for his final chapters.

Far in the background of Turner's painting, *The Garden of the Hesperides*, the dragon which traditionally guards the golden fruit lies full length on a mountain top, jaws ferociously and frighteningly agape. And it is this dragon, in this picture, which draws and holds Ruskin's horrified attention and imagination in the next chapter, 'The Nereid's Guard'. He determines to analyse the picture 'completely' and this means going as far back and down into the fable of the Hesperides as he can. From the start, he sees the fable as having both natural and moral meaning. 'The nymphs of the west, or Hesperides, are therefore, I believe, as natural types, the representatives of the soft western winds and sunshine.' But their moral significance lies far deeper and, drawing on Hesiod, Ruskin sees them also as 'nymphs of the sunset, and . . . daughters of the night'. As such they are related to the other darker offspring of Night, as recorded by Hesiod – Sleep, Censure, Sorrow, the Destinies. 'We have not, I think, hitherto quite understood the Greek feeling about these nymphs and their golden apples, coming as a light in the midst of cloud; between Censure, and Sorrow – and the Destinies.' He gives the names of the four nymphs, the most important of which (for Ruskin) is 'Ægle' – Brightness – with a footnote spelling out that the name 'signifies especially the spirit of brightness and cheerfulness; including even the subordinate idea of household neatness or cleanliness'. He then considers the significance of the fruit and its guardians in an amazing burst of imaginative myth-interpretation. It is an arresting thought that the originating moment for the excursus which follows was – in terms of this book – the thought of the young Turner staring in wonder at the golden oranges piled on the barrows in wrecked and litter-strewn and distinctly not so Hesperidean Covent Garden.

> And was it not well to trust to such keepers the guarding of the golden fruit which the earth gave to Juno at her marriage? Not fruit only: fruit on the tree, given by the earth, the great mother, to Juno (female power), at her marriage with Jupiter, or *ruling* manly power. . . . I call Juno, briefly, female power. She is, especially, the goddess presiding over marriage. . . . Juno is pre-eminently the housewives' goddess. She, therefore, represents, in her character, whatever good or evil may result from female ambition, or desire of power; and, as to a housewife, the earth presents its golden fruit to her, which she gives to two kinds of guardians. The wealth of the earth, as the source of household peace and plenty, is watched by the singing nymphs – the Hesperides. But, as the source of household sorrow and desolation, it is watched by the Dragon. We must, therefore, see who the Dragon was, and what kind of dragon. (*CW* 7, 392–6)

And Ruskin sets out to trace 'the whole line of descent', seeking out all that is dragonish in religion, myth and literature – Phorcys and Ceto, Gorgons and Harpies, Typhon and Erchidna, Medusa and Geryon – concluding with Dante.

We now have, he says, 'enough . . . collected to get at the complete idea of the Hesperian dragon, who is, in fine, the "Pluto di gran nemico" of Dante; the demon of all evil passions connected with covetousness; that is to say, essentially of fraud, rage, and gloom' (*CW* 7, 401).[12] The phrase from Dante concludes canto VI of the *Inferno* and the complete line together with the one preceding it reads:

> venimmo al punto dove si digrada;
> quivi trovammo Pluto il gran nemico.
>
> ('we reached the point where the descent begins;
> here found we Plutus, the great enemy.')[13]

Ruskin included a drawing of the dragon in Turner's painting and he entitled it, cryptically enough for the unlearned reader, 'Quivi Trovammo'. It seems that Dante followed a medieval tradition of not distinguishing between Pluto, god of the lower regions, and Plutus, the god of riches and, more generally, wealth incarnate. The confusion and conflation serves Ruskin's purposes well, as he sought to excoriate the infernal materialism of his contemporaries. Just look around now and – 'quivi trovammo'. *Now* Ruskin is ready to interpret the moral meaning of Turner's dragon which he almost viscerally evokes: 'note the grovelling and ponderous body, ending in a serpent, of which we do not see the end. He drags the weight of it forward by his claws, not being able to lift himself from the ground

("Mammon, the least erected spirit that fell"); then the grip of the claws themselves as if they would clutch (rather than tear) the earth to pieces' (*CW* 7, 402).

> That power, it appears, on the hill-top, is our British Madonna; whom reverently, the English devotional painter must paint, thus enthroned, with nimbus about the gracious head. Our Madonna – or our Jupiter on Olympus – or, perhaps more accurately still, our unknown god, sea-born. . . . This is no irony. The fact is verily so. . . . In each city and country of past time, the master-minds had to declare the chief worship which lay at the nation's heart; to define it; adorn it; show the range and authority of it. Thus in Athens, we have the triumph of Pallas; and in Venice the assumption of the Virgin; here, in England, is our great spiritual fact for ever interpreted to us – the Assumption of the Dragon. No St George any more to be heard of; no more dragon-slaying possible: this child, born on St George's Day, can only make manifest the dragon, not slay him, sea-serpent as he is; whom the English Andromeda, not fearing, takes for her lord. The fairy English Queen once thought to command the waves, but it is the sea-dragon now who commands her valleys; of old the Angel of the Sea ministered to them, but now the Serpent of the Sea; where once flowed their clear springs now spreads the black Cocytus pool; and the fair blooming of the Hesperid meadows fades into ashes beneath the Nereid's Guard. (*CW* 7, 407–8)

England fading into ashes now, not Venice. England – a place where myths and legends get scrambled, abort themselves, go into vertiginous reverse or dark and delirious transformations. England, the negation and antithesis of 'Venice' now, and where Venice and Turner, amidst the litter which is London and the Death which is Europe, are moving towards a final confluence in Ruskin's darkening imagination.

Opposite the opening page of the next chapter, Ruskin places the engraving of the Giorgione fresco of the nude which he appropriates or enlists for his own purposes by entitling her 'The Hesperid Ægle' – also the title of the chapter. It is fitting that this figure should stand guard, or herald, at the start as she reappears, gloriously, at the close. But she has little control or direct influence on the intervening material, as Ruskin broods and meditates on Turner's greatness which he all but infinitizes. He starts by considering another dragon picture – 'the Python, slain by Apollo' – and promises to explicate the true identity of the 'vaporous serpent' presently. The hostility which greeted the picture Ruskin interprets as another example of how the old myths are being reversed by contemporary England: 'They would neither look nor hear; – only shouted continuously, "Perish Apollo. Bring us back

Python."' But before he 'reads' the painting for its larger portents, he pauses once again to assert and extol the supreme virtue and importance of *colour* – 'the type of love', as he never tires of repeating. Turner is a supreme colourist, and his peculiar genius concerns his use of scarlet: nobody has painted clouds and shadows scarlet before Turner; 'the peculiar innovation of Turner was the perfection of the colour chord by means of *scarlet* (*CW* 7, 409, 412–13). Ruskin's passion is that *scarlet* – colour, as he says, of the rose of dawn and sunset, colour of blood, colour of the Giorgione fresco.[14] Colour, as he does not say, supremely of desire. It is the colour with which the chapter finally, in every sense, climaxes. In the vermilion glow produced by his words, Ruskin can now turn to Apollo and the Python. This Python is no 'merely devouring dragon. . . . It must possess some more terrible character to make the conquest over it so glorious. Consider the meaning of its name, "THE CORRUPTER". That Hesperid dragon was a terrible-guardian. This is the treasure-destroyer, – where moth and rust doth corrupt – the worm of eternal decay.' 'Apollo's contest with him is the strife of purity with pollution; of life, with forgetfulness; of love, with the grave.'

> Well did Turner know the meaning of that battle: he has told its tale with fearful distinctness. The Mammom dragon was armed with adamant; but this dragon of decay is a mere colossal worm: wounded, he bursts asunder in the midst, and melts to pieces, rather than dies, vomiting smoke – a smaller serpent-worm rising out of his blood. Alas, for Turner! This smaller serpent-worm, it would seem, he could not conceive to be slain. In the midst of all the power and beauty of nature, he still saw this death-worm writhing among the weeds. A little thing now, but enough. (*CW* 7, 420–1)

In contemporary England, you can only scotch the snake, not kill it – and that only on the canvas. Outside it, as Ruskin saw it, Python was everywhere triumphant over all things Apollonian. Why, he asks, is there this deep sadness in Turner? He has his answer.

> He was without hope.
>
> True daughter of Night, Hesperid Ægle was to him; coming between Censure and Sorrow, – and the Destinies.
>
> What, for us, his work may yet be. I know not. But let not the real nature of it be misunderstood any more.
>
> He is distinctively, as he rises into his own peculiar strength, separating himself from all men who had painted forms of the physical world before, – the painter of the loveliness of nature, with the worm at its root: Rose and canker-worm – both with his utmost strength; the one *never* separate from the other. (*CW* 7, 421–2)

This Hesperid Ægle is the daughter of the night, the nymph of sunset, brightness amidst darkenings. As she was also, in Ruskin's mind, Giorgione's nude, she was also virtually an epiphany of scarlet. Writing in 1760, A. M. Zanetti, describing this monumental and stupendous fresco, described it as 'a great fire . . . flowing in the strong shadows and in the heavy redness overall'.[15] But whatever she brought him by way of visions of roseate loveliness, Ruskin sees more evidence of the work of the worm in Turner's canvases – literally in that many were found in an advanced state of deterioration and decay, which becomes a powerful trope for the more general neglect, and failure fully to appreciate, which Ruskin thought contemporary England had meted out to him.

> But they cried out for Python, and Python came; – came literally as well as spiritually; – all the perfectest beauty and conquest which Turner wrought is already withered. The canker-worm stood at his right hand, and of all his richest, most precious work, there remains only the shadow. Yet that shadow is more than other men's sunlight; it is the scarlet shade, shade of the rose. Wrecked, and faded, and defiled, his work still, in what remains of it, or may remain, is the loveliest ever yet done by man, in imagery of the physical world. Whatsoever is there of fairest, you will find recorded by Turner, and by him alone. (*CW* 7, 422)

Ruskin is gathering his hyperboles around himself, defiantly, self-protectively. For, as he suddenly admits, though he writes 'you' he does not know 'to how few I speak', particularly nowadays when, wherever he goes, all he can see is men intent on *destroying* beauty. How could Turner's beauty have survived in such a world? Perhaps it is only fitting that his paintings should fade into their own sunsets with only Ruskin to commemorate the loveliness that was, 'the beauty been'.

At this point Ruskin has a sudden hesitation, lapsing partly into the kind of utilitarian vocabulary he has elsewhere scorned – what, really, is the good of art, what use is it?

> I would have tried to enter here into some examination of the right and worthy effect of beauty in Art upon the human mind if I had been myself able to come to demonstrable conclusions. But the question is so complicated with that of the enervating influence of all luxury, that I cannot get it put into any tractable compass. . . . What the final use may be to men, of landscape painting, or of any painting, or of natural beauty, I do not yet know. (*CW* 7, 423)

This is odd, since Ruskin can usually find a hundred ways of asserting the morally beneficial, if not indeed the mentally and physically beneficial, effects of perceiving and appreciating beauty in landscape, whether in nature or on canvas. Perhaps he is suspicious of the sheer pleasure to be derived from contemplating Turner, since such pleasure may be hard to disentangle from, indeed distinguish from, 'luxury', and luxury, like some other sensual pleasures, 'enervates'. And such pleasurable enervation cannot be a good thing. Ruskin is indeed preparing to redefine the scope and aim of his work in contemporary England and anticipates the time when he will no longer work primarily as an art critic. Obviously he would hardly have considered it an adequate justification for writing about Turner, or anything else, simply to say: I am a man who is mad about scarlet. Though, fortunately for us, he clearly was.

Ruskin tries to find some positive things to say under the aegis of 'the rose' and suggests various ways in which a healthy life of labour may also be refined and ennobled. But he is more obsessed with 'the Worm' and, returning to Turner, Ruskin notes how this sad man of no hope ('friendless in youth – loveless in manhood, – and hopeless in death'), wherever he looked, saw ruin.

> Ruin, and twilight. What was the distinctive effect of light which he introduced, such as no man had painted before? Brightness, indeed, he gave, as we have seen, because it was true and right; but in this he only perfected what others had attempted. His own favourite light is not Ægle, but Hesperid Ægle. Fading of the last rays of sunset. Faint breathing of the sorrow of night.
>
> And fading of sunset, note also, only ruin. . . . None of the great early painters draw ruins, except compulsorily. The shattered buildings introduced by them are shattered artificially, like models. There is no real sense of decay; whereas Turner only momentarily dwells on anything else than ruin. . . . There is no exultation in thriving city, or mart, cr in happy rural toil, or harvest gathering. Only the grinding at the mill, and patient striving with hard conditions of life . . . note the pastoral by the brook-side, with its neglected stream, and haggard trees, and bridge with the brokenrail, and decrepit children – fever-struck. . . . Then the Water-mill, beyond the fallen steps overgrown with the thistle: itself a ruin, mud-built at first, now propped on both sides; – the plank torn from its cattle-shed; a feeble beam, splintered at the end, set against he dwelling-house from the ruined pier of the watercourse; the old millstone – useless for many a day – half buried in slime, at the bottom of the wall; the listless children, listless dog, and the poor gleaner bringing her single sheaf to be ground. (*CW* 7, 432–3)

Ruskin increasingly enlarges this topography of ruin in Turner until we are once again confronted with the European death of the nineteenth century:

'Tyre at sunset, with the Rape of Europa, indicating the symbolism of the decay of Europe by that of Tyre, its beauty passing away into terror and judgment' (*CW* 7, 435). Ruskin indicates, in and by a characteristically self-extending footnote, that he could go on indefinitely about this sense of desolation to be found in Turner's works, fastening on this, among others:

> one of the saddest and most tender is a little sketch of dawn, made in his last years. It is a small space of level sea-shire; beyond it, a fair, soft light in the east; the last storm clouds melting away, oblique into the morning air; some little vessel – a collier, probably – has gone down in the night, all hands lost; a single dog has come ashore. Utterly exhausted, its limbs flailing under it, and, sinking into the sand, it stands howling and shivering. The dawn-clouds have the first scarlet upon them, a feeble tinge only, reflected with the same feeble blood-stain on the sand. (*CW* 7, 438)

Ruskin's quite incomparable eye and his unmatched ability to empathize into every nook and cranny of a canvas are here, as so often, unerring. This painting, still to be seen in London, is surely one of the most desolate pictures ever conceived and executed. I note here, in view of what is to follow, that in this footnote Ruskin returns to Turner's use of scarlet: 'And remember, also that the very sign in heaven itself which, truly understood, is the type of love, was to Turner the type of death. The scarlet of the clouds was his symbol of destruction.' Scarlet signifies – is – life *and* death, desire *and* destruction, the one, perhaps, never entirely separate from the other. By now Ruskin is ready for the amazing consummation of this chapter.

> I will only point, in conclusion, to the intensity with which his imagination dwelt always on the three great cities of Carthage, Rome and Venice – Carthage in connection especially with the thoughts and study which led to the painting of the Hesperides' Garden, showing the death which attends the vain pursuit of wealth; Rome, showing the death which attends the vain pursuit of power; Venice, the death which attends the vain pursuit of beauty.
>
> How strangely significative, thus understood, those last Venetian dreams of his become, themselves so beautiful and so frail; wrecks of all they were once – twilight of twilight!
>
> Vain beauty; yet not all in vain. Unlike in birth, how like in their labour, and their power over the future, these masters of England and Venice – Turner and Giorgione. But ten years ago, I saw the last traces of the greatest works of Giorgione yet glowing, like a scarlet cloud, on the Fondaco de Tedeschi. And though that scarlet cloud (sanguigna e fiammeggiante, per cui le pitture cominciarono con dolce violenza a rapire il cuore delle genti) may, indeed, melt away into

> paleness of night, and Venice herself waste from her islands as a wreath of wind-driven foam fades from their weedy beach; – that which she won of faithful light and truth shall never pass away. Deiphobe of the sea, – the Sun God measures her immortality to her by its sand. Flushed, above the Avernus of the Adrian lake, her spirit is still seen holding the golden bough; from the lips of the Sea Sibyl men shall learn for ages yet to come what is most noble and fair; and, far away, as the whisper in the coils of the shell, withdrawn through the deep hearts of nations, shall sound for ever the enchanted voice of Venice. (*CW* 7, 439–40)

'How things bind and blend themselves together!' as he will later write. How, indeed. One can only wonder at such magical coalescences, such beautiful blendings. Turner, Giorgione and Venice flow together, and flare up one last time in a scarlet cloud even as they are fading away into a twilight of twilights – fairer through fading, if we may adapt Emily Dickinson's words. At the centre is Giorgione's incomparable nude – one might almost call her the woman in scarlet – melting away into the night. The fading fresco was once (Ruskin recuperates through Zanetti whose engraving he copied for the Hesperid Ægle) 'sanguigna e fiammeggiante' – blood-red and shining or blazing – and Ruskin has allowed himself to be ravished ('rapire') by her sweet violence ('dolce violenza'). The shining is as important as the redness; Venice is matched with 'Deiphobe of the sea', and Phoebe is literally the Shining One. Everything here seems to be withdrawing, back into wreckage, back into waste, back into night. But also back into immortality. Venice may become as distant as a whisper in a shell, but the murmur is 'for ever'. Instead of being desecrated, Venice is here deified: her spirit holds the golden bough and she speaks with the voice of a Sea Sybil.

But how do things bind and blend themselves together – as and when, and *if* they do? Is it through the magical interweavings and imponderable adhesions of memory? Or the unfathomable coalescences and inexplicable associations in the unconscious? And *do* they, always? They certainly blended in a similar way for James when he embarked on his autobiography, where, from the start, he describes having 'to find discrimination among the part of my subject again and again difficult – so inseparably and beautifully they seemed to hang together and the comprehensive case to decline Mutilation or refuse to be treated otherwise than handsomely.'[16] But, as we shall see, for Hofmannsthal things most dismayingly did not bind themselves together. For Proust they redeemingly did. For Pound, excitingly and vexingly, they did and they didn't.

And Ruskin has answered his own earlier question, posed by Gerard Manley Hopkins some twenty-five years later in a poem entitled 'To what serves Mortal Beauty?' – mortal beauty which is, as the poem proclaims, 'dangerous; does set dancing blood'. Hopkins's answer has two stages. First: 'See: it does this: keeps warm Men's wits to the things that are' – that enraptured attention to the thisness and thereness, the quiddity and haecceity, of the given world, so characteristic of Hopkins. Then the step back, the letting go – equally characteristic.

> What do then? how meet beauty? Merely meet it, own,
> Home at heart, heaven's sweet gift; then leave, let that alone.
> Yea, wish that though, wish all, God's better beauty, grace.[17]

Hopkins turns away from the 'Pied Beauty' of the world with all its 'dappled things' – with desperate reluctance as one always feels – and admonishes and advises us, but more urgently himself, to leave and let that alone, wishing for 'God's better beauty', hoping that it exists. Ruskin could not quite give this answer, not any more. He certainly wanted to warm up men's wits to things that are, the beautiful and the damnable, but he could not now be certain of God's grace, nor that there was or could be any 'better beauty' than that to be found in Turner–Giorgione–Venice, that matchless, priceless triad. The use of *that* beauty was that from it 'men shall learn for ages yet to come what is most noble and most fair.' There is a sadness and poignancy in the passage, as of regretful relinquishment as he see both the paintings and the city receding from him, from the world. But he makes the nobility and fairness, and the light and truth, and that blood-red beauty, glow and shine forth in a merging, commemorative moment of incomparable beauty. Vain beauty? Perhaps, since from one perspective all is vanity. Yet certainly, most certainly, not all in vain. There is a celebration or affirmation in the elegiac wave of the passage.

Venice-Deiphobe never shone quite so again for Ruskin, at least in his writing. But that it had served as a shining light, in every sense, for Ruskin there can be no doubt – which gives added resonance to the concluding paragraph of *Praeterita*, another of the great moving moments in English prose:

> How things bind and blend themselves together! The last time I saw the Fountain of Trevi, it was from Arthur's father's room – Joseph Severn's, where we both took Joanie to see him in 1872, and the old man made a sweet drawing of his pretty daughter-in-law, now in her schoolroom; he himself then eager in finishing his last picture of the Marriage in Cana, which he had caused to take place under a wine trellis, and delighted himself by painting the crystal and ruby glittering of the changing rivulet of water of out the Greek vase, glowing into wine. Fonte Branda I last saw with Charles Norton, under the same arches where Dante saw it. We drank of it together, and walked together, that evening on the hills above, where the fireflies among

> the scented thickets shone fitfully in the still undarkened air. *How* they shone! moving like fire-broken starlight through the purple leaves. *How* they shone! through the sunset that faded into thunderous night as I entered Siena three days before, the white edges of the mountainous clouds still lighted from the west, and the openly golden sky calm behind the Gate of Siena's heart, with its still golden words, 'Cor magis tibe Sena pandit', and the fireflies everywhere in sky and cloud rising and falling, mixed with the lightning, and more intense than the stars. (*CW* 35, 561–2)

Dante saw God in terms of light ('luce eterna') and 'shining being' ('chiara susistenza'), and he concluded each book of the *Divine Comedy* with a star or stars. Ruskin concludes with stars as well, but for him but they are memories of fireflies rather than intimations of God, and their ephemeral, miraculous glow passes quickly away, even as that of Venice would one day fade. After that incandescent evocation at the end of *Praeterita* we may say the brightness fell from the air for Ruskin as he entered a terminal twilight in which nothing much shone any more.

On 1 January 1871 Ruskin wrote the first of those extraordinary 'letters' addressed to 'The Workmen and Labourers of Great Britain' which he entitled *Fors Clavigera*. The last one was written at Christmas 1884 and subtitled 'Terminal'. In all there are ninety-six letters. They are avowedly 'desultory and accidental – written on any matter *chanced* to interest me, and in any humour which *chance* threw me into' and Ruskin makes no apologies for his 'unfettered method' (*CW* 29, 315). Such an abandonment or commitment to a completely aleatory mode of writing, allowing free rein to random associations and giving *carte blanche* to the considerable digressive tendencies of his passionate and capacious mind, is virtually unprecedented before this century. Since that mind was full of every kind of knowledge, brimming over with the accumulations of his voracious reading, steeped in myth, legend and religion, and dreaming of a new society based on a revived and revitalized appreciation of feudalism and the ancient chivalries, the result is not unlike a nineteenth-century *Cantos*, or, as we should probably more properly say, Pound's *Cantos* are not unlike a twentieth-century *Fors Clavigera*.[18] Both writers also felt the wing of madness brush over them at times. Ruskin's case is particularly moving as he foregrounds his fears of going mad and makes no effort to disguise the strained disorderliness of his thoughts or to conceal any of his self-doubts and tribulations. 'Let me not be mad' – and there are indeed Lear-ish moments in these letters. 'I have been so puzzled lately by many matters that once seemed clear to me, that I seldom now feel sure of anything' (*CW* 27, 200). The siege and burning of Paris in 1871 'broke up what little consistency of plan had formed, besides putting me into a humour in which I could only write incoherently; deep domestic vexation occurring to me at the same time, till I fell ill, and my letters and vexations had like to have ended together. So I must patch the torn web as best I can . . . and, if the work goes on, – But I had better keep all Ifs out of it' (*CW* 27, 382). Patching the torn web and trying to keep out the Ifs – the increasing swarms of unendurable contingencies and unbearable possibilities – this is what we can see Ruskin trying to do in these letters. At times it is heart-breaking as we feel adumbrations of that time that was to come when the web of that mighty mind was torn beyond patching and vexed beyond consolation. Particularly poignant is the communicated sense of his feelings of complete isolation. 'I am left utterly stranded, and alone, in life and thought' (*CW* 28, 14). 'I feel the separation between me and the people around me, so bitterly, in the world of my own which they cannot enter' (*CW* 28, 146). 'I stand – so far as I can discern – alone in conviction, in hope, and in resolution, in the wilderness of this modern world' (*CW* 28, 425). As he tries almost single-handedly and single-mindedly to pull the modern world back on to the right track and make it see the error – the madness – of its ways, one can sense the growing anger and sense of futility as he despairs of ever getting any truth 'into the desperate, leathern-skinned, death-helmeted skull of this wretched England' (*CW* 28, 696). At times this spills over into nauseated vituperation and we have more of Timon than Lear – 'this festering mass of scum of the earth, and miserable coagulation of frog-spawn soaked in ditch-water' (*CW* 28, 427), etc. etc. At times he seems to sink back exhausted after another bout of futile '*verbal* hammering', no longer able to find adequate terms of abuse – 'I am bankrupt in terms of contempt' (*CW* 29, 429).

What Ruskin hoped for his letters he makes clear: 'they are a mosaic-work into which I can put a piece here and there as I find glass of the colour I want; what is as yet done being set, indeed, in patches, but not without design' (*CW* 27, 669) – this was to be exactly Pound's method, and hope ('not without design') in the *Cantos*. Ruskin's aspiration and endeavour was 'to bring the absolute truth out into pure crystalline structure' (*CW* 28, 650) but in truth a more waywardly organic metaphor was more suitable, as he realizes.

> A friend . . . remonstrated with me, the other day, on the desultory character of Fors; and pleaded with me for the writing of an arranged book instead. But he might as well plead with a birch-tree growing out of a crag, to arrange its boughs before hand. The winds and floods will arrange them according to their wild liking; all that the tree has to do, or can do, is to grow gaily, if it may be; sadly, if gaiety be impossible; and let the black jags and scars rend the rose-white of its trunk where Fors shall choose. (*CW* 28, 254)

Ruskin will, and can only, also write to his 'wild liking', allowing all the jags and scars to show. Yet even a tree will not really serve as a suitable metaphor for these letters, this writing. For this is writing continually threatening to get out of control, barely skirting chaos. In one letter, he starts to consider bees (what would a bee's chin look like, he wonders at one point), then he gets on to noses and the difference between an elephant's proboscis and a bird's beak (is the beak a nose?), then he starts thinking about why elephants don't build houses with their noses as birds do, and then he wonders . . . and then he thinks . . . and 'finally, I think I had better stop thinking' (*CW* 28, 278). One thing leads to a hundred others – 'I *must* try to keep to my business' (*CW* 29, 55) is a recurring cry and doomed resolve. Clearly he would have liked to be as he imagines Walter Scott to have been; he 'wrote in gladness the fast-coming fancies . . . with the same heavenly involuntariness in which a bird builds her nest' (*CW* 29, 265). But his mind was too tormented – too many 'jags and scars' – and one constantly feels that he senses the possible danger of yielding to an 'involuntariness' which might prove to be the reverse of heavenly. He keeps trying to 'keep to my one point' and keeps failing.

> Were I to yield, as I was wont in the first series of these letters, without scruple, to the eddies of thought which turned the main stream of my discourse into apparently irrelevant, and certainly unprogressive inlets, I should in this place proceed to show how true-love is inconsistent with railways, with joint-stock banks, with the landed interest, with parliamentary interest, with grouse shooting, with lawn tennis, with monthly magazines, spring fashions, and Christmas cards. (*CW* 29, 445)

He yields to the eddies even in the very act of trying to avoid them – to our great gain to be sure, but perhaps to his ultimate confusion. I think I had better stop thinking: the Beckett-like formulation enacts the impossibility of the self-cancelling resolve. That way madness lies – and of course, for Ruskin, that way madness lay.

Ruskin returned to Venice for brief visits in 1869 – the first time for seventeen years. During those visits he started looking at Carpaccio's paintings really seriously for the first time – particularly *The Dream of St Ursula*. He was back in Venice for three weeks in 1872, during which time he wrote about that painting in one of his *Fors* letters. By the time of his next visit in 1876–7, Rose La Touche – who of course had much to do with his obsession with St Ursula – had died (1875), and during the course of the winter of 1876 it seems that Ruskin experienced his first bout of unmistakable madness. During this period he wrote again about the St Ursula painting, in a very different vein. He made one last visit to Venice in 1888 after he had experienced a number of breakdowns, but the 1876–7 visit occasioned what was effectively his last writing involved with Venice. Contemporary Venice had become for him a place of ugly, raucous, soulless modernity – a noisy, distracting mess. It is perhaps apt that the first words he sets down on his return to Venice in 1872 depict a Venice that *prevents* writing, when previously it has served to inspire it: 'I can't write this morning, because of the accursed whistling of the dirty steam-engine of the omnibus for Lido, waiting at the quay of the Ducal Palace for the dirty population of Venice, which is now neither fish nor flesh, neither noble nor fisherman' (*CW* 27, 328). Interestingly enough, the first words he writes on his 1876 visit again refer to an impeded, rather than a facilitated, inscribing: 'I am weary this morning, with vainly trying to draw the Madonna – herb clustered on the capitals of St Mark's porch' (*CW* 28, 724). It is on this visit that Venice becomes a nightmare as his mind begins to tear:

> And little enough mind I have for any work, in this seventy-seventh year that's coming to our glorious century, wider than I could find in the compass of my cockle-shell. But alas! my prudent friends, little enough of all that I have a mind to may be permitted me. For this green tide that eddies by my theshold is full of floating corpses, and I must leave my dinner to bury them, since I cannot save; and put my cockle-shell in cap, and take my staff in hand, to seek an unencumbered shore. This green sea-tide! – yes, and if you knew it your black and sulphurous tides also – Yarrow, and Taviot, and Clyde, and the stream, for ever now drumly and dark as it rolls on its way, at the ford of Melrose. (*CW* 28, 757–8)

For Ruskin the unburied corpses – the European death of the nineteenth century – were everywhere and increasing, and he never was to find an 'unencumbered shore', unless he found it in that realm where thinking has torn itself beyond care and coherence.

Of Ruskin's two descriptions of the Carpaccio St Ursula, Jean Clegg rightly points out that the first offers a domestic Ursula while the second spiritualizes her, the change no doubt having a lot to do with the difference to Ruskin of Rose alive and Rose dead. Though, presciently or not, Ruskin had prematurely buried Ursula in his first (1872) account. 'The coverlid is scarlet, the white sheet folded half way back over it; the young girl lies straight, bending neither at waist or knee, the sheet rising and falling over her in a narrow unbroken wave, like the shape of the coverlid at the last sleep, when the turf scarcely rises.' But it is a temporary death – she had died into a dream. 'So dreams the princess, with blessed eyes, that need no earthly dawn. It is very pretty of Carpaccio to make her dream out the angel's dress so particularly, and notice the slashed sleeves; and to dream so little an angel – very nearly a doll angel – bringing her the branch of palm and message.' This is soothing nursery stuff – a princess dreaming of her dolls. This princess will wake and live. 'But the lovely characteristic of all is the evident delight of her continual life. Royal power over herself, and her happiness in flowers, her books, her sleeping and waking, her prayers, her dreams, her earth, her heaven' (*CW* 27, 344). In the troubled winter of 1876, however, Ruskin will kill her in good earnest. But before considering his revised interpretation of the painting it is worth noting how Ruskin uses his conjured image of the sleeping St Ursula to show up by contrast modern girlhood. In a way which anticipates many such passages in Henry James, Ruskin takes 'two American girls' and their conduct in Europe, to exemplify in extreme form the sort of femininity being produced by modern times. He sees them in a train travelling to Verona:

> And here they were, specimens of the utmost which the money and invention of the nineteenth century could produce in maidenhood, – children of its most progressive race, – enjoying the full advantages of political liberty, of enlightened philosophical education, of cheap pilfered literature, and of luxury at any cost. Whatever money, machinery, or freedom of thought could for these two children, had been done. No superstition has deceived, no restraint degraded them: – types, they could not but be, of maidenly wisdom and felicity, as conceived by the forwardest intellects of our time.
>
> And they were travelling through a district which, if any in the world, should touch the hearts and delight the eyes of young girls. Between Venice and Verona! What a princess's chamber, this, if these are princesses, and what dreams might they not dream, therein!
>
> But these two American girls were neither princesses, nor seers, nor dreamers. By infinite self-indulgence, they had reduced themselves simply to two pieces of white putty that could feel no pain. The flies and the dust stuck to them as clay, and they perceived, between Venice and Verona, nothing but the flies and the dust. They pulled down the blinds the moment they entered the carriage and then sprawled, and writhed, and tossed among the cushions of it, in vain contest, during the whole fifty miles, with every miserable sensation of bodily affliction that could make time intolerable . . . And so they went their way, with sealed eyes and tormented limbs, their numbered miles of pain.
>
> There are two states for you, in clearest opposition; Blessed, and Accursed. The happy industry, and eyes full of sacred imagination of things that are not, (such sweet cosa, e la fede,) and the tortured indolence, blind even to the things that are. (*CW* 27, 345–7)

One may well choose to believe that these two hapless and benighted American girls owe as much to Ruskin's need for 'clearest opposition' as to any historical railway encounter. They are more like constructs, compilations and assemblages of all that Ruskin loathes about the latter nineteenth century, quintessences of bad and horrid modernity. (Which is not to say that their recorded behaviour and deportment is either implausible or unrecognizable.)

They are also representative of a type that Ruskin was coming to dislike more and more. He came to Venice to dream princesses – and he kept seeing tourists. Although Venice had long attracted people on tours, travellers, even incurious pleasure-seekers, both the scale and the type of modern tourist were something new, and to Ruskin both symptomatic and ominous – another miasmic product of his ever-darkening times. From Ruskin's time on, a question will often arise to cause discomfort, anxiety and unease to the would-be serious visitor to Venice: when is a tourist not a tourist? Or: in coming to Venice can you be anything other than a tourist, or does 'tourism', irresistibly though uninvitedly, claim you for its own with all the contaminating homogenization it secretes, robbing you of the difference you hoped you came with?

It should be noted that, perhaps because he felt compelled to try to educate everybody, Ruskin provided his own kind of travel guides to Venice – to be sure, making them as offensive and insulting to the putative reader as he could. This unfinished fragment of a work, *St Mark's Rest*, is an unhappy dim echo of the major majestic work of his youth. Ruskin looks back at this earlier work and regrets that when he wrote it 'the old Protestant palsy still froze my heart, though my eyes ere unsealed' (*CW* 24, 278). In this work his heart is not in very good order and if it is not frozen the writing, comparatively, is. There are no exfoliating irradiations but rather impatient instructions, hectoring sermons, signs of a snappish temper – and periodic abuse aimed directly at the putative reader, invariably, for some reason, presumed to be cockney: 'Glib-tongued Cockney friend'; 'oh my civilised friend' (heavily ironic); 'congratulatory modern ambassador' (this also); 'You wretched little cast-iron gas-pipe of a Cockney that you are' (this not) (*CW* 24, 210, 216, 233, 279). There are gibes at Murray, and in some ways it may be seen as an anti-tourist-guidebook, certainly anti the tourists it so pessimistically and protestingly deigns to instruct and enlighten. But clearly Ruskin is writing this in a period of acute mental strain and distress, and for the most part it is, more than anything else, a sad document. As always with Ruskin, there are moments when the writing seems to break through into serenities of wonder and appreciation, and he is at his best here when he is transcribing his newly found delight in the work of Carpaccio, and how all the elements in his pictures come together in 'one music of moving peace' (*CW* 24, 369). 'Peace' was something which Ruskin would be seeking from now on with increasing desperation.

Contemporary Venice – and 'that mixed mess of dust and spittle with which modern progressive Venice anoints her marble pavements' (*CW* 24,

273) – clearly pained him even to madness. The Book of Venice (the city and its art) 'once lay open on the waves, miraculous, like St Cuthbert's book, – a golden legend of countless leaves: now, like Baruch's roll, it is being cut with the penknife, leaf by leaf, and consumed in the fire of the most brutish of fiends' (*CW* 24, 204). A reader may be forgiven for missing the reference to the story of the prophetic book of Baruch which is cut up and burnt by Jehudi, as told in Jeremiah 36 (as Cook and Wedderburn with their usual helpfulness inform us), but there is no mistaking Ruskin's sense of witnessing the despoliation of the text and texture of the City Beautiful. 'I only asked you to look at the fresco just now, because therein is seen the end of *my* Venice, – the Venice I have to tell you of. Yours, of the Grand Hotels and the Peninsular steamers, you may write the history of yourself' (*CW* 24, 234). Ruskin has written *his* Venice Book. He is desperately little inclined, one feels, to try to write another. Yet, even in this mood, the city can still inspire and provoke him to unexpected wonders of trope or figure – 'this amphibious city – this Phocaea, or sea-dog of towns, – looking with soft human eyes at you from the sand, Proteus himself latent in the salt-smelling skin of her' (*CW* 24, 263). Venice as seal; Venice as Proteus – what striking images for the seductive-elusive city which the ever-ambivalent Ruskin could never finally hold in any one fixed shape!

When Ruskin returns to consider Carpaccio in 1876 he is concerned with what he will call 'the Myth of Venice', of which Carpaccio is a supreme (Ruskin calls him) writer: 'His message is written in the Venetian manner, by painting the myths of the saints, in his own way' (*CW* 28, 732) – more succinctly, 'painting is the way Venetians write' (*CW* 27, 314). He concentrates on the myth 'because a great myth *can* only be written in the central time of a nation's power' (*CW* 28, 732). So if you want to find the power, as Ruskin invariably did, look for, and into, the crucial myth. Which for Ruskin now means, not Tintoretto or Veronese or Titian, but 'Carpaccio, or Angelico, and Dante, and Giotto, and Filippo Lippi, and Sandra Botticelli' (*CW* 28, 763) – above all, Carpaccio: 'This prophecy of Carpaccio's may be thought by you as the sweetest, *because* the truest, of all that Venice was born to utter' (*CW* 28, 732). Carpaccio, Ruskin points out, paints chiefly the stories of three saints St Jerome, St George and St Ursula. The first saint is 'a quite real one'; the second 'a very dimly real one' ('a very ghostly saint, – armour and all too light to sink a gondola'); but of the third he cannot find 'the slightest material trace. Under scholarly investigation, she vanishes utterly into the stars and the aether' (*CW* 28, 732) – another brightness, not yet fallen from the air.

> The whole of her utility is Immaterial – to us in England, immaterial, of late years, in every conceivable sense. But the strange thing is that Carpaccio paints, of the substantial and indisputable saint, only three

> small pictures; of the disputable saint, three more important ones; but of the entirely aerial saint, a splendid series, the chief labour of his life. The chief labour; – the chief rest, or play it seems also: *questionable in the extreme as to the temper of Faith in which it is done.* (*CW* 28, 734; my italics)

The stress on immaterial utility is part of Ruskin's lifelong battle against Mill's insistence on material utility. But there is something more interesting going on in this championing of immateriality, which we might crudely summarize as: less matter means more art. Before attempting to amplify this, I want to introduce a revealing assertion made by Ruskin in a much earlier letter (in fact the first he wrote after returning from his 1872 visit to Venice): 'it is fatally certain that whenever you begin to seek the real authority for legends, you will generally find that the ugly ones have good foundations, and the beautiful ones none. Be prepared for this; and remember that a lovely legend is all the more precious when it *has* no foundation' (*CW* 27, 357). St Ursula is all the more valuable, all the more to be cherished, because she is not even 'very dimly real' but 'entirely aerial'. Did Carpaccio *believe* in her and her legend, or *how* did he believe? Ruskin's answer is interesting in the extreme. Suppose he believed in them much as Shakespeare believed in fairies, and, like Shakespeare's *Midsummer Night's Dream*, *The Dream of St Ursula* was painted for 'popular amusement'. Ruskin is willing to go along with that: 'This play, this picture . . . were, both of them we will say, toys, for the English and Venetian people.' But Ruskin wants to go further than this.

> I am willing, however, for my own part, to take Carpaccio a step farther down in the moral scale still. Suppose that he painted this picture, not even to amuse his public – but to amuse himself! To a great extent I *know* that this is true. I know . . . that he painted this picture greatly to amuse himself, and had extreme delight in the doing of it; and if he did not actually believe that the princess and angels ever were, at least he heartily wished there had been such persons, and could be. Now this is the first step to real faith. There may never have been saints: there may be no angels. – there may be no God . . . Well: possibly there isn't; but, my good Sheffield friends, do you wish there was? (*CW* 28, 734–5)

Ruskin attempts to modify this very large concession – namely, that desire *is as good as* belief and may substitute for it – by saying that it is a matter of getting yourself in a 'state to fit you for being approached by the Spirits that you wish for', but he quickly realizes that this is a distinction without a difference, and, changing direction, says that there is no harm in longing for Aladdin's lamp while you are reading the *Arabian Nights*, even if you know that rubbing real lamps will get you, and your desire, nowhere. 'Well – concerning these Arabian nights of Venice and the Catholic Church. Carpaccio thinks, – "Oh, if there had but been such a Princess as this – if there could but be! At least I can paint one, and delight myself in the image of her."' (*CW* 28, 736). Such a notion of art as essentially a self-pleasuring activity comes close to suggesting auto-eroticism. It takes Ruskin, on his own terms, further down the moral scale than he can ever have imagined going. For this is to make art a substitute for the God, the angels, the princesses, the little girls who may not, may no longer, exist – precisely wish-fulfilment. Delight in the image of your desire. Venice has become an Arabian Nights in which you follow your wishes and make them come true by imagining, imaging, them. Surely the Venice of 'The Fall' could hardly have more wholeheartedly given itself over to self-gratification.

There is, of course, a major difference: Ruskin could scarcely be further from having sensual satisfaction in mind. He has come to bury St Ursula, not to bed her, or rather to bed her in her bier. When he now reads, or re-reads, Carpaccio's picture, a darker text reveals itself to his deeply searching, closely scrutinizing eyes. (He is literally closer to it, the authorities having taken it down to allow him minute inspection at his leisure.) 'Carpaccio begins his story with what the myth calls a dream' – as did Ruskin in 1872– 'But he wishes to tell you that it was no dream – but a vision; – that a real angel came, and was seen by Ursula's soul, when her mortal eyes were closed. "The Angel of the Lord," says the legend. What! – thinks Carpaccio; – to this little maid of fifteen, the angel that came to Moses and Joshua? Not so, but her own guardian angel.' It was an angel 'concerning her marriage. Shall not such an angel be crowned with light, and strew her chamber with lilies? But there is no glory, no gold. The angel's wings are colourless, the robes are gray.' Looking more closely, Ruskin decides that he is now carry-ing, not the palm branch and the scroll, but the martyr's palm, the fillet of victory and – something he could not see before tucked up in the hand and under the wrist – 'folds of shroud'. Ruskin made it quite clear what he now reads. 'He comes to her, "in the clear light of morning"; the Angel of Death.' Gone is 'the delight of her continual life': everything presages the 'divine rest' of a sanctified death. Material, materiality, carnality, our whole maculate condition have been blessedly renounced and transcended. She is all air, unscorched, untouched by the Cleopatran fire. 'For this is the first lesson which Carpaccio wrote in his Venetian words for the creatures of this restless world, – that Death is better than *their* life; and that no bridegroom rejoices over bride as they rejoice who marry not, nor are given in marriage, but are as the angels of God, in Heaven' (*CW* 28, 744–6). Ruskin is quite explicit in a footnote: St Ursula lying on her bed is indistinguishable from Ursula lying on her bier in a later picture. In her utter purity she was always already dead to this world. *This* is now the Myth of Venice. Venice has travelled a long way since he imagined the raising of those first stones.

Ruskin had one more important lesson to draw from Venice re-visited. In 1872 he encountered a sad-faced boy selling figs in front of the Ducal Palace – 'half-rotten figs, shaken down, untimely, by the midsummer storm' (*CW* 27, 36). It was, says Ruskin, a very impressive 'sign' to him, but he gave no further explanation until January 1877. It is important to remember that the Ducal Palace 'is the perfect type of such a building as should be made the seat of a civic government exercising all needful powers' (*CW* 29, 33). The poor lad could only sell his rotten figs there now 'because the Lords of Venice were fallen . . . because the laws of the greater Lords of Venice who *built* her palaces were disobeyed in his modern liberties.' He then quotes from some early sixteenth-century Venetian laws, starting: '19th June 1516 – "It is forbidden to all and sundry to sell bad fruits. Figs, especially, must not be kept in the shop from one day to another, on pain of fine twenty-five lire."' He gives more examples of 'these most wholesome ordinances of state'. Of course, Ruskin is pointing to what he sees as the superior mode of government of aristocratic Venice – 'Nor did the government once relax its insistence, or fail to carry its laws into effect, as long as there was a Duke of Venice.' Now the people are 'Free' and as a result it is impossible to buy fruit which is 'not *both* unripe and rotten'. What Ruskin is holding up for admiration – and emulation, if only in his Guild of St George – is 'the methods taken by the Duke and statesmen of Venice for the ordering of her merchandize, and the aid of her poor' (*CW* 29, 37–41). In a later letter Ruskin records his discovery of 'the first recorded words of Venice herself, on her Rialto – words of the ninth century inscribed on her first church, St James of the Rialto'. These words include '"Around this temple, let the merchant's law be just – his weights true, and his arguments guileless." These, so please you, are the first words of Venice to the mercantile world' (*CW* 29, 99). This letter also mentions that he has had occasion 'to declare again in its full breadth the great command against usury'. In letter LXXVII he again speaks out against 'modern usury' and vituperates and fulminates against his contemporaries – 'Your political cowardice is new, and your public rascality, and your blasphemy, and your equality, and your science of dirt' – and he embarks on his modern Decalogue: '"Thou shalt have any other God but me. Thou shalt worship every beastly imagination on earth and under it . . ."' (*CW* 29, 133–4), and so on. More than once he engages in a nauseous discharge against his usurious age, as for instance when he addresses a bishop who had apparently defended modern capitalism and asks him 'whether he consider usury a work of the Lord?' and vents his disgust at the 'loathsome fallacy and fatuity pervading every syllable of our modern life'.

With usura hath no man a house of good stone
each block cut smooth and well fitting
that design might cover their face,
with usura
hath no man a painted paradise on his church wall
harpes et luz . . .

with usura, sin against nature,
is thy bread ever more of stale rags
is thy bread dry as paper,
with no mountain wheat, no strong flour
WITH USURA
wool comes not to market
sheep bringeth no grain with usura
Usura is a murrain, usura
blunteth the needle of the maid's hand
and stoppeth the spinner's cunning. Pietro Lombardo
came not by usura
Duccio came not by usura
nor Pier della Franceca; Zuan Bellin' not by usura
nor was 'La Calunnia' painted.
Came not by usura Angelico; came not Ambrogio Praedis,
Came no church of cut stone signed: *Adamo me fecit.*[19]

Came not by usura Ruskin's Venice. There is continuity between Ruskin's economics and Pound's, which has been noticed.[20] Here I want to note a similarity of tone – a vehement loathing, at times in Ruskin deranged, at times in Pound demented; a disgust which, sometimes in Ruskin, often in Pound, becomes itself disgusting – provoked by the thought, the spectacle, the nightmare phantasmagoria of a society, a species, a world given over to usury and all that that implied. It took both men into madness. Both men tried to outline and articulate a notion of the good society, a new or – as they depicted it – restored ideal non-usurious culture, Pound following Ruskin back to medieval and early Renaissance Venice for exemplars of good governance. Attempts to literalize and concretize this ideal in the contemporary world led Ruskin to found the touchingly quixotic and harmlessly eccentric Guild of St George which amounted to little more than a personal club in which Ruskin could play at his version of feudalism. It led Pound to his appalling misreading and perverted embrace of fascism – and we know what, and to what effect, that played at. Both men were shattered into long terminal silences by a sense of failure and futility – Ruskin, as we have seen, because he felt he was a lone prophet crying in the wilderness who had exhausted a lifetime of energy and passion and caring and warning to absolutely no avail. ('I went mad . . . because nothing came to my work'; *CW* 29, 386.) With Pound this sense of failure was compounded by a belated recognition of his error – impossible to assess how heart-felt and mind-deep, since traces of self-justification keep filtering back – and a never abandoned conviction of the rightness of his aspirations and intentions.

> But the beauty is not the madness
> Tho' my errors and wrecks lie about me.
> And I am not a demigod,
> I cannot make it cohere.
> If love be not in the house there is nothing . . .
>
> i.e. it coheres all right
> even if my notes do not cohere.
> Many errors,
> a little rightness,
> to excuse his hell
> and my paradiso.
> And as to why they go wrong,
> thinking of rightness
> And as to who will copy this palimpsest? . . .
>
> To confess wrong without losing rightness:
> Charity I have had sometimes,
> I cannot make it flow thru.
> A little light, like a rushlight
> to lead me back to splendour.
>
> (canto CXVI)

I am not alone in finding these late lines both very moving and beautiful. Problems certainly remain. This same canto begins:

> Came Neptunus
> his mind leaping
> like dolphins,
> These concepts the human mind has attained.
> To make Cosmos –
> To achieve the possible –
> Muss., wrecked for an error,
> But the record
> the palimpsest –
> a little light
> in great darkness
>
> (canto CXVI)

It has been confirmed that Neptunus is Hitler, and it is utterly offensive and unacceptable to have that beautiful dolphin metaphor bestowed on the mind of such a man. No doubting who 'Muss' is, and to try to let him off the hook on which he was, as it were, finally and all too understandably impaled, by saying he was 'wrecked for an error', is so ludicrous that one does not know whether to laugh or weep. One begins to wonder just what exactly is this palimpsest, this record, which he is so worried about, and what those concepts are which the human mind – which human's mind? – has attained. There are no such ambiguities in Ruskin. Even his dottiest ideas – indeed, especially his dottiest ideas – are articulated with absolute if impatient clarity. And most of his ideas were quite the reverse of dotty. Even at his most intemperate and desperate Ruskin never begins to lose his way in the catastrophic manner of Pound.

But Ruskin could certainly have written and would surely have concurred with these lines by Pound, including the achingly sad lament they start with –

> M' amour, m'amour
> what do I love and
> where are you?
> That I lost my center
> fighting the world.
> The dreams clash
> and are shattered –
> and that I tried to make a paradiso
> terrestre.

– though he might not have felt the need to add the moving, contrite lines asking for absolution and remission which follow:

> Let the Gods forgive what I
> have made
> Let those I love try to forgive
> what I have made.

But the central aim which both men shared is perfectly expressed in the one line from these same 'Notes' (for canto CXVII and following):

> I have tried to write Paradise

Ruskin hoped that *Fors* would prove to be a mosaic – 'indeed, in patches, but not without design' – a 'pure crystalline structure' ('Crystal, we beseech thee' – Pound's addendum for canto C; but see chapter 6).[21] Yet the prevailing feeling is: 'this letter is all made up of scraps', 'I must construct my letters still . . . of swept-up fragments' (*CW* 28, 70, 90). Pound's aim was also a mosaic, a massive reconstitutive reassemblage of key cultural and historic – and economic – 'patches', which would finally crystallize, as it were; but he too found himself with an accumulation of fragments which he could not make cohere. Dante had written Paradise – that both men were intensely aware of. The question was, could things be brought together and resolved, transformed into such a coherent, concentric radiance, in their own times? Could a paradise be found to write? In life it would seem that Ruskin finally found an intimation of it with his own little personal St Ursula: 'I draw back to my own home, twenty years ago, permitted to thank heaven once more for the peace, and hope, and loveliness of it, and the Elysian walks with Joanie, and Paradisiacal with Rosie, under the peach-blossom branches by the little glittering stream which I had paved with crystal for them' (*CW* 35, 560). *There* was his crystal: paradise some remembered moments, some moments of memory. The Paradise he wrote was Venice – Venice revisited, rebuilt, reimagined. But, as we have seen, that Paradise kept turning into an Inferno. Ruskin only escaped from this purgatorial oscillation when Venice was stilled and distilled into Myth – a myth of peace and immateriality and death. Beyond desire.

Pound was also to ground his written paradise in Venice, but that is matter for another chapter. Having unbuilt and rebuilt Venice – 'I was never weary of building, *un*building . . . and rebuilding' (*CW* 35, 58) – Ruskin had finally put it to bed, under the summons of the Angel of Death. When he came to write his autobiography, as I said, he tried to diminish and relegate his much-loved city, as he covered his troubling wife in silence. He literally dispatches Venice to the margins of his life:

> I must here, in advance, tell the general reader there have been, in sum, three centres of my life's thought: Rouen, Geneva, and Pisa. All that I did at Venice was bye-work, because her history had been falsely written before, and not even by any of her own people understood; and because, in the world of painting, Tintoret was virtually unseen, Veronese unfelt, Carpaccio not so much as named, when I began to study them; something also was due to my love of gliding about in gondolas. (*CW* 35, 156)

But he could not, finally, reduce his relationship to Venice to a taste for gondola rides, and in a later passage (*CW* 35, 296) the repressed returns and, honourably, he gives himself the lie. He has touched on Venice again and suddenly finds himself compelled to insert:

> I find a sentence in my diary on 6th May, which seems inconsistent with what I have said of the centre of my work.
>
> 'Thank God I am here; it is the Paradise of cities.'

That is what he wrote.

4

Henry James: Perpetual Architecture, Perpetual Fluidity

HENRY James was walking in the piazzas or gliding down the canals of Venice in September 1869 when he was twenty-six. He had met Ruskin in London earlier that year, and he duly set about seeing Venice with Ruskin in his pocket. Venice was, to use a word he himself employed in another context, 'Ruskinized'. And although his relationship to Ruskin's Venice was nothing like so crucial and dramatic as Proust's, I think we can detect an arguably Ruskinian ambivalence in James's response to the city. It was, of course in many ways simply one of the riper fruits, the rarer and richer dishes, in that 'banquet of initiation' which was Europe for James. Europe was above all Italy, and Venice was 'perfectly *Italianissima*'. And James was like any other bemused and enraptured tourist – only, being James, superlatively so: *touristissimo.* We can tell from his first letters from Venice that he was much the 'Passionate Pilgrim' he was soon to inscribe in his fiction. From the start, Venice – or his response to it – is marked by excess. Excess and unreality. And sad decay. Irresistible and yet too much.

> I have received far more 'impressions' than I know what to do with. One needs a companion to help him to dispose of this troublesome baggage. Venice is quite the Venice of one's dreams, but it remains strangely the Venice of dreams, more than of any appreciable reality. The mind is bothered with a constant sense of the exceptional character of the city: you can't quite reconcile it with common civilization. It's awfully sad too in its inexorable decay.[1]

These are perhaps the first words penned by James about Venice, in a letter to John Le Farge written shortly after his arrival there in September 1869. In his first reactions and responses to the city which was to play such a crucial role in his fictional topography, James reveals initial apprehensions of mutual unassimilability – rather than drawing him in it seems to throw him back upon himself.

> This Italian tone of things which I then detected, lies richly on my soul and gathers increasing weight, but it lies as a cold and foreign mass – never to be absorbed and appropriated. The meaning of this superb image is that I shall never look at Italy – Venice, for instance – but from without. . . . Ruskin recommends the traveller to frequent and linger in a certain glorious room at the Ducal Palace where Paolo Veronese revels on the ceilings and Tintoret rages on the walls, because he 'nowhere else will enter so deeply into the heart of Venice'. But I feel as if I might sit there forever (as I sat there a long time this morning) and only feel more and more my inexorable yankeehood. (*L* I, 137)

However, in the course of this long letter to his brother William he seems to sense that this 'watery paradise' has probably had more and deeper effect on him than he can immediately realize: 'I'm curious to know how this enchanted fortnight will strike me, in memory eleven years hence – for althou' I've got absurdly used to it all, yet there is a palpable sub-current of deep delight' (*L* I, 142). To his sister Alice he conveys a sense of somehow not having done Venice justice:

> Yes, Venice too has become a figment of the past – she lies like a great dazzling spot of yellow paint on the backward patch of my destiny. Now that I behold her no more I feel sadly as if I had done her wrong – as if I had been cold and insensible – that my eyes scowled and blinked at her brightness and that with more of self-oblivion I might have known her better and loved her more. Wherever we go we carry with us this heavy burden of our personal consciousness and wherever we stop we open it over our heads like a great baleful cotton umbrella, to obstruct the prospect and obscure the light of heaven. Apparently it's in the nature of things. To come away vaguely dissatisfied with my Venetian sojourn is only one chapter in the lesson which this hardened old Europe is forever teaching – that you must rest content with the flimsiest knowledge of her treasures and the most superficial insight into her character. I feel sadly the lack of that intellectual outfit which is needful for seeing Italy properly and speaking of her words which shall be more than empty sounds – the lack of facts of all sort – chiefly historical and architectural. (*L* I, 145)

James is comparatively young – twenty-six. This is his first visit to Europe and he has only a few American tales to his credit. He was to discover his own way of absorbing and appropriating what he calls 'the aesthetic presence of the past' as he experienced it in Italy, and it would be a way which was not dependent on accumulations of facts; rather it sedulously and sinuously avoids and evades the factual as if in tacit deprecation of that kind of impersonal information. He learned how to yield to the seduction of Venice in such a way that it would provide him with tropes and topoi for what might be regarded as his finest work – *The Wings of the Dove.* What is notable here is his discovery of 'personal consciousness' as a 'baleful umbrella' which one may self-protectively open when faced with a range of new and rich sensations. A major Jamesian theme is here adumbrated – the endlessly various extents to which an inexperienced consciousness may put up the 'baleful umbrella', or may abandon it, when exposed to the bewildering and ambiguous accumulations of the past for which Venice may stand as superlatively representative. He also feels 'dissatisfied'; Venice makes him feel ignorant of history, of architecture – and doomed to the 'most superficial knowledge' of the character of the place. He is aware of a general intellectual and factual 'lack' which prevents him from 'speaking of her in words which shall be more than empty sounds'. Venice thus confronts him with his overall 'lack' – his ignorance and general inadmissibility; thrusts him back into his Americanness, and under the baleful umbrella of self-consciousness; and condemns him to 'empty' words. Venice is the most desirable aspect of the most desired object – Italy *Italianissima.* At the same time, it excludes as it eludes. To visit it was to be banished from it – back to Newport, to Yankeehood, encumbered with the 'troublesome baggage' of its unusable excess. He writes of 'transforming' the names of Italian towns like Venice 'into places'. But the place Venice resists his appropriation and transformation, and sends him on his way with only 'empty words'. But of course there was still and always that 'sub-current' throbbing in memory. This was, of course, very far from the last word James had to say about Venice – not, that is, his last Venetian word.

When James returned to America the following year (1870), he wrote his first piece of fiction deploying a scenario which he would virtually make his own – an impressionable young American girl encountering Europe for the first time. And James chose to set the story predominantly in Venice. 'Travelling Companions' is seemingly slight as a narrative, concerning as it does mainly the somewhat indecisive but finally successful courting of the American girl, Charlotte Evans, by the first-person narrator, who is a young American tourist undertaking, as James had just done, his first 'Italian pilgrimage'. The character analysis does not probe very deeply but it is interesting to see James feeling his way into how he might weave his feelings about art into a narrative – or weave a narrative out of his feelings about art. The story indeed opens with an evocation of a supreme work of Italian art, then in a state of complete decay, Leonardo's *Last Supper.* It is notable that a part of the pleasure for this young American aspirant artist is just 'the very completeness of its decay'. 'The mind finds a rare delight in filling each of its vacant spaces, effacing its rank defilement, and repairing, as far as possible, its rank disorder.'[2] To the extent that European art has receded into blankness and faded into defilement it perhaps opened up space for the creative – the re-creative – contribution of an American artist. Certainly one can sense James wanting to put himself into a position of relationship with the great art of the past, fading yet awesomely majestic and powerful in its ruin; and, I think, to draw from thence some grounding and legitimation for his own as yet inchoate sense of the possible mystery and seriousness of the work of art.

> One by one, out of the depths of their grim dismemberment, the figures trembled into meaning and life, and the vast, serious beauty of the work stood revealed. What is the ruling force of this magnificent design? Is it art? is it science? is it sentiment? is it knowledge? I am sure I can't say; but in moments of doubt and depression I find it of excellent use to recall the great picture with all possible distinctness. Of all the works of man's hands it is the least superficial. (*T* II, 172)[3]

This, I feel, is James rather than his character.

His character, Mr Brooke, duly follows Charlotte Evans to Venice, whither she is urged to go by her father, who is always in a hurry. It is, incidentally, interesting that James should have introduced another type of character in this story who is to recur in his fiction from the first novel to the last – the American retired businessman (often the father of the girl) who has been successful with American money and is somewhat suspicious and defensive when it comes to Europe and culture.

> The gentleman, who was obviously her father, bore the national stamp as plainly as she. A shrewd, firm, generous face, which told of many dealings with many men, of stocks and shares and current prices, – a face, moreover, in which there lingered the mellow afterglow of a sense of excellent claret. . . . Without taste, without culture or polish, he nevertheless produced an impression of substance of character, keenness in perception, and intensity in will, which effectually redeemed him from vulgarity . . . with his general expression of unchallenged security and practical aptitude and uncurious scorn of tradition, he impressed the beholder as a man of incontestable force. (*T* II, 173, 198)

Adam Verver is there from the start. The narrator purports to 'relish him vastly' but there is surely a slight shadow of the ominous about him as he sits drinking his absinthe and discoursing on the superiority of things American. And as he has the money he has the power. The Evanses stay at the Hotel Danielo, which is certainly a more luxurious hotel than the Europa, where Mr Brooke resides. Money matters do not loom in this story – at least among the visitors (there is a desperately poor Italian family with a dying daughter who pathetically persuade Mr Brooke to buy a supposed Correggio to alleviate their poverty: a sign surely of some narrative unease, even guilt, on the part of the American aesthetic pilgrims). But matters financial and sexual – of quite sordid power – will be inextricably intertwined with the Venetian scene when James returns to it for two of his major works. Mr Evans is not threatening; but he represents a world of cold, possibly ruthless, male American money and force which might be willing to buy Europe without ever deigning to appreciate it – those baleful umbrellas very firmly and massively up – and which casts a long shadow in James's fiction.

Mr Brooke makes his way to Venice, though his approach is not unclouded. 'As I hurried along in the train toward the briny cincture of Venice, my heart was heavy with the image of that sombre, dying Italian maiden' – the one he had seen in Vicenza. 'Her face haunted me. What fatal wrong had she suffered?' (*T* II, 191). He looks forward to, as it were, effacing this image in the company of his 'bright American friend'. Not much is made of this superimposition, but it is to me very suggestive that under the face of that rich American brightness lies suppressed or erased a counter-image of the ravaged face of an impoverished Italian dereliction. We are dealing with relatively simple strokes here, and the hidden face of grief and mortality – and a fatal wrong suffered – does not resurface or in any way disturb the relatively unobstructed progress of the two young people and their only slightly faltering love. American brightness prevails, and with the timely death of the always potentially obstructive father, the story can conclude with that rare phenomenon in James – a confident marriage of mutual love. But in later James work the sense of the image concealed by the image – a feeling for the thing behind the ostensible, beneath the profferred – becomes increasingly powerful and disturbing.

Of his first encounter with Venice Mr Brooke makes the usual disclaimers. 'I have no space to tell the story of my arrival in Venice and my first impressions', with customary deprecations about 'my feeble pen', the usual anxiety and sense of inadequacy of all post-Ruskin visitors to Venice. But there is a certain kind of instability in his approach to the city. 'I exhausted three gondoliers and saw all Venice in a passionate fury and haste. I wished to probe its fulness and learn at once the best – and the worst' (*T* II, 192). The worst, we might say, is that history comes to seem very large and he himself ludicrously small.

> I had left Europe. I was in the East. An overwhelming sadness of man's spiritual history took possession of my heart. The clustering

> picturesque shadows about me seemed to represent the darkness of a past from which he had slowly and painfully struggled. The great mosaic images, hideous, grotesque, inhuman, glimmered like the cruel spectres of early superstitions and terrors. There came over me, too, a poignant conviction of the ludicrous folly of the idle spirit of travel. How with Murray and an opera-glass it strolls and stares where omniscient angels stand diffident and sad! How trivial and superficial its imaginings! To this builded sepulchre and trembling hope and dread, this monument of mighty passions, I had wandered in search of pictorial effects. A vulgarity! Of course I remained, nevertheless, still curious of effects. (*T* II, 205–6)

The ontological displacement – or embarrassment – induced by the sheer spectacle of Venice constantly manifests itself in this uneasy oscillation between feeling a mere vulgar tourist and a none the less impassioned observer.

The best of Venice for Mr Brooke might be said to be the Tintoretto paintings. Tintoretto was to play an important part in James's developing notions of art and the artist, and there is a rich passage in the story in which Mr Brooke takes Charlotte, first, to see Tintoretto's *Crucifixion* (in San Cassiano). Here again we can see James finding terms for the kind of art which most moved him.

> Never, in the whole range of art, I imagine, has so powerful an effect been produced by means so simple and select; never has the intelligent choice of means to an effect been pursued with such a refinement of perception. . . . The reality of the picture is beyond all words: it is hard to say which is more impressive, the naked horror of the fact presented, or the sensible power of the artist. (*T* II, 205–6)

This last question is clearly of some moment for James and it recurs in a revealing exchange between the two of them as they look at the painting.

> 'What is it here' I asked 'that has moved you the most, the painter or the subject?'
>
> 'I suppose it's the subject. And you?'
>
> 'I'm afraid it's the painter.' (*T* II, 206)

The apologetic note indicates sufficiently that this would not have been a common answer at this time. It is the Ruskin problem again. What moves more? The subject – or the art with which it is depicted? James is already laying down a line which stresses the supreme importance of treatment – the actual production of effects, the processes and procedures, in a work of art – which in time will enable him to articulate a new conception of the obligations and priorities and enablements of the artist, in particular the novelist. He always regarded Tintoretto as exemplary.

After pondering the awesome and brutal 'reality' of this *Crucifixion*, Mr Brooke suggests that they at once proceed to the Ducal Palace to look at Veronese's *Rape of Europe* and the *Bacchus and Ariadne* by Tintoretto. To pass 'immediately' from a canvas depicting the most solemn moment of the Christian faith to two canvases portraying – celebrating – the sexual opportunism of the pagan Zeus and Dionysus might strike us as somewhat unseemly, a slight failure of taste. To hasten from an image of the male body crucified to images of the female body in a state (arguably) of erotic expectancy may indicate a felt need to escape from a too oppressively 'real' image of cruelty and death to images of 'unprotesting joy'; it may be – one hopes it isn't – a rather unsubtle move in Mr Brooke's courtship-by-pictures. Even if it is only a sign of the desperately indiscriminate assimilatory eclecticism of the tourist, it is hardly an innocent move. But innocent moves are hardly possible in this Venice in which the accumulated images are too numerous and dense, too contradictory and contiguous to allow of simple vision. Charlotte Evans, who may be presumed to have the famous innocent eye, indeed indicates her preference for the Tintoretto which offers a good deal more nakedness than the Veronese (in which 'the rosy-footed, pearl-encircled, nymph-flattered victim of a divine delusion rustles her lustrous satin against the ambrosial hide of bovine Jove'!). Mr Brooke thinks she is right, for the Tintoretto offers no 'shimmer of drapery' but only 'the shining purity and symmetry of deified human flesh' (*T* II, 206–7). This is a very different divinization of the flesh than that celebrated in the *Crucifixion* – eroticized flesh does indeed come at the spectator from all directions – and it is perhaps surprising that a young American girl should thus unblushingly be able to indicate her preference for it. It suggests that there is a way of regarding Venice and Venetian paintings which filters out the powerful sensual suggestiveness of the subject matter and looks only at the colour and the light. This could be both a self-protective (the 'baleful umbrella') and a self-deceptive vision, and James will return to it – in a very different and more perverse form – in *The Aspern Papers*.

Her stated preference clearly strikes Mr Brooke as propitious – he seems if anything over-responsive to the pagan scenes – and he suggests 'a long day on the lagoon, beyond sight of Venice'. It is as if he wants to take her beyond the crowded realm to make his own bid for what, eventually, will lead to sexual satisfaction. This separating out of Charlotte from Venice is necessary for another reason. At an earlier stage in their acquaintance he used to walk in the city alone. 'I wandered far; I penetrated deep, it seemed to me, into the heart of Venetian power . . . but on my return . . . I always found my sweet young countrywoman waiting to receive me' (*T* II, 197). It suggests, among other things, that the American girl with her 'positive maidenhood' is always waiting to save him from his dangerous errancy in the labyrinthine interior of the old seductress, the city. It is certainly a city that has lost its 'maidenhood' and, always, invites 'penetration'. But Venice and Charlotte start to merge for Mr Brooke – 'In my own mind, Charlotte Evans and Venice had played the game most effectively into each other's hands' (*T* II, 199). So, he goes on, if he had to paint her portrait he would situate her in a Venetian setting and if he had to do a sketch of Venice he would put her in it leaning from a window. There is clearly some reciprocal eroticization going on and one might surmise that the desire to 'penetrate' the one is becoming indistinguishable from the desire to penetrate the other.

Not that Mr Brooke strikes us, or himself, as a passionate man. Rather as is the case with an Arthur Hugh Clough figure, for him to wonder whether he is in love is immediately to question the reality, authenticity, sincerity of the feeling – perhaps 'I only wanted to talk of love' (*T* II, 29). His discourse of love to Charlotte is comically gauche and unconvincing and Charlotte is quite right to distrust and dismiss it. She sees that Venice has 'thrown you into a romantic state of mind' and that he is in love with a 'painted picture' (*T* II, 203). They make a little expedition to Padua and miss the last train back to Venice. This means they have to stay the night at the same hotel – horror! – and this in turn leaves Mr Brooke wondering whether Charlotte is now 'Compromised' and will have lost her 'reputation'. It will be seen that the appreciation of the ardours of the canvas does not carry over into real life. Quite the reverse in all probability; the repressive etiquettes and conventions of the day stimulating a displacement of affect into the permitted and regulated – and safe – relish of the painted images of sexual abandon. Mr Brooke conducts another Clough-like interior monologue about love and marriage, all hesitation, uncertainty, self-undermining – and self-emasculating – self-questioning. 'Was I or was I not in love? I was able to settle nothing. I wandered musingly further and further from the point' (*T* II, 214). And further and further from marriage.

'I felt that I was not possessed by a passion; perhaps I was incapable of passion.' The tentative concession is of course self-fulfilling and makes passional incapacity certain. After a subsequent attempt at proposal – a limp affair guaranteed not to succeed – he feels a 'sense of freedom and relief' and 'in my deepest heart I admitted the truth, the partial truth at least, of her assertion of the unreality of my love' (*T* II, 214, 219). After looking at the Giotto paintings in Padua, Charlotte says to him, 'Mr Brooke we ought to learn from all this to be *real*; real even as Giotto is *real*; to discriminate between genuine and factitious sentiment; between the substantial and the trivial; between the essential and the superfluous; sentiment and sentimentality' (*T* II, 210–11). (Clough was also worried about 'factitious sentiments' and whether he could be sure of having any that weren't.) The problem – and Venice makes the problem particularly acute, not only for James – is how to locate and recognize and be sure of the '*real*'. Tintoretto's

Crucifixion was real ('The reality of the picture is beyond all words'), and that is an artistic image housed within a city of art; Mr Brooke's self-inventing, self-erasing 'love' is 'unreal'. Perhaps the overwhelmingly authoritative reality of the former in part guarantees the self-doubting unreality of the latter. Who can be sure of their feelings? The wealth of congregated images, the image of the city itself – these serve to call into question the authenticity of the emotions they arouse. Notoriously Venice problematizes the locus of 'the real' – and '*le vrai*'.

Certainly Mr Brooke feels more moved – more aroused – by Charlotte the closer she is to a picture, the deeper she is in Venice. In the event he does marry her after the death of her father, though here again it takes a Venetian painting and memories of Venice to bring them together in a contractual kiss. The painting possibly wrongly entitled *Sacred and Profane Love*, glows with 'the true Venetian fire'. The presence of unambiguous sexuality on the canvas is made to do ambiguous work: 'Beside a low sculptured well sit two young and beautiful women: one richly clad, and full of mild dignity and repose; the other with unbound hair, naked, ungirdled by a great reverted mantle of Venetian purple, and radiant with the frankest physical sweetness and grace' (*T* II, 224). They agree that one stands for the love Charlotte denied and one for the love she now accepts but, collusively, they don't say which is which. Rather, they equivocate themselves into a kiss which, we learn, sealed their marriage. Either way, it seems fairly certain that, without the painted flesh of Titian's and Tintoretto's canvases, Mrs Brooke would have remained a lifelong bachelor. And indeed it is – as James seems to recognize – an unconvincing ending of the kind that he was not to repeat. Mr Brooke initiates a long line of males in James's fiction – up to and including Strether – who are, constitutionally and constitutively, not the marrying kind. What Mr Brooke is really in love with is Observation. When he arrives in Italy en route for Venice – 'Imagination, panting and exhausted, withdrew from the game; and Observation stepped into her place, trembling and glowing with open-eyed Desire' (*T* II, 175). The personification, the personal pronoun, the nature of the participles all arguably serve to feminize Observation and thus, perhaps, Mr Brooke – and thus, perhaps, Henry James. Passion has all run into the eye and the eye is trembling to be taken.

The stance and role of the observer figure – with all that it implies of refusal of participation and possible attendant sterilities – were to come under scrutiny by James, himself a supreme observer, throughout his work. And here at the start, with virtually his first American observer figure in Europe, he marks a possible anxiety and unease in the position. With Charlotte Mr Brooke visits a Catholic church and articulates a regret which has become more familiar in the more than one hundred years since the tale was written but which, I think, was fairly novel when James and Mr Brooke gave voice to it. '"What a real pity that we are not Catholics; that that dazzling monument is not something more to us than a mere splendid show! What a different thing this visiting to churches would be for us, if we occasionally felt the prompting to fall on our knees. I begin to grow ashamed of this perpetual attitude of bald curiosity"'. And of an Italian couple they see praying together he says, 'I keenly envied them.' 'Be they husband and wife, or lovers, or simply friends, we I think, are rather vulgar beside them' (*T* II, 208–9). The vague sense of guilt, and a compound of envy, nostalgia, cultural depletion and personal impoverishment, which can be aroused by treating the ethos, beliefs, rituals, even daily life, of others – other countries, other races, other religions – as mere spectacle; indeed, the latent dangers (of alienation for the observer, of reification for the observed) of the whole 'othering' process which can result from certain modes of vision or observation, have increasingly come to occupy the minds of Western writers (not only novelists of course – anthropologists, philosophers, sociologists, etc.), and in this relatively simple little scene and response James touches on a guilt and a regret which were to become more familiar to the Western mind in the years to come.

James had come to see the 'essential misery' that lies 'Behind the Picturesque' (*T* II, 183) as Ruskin so powerfully did – and was also registering some of the potential improprieties in the habit of privileged spectatorship. He was already becoming aware that the voluptuous figure of Observation, tremulous with desire, might degenerate into a habit of 'bald curiosity', might, indeed, not easily be distinguished from it if you stripped it of its self-protective Personification: and aware that the artist-observer could not always and never confidently be separated from the tourist-voyeur. Aware, too, that there was a possible shame and a possible vulgarity in the one shading into the other. In his first European tale which, appropriately, is a Venetian tale, James in fact touched on, adumbrated, glanced at, themes and subjects, preoccupations and problems and possible riches, which he would come back and back to in his subsequent writing. I do not think it is too much to say to suggest that James's important fiction starts in Venice. A final exchange from the two Americans – Mr Brooks speaks first:

> 'The reality of Venice seems to me to exceed all romance. It's romance enough simply to be here.'
>
> 'Yes; but how brief and transient a romance!'
>
> 'Well,' said I, 'we shall certainly cease to be here, but we shall never cease to have been here.' (*T* II, 194)

If Venice as a setting drops out of James's work for over twenty years – as being a romance in itself it might always threaten to dwarf or drain any 'romance' that was situated there – it is certainly true to say that, distinctly, he never ceased to have been there.

James reserves Venice as a setting for just two of his later fictions, for reasons which I think become clear, as I shall suggest later. But James returns to writing about Venice in a number of essays written between 1872 and 1902 – he never ceases to have been there and he returns and returns, more often in writing than in person. James maintained a fluctuant and ductile authorial presence, or persona, in his travel writing. He can be, or he can posit and hypothesise, 'the sentimental tourist', 'the cold-blooded stranger', 'the restless analyst', 'the brooding analyst', 'the passionate pilgrim', 'the shuddering pilgrim', 'the fond spectator', 'the hovering kindly critic'. 'Hovering' is what he mainly does in his Venetian essays; hovering, and looking, strolling, resting, floating, hanging – preferably over a balcony, his own preferred site and an increasingly important one in his fiction. The particular interest of his Venetian essays – apart from the intrinsic interest in watching him approach and reapproach the city, essaying different modes of 'possession' and 'appropriation' – is that they effectively span his writing career and offer illuminating supplements to his fiction. Thus the first essay follows soon after the completion of *Roderick Hudson* in 1872; the second is written shortly after the completion of *Portrait of a Lady* in 1882; the third follows the relative (commercial) failure of *The Tragic Muse*, when James realizes he will never produce successful novels of Balzacian realism, and his writing takes a turn (1892); the fourth comes close to the end of a decade of increasingly experimental, and in some ways increasingly dark, fiction and follows the completion of *The Awkward Age* in 1899; while the last comes shortly after he finished *The Wings of the Dove* in 1902. (These essays were collected with others and published by James in 1909 as *Italian Hours.* Being James, of course he could not resist the chance to amend and supplement his 'stammering notes of years before',[3] deprecating 'the scantness of such first-fruits of my sensibility' and occasionally offering 'to amplify it by other memories'.[4] However, he does let the stammering and the scantness stand, and if we look through the added refinements and ornamentations we can still read the James of years before.)

Of course James wishes to avoid the clichéd ruts of the genre, and increasingly he allows his imagination and memory to roam free and float wide and hang high over the city, promising to be 'systematically superficial' (and perhaps surfaces are all we have, all we can know) and referring to his 'devious discourse' (for what is the use of the blunt frontal assault?). It is notable that in his travel writings he recurrently inscribes his awareness of the latent superficiality and even cruelty of the mode, both the stance and the writing. As in an essay in 1877:

> To travel is, as it were, to go to the play, to attend a spectacle; and there is something heartless in stepping forth into foreign streets to feast on 'character' when character consists simply of the slightly different costume in which labour and want present themselves . . . half the time we are acclaiming the fine quality of the Italian smile the creature so constituted for physiognomic radiance may be in a sullen frenzy of impatience and pain. Our observation in a foreign land is extremely superficial, and our remarks are happily not addressed to the inhabitants themselves, who would be sure to exclaim upon the impudence of the fancy-picture. (*IH* 116)

I think he felt this particularly in Venice, where the discrepancy between the actual conditions of local contemporary life and the overall atmospheric beauty was so glaring. Indeed, it would seem that it is in all ways preferable (and more comfortable) not to animadvert on the local immediate conditions, and James seldom does – though his awareness of them is constantly breaking through. As he writes in his first essay on Venice in 1872:

> The light here is in fact a mighty magician and, with all respect to Titian, Veronese and Tintoret, the greatest artist of them all. You should see in places the material with which it deals – slimy brick, marble battered and befouled rags, dirt, decay. Sea and sky seem to meet half-way, to blend their tones into a soft iridescence, a lustrous compound of wave and cloud and a hundred nameless local reflections, and then to fling the clear tissue against every object of vision. (*IH* 212)

After Turner it was always possible to see the material Venice perpetually dissolving into the radiant indistinctness of water, air, and light, and I think it is this way of looking at Venice which dictates James's remarks that 'for my own part' the whole subject of Venice 'can't be too diffusely treated' (*IH* 54). (Compare his 1906 letter to Alvin Coburn, who was taking photographs to illustrate the collected edition of James's work, in which, after very detailed instructions of where to go and which buildings to photograph, he concludes: 'And do any other odd and interesting bit you can, that may serve for a short symbolized and generalized Venice in case everything else fails; preferring the noble and fine aspect, however, to the merely shabby and familiar' (*L* IV, 428). How a 'symbolized and generalized Venice' figures in his fiction I will be considering more closely.) Whatever else it does, 'diffusionism' takes the hard accusing edge off material squalor and manifest indigence.

But James does introduce a dark note near the end of the 1872 essay. He is describing, as he invariably does when writing about Venice, the extraordinary power of Tintoretto's paintings – 'he *felt*, pictorially, the great, beautiful, terrible spectacle of human life very much as Shakespeare felt it poetically' – and he animadverts on the terrible condition of the (then unrestored) main collection of Tintoretto's works in Venice: 'Nothing indeed can well be sadder than the great collection of Tintorets at San Rocco. Incurable blackness is settling fast upon all of them, and they frown at you across the sombre splendour of their great chambers like gaunt twilight phantoms of pictures' (*IH* 59). Shades of Ruskin on Turner's fading canvases. This sense of an 'incurable blackness' settling in the city is articulated again in the 1882 essay which again returns to San Rocco: 'It is not immortality that we breathe at the Scuola di San Rocco, but conscious reluctant mortality' (*IH* 22). However, he immediately passes from there to the Ducal Palace – and brightness fills the air.

> There is no brighter place in Venice. . . . The reflected sunshine plays up through the great windows from the glittering lagoon and shimmers and twinkles over gilded walls and ceilings. All the history of Venice, all its splendid stately past, glows around you in a strong sea-light. Every one here is magnificent, but the great Veronese is the most magnificent of all . . . the white colonnades sustain the richest canopies, under which the first gentlemen and ladies in the world both render homage and receive it. Their glorious garments rustle in the air of the sea and their sun-lighted faces are the very complexion of Venice. (*IH* 23)

With the brightness of the Ducal Palace juxtaposed with the darkness of San Rocco, James has already sketched out the lineaments of his great Venetian novel, *The Wings of the Dove.* For what Milly Theale will most desire will be, exactly, to emulate one of those first ladies in glorious garments in a re-created Veronese painting – rendering and receiving homage, all Venetian history glowing around her. But what, at some level, she is having to experience and live with – and from which there is finally no escape into art – is, indeed, 'conscious, reluctant mortality'. There could be no more accurate words to describe her fate, her doom.

Since Venice was 'Ruskinized' and since Ruskin had 'given up' Venice – with a vengeance – James has to come to terms with Ruskin's moralism (as Proust would have to do, though for him it was both a harder and a more crucial achievement). James maintains a continuous discrimination between Ruskin the matchless aesthetic appreciator and Ruskin the uncompromising ascetic judge, urbanely disengaging himself from the narrow-minded blight of the latter. As, in a later essay on Venice, having acknowledged the Ruskin who helped us all to 'enjoy' Venice he continues: 'he has indeed lately produced several aids to depression in the shape of certain little humorous – ill-humorous – pamphlets . . . which embody his latest reflections on the subject of our city and describe the latest atrocities perpetrated there'

(*IH* 2). Probably *St Mark's Rest.* This ironic distancing of himself from the Ruskin tone is particularly important in the context of Venice because 'it hasn't a genius for stiff moralism, and indeed makes few pretensions in that direction'. 'Fortunately,' he adds, 'one reacts against the Ruskin contagion' (*IH* 17, 2). But his most direct attack on, or confrontation with, Ruskin occurs in the 1877 essay on 'Italy Revisited'. There he expresses his dislike of Ruskin's 'personal ill-humour' and asks 'by what right this infernal votary of form pretended to run riot through a poor charmed *flâneur's* quiet contemplations'. Ruskin, he maintains, does not bear the test of being read in Italy, 'where art was spontaneous, joyous, irresponsible'. He unashamedly makes the hedonistic case. 'Art is the one corner of human life in which we may take our ease. To justify our presence there the only thing demanded of us is that we shall have felt the representational impulse' (*IH* 128–9). Here is his strongest denunication of Ruskin:

> as for Mr Ruskin's world being a place – his world of art – where we may take life easily, woe to the luckless mortal who enters it with any such disposition. Instead of a garden of delight, he finds a sort of assize court in perpetual session. Instead of a place in which human responsibilities are lightened and suspended, he finds a region governed by a mind of Draconian legislation. His responsibilities indeed are tenfold increased; the gulf between truth and error is for ever yawning at his feet; the pains and penalties of this same error are advertised, in apocalyptic terminology, upon a thousand sign-posts; and the rash intruder soon begins to look back with infinite longing to the lost paradise of the artless.

On the contrary, when it comes to art, 'A truce to all rigidities is the law of the place; the only thing absolute there is that some force and some charm have worked. . . . We are not under theological government' (*IH* 130). It is firmly – and fairly – said. But it is not quite the whole story. James was not – not by any means – wholly a *flâneur*, and, while 'the representational impulse' and 'force and charm' are indeed necessary conditions for Jamesian art, they are not really, thus unqualified or unsupplemented, sufficient. In 'Florentine Notes' he had recently written that 'on some days we ask but to be somewhat sensibly affected; on others, Ruskin-haunted, to be spiritually steadied'. The tone and phrasing clearly privilege the latter. On such Ruskin-haunted days, says James, he finds himself deeply appreciative of the paintings of Andrea del Sarto – for their 'unerring grace'; for their 'withdrawn sobriety'; 'and best of all, as well as rarest of all, an indescribable property of relatedness as to the moral world' (*IH* 289). We would hardly find a more felicitous phrase to describe an indispensable element of James's own art.

'It is a great pleasure to write the word' – thus James starts his most sustained and prolonged essay on 'Venice' in 1882. It is possible to think that for James there was by now more pleasure in writing the word, *writing* Venice, than visiting it. Undiffused, Venice still obtrudes its present poverty. 'The misery of Venice stands there for all to see – it is part of the spectacle. . . . The Venetian people have little to call their own – little more than the bare privilege of leading their lives in the most beautiful of towns. Their habitations are decayed; their taxes heavy; their pockets light; their opportunities few.' By way of reaction James seems to turn his anger on the 'herd of fellow-gazers', the tourists who swarm and 'infest' the city. It is as though these 'herds' – sometimes 'hordes' – are exhausting all possibility of individual response to the city: 'there is nothing left to discover or describe, and originality of attitude is completely impossible' (*IH* 1–5). Venice – as a city of the present – is all but obliterated. 'The barbarians are in full possession and you tremble for what they may do. You are reminded from the moment of your arrival that Venice scarcely exists any more as a city at all; that she exists only as a battered peep-show and bazaar' (*IH* 7). In the face of this present squalor and despoliation of the city disappearing under tourism, James writes himself his own Venice – Venice as woman, Venice as Venus as we might say, not an identity, to be sure, but, rather, a coercive lexical transformation.

> The creature varies like a woman, whom you know only when you know all the aspects of her beauty. She has high spirits or low, she is pale or red, grey or pink, cold or warm, fresh or wan, according to the weather or the hour. She is always interesting and almost always sad; but she has a thousand occasional graces and is always liable to happy accidents. You become extraordinarily fond of these things; you count upon them; they make part of your life. Tenderly fond you become; there is something indefinable in those depths of personal acquaintance that gradually establish themselves. The place seems to personify itself, to become human and sentient and conscious of your affection. You desire to embrace it, to caress it, to possess it; and finally a soft sense of possession grows up and your visit becomes a perpetual love affair. (*IH* 6–7)

In writing, *with* writing, he takes almost by force the city which would not let him or anyone in.

No other city – not Florence, nor Rome – is so fully feminized and frankly eroticized by James. And I think this eroticization surfaces at various points in the text.

> From the moment, of course, that you go into any Italian church for any purpose but to say your prayers or look at the ladies, you rank

> yourself among the trooping barbarians I just spoke of; you treat the place as an orifice in the peep-show. Still it is almost a spiritual function – or, at worst, an amorous one – to feed one's eyes on the molten colour that drops from the hollow vaults and thickens the air with its richness. (*IH* 10)

James is trying to mark a difference between his mode of being-in Venice and that of the barbarians. Yet he can scarcely do more than to project himself as a superior – and arguably more aroused – voyeur. The very phrases – 'look at the ladies . . . orifice in the peep-show . . . feed one's eyes' – suggest that the 'amorous' has decidedly absorbed, usurped, transformed and melted the 'spiritual function'. Or, in Venice, looking at ladies is a way, *the* way, of saying his prayers. To enter a church with that desire and intention is perhaps not so very different as treating the place as 'an orifice in the peep-show' – in the presence of imaginary ladies the phrase is suggestive enough. Sexuality is certainly in the air in Venice for James, even in his own boarding-house (he calls it an 'installation') where he finds the relationships between the occupants teasingly 'mysterious'. 'It was an interesting problem for instance to trace the subtle connection between the niece of the landlady and the occupancy of the fourth floor. Superficially it was none too visible' (*IH* 12) and, of course, the less superficially visible are the subtle connections between putative or potential lovers, the better James likes it.

The painting he finds most 'interesting' in Venice is by Sebastiano del Piombo and is in San Giovanni Crisostomo. It is not the patron saint but the 'worldly votaries' who arrest his attention. There are three ladies holding little white baskets. Two are in profile but the third turns her face to the spectator.

> This face and figure are almost unique among the beautiful things of Venice, and they leave the susceptible observer with the impression of having made, or rather having missed, a strange, a dangerous, but a most valuable acquaintance. The lady, who is superbly handsome, is the typical Venetian of the sixteenth century, and she remains for the mind the perfect flower of that society. She walks a goddess – as if she trod without sinking the waves of the Adriatic. It is impossible to conceive a more perfect expression of the aristocratic spirit either in its pride or in its benignity. This magnificent creature is so strong and secure that she is gentle, and so quiet that in comparison all minor assumptions of calmness suggest only a vulgar alarm. But for all this there are depths of possible disorder in her light-coloured eyes. (*IH* 26–7)

Was ever a painting of a woman so lovingly, so adoringly, so perceptively, so creatively looked at? James will hardly introduce a more memorable heroine than this. She is the quintessence of the lady; she is aristocratic; she is a sea-born goddess (as, of course, was Venus). She is strong; she is gentle. She is all woman, all women – goddess, queen, mother, lover. And she is also dangerous, strange – with 'depths of possible disorder' in her eyes. She is, exactly, all that a man could desire. She is 'unique among the beautiful things in Venice' – and she is a painting, a Venetian picture, a picture of Venice herself as James has rewritten her.

It is appropriate, even inevitable, that James should find his 'realest' Venice in a painted image, since in Venice 'art and life seem so interfused and, as it were, consanguineous. . . . All Venice was both model and painter, and life was so pictorial that art couldn't help becoming so' – this, some time before Oscar Wilde would maintain that nature imitated art. In James's fluent phrasing of it you can't tell the place from the art nor, really, which had originated the other, art and life becoming in Venice interchangeable terms. This is to occlude, of course, both the visible misery and the bestial barbarians, and James's dream of Venice – or dream-Venice – is one seen from what might called the gondola perspective; 'perpetual architecture above you and perpetual fluidity beneath' (*IH* 19–20). For the rest 'the magic name I have written above these pages' evokes 'little mental pictures' (*IH* 13) – a patch of green water, a girl on a bridge, an old pink wall, a glimpse of roses in a garden, a flight of slimy water-steps. 'It is very hot and still, the canal has a queer smell, and the whole place is enchanting.' This, if you like, is part of the diffusive or perhaps disintegrative vision; Venice decomposed into dream-like fragments. Indeed, in writing, no city seems to resist more the totalizing and synthesizing or analysing vision – or perhaps less invites it. The perpetual architecture is perpetually dissolving into the perpetual fluidity. It is the images that hold firm. The gondola perspective, and also the balcony perspective. This is where he concludes this essay – 'If you are happy you will find yourself . . . on a balcony that overhangs the Grand Canal.' It is late evening, with gondolas gleaming and lanterns mysteriously moving in the darkness. There is some serenading too. 'The serenading in particular is overdone; but on such a balcony as I speak of you needn't suffer from it, for in the apartment behind you – an accessible refuge – there is more good company, there are more cigarettes. If you are wise you will step back there presently.' It is an amiable, even intimate conclusion – drawing the reader into the scene and on to the balcony. Yet, just as stated, it is full of adumbrations. Standing or leaning on the balcony comes to be perhaps the most preferred coign of vantage – simply, the best place to be-in James's later work. At three critical moments in *The Ambassadors* Strether is seen on a balcony overlooking Paris – taking ocular and imaginative possession, and yet above it, and thus safely out of it. *The* Jamesian stance. As here, there is a balcony to hang over, but there is an 'accessible refuge'. Into which the wise presently step.

Venice next figures in James's fiction in an interestingly oblique relationship to the main narrative setting and action. It appears in a letter. James set about writing *The Princess Casamassima* during the years 1885–6. There was a good deal of social unrest and anxiety at the time, with Irish bomb attempts on the Houses of Parliament and the Tower. James was clearly trying to address the contemporary state of society in this novel, ostensibly about a revolutionary group in London. The protagonist of the novel is a young bookbinder with the name of Hyacinth Robinson. The illegitimate son of a dissolute aristocrat and an abused woman of the people who avenges herself on her seducer and dies for it, he is shown to be under the conflicting influences of his mixed blood. Himself suffering poverty and deprivation and intimate with the impoverished lives of the exploited, he is converted to the – always rather vague and shadowy – revolutionary cause. He even so far commits himself as to take an oath to assassinate some 'blatant humbug in a high place' (revolutionary socialism tends to blur into mere anarchy in James's novel – and probably his mind). One may question the chances – the plausibility – of a male character labouring under the name of 'Hyacinth' ever seeing a violent revolutionary act through, but he is given a famous speech denouncing the current state of society and warning of things to come:

> It's beyond anything I can say. Nothing of it appears above the surface; but there's an immense underworld people with a thousand forms of revolutionary passion and devotion. The manner in which it's organized is what astonished me. I knew that, or thought I knew it, in a general way, but the reality was a revelation. People go and come, buy and sell, and drink and dance, and make money and make love, and seem to know nothing and suspect nothing and think of nothing; and iniquities flourish, and the misery of half the world is prated about as a 'necessary evil' and generations rot away and starve in the midst of it, and day follows day, and everything is for the best in the best of possible worlds. All that's one half of it; the other half is that everything's doomed.[5]

As Barbara Melchiori has pointed out, these are hardly the words of an ardent young revolutionary socialist looking forward to the dawning of a new society. If anything he seems to share some of the fears articulated by the conservative press of the time. His commitment to revolution is tentative and precarious at best, and he is drawn to the Princess, not because of the radical ideas she plays with, but on account of the life of privilege and tasteful amenity she inevitably represents. Hyacinth's habitual tone is that of a yearning outsider whose desire is not to dismantle and destroy, but to gain admittance to, and enjoy, a social-aesthetic world from which he is, and knows he is, by origin, situation and definition, excluded. A small bequest enables him to take a trip to Europe before he has to commit his fatal deed, and there his disaffection and disassociation – emancipation as he might feel it – from revolutionary politics (from politics *tout court* really) is completed. It is articulated in a letter to the Princess written from Venice. The conversion to what we might call the 'perpetual architecture' of old Europe (which perforce entails an acceptance of the social and class architecture which it both supports and is supported by – no matter how much confessed injustice it produces and perpetuates) starts in Paris and is completed in Venice. The decision to relate the drastic shift of allegiances in a letter has certain obvious advantages for James, advantages which can be seen as evasions and avoidances and a very happy (for James) short-cut. The actual material life of contemporary Venice does not have to be engaged with.

Hyacinth writes as a Jamesian observer, and Venice once again is treated as spectacle – with both the 'visible misery' and the 'barbarian' tourists effectively elided, overlooked, absent. It becomes simply a site for felicitous aesthetic epiphanies: 'what ineffable impressions, what a revelation of the exquisite!' he writes. The letter continues like a James essay, a meandering itemization of charming fragments and glimpses. He notices the girls, the flowers, the leather curtains in the church doorways, the fountains, the brick tiles, and so on. Of course, James lends a certain air of naïve wonder to Hyacinth's tone but it is still very much the young Henry James in Venice. The impressions serve as a prelude – no doubt intended as part of an explanation and justification – to the fully articulated conversion or volte-face which follows:

> It's not that it [i.e. the 'sacred cause' to which he has committed himself] hasn't been there to see, for that is perhaps the clearest result of extending one's horizon – the sense, increasing as we go, that want and toil and suffering are the constant lot of the immense majority of the human race. I've found them everywhere and have not minded them. . . . What has struck me is the great achievements of which man has been capable in spite of them – the splendid accumulations of the happier few, to which doubtless the miserable many have also in their degree contributed. . . . I feel myself capable of fighting for them. . . . The monuments and treasurers of art, the great palaces and properties, the conquests of learning and taste, the general fabric of civilization as we know it, based if you will upon all the despotisms, the cruelties, the exclusions, the monopolies and the rapacities of the past, but thanks to which, all the same, the world is less of a 'bloody sell' and life more of a lark – our friend Hoffendahl seems to me to hold them too cheap and to wish to substitute for them something in

> which I can't somehow believe as I do in things with which the yearnings and the tears of generations have been mixed. You know how extraordinary I think our Hoffendahl – to speak only of him; but if there's one thing that's more clear about him than another, it's that he wouldn't have the least feeling for this incomparable, abominable old Venice. He would cut up the ceilings of the Veronese into strips, so that every one might have a little piece. I don't want every one to have a little piece of anything and I've a great horror of that kind of invidious jealousy which is at the bottom of the idea of distribution.[6]

At a stroke – or as many strokes of the pen required to write the letter – Hyacinth's disenchantment with, and disengagement from, any idea of revolution or change, indeed his enlistment in support of the status quo and privilege-kept-in-place, is enacted and completed. If you give up any idea of 'redistribution' you may as well give up on politics and commit yourself to the inertia of as-is. As Hyacinth very literally does when he commits suicide rather than go through with the assassination to which he pledged himself in his early enthusiasm for 'the sacred cause'.

Barbara Melchiori maintains that it is inherently implausible to have this aggrieved and deprived little Soho bookbinder write a letter from a completely conservative, bourgeois point of view in terms and with arguments suspiciously like James's own, and she goes on to point out that it is a deliberate misrepresentation to suggest that socialism entailed vandalism.[7] This seems to me right, but then Hyacinth as a character is implausible from start to finish, and James did well to avoid, in his subsequent fiction, trying to relate his critical insights into the *mores* and conduct of contemporary society to overt political involvement on the part of his characters. Whether unmediated politics in a novel can ever be anything other than Stendhal's pistol shot at a concert is a matter of argument, but James, seemingly unable to tell socialism from anarchism, was not the novelist calculated to succeed in the attempt. What is revealing in *The Princess Casamassima* is the use of Venice-as-spectacle as a site of total and terminal depoliticization. It could be James's last letter to himself and, effectively, it subverts the whole novel. After this letter there is simply nowhere for Hyacinth to go and, really, nothing for him to do. Except what, finally, he does. The letter is an only slightly premature suicide note.

James was very careful about the settings, the topography, of his fictions, so we should note that he deliberately changed the setting of *The Aspern Papers* from Florence, where the actual story he was told was set, to Venice. The story he was told concerned a Boston 'Shelley-worshipper' who learned that, improbably enough, a '*ci-devant* mistress' of Byron was still alive and living in Florence – and that, even more importantly, she had many 'interesting papers', including letters by Shelley and Byron. The American Shelley-worshipper formed a scheme to get hold of the papers by insinuating himself into the house of the old lady (and her niece) as a lodger. The old lady died, the niece offered him the papers if he would marry her, and he fled. What particularly struck James was 'the plot of the Shelley fanatic – his watchings and waitings – the way he *couvers* the treasure'.[8] *Couver* means to hatch or brood on, and by anglicizing the verb with an 's' James perhaps wants us to hear 'covets' and 'covers' as well. Be that as it may, his interest is clearly in the fanaticism, the monomania, the *plotting*. And he has moved this plotter to Venice, just as he will, in due course, bring those two great plotters, Kate Croy and Morton Densher, to Venice as well. What happens to plots in Venice might be said to be a concern of both works involving these characters. At the very least we can say that in both cases the plotting comes to – and leads to – grief.

In the Preface to *The Aspern Papers* which James wrote for the New York edition, he refers to this anecdote as a 'curious flower' thrown off 'in an out-of-the-way corner of the great garden of life' – an interesting image, given the importance of a real garden in the story, which, however, is rather vigorously, one might say ruthlessly, 'worked'. The Preface takes James back to Italy – not only its inexhaustible charm and appeal, but also its final unknowability, unencompassability, impenetrability. 'So, right and left, in Italy – before the great historic complexity at least – penetration fails; we scratch at the extensive surface, we meet the perfunctory smile, we hang about in the golden air.'[9] Penetration fails . . . *The Aspern Papers* is itself about an attempted violation which involves a failed penetration, and this by a narrator who not only scratches but vigorously 'rakes' the surface – not only literally of a garden, but metaphorically of the present, digging up the past as we say. How close this brings him to James himself we may have to consider. But certainly it is well to bear in mind the following expression of a sentiment, a pleasure.

> I delight in a palpable imaginable visitable past – in the nearer distances and the clearer mysteries, the marks and signs of a world we may reach over to us as by making a long arm we grasp an object at the other end of our own table. . . . That, to my imagination, is the past fragrant of all, or of almost all, the poetry of the thing outlived and lost and gone, and yet in which the precious element of closeness, telling so of connexions, but tasting so of differences, remains appreciable.

There is a touch of greed, a hint of transgression, in the image. Good manners draw a fairly firm, if invisible, limit within which it is permissible to reach out and help yourself at a meal, and the long arm stretched out to reach an object at the other end of the table surely goes well beyond it. It doesn't do to lean too heavily on James's often delightfully informal images; and, as Browning insists, a man's reach should outstretch his grasp anyway. The point here is that the story does raise the matter of how licit it is to reach for – rake for – a past which is indeed literally '*visitable*'. The dead poet's mistress is still alive, and her palace – at least – is 'penetrable'. James is curiously unforthcoming – or disingenuous – concerning why he moved the setting to Venice, and why he invented a 'great' American lyric poet for a period of American history which could not, remotely, boast of such a figure. He doesn't really go much beyond saying that 'it was a question, in fine, of covering one's tracks'.[10] We might be inclined, and feel permitted, to dig a little deeper. But it is time to consider the story itself.

James opted to invoke Venice as a significant – a constitutive – setting in only two of his major fictions, and in both works it serves as a site for two cardinal transgressions, and of profound and irreparable loss – the kind of loss which Browning seems to associate with Venice in the lines from 'A Toccata of Galuppi's':

> As for Venice and its people, merely born to bloom and drop,
> Here on earth they bore their fruitage, mirth and folly were the crop,
> What of soul was left, I wonder, when the kissing had to stop.[11]

In *The Wings of the Dove* the kissing most certainly starts and, as certainly, has to stop. In *The Aspern Papers* the kissing never starts, which, arguably, is just the trouble. Kissing is, perhaps, not of the essence – but a possible loss of soul is. What is true of both works is that, in them, Venice figures as the place where the *plotting* has to stop.

The Aspern Papers is recounted by a first-person narrator: this is rare in James, who deprecated and suspected what he called 'the fatal fluidity of personal revelation'. It is deployed, in his major fiction, most notably in *The Turn of the Screw* and *The Sacred Fount* – to which *The Aspern Papers* may, indeed, be compared. All three narrators are, to some extent or other – and the differences are of course crucial – mentally deranged or obsessed. The narrator of *The Aspern Papers* – editor, adulator, hagiographer of that great American poet, the late Jeffrey Aspern – gives his account of his ultimately frustrated, though exceedingly costly, attempt to get his hands on some hitherto unknown private writings of the poet in the possession of a now ancient ex-mistress, Juliana, who is sitting (brooding) on them in Venice (as it now is) in the company of her seemingly hapless and forlorn niece, Tita. By an inexorable law of first-person narratives, we have to make a distinction between the 'now' of the writing and the 'then' of the events being described. By a no less inexorable law we only know what the narrator tells us, only, we may say, have *his word* for how things were, so that we not only have to read what he writes, but read *him* as he is writing it. Is he confessing, redressing; revealing, concealing? Squaring the accounts or falsifying them? Making something good (a past mistake), making someone *bad* (his own past self)? Is it a self-justification or self-indictment? Do we infer an omission, do we intuit a falsification? Why is he writing anyway – to get something off his chest, or simply to get something on the page? Is this an expiation or merely a distraction. No definitive answers can, of course, be forthcoming; but such questions must be in our minds as we read his papers about the Papers.

The point of this preamble is that the narrator puts his earlier self, engaged in his Venetian plotting, in a very bad light (in the 1908 version which James, of course, revised, he puts himself in, marginally, a worse one). Do we give him credit for this – as, invariably, we do when someone owns up to, and specifically and judgementally names, his own misconduct? Or – as we sometimes also do – do we say that the seductive pleasures of indulged self-recrimination – ah, how *bad* I was! – should not too easily be allowed to do duty for self-exculpation? If it is *he* who demonstrates how ill he behaved *then* – and it can only *be* he – do we fee how well and maturely he is writing *now*? Or do we feel he is another Bourbon who has forgotten nothing and learned nothing? Again, no answers – it all depends, literally, on how you read him, and he has been read differently enough, goodness knows, by the critics over the years. But let us see how – by his own account – he was, and behaved, in that earlier Venice.

We can say at once that he does not see Venice as Henry James the travel-writer sees Venice. But then, he is not a traveller but a plotter. He has other fish to fry. Arguably, he scarcely sees Venice at all – at best, intermittently and with scanting attention. He says he 'adored the place' and is 'intensely fond' of it, and refers to its 'golden glow' (*T* VIII, 281). But his terms of approval are invariably equivocal (when they are not simply tourist-book clichés) and not infrequently mingled with deprecations. To refer to Venice as 'a city of exhibition' verges on the disparaging; 'characteristic Venetian shabbiness' is petulantly patronizing (*T* VIII, 279, 307). He talks of 'exquisite impressions', and there is one sentence about the Piazza which could, just about, find a place in one of James's essays. But more characteristically he remarks on the 'odour' of the canals; and while acknowledging, parenthetically, that '(the moonlight of Venice is famous)' he is more unparenthetically exercised at that moment of recall by the 'swarm of noxious insects' troubling him (*T* VIII, 311–12). He refers contemptuously to the 'invertebrate dialect' of Venice (*T* VIII, 318), while James speaks warmly of its 'delightful garrulous language' (*IH* 16). He views the garden of Juliana's palace with a kind of instrumental cynicism as he 'works' it as part of his scheme of insinuation; James himself, by contrast, is little short of ecstatic about the gardens of Venice – 'Of all the reflected and liquefied things in Venice ... I think the lapping water loves them most' (*IH* 43). He takes Tita on an expedition into the city and gives the too-long-sequestered woman some guidebook information before moving on to the serious business of 'the papers'. 'What had I come back to Venice for but to see them, to take them?' (*T* VIII, 370). Tunnel vision with a vengeance: no wonder that Venice in itself and for itself hovers vaguely at the extremest edge of his peripheral vision. Abroad in the city, he gets 'all but inextricably lost, as I did whenever I went out in Venice.' He is, his story serves fairly to bear out, lost in a more than topographical tangle. On one occasion he says that Tita's old-fashioned references seem to 'carry one back to the queer rococo Venice of Casanova' (*T* VIII, 319); in 1908 James doubled the irony and added 'and Goldoni'. Sexually active lover of women is very exactly what the narrator is not, and, unlike those of the first Venetian dramatist, his plots are neither comic, nor do they have happy endings. His last walk in Venice, after he has fled from Tita's effective proposal, brings him, brings us, an encounter with the great statue of Bartolommeo Colleoni, of which more later. It also brings him to a sense of Venice as 'an immense collective apartment' in which palaces and churches 'play the part of great divans of repose, tables of entertainment, expanses of decoration'. His, certainly, is *not* the Ruskinian eye. As for the inhabitants – well, 'the Venetian figures, moving to and fro against the battered scenery of their little houses of comedy, strike you as members of an endless dramatic troupe' (*T* VIII, 379). And, no doubt, like Juliana and her niece, 'untidy persons, with a low Italian standard' (*T* VIII, 299). Thank God I'm an American – clean, tidy, hygenic. And very male.

James has the narrator make himself out to be, to have been, a quite unashamed patriot and a tolerably crude misogynist. His phrase for poor Miss Tita is a 'piece of middle-aged female helplessness', while her aunt is, concisely, the 'old witch' (*T* VIII, 369, 378). To the extent that Venice figured for James always, as surpremely feminine, we may not be too surprised that the narrator deals with her fairly brusquely too, despite professed 'adoration' of, to me, a formulaic and unconvincing kind. And what of his favourite, revered poet? Jeffrey Aspern was 'not a woman's poet'; but women used to fling themselves at him – a 'pernicious fashion', comments the narrator, adding that Aspern strikes him as having been kinder to these tiresome women than 'in his place ... I should have been' (*T* VIII, 277–8). Not only was Aspern not a women's poet, he was an uncompromisingly American one. The narrator indeed regrets that Aspern 'had known Europe at all'. But, in the event, it did not matter. Europe had no effect on him: he proved to be impenetrably (irredeemably?) American. 'His own country after all had most of his life, and his muse, as they said at that time was essentially American. That was originally what I had loved him for: that at a period when our native land was nude and crude and provincial, when the famous "atmosphere" it is supposed to lack was not even missed' – no one more insistent on that 'lack' than James himself of course – 'when literature was lonely there and art and form almost impossible, he had found means to live and write like one of the first; to be free and general and not at all afraid; to feel, understand and express everything' (*T* VIII, 311). *Everything*? What kind of omnivorously inclusive, omni-porous poetry can this have been? Perhaps something like the poetry of Walt Whitman, a poet whom the younger James loudly despised, and the old James quietly adored? Certainly, Aspern has found in the narrator an ideal devotee or high priest (Aspern is his 'god') – crude, provincial and, if not exactly 'nude', fairly naked of real manners; devoid of, and blind to, true art and form, and necessarily lonely, since manifestly incapable of human relationships. We can begin, perhaps, to see what James was doing in making the changes to the original story he did. He is going to project an extreme version of his favourite American-in-Europe theme. Venice, of course, is art, the feminine, sexuality, but also style and manners, a habitable Veronese painting, the supreme site of the accumulated riches and amenities of European civilization. And into *this* city James is introducing an American in the grip of a 'fixed idea' or (1908) 'monomania' which makes him, self-avowedly, ruthless and predatory. In the process he displays a patriotism which is touched with crassness, and a misogyny tending to gracelessness. The irritated contempt with which he speaks of both Europe and women masks, one can only infer, a fear and incomprehension of both. On the one hand there will be the sequestered privacies of a precious past; on the other we will watch a very determined New World intruder who wants to 'rake' it up. There is the threat of a violation which might be also a desecration, a profanation. Only, finally, nothing happens. Except – just that. By which, rather Jamesianly perhaps, I mean that what happens *is* that nothing happens. The papers are burnt; the narrator has fled – Venice relinquished, Tita untouched. There has been a perverse exchange whereby passion has attached itself to paper, while woman has been treated as litter (we speak of a piece of paper; the narrator of a piece of female helplessness). The kissing does not stop because, perhaps perversely, it never started. And there is just a little soul left – or engendered – at the end.

The narrator is something more than open about his lack of scruple. There is a touch, almost, of boasting as he admits to 'hypocrisy', 'duplicity', 'ingratiating diplomatic arts' – because 'there's no baseness I wouldn't commit for Jeffrey Aspern's sake.' He 'sails under false colours', using a 'name that was not my own' (*T* VIII, 283) – not that we readers learn *either* name. His siege of and assault on the house of the women (on the women) has to be indirect, devious. 'If I should sound that note first I should certainly spoil the game. I can arrive at the papers only by putting her off her guard' (*T* VIII, 282). In 1908 that second sentence became: 'I can arrive at my spoils only by putting her off her guard': 'papers' become 'spoils' more than once in the revisions, just as 'documents' become the more generalized treasures of 'relics and tokens'. Of course, by the time of the revisions James had written *The Spoils of Poynton* and had become more interested in and aware of the many and various campaigns for different kinds of booty, loot and stolen treasure that are conducted at all levels of so-called civilized life. With his revisions James has come a fair way toward giving us a work which might, not inappropriately, be subtitled 'The Spoils of Venice'.

But the 'spoils' are spoilt; or, somewhere, there is a spoiling (in *The Spoils of Poynton* Mrs Gareth is 'despoiled of her humanity'). At the centre of the narrator's account there is a very imperfectly hidden display of a displacement of the sexual drive – from woman to paper. Banteringly, at the start, he announces to a Venetian acquaintance his willingness or plan to 'make love to the niece' (*T* VIII, 284) in order to procure the papers. In the event he both does and does not make love to her, and loses both woman *and* papers – and perhaps more. At one point he wishes that his servant, Pasquale, had fallen in love with the ladies' maid, or had 'taken her in aversion . . . but I afterwards learned that Pasquale's affections were fixed upon an object that made him heedless of other women' (*T* VIII, 304). Some projection here: the 'object' on which Pasquale's affections are fixed is another *woman*; it is the narrator who has fixed his affections upon an *object* which, exactly, makes him, in a deep sense, 'heedless of other' – of all – 'women'. Even as he, briefly, contemplates attaching himself to Tita, it is clear that if he could bring himself to 'take her' it would indeed be 'in aversion'. His whole account is full of erotic displacements. Somewhere in the very heart of the house, in a way *inside* the women guarding the secret treasure, are the papers and, in some way, he will have to penetrate both house and women to get at them. The hints could hardly be more sexually nuanced. Wondering where the papers might be hidden, his probing eye fixes on a 'tall old secretary'. He looks at it and notes with irritation its 'peevish little lock' (*T* VIII, 349) – he looks at it so hard that Tita (tighter?) blushes. When, later, he finds himself alone with the secretary, he sees that in addition to the lock there is a little 'button' on the lid and his 'theory' is that Tita has left the secretary 'unlocked' for him, and that 'the lid would probably move if I touched the button' (*T* VIII, 362). He reaches out and just 'touched the button with my hand' when he is caught in the act of, as it were, this foreplay by Tita's aunt, who, among other roles, would be the notional guardian of her niece's virginity. At an earlier point, the narrator had imagined the old woman dying and then 'I could seize her papers' (*T* VIII, 291). The 1908 narrator, laying himself somewhat more vigorously bare, says: 'I could pounce on her possessions and ransack her drawers.' It would be vulgar of me to suggest that throughout he reveals himself to be bent on ransacking the wrong kind of drawers, but it is a conclusion resisted only with difficulty.

The garden, which he so assiduously cultivates (with paid labour) in an effort both to woo and to mislead the two women, offers itself as a fairly obvious metonymic object. It is a 'blind' to mask his real desire and objective; raking up gardens is his way of both indicating and concealing the fact that he actually wants to 'rake up the past' – not grow flowers but purloin letters. Yet we can see it as another 'blind' as well. It may be masking from the narrator his own ambiguous sexual needs and desires. The garden stands for the papers – 'I must work the garden, I must work the garden' (*T* VIII, 284) – but it could also be a metonymy for Tita, or woman. That is to say that, while consciously it substitutes for the papers, unconsciously it could come to substitute for her. His semi – or pseudo-seduction of her takes place in the garden which is, indeed, a 'bower', but less of bliss and more of something that smacks of sexual exploitation and manipulation. It is certainly possible to gain the impression that unwittingly he desires a relationship with Tita, despite his reiterated aversion and distancing disavowals. On this reading we would then have to say that he can pursue his courtship of Tita by pretending to himself that he is only pretending. It is a dangerous game – devious, deviant. The garden in Venice thus becomes a site of displaced desire – misdirected drives, feelings gone wrong. It proves to be a rather barren garden – 'for a good many days unlimited litter was all my gardener had to show for his ministrations.' This is apt enough: if you, as it were, sow paper passions you might expect to reap litter. The narrator is using the wrong seed. And when the flowers do come they are perverted into weapons: 'I would bombard the citadel with roses. Their door would have to yield to the pressure when a mound of fragrance should be heaped against it' (*T* VIII, 307). This is comical enough, in all conscience; but to twist the amorous language of flowers into terms of military assault does, at least, suggest some confusion, or overdetermination, of motive.

Money also looms large – the literal meaning acquiring strong metaphorical portent. The narrator and Juliana talk constantly the language of money – rent, price, expense, spending: the narrator is very conscious of 'spending time and precious money'. While the narrator is mainly concerned with the question of the buying/selling of the papers, the whole financial discourse comes to centre on the unspoken matter of the buying/selling of Tita. In the event the narrator spends too much, overspends. And finally loses effectively everything. His sexual energy, like his money, has been misspent. At one point he talks to Tita of the 'pleasure' he would get from the papers for which he is spending so much ('too much' as Tita thinks), Tita comments: 'Oh, pleasure, pleasure – there's no pleasure in this house'. (*T* VIII, 303). No pleasure, because no love. When the narrator returns to the house after the death of Juliana – 'Tita Bordereau's countenance expressed unqualified pleasure in seeing her late aunt's lodger.' 'Unqualified pleasure' is now on offer. But the narrator's sexual drive has been perverted – 'spoilt' – and he flees back to a pleasureless life, leaving behind an (again) pleasureless house.

When Tita, after her aunt's death, directly (though with desperate modesty) offers him the papers if he will marry her, he recoils 'in aversion'. He flees. He upbraids and reproaches himself, denying to himself that he had made love to her, but making the important self-inculpating concession that 'I had unwittingly but none the less deplorably trifled.' Any attempts to credit the narrator with a growth of conscience must start from this remark. But his language remains commercial – he just cannot bring himself to 'pay the price'. 'I could not, for a bundle of tattered papers, marry a ridiculous, pathetic, provincial old woman' (*T* VIII, 377). One feels he regards Tita as being as tattered as he imagines the papers to be. Perhaps it's all turning to litter to his coarse and recoiling eye. (There is, incidentally, evidence in his determined negations that Tita might be, in fact, a potentially striking woman – large eyes, abundant hair, fine hands; perhaps he is 'fortifying' himself against desire.) He is refusing the one purchase which would, perhaps, *have* been 'worth the price'. He indeed refers to his 'literary concupiscence' (*T* VIII, 380) and how it has prevented his noting a change in Tita – and that seems about right inasmuch as it indicates some sense of the way in which his normal sexual instincts have been deformed or misdirected into a lascivious lust for paper. That phrase – 'literary concupiscence' – was changed in 1908 to 'stratagems and spoils'. This, as Adrian Poole notes in his excellent edition of the work,[12] is, consciously or not on the narrator's part, an allusion to crucial lines in *The Merchant of Venice*:

> The man that hath no music in himself,
> Nor is not moved with concord of sweet sounds,
> Is fit for treasons, stratagems, and spoils;
> The motions of his spirit are dull as night,
> And his affections dark as Erebus:
> Let no such man be trusted.
>
> (V. i. 83–8)

'Painfully pertinent' Poole calls these lines, and that seems about right, too. Pertinent for this latter-day would-be merchant in Venice – a foiled, spoiled merchant whose spiritual motions are dull indeed. Don't trust him.

What, in 1888, had been 'a preoccupation that was almost profane' (*T* VIII, 352) becomes in 1908 'an appetite well-nigh indecent' – which fairly dots the 'i' and crosses the 't'. Where a decent appetite might have taken him he is perhaps never to know. When, after running away from her 'heroic' offer, he does return to her, he now notes 'an extraordinary alteration in her' – which his 'literary concupiscence' had previously prevented him from noticing. She stands in front of him 'with a face of mildness bent upon me, and her look of forgiveness, of absolution made her angelic; she was younger; she was not a ridiculous old woman. This optical trick gave her a sort of phantasmagoric brightness.' This last sentence becomes, in 1908, 'This trick of her expression, this magic of her spirit, transfigured her.' Perhaps, in fact, he is actually seeing her for the first time. But note the terms – forgiveness, absolution, angelic, brightness, magic, spirit, transfiguration. To which we should add some more words which follow shortly – he registers her 'infinite gentleness' – 'now she had a force of soul – Miss Tita with a force of soul was a new conception – to smile at me in her humiliation' (*T* VIII, 380–1) ('abjection' in 1908). 'What of soul was left . . .' – well, this much at least. 'Soul' is a 'new conception' to the narrator because his discourse has been relentlessly materialist – instrumental, appropriative. All the words I have emphasized, from 'abjection' to 'transfiguration', and taking in 'absolution', 'infinite' and 'spirit' along with 'mildness' and 'gentleness', are of course religious terms; more specifically, they refer us to Christian virtues, values and beliefs (or hopes). It opens up a new dimension – what, in *The Spoils of Poynton*, Fleda Vetch calls 'a fourth dimension'. Call it the 'spiritual'. Call it, if you prefer, 'magic'. A year after *The Spoils of Poynton* James published *The Two Magics* (1898), which consisted of *The Turn of the Screw* and *Covering End* – black and white magic, with (arguably) a woman who kills and a woman who saves. The 'magic of her spirit transfigured her' – it is what happens to Tita in Venice, it is what happens to and through Milly Theale, also in Venice, in *The Wings of the Dove*, where there is a late, indeed posthumous, attempt of the spiritual somehow to supersede and supplant the merely material-sexual. Brightness falls from the air.

But the narrator glimpses, perceives, Tita's 'phantasmagoric brightness' and/or 'the magic of her spirit' (1908 simply spells out 1888 in another way) only very briefly. Early on, he recalls a previous conviction that Tita was 'deeply futile, because her inefficiency was spiritual' (*T* VIII, 279). It is an odd formulation because we do not usually think of the 'spiritual' in terms of degrees of 'efficiency' – though I suppose an American pragmatist might. In 1908 James changed 'spiritual' to 'inward'. Either way, any 'inefficiencies', spiritual or inward, on display in this narrative are unmistakably the narrator's. One might say that we only discern this because he makes it clear to us, and that, inasmuch as he does so, the exposure is, at least, admirable. But what of soul is left? interestingly, in 1888 only Tita is, speculatively, invested with a 'force of soul' – and that is the sole use of the word. But in 1908 James doubles up on the usage and gives the narrator a soul as well; so that when the slow-to-bloom garden is giving him a trying time in 1888 'I composed myself' (*T* VIII, 308). As any half-way reasonable plotter would. But in 1908 this becomes 'I possessed my soul', which is perhaps even a little portentous for a restless editor (no born horticulturist he) waiting for the confounded flowers to come out. But by the very disproportionateness of the phrase to the context James is surely signalling that, if *that* is what he thinks he possesses, he can have precious little true soul – either to have or to lose. He has not yet seen Tita transfigured, radiating an entirely unforeseen brightness.

Under the spell of that brief brightness, the narrator even begins to think over her proposal – 'Why not, after all – why not?' But when she tells him that she has destroyed the papers (they are 'burnt' in the night, like 'the old things' of Poynton) then 'a real darkness for a moment descended upon my eyes.' After the moment of glimpsed brightness – a moment which has everything to do with sacrifice and absolution – the darkness descends, or is it *re*descends? Tita shrinks again to battered tatters: 'the transfiguration was over and she had changed back to a plain, dingy, elderly person.' Which was the 'true' vison of Tita? We – and he – can never know. But, either way, whatever she might have possessed of value, beauty, desirability (perceived or in the eyes of the perceiver – who, ever, knows which?), all vanishes for the narrator with the papers. I am simply suggesting that the perverse confusion of the papers with the woman – and what I want to call the soul-destroying subordination of the latter to the former – is with the narrator to the end, despite whatever agitations of conscience break through. The last sentence inadvertently – though twenty years later with growing advertence – confesses this. He reveals the fact that he has sent Tita a large sum of money for the portrait of Jeffrey Aspern which he did manage to take away from Venice – the sum of his 'spoils'. Perhaps this was guilt money. Whatever, he pretends to Tita that he has sold the portrait and thus raised the money. In fact he has kept it and it is still, at the time of writing, hanging above his writing-table. This is certainly fitting. Aspern ('not a woman's poet'), the tutelary 'divinity' (he is the narrator's 'god'), supervising his papery, bachelor and thus sterile abode: the portrait of a dead writer instead, perhaps, of the body of a live woman – a bad exchange, a poor purchase for which he paid 'too much'. He concludes in 1888 – he is referring to the portrait – 'When I look at it my chagrin at the loss of the letters becomes almost intolerable' (*T* VIII, 381–2). In 1908, a wobbling doubt is surfacing: 'When I look at it I can scarcely bear my loss – I mean of the precious papers.' The inserted hesitation, the introduced pause of uncertainty, speaks, as we say, volumes. What else *might* he have meant, apart from the papers? He now seems to be suppressing an incipient awareness of another, a greater, loss. It is not, clearly, the money. We are bound to feel that it is, perhaps, Tita – whom he, apart from a magic moment, scarcely saw, just as, I maintain, he scarcely sees Venice – 'the magical name' (*IH* 13). No magics for this narrator. He has 'lost' Tita, the old but perhaps still-beautiful woman, just as he has relinquished Venice, the old, but certainly still-beautiful city – both beautiful if you have unplotting eyes to see them. This is the loss beneath the loss; the loss the narrator dare not name yet somehow seems to sense while refusing to know. It is indeed scarcely bearable, 'intolerable'. And the loss beneath the loss beneath the loss may be even greater. What of soul was left? In the case of this narrator we can give no very confident answer.

Wondering how to address himself to Tita after he has gracelessly fled from her, and seeking to 'exclude brutal solutions', he walks blindly around Venice until he has perhaps his most vivid and arresting encounter with a feature of the city.

> I only know that in the afternoon, when the air was aglow with the sunset, I was standing before the church of Saints John and Paul and looking up at the small square-jawed face of Bartolommeo Colleoni, the terrible *condottiere* who sits so sturdily astride of his huge bronze horse, on the high pedestal on which Venetian gratitude maintains him. The statue is incomparable, the finest of all mounted figures, unless that of Marcus Aurelius, who rides benignant before the Roman capitol, be finer: but I was not thinking of that; I only found myself staring at the triumphant captain as if he had an oracle on his lips. The western light shines into all his grimness at that hour and makes it wonderfully personal. But he continued to look far over my head, at the red immersion of another day – he had seen so many go down into the lagoon through the centuries – and if he were thinking of battles and stratagems they were of a different quality from any I had to tell him of. He could not direct me what to do, gaze up at him as I might. (*T* VIII, 378)

Bartolommeo was a particularly ruthless mercenary and you may be sure that *he* never excluded 'brutal solutions'. As Adrian Poole notes,[13] his emblem was a pair of *coqlioni* (testicles) and these, one might fairly say, are what the narrator so signally lacks, if only metaphorically speaking. He will neither be 'brutal' in the all too virile manner of Bartolommeo, but he certainly has not learned any 'benignity' from the figure of Marcus Aurelius either. He can only look dumbly and unemulatingly up to his more manly, illustrious predecessors. But, in a necessarily more contracted manner, he *has* been plotting and following 'battles and stratagems', and one might feel that in his own way and on his own territory – battles of the drawing-room – he has, in all conscience or rather consciencelessness, been brutal enough. 'Civilized' brutality is to return to the Venetian air in *The Wings of the Dove* as well.

When Tita makes her desperate and direct proposal to him, he records that he hoped, at that moment, that 'though my face showed the greatest embarrassment that was ever painted on a human countenance it was not set as stone.' Medusa is not named, but it is two female 'looks' which definitively unman him. His last memory of Tita is just this – 'she paused long enough to give me one look. I have never forgotten it' (*T* VIII, 382). But it is Juliana who effectively stares him into ashamed impotence. There are many references to the 'horrible green shade' which perpetually covers her reputedly once marvellous eyes. At the same time, she tells the narrator, '"I want to watch you – I want to watch you!"' (*T* VIII, 348). Given what he has in mind he will, from her point of view, certainly bear some watching. And of course it is Juliana who catches him in the nocturnal act which is, in effect, the climax of his campaign – touching the button if not actually ransacking the drawers. 'Miss Bordereau stood there in her nightdress, in the doorway of her room, watching me; her hands were raised, she had lifted the everlasting curtain that covered half her face, and for the first, the last, the only time I beheld her extraordinary eyes. They glared at me, they made me horribly ashamed' (*T* VIII, 362). That last sentence becomes, in 1908, 'They glared at me; they were like the sudden drench, for a caught burglar, of a flood of gaslight; they made me horribly ashamed.' Fair cop, indeed. But it is the sense of the shaming power of the female gaze, or glare, I wish to stress. If he was not emasculated before this moment, he surely is, definitively, now.

Juliana utters only one reproach to the caught burglar: '"Ah, you publishing scoundrel"' (*T* VIII, 363). But this concisely points to one of the most important issues raised by this story, an issue which is squarely concerned with matters of privacy and sexuality – rummaging for secrets, ransacking drawers. Here is a crucial exchange between Juliana and the narrator – she has, perhaps, begun to rumble his game; he has, tentatively, begun to come into the open. She speaks first:

> 'Do you think it's right to rake up the past?'
>
> 'I don't know that I know what you mean by raking it up; but how can we get at it unless we dig a little? The present has such a rough way of treading it down.'
>
> 'Oh, I like the past, but I don't like critics,' the old woman declared, with her fine tranquillity.
>
> 'Neither do I, but I like their discoveries.'
>
> 'Aren't they mostly lies?'
>
> 'The lies are what they sometimes discover,' I said, smiling at the quiet impertinence of this. 'They often lay bare the truth.'
>
> 'The truth is God's, it isn't man's; we had better leave it alone. Who can judge of it – who can say?'
>
> 'We are terribly in the dark, I know,' I admitted; 'but if we give up trying what becomes of all the fine things?' (*T* VIII, 341)

The fine things – the old things: in this exchange James is, in fact, standing very close to his narrator.

Here I must digress a little. All his life James deprecated, when he did not simply detest, 'publishing scoundrels' – in the form, particularly, of journalism making its quite unabashed inroads and encroachments into and on to 'private life'. You can see this in *The Bostonians* and *The Reverberator* but also everywhere in his notebooks and letters. At the same time, if the journalists were inquiring a good deal too curiously into what was none of their business, the novelists had, markedly, not been inquiring curiously enough into what, most surely, should be *their* business. Thus James, in 1899 ('The Future of the Novel') writing about what had happened to the nineteenth-century novel:

> There came into being a mistrust of any but the most guarded treatment of the great relation between men and women, the constant world-renewal, which was the conspicuous sign that whatever the prose picture of life was prepared to take upon itself, it was not prepared to take upon itself not to be superficial. Its position became very much: 'There are other things, don't you know? For heaven's sake let that one pass!' And to this wonderful propriety of letting it pass the business has been for these so many years . . . largely devoted . . . there is an immense omission in our fiction.[14]

Particularly in his later works, James did what he could to repair that omission, in his own often elliptical way. But joining these two complaints together we can, very crudely, summarize by saying that James felt that in one kind of writing (mainly journalism) there was too much interest in, particularly, the 'constant world-renewal' (one of his code phrases for sex) and related private matters in the lives of prominent (or indeed not so prominent) people; while in fiction there was all too little attention paid to those aspects of the lives of the fictional characters.

In 1896, an article James had written for *Century Magazine* was returned to him because it had shocked the editor's prudery. It immediately gave James an idea for an 'illustrative little action', as he jotted down in his notebook: a 'little action illustrative of the whole loathsomely prurient and humbugging business'.

> One must figure out a little story in which that bétise is presented. There must be the opposition – embodied in 2 young men, the serious, intelligent youth who, à propos of a defunct great, fine, author, makes an admirable little study or statement; and the other fellow who, canny, knowing, vulgar, having the instinct of journalistic vulgarity, doesn't say a valuable thing, but goes in for superficial gossip and twaddle. (*N* 155)

This became, in 1898, his story, 'John Delavoy'. The narrator is a version of the first of the two young men James envisaged. The great writer, John Delavoy, has recently died. He was, fortunate man, 'the most unadvertised, unreported, uninterviewed, unphotographed, uncriticized of all originals. Was he not the man of the time about whose private life we delightfully knew least?' (*T* IX, 405). The narrator writes an appreciative article on the great writer's work which he submits to an editor – a version of the second young man. He is a successful editor of a popular magazine and at first he accepts the article – unread. He wants something on the great man. When he does read it, he is shocked and rejects it as quite unprintable. Clearly, John Delavoy was a writer who *did* explore 'the great relation between men and women', and the editor wants none of that in *his* magazine. '"You're not writing in *The Cynosure* about the relations of the sexes. With those relations, with the questions of sex in any degree, I should have supposed you would already have seen that we have nothing whatever to do. If you want to know what our public won't stand, there you have it"' (*T* IX, 424). What he wanted was, exactly, 'superficial gossip and twaddle' about the private life of the author. John Delavoy's *work* is '"the sort of thing that's out of our purview!"' The narrator has to content himself with an exclamation which contains incredulity, and something more. '"Wonderful, wonderful purview!" I quite sincerely, or at all events very musingly, exclaimed' (*T* IX, 438).

So much is clear enough, and to the extent that the narrator of *The Aspern Papers*, another editor, desperately wants to find out details about Aspern's private *life* as opposed to evaluating his *work*, he must share in the reprobation meted out unequivocally to the editor in 'John Delavoy'. However, to be fair, we must replace 'as opposed to' with 'in addition to' – he clearly, rightly or wrongly, highly esteems the work as well. And here we approach the problem, both in James, and for James. In 1909 James was involved in looking over some letters – papers, we might say given the context – of Byron, concerning his relationship with his half-sister, Augusta Leigh. There is a famous account by John Buchan – also involved in considering the letters – of their different reactions to some of the things revealed in the letters. They nearly made Buchan sick, but 'my colleague never turned a hair.' If they came across some 'special vileness' James would say '"Nauseating perhaps, but how quite inexpressibly significant"' (*T* IX, III note). James was clearly deeply fascinated by the revelations which could be afforded by what he could conceivably have indicted as scoundrelly publishing.

The matter comes to a head over the case of George Sand. Between 1868 and 1914 James wrote eight pieces concerning George Sand. He wrote about her more often that he wrote about any other novelist, and quantitatively only Balzac and Hawthorne have, marginally, more space given to them (and, in Hawthorne's case, only because of a comissioned book).

What so fascinated James about George Sand is scarcely far to seek – 'George Sand lived her remarkable life and drove her perpetual pen.'[15] *How*, how on earth, did she manage to write so much ***and***, at the *same time*, participate so perpetually in the 'constant world-renewal'? How much of wonder, envy, fascination and sheer prurient fantasizing might have been involved in James's lifelong obsession with the figure, the example, of George Sand is hardly to be pondered. The point here is that most of the pieces James wrote about her were consequent and ensuant on the publication, after her death, of more and more documents – papers – concerning her life; her life of loving and her life of writing. Published by scoundrels? The matter is not so simple.

In 1912, reviewing yet another volume, based on documents, on George Sand's life and work, James commends the author and his pages for representing 'quite the high-water mark of patience and persistence, of the ideal biographic curiosity'.[16] But what is the *ideal* biographic curiosity? Did the narrator of *The Aspern Papers* have it? He certainly had 'patience and persistence'. And what about this image from a little later in the review? James refers to 'the figure now shown us, blazed upon to the last intensity by the lamplight of investigation, and with the rank oil consumed in the process fairly filling the air'.[17] By a curious inversion, the hapless victim of the 'investigating' powers has become a figure reminiscent of the 'caught burglar', which makes the delving editor some sort of authorized policeman. But that cannot be right either.

An earlier essay on George Sand (1897, around the time James was writing 'John Delavoy') faces the issue squarely when James defines 'the greatest of literary quarrels' – 'the quarrel beside which all others are mild and arrangeable, the eternal dispute between the public and the private, between curiosity and delicacy'.[18] As James concedes, 'When we wish to know at all we wish to know everything' – and he most certainly wished to know about George Sand. To the imagined reproach that it is 'none of your business', James says that 'the genuine analyst' (with which generic figure James would surely identify) may ask in turn '"What *is* then forsooth of our business?"' Just where the 'genuine analyst' shades into, or shades off from, the 'publishing scoundrel' is becoming very difficult to discern. As James goes on to admit; it is hard to work out any rule 'by which we shall know when to push in and when to back out'.[19] Arguably, the narrator of *The Aspern Papers* tried to push in too crudely before backing out too gracelessly – but he might well, the while, have considered himself some sort of 'genuine analyst'. James has, of course, a quite superior 'delicacy', but no one, surely, could have had a hungrier 'curiosity'. To be sure, he wrote often and at length about George Sand's works, at times elevating and praising them in terms which we might now find surprising. But he certainly was equally happy, indeed eager, to 'push in' to her life – as far as possible.

Not by his own agency to be sure – that *would* be indelicate; but through the means (the gaslights, the lamplights) of letters and well-documented biographies – 'The George Sand Papers' as it were.

Some of the things at stake, some of the matters involved – sexual, ethical, literary – in this desire to know, particularly to know 'everything' about the life of this woman writer, are suggested in an extraordinary paragraph from later in this essay which I must quote at length.

> When we meet on the broad highway the rueful denuded figure we need some presence of mind to decide whether to cut it dead or to lead it gently home, and meanwhile the fatal complication easily occurs. We have *seen*, in a flash of our own wit, and mystery has fled with a shriek. These encounters are indeed accidents which may at any time take place, and the general guarantee in a noisy world lies, I judge, not so much in any hope of really averting them as in a regular organization of the struggle. The reporter and the reported have duly and equally to understand that they carry their life in their hands. There are secrets for privacy and silence; let them only be cultivated on the part of the hunted creature with even half the method with which the love of sport – or call it the historic sense – is cultivated on the part of the investigator. They have been left too much to the natural, the instinctive man; but they will be twice as effective after it begins to be observed that they may take their place among the triumphs of civilization. Then at last the game will be fair and the two forces face to face; it will be 'pull devil, pull tailor', and the hardest pull will doubtless provide the happiest result. Then the cunning of the inquirer, envenomed with resistance, will exceed in subtlety and ferocity anything we to-day conceive, and the pale forewarned victim, with every track covered, every paper burnt and every letter unanswered, will, in the tower of art, the invulnerable granite, stand, without a sally, the siege of all the years.[20]

There is such a growing sense of violence here that one is indeed inclined to send for the police, if not call up the army. We start with a naked figure – the woman writer stripped bare by her biographers, even – running away with a shriek, and conclude with a 'pale victim' – the same figure? – about to be fallen on with hitherto unparalleled ferocity, as by some envenomed pack of hounds. The hunting image is demanded since the 'historic sense' has now become indistinguishable from 'love of sport'. At which stage it becomes difficult to tell 'the triumphs of civilization' from the trophies of the field. Walter Benjamin would have commended the insight. It is hard to separate civilization's gains from its barbarities. And this indeed is the world of James's later work. There are, in *The Wings of the Dove*, only 'the workers and the worked', and if you don't want to be the one you had certainly better try to be, or resign yourself to being, the other. Though in that world you will almost certainly end up being both. The manifestly 'worked' yet seemingly saintly Milly Theale 'works' – triumphantly – from beyond the grave. The workers and the worked: the reporters and the reported – *à la guerre c'est comme à la guerre*, and to the victor the spoiled spoils. For his own part James was bent on heading for the 'tower of art' – not so much the ivory one of retreat as the granite one of resistance. Perhaps, now, it is easier to have a sense of what momentous issues are, even if only implicitly, at stake in James's first extended Venetian fiction, *The Aspern Papers.* Is it a coincidence that one of George Sand's most notorious and scandalous affairs – more than once singled out by James – took place in Venice?

It is notable, and in a sense premonitory, that James should decide to situate the final degrading scene, or scene of degradation, of 'The Pupil', that grim story of the absolutely shameless, absolutely conscienceless parents, the Moreens, 'speculative and rapacious and mean', in Venice. With a final brazen impertinence Mrs Moreen will ask the impoverished tutor, Pemberton, for a loan of 60 francs. They have utterly exploited his affection for their poor neglected son, Morgan, not paying him, and abusing his decency and loyalty in every way. He has come to Venice because they have told him that Morgan needs him – the pathetic boy will indeed die soon – and the first thing the mother does is to try to borrow money from the very man they have reduced to penury. It is a kind of utmost in human impudence, shamelessness and selfishness and you will hardly find a more fundamentally squalid couple depicted in the whole of James. It takes place in Venice but a Venice turned ugly and desolate.

> One sad November day, while the wind roared round the old palace and the rain lashed the lagoon, Pemberton, for exercise and even somewhat for warmth (the Moreens were horribly frugal about fires – it was a cause of suffering to their inmate), walked up and down the big bare *scala* with his pupil. The scaliola floor was cold, the high battered casements shook in the storm, and the stately decay of the place was unrelieved by a particle of furniture. Pemberton's spirits were low, and it came over him that the fortune of the Moreens was now even lower. A blast of desolation, a prophecy of disaster and disgrace, seemed to draw through the comfortless hall. (*T* VII, 444)

For James, as for Ruskin and later for Proust, there was another side or aspect to the dazzling, iridescent, shimmering city in which life and art were 'interfused . . . consanguineous' – a dark Venice, a place of admonition, premonition and negation. Another Venice, the Venice behind, a place of death, loss and supersession starts increasingly to show through and figure in his writing. In an essay on 'The Grand Canal', written a year after 'The Pupil' in 1892, Venice has simply died.

> Venetian life, in the old large sense, has long since come to an end, and the essential present character of the most melancholy of cities resides simply in its being the most beautiful of tombs. Nowhere has the past been laid to rest with such tenderness, such a sadness of resignation and remembrance. Nowhere else is the present so alien, so discontinuous, so like a crowd in a cemetery without garlands for the graves. . . . The vast mausoleum has a turnstile at the door, and a functionary in a shabby uniform lets you in, as per tariff, to see how dead it is. (*IH* 32)

Two years later (1894) Venice would become associated with death in a much more literal and shocking way when his old friend Constance Fenimore Cooper committed suicide there. (I will return to this relationship.) The Venice of the 'Grand Canal' essay is indeed 'at the fag-end of greatness' (*IH* 40). But as James turns to 'look down the great throat, as it were, of Venice' and sets out down the Grand Canal – thus, by his own image, allowing the city to 'swallow' him – he succumbs to a myriad 'vague infatuations'. The vagueness is of the essence. 'There are no references, I ought to mention, in the present remarks, which sacrifice to accident, not to completion. A rhapsody on Venice is always in order, but I think the catalogues are finished. I should not attempt to write here the names of all the palace' (*IH* 34). Names, and what he used to call 'solidity of specification', become ever rarer in James's later travel writing (indeed there is an increasing attenuation and avoidance of naming in general in all his later work), as James chooses happily to submit to 'all the sweet bribery of association and recollection'. *That* was how things bound and blended themselves together for him. And cataloguing is drowned in rhapsody.

Rhapsody of a particularly Jamesian kind which has much to do with imaginative possession – to compensate, perhaps, for felt failures of penetration. Describing his sensations of anger and dismay in the shops of some curiosity and antique dealers – 'bad moments . . . in their halls of humbug' – James goes on to indicate how he consoles himself for the sense of despoliation and dispersal of noble homes that such shops give him. 'You reconstruct the admirable house according to your own needs' and then, when that's done, you lean on the balcony (of course), look down into the little green garden (presumably part of your own reconstruction) 'and end by feeling it a shame that you yourself are not in possession'. But, surely, by this time you are. '(I take for granted, of course, that as you go and come you are, in imagination, perpetually lodging yourself and setting up your gods; for if this innocent pastime, this borrowing of the mind, be not your favourite sport there is a flaw in the appeal that Venice makes to you.)' As James floats down the canal looking at the older, earlier palaces – 'they have lived on as they could and lasted as they might' (*IH* 37–8) – cutting out the 'glare' of the brand new cafés with their electric lights, steering away from the 'awful *vaporetto*' and resolving 'to keep out of the great vexed question of steam on the Canalazzo', he indulges in that 'borrowing of the mind' which is all his joy. It is a well-chosen word. You do not try to 'buy' Venice (he refers to relics of the older city being 'purchased by the devouring American'); nor, *a fortiori*, do you attempt to 'bracket it out' (by some sort of Emersonian self-blinding) – no, you *borrow* Venice. Then you move in and set up your gods. Pastime indeed. And the most remarkable thing about this Venice, seemingly become its own tomb – a stretch of the Grand Canal strikes him as having a 'Deluge air' and looking like 'a flooded city' – is that, time and again, 'the whole scene profits by the general law that renders decadence and ruin in Venice more brilliant than any prosperity. Decay is in this extraordinary place golden in tint and misery *couleur de rose*' (*IH* 49). To this particular borrower, ruin and decay offered a far more grateful spectacle than the modern innovations of electricity and steam; they were perhaps more permissively open to the hand reaching down the table trying to grasp a still – just – '*visitable* past'. As we shall see, in his next and penultimate essay on Venice, that hand is more eagerly, perhaps more desperately, busy than ever.

Leon Edel has detailed the story of the relationship between James and Constance Fenimore Cooper – they met in 1880 – and any further speculation about the degree of intimacy it entailed, or attained, is pointless (*L* III, 523–4). Clearly she admired him greatly – 'your writings', she wrote, 'are my true country, my real home' (*L* III, 551) – and, one may well feel (on the strength of such letters to him as survive), loved him. In one of those letters (24 May 1883) she had written:

> why not give us a woman for whom we can feel a real love? There are such surely in the world. I am certain you have known some, for you bear the traces – among thicker traces of another sort. – I do not plead that she should be happy; or even fortunate; but let her be distinctly lovable; perhaps, let someone love her very much; but, at any rate, let *her* love, and let us see that she does; do not leave it merely implied. In brief, let us care for her, and even greatly. If you will care for her yourself as you describe her, the thing is done. (*L* III, 559)

Not, perhaps, a declaration; but more, surely, than a purely scriptural exhortation. Constance Wilson was a lonely middle-aged spinster, deaf and depressive. She was a writer and fairly peripatetic. She was driven back and back to Venice from where she wrote to James in 1883:

> I either take a gondola and float through all the colour until six; or else I go, on foot, to all sorts of enchanting places – like Santa Maria dell'Orto, – over myriad bridges, losing my way all the time and enjoying it, and wondering only now and then how I shall ever be able to get away from Venice; whether the end of the riddle of my existence may not be, after all, to live here, and die here, and be buried on that plateau in the lagoon. (*L* III, 550)

Die there she did, in 1894, though whether she jumped or simply fell from the window in Casa Semitecolo remains necessarily unascertainable. But James – along, it must be said, with everyone else – believed it was the former, and the effect on him was little short of shattering. He wrote of her to John Hay: 'a woman so little formed for happiness that half one's affection for her was, in its essence, a kind of anxiety . . . what a picture of lonely unassisted suffering! It is too horrible for thought!' (*L* III, 460). And to Francis Boott: 'I am still too sickened with the news – too haunted with the image of the act – and too much, generally, in darkness.' Perhaps, he went on to Boott, it was partly due to 'the sadness of her lonely Venetian winter' (*L* III, 462). To a Dr Baldwin he wrote that she was 'exquisitely morbid and tragically sensitive' and 'the victim of chronic melancholia' (*L* III, 464). Less diagnostically, but perhaps more feelingly, he wrote to Katherine De Kay Bronson: 'But it is all too pitiful and too miserable to dwell on – too tragic and too obscure' (*L* III, 465).

James came over to Venice, not least it seems (though one must be wary of ascribing motives) to enable him to be present when Constance Wilson's rooms were opened when he could repossess himself of his letters to her. But it would appear that he had other obligations to fulfil with regard to her effects, as emerged in an account given by Mrs Huntingdon of something James told her when he came to Florence immediately after leaving Venice:

> Some very famous person died in Venice and left him *executeur administraire*. . . . in her will she left that he had to do certain things, and one of the things was that he had to bring all her belongings out in a gondola and throw them in the water, in the laguna, and he made a frightfully funny story, I thought, of it, because he said he took all these things out into the laguna and there were a lot of clothes, a lot of her black dresses, so he threw them in the water and they came up like balloons all round him, and the more he tried to throw them down, they got all this air, the more they came up and he was surrouned by these horrible black balloons. . . . he kept on saying he . . . tried to

> beat these horrible black things down and up they came again and he was surrounded by them.[21]

This is one of those occasions when art lays down its tools at the feet of life, for who would have dared to imagine a scenario in which Henry James is trying to 'drown' the black dresses of a woman who had committed suicide (perhaps out of frustrated love for him) in the 'perpetual fluidity' of the Venetian waters, and envision those dresses, like the most shameless and shaming return of the repressed, keep returning again and again to the surface like 'horrible black balloons' which 'the more he tried to throw them down . . . the more they came up', until he was surrounded by 'horrible black things'. The suggestiveness of the episode and account is boundless: further comment would be superfluous.

Whether or not Constance Wilson's suicide was a generative or determining factor in James's decision to incorporate a 'death in Venice' in his subsequent fiction – his notebooks of 1895 contain the title *La Mourante* for a proposed work (*N* 146) – is of course unknowable. 1895 also saw the publication of 'The Altar of the Dead' – an altar at which James himself was lighting an increasing number of candles. His subsequent writing on Venice seems imbued with an even stronger sense of sadness and decline, though as always the ruins have a phosphorescent glow. An 1899 essay is entitled 'Two Old Houses and Three Young Women', and this in itself is enough to signal a radical shift of approach. Is this to be travelogue? autobiography? fiction? In truth it is all three; or, rather, the differences have ceased to matter. From the start, we notice how gently James reaches out and back for his subject. 'There are times and places that come back yet again, but that, when the brooding tourist puts out his hand to them, meet it a little slowly, or even seem to recede a step, as if in some slight fear of some liberty he may take. Surely they should know by now that he is capable of taking none. He has his own way – he makes it all right' (*IH* 64). The narrator of *The Aspern Papers* was never so courteous and considerate as this. He had *his* own way – and made it all wrong. For James the places ('Italian') and times ('Hours') come back, unsolicited as it were, and have simply to be greeted and met with appropriate decorum. Yet, not quite. He refers to 'your practised groping gaze', by which he means his own, and if the eye can become a hand so can memory. 'Hold to it fast that there is no other such dignity of arrival as arrival by water'. 'Hold to it' – he repeats the injunction. And then repeats it again. 'Hold to it, at any rate, that if a lady, in especial, scrambles out of a carriage, tumbles out of a cab, flops out of a tram-car, and hurtles, projectile-like, out of a "lightning-elevator", she alights from the Venetian conveyance as Cleopatra may have stepped from her barge' (*IH* 66). Perhaps between merely meeting and firmly holding we need a middle term and, of course, James exactly has it. Thus at the end of this essay James depicts himself hanging back – 'to woo illusions and invoke the irrelevant' (*IH* 76). James is a wooer of the past. 'I can woo it all back' is a recurrent cry of felicity in his late Autobiographical writings.

To James's eyes Venice is older than ever, but that only increases her 'ambiguity'. 'Dear old Venice has lost her complexion, her figure, her reputation, her self-respect; and yet, with it all, has so puzzlingly not lost a shred of her distinction.' But perhaps that is just the point. Perhaps 'the misfortune of Venice' is 'the essence of her dignity'. Resolutely, then, he clings 'to one's prized Venetian privilege of making the sense of doom and decay a part of every impression'. James follows his train of thought, or feeling, to its logical, rather scandalous, conclusion. 'What was most beautiful is gone; what was next most beautiful is, thank goodness, going – that, I think, is the monstrous description of the better part of your thought. Is it really your fault if the place makes you want so desperately to read history into everything?' (*IH* 64–5). Reading history in seems to come perilously close to reading life out.

As James starts to hang his 'three pictures', as he puts it, he finds himself turning over this central question: 'if that inveterate "style" of which we talk so much be absolutely conditioned – in dear old Venice and elsewhere – on decrepitude' (*IH* 64). A definition of 'style' was as elusive (as the word was as important) as the notion of the 'gentleman' was for Trollope: 'what in the world was the secret of style, which you might have followed up and down the abysmal old Italy for so many a year only to be still vainly calling for it?' (*IH* 354). His first 'picture' is set in 'a high historic house' (unnamed, of course, but identified by D. C. Woodcox as Palace Mocenigo[22]), and here again 'one' – but it is James – 'grasped at the idea of something waning and displaced, and might even fondly and secretly nurse the conceit that what one was having was just the last' (*IH* 67–8). At the end of the essay he laments, 'There was still the sense of having come too late' – the torment of belatedness, as Harold Bloom was to designate the feeling – 'yet not too late, after all, for this glimpse and this dream' (*IH* 76). Late: but not too late to see the last. Thank goodness.

The occasion in the old house was in fact a betrothal celebration, but James's emphasis is hardly on the matrimonial. 'Such old, old women with such old, old jewels; such ugly, ugly ones with such handsome, becoming names; such battered, fatigued gentlemen with such inscrutable decorations; such an absence of youth, for the most part, of either sex – of the pink and white, the "bud" of new worlds; such a general personal air, in fine, of being the worse for a good deal of wear in various old ones' (*IH* 68). Thou mettest with things new-born; I with things dying. James is not interested in renewals but in 'Terminations' (the title he had, indeed, given to a collection of tales published in 1905). Such decrepitude. But – do we infer? – such style!

'If "style", in Venice, sits among ruins, let us always lighten our tread when we pay her a visit.' His steps, when he visits the home of the 'three young women' – they are in fact 'three sisters' – are quiet and soft enough for (what else?) 'a death chamber'. He sees so much in this old house that he feels fiction-making redundant. But that's 'the sad-eyed old witch of Venice' for you ('she so easily puts more into things that can pass under the common names that do for them elsewhere'). As he sees the three sisters in their setting – 'their beautiful blighted rooms, the memories, the portraits, the shrunken relics' – Henry James the novelist can only sigh. The scene is already resolving itself into the possibility of chapter after chapter. 'What on earth is the need to "invent", in the midst of tragedy and comedy that never ceases. . . . The charming lonely girls, carrying so simply their great name and fallen fortunes, the despoiled *decaduta* house, the unfailing Italian grace, the space so out of scale with actual needs, the absence of books, the presence of ennui, the sense of the length of the hours and the shortness of everything else' – it is striking how much this atmosphere has in common with Chekhov's *Three Sisters*, written, somewhat uncannily, a year later. For James, 'all this was a matter not only for a second chapter and a third, but for a whole volume, a *dénoûment* and a sequel. This time, unmistakably, it *was* the last – Wordsworth's stately "shade of that which once was great"; and it was almost as if our distinguished young friends had consented to pass away slowly in order to treat us to the vision' (*IH* 72–3). This time it really *is* the last. Thank goodness – and thank Venice and the three sisters, the old witch of a city and the young girls, alike, decaying and passing away so slowly, so unmistakably, and with such style. James imagines the girls being present when their impoverished elders – realizing what they had done in selling off the family treasures – 'looked at each other with the pale hush of the irreparable'. And, James notes, 'these were matters to put a great deal of old, old history into sweet young Venetian faces' (*IH* 74). City and girls sinking under the weight, sinking *into* the weight, of history – but, for James, glowing into vision. Fairer through and while fading. And hold fast to *that*.

This late Venice is saluted by James 'supremely as the refuge of endless strange secrets, broken fortunes and wounded hearts' (*IH* 69). A similar note is struck in the last essay he wrote on Venice, 'Casa Alvisi', which was in fact an introduction to a volume of reminiscences called *Browning in Venice* by Mrs Katherine De Kay Bronson. Casa Alvisi was the name of her house, and James had often enjoyed her hospitality there. He seems to be evoking the figures who had passed through it, passed through Venice:

> it is in Venice again that her vanished presence is most felt, for there, in the real, or certainly the finer, the more sifted Cosmopolis, it falls into its place among the others evoked, those of the past seekers of

> poetry and dispensers of romance. It is a fact that almost every one interesting, appealing, melancholy, memorable, odd, seems at one time or another, after many days and much life, to have gravitated to Venice by a happy instinct, settling in it and treating it, cherishing it, as a sort of repository of consolations; all of which to-day, for the conscious mind, is mixed with its air and constitutes its unwritten history. The deposed, the defeated, the disenchanted, the wounded, or even only the bored, have seemed to find there something that no other place could give. (*IH* 82)

These words were published in February 1902; six months before the publication of *The Wings of the Dove.*

Early in the novel Morton Densher asks Kate Croy, on one of their walks, what her disgraced father '"had originally done?"'. Kate's answer is, in an odd way, premonitory.

> 'I don't know – and I don't want to . . . my sister first made out that he had done something. I can hear her now – the way, one cold black Sunday morning when, on account of an extraordinary fog, we hadn't gone to church, she broke it to me by the school-room fire. I was reading a history-book by the lamp – when we didn't go to church we had to read history-books – and I suddenly heard her say, out of the fog, which was in the room, and apropos of nothing: "Papa has done something wicked." And the curious thing was that I believed it on the spot and have believed it ever since, though she could tell me nothing more – neither what was the wickedness, nor how she knew, nor what would happen to him, nor anything else about it. . . . That has been part of the silence, the silence that surrounds him, the silence that, for the world, has washed him out.'

Densher presses a little: '"What has he done, if no one can name it?" "He has done everything." "Oh everything! Everything's nothing."' But he presses no further: '"I wouldn't find out for the world."'[23] There is a lot of quintessential James in this little scene and response. Alternating between the institutionally backed and securely grounded knowledge of church and history, the child suddenly experiences a different kind of 'knowledge' which emerges out of the fog – or, rather, as a fog. It is a knowledge which is not a knowledge. It is unnamed, unnameable, and no one wishes to know or name it. It is surrounded by a silence, a tacit conspiracy of not-asking. While it necessarily stimulates curiosity, the Jamesian response is – 'I wouldn't find out for the world.' It may be covered by mystifying superlatives and hyperboles – the wickedness stretches to 'everything'. But this is only to compound the vagueness, thicken the fog. The word is often employed by the schemers, covering a multitude of – what? – sins, possibilities? But Densher is right. 'Everything' means 'nothing', but expresses the desire to not name. Very often in James we find an aroused curiosity and a consequent move towards acquiring knowledge, coupled with a systematic eluding and deferring of it. With regard to knowledge – knowledge, often sexual – the instinct in James seems to be: approach and avoid. The matter of Mr Croy's nefariousness never comes up again, but the novel is to centre on another fog surrounded by a collusive silence – Milly Theale's illness. As to the nature, the seriousness, the prognosis, even the very existence of this illness, the characters – including Milly herself – 'wouldn't find out for the world'. By the same token, the reader *cannot* find out – for the world. Yet Milly dies, and dies in Venice. And there, late in the book, as Densher watches Sir Luke Strett leave him to make his last visit to Milly, he is given a crucial meditation and realization:

> He hadn't only never been near the facts of her condition – which counted as a blessing to him; he hadn't only, with all the world, hovered outside an impenetrable ring fence, within which there reigned a kind of expensive vagueness made up of smiles and silences and beautiful fictions and priceless arrangements, all strained to breaking; but he had also, with every one else, as he now felt, actively fostered suppressions which were in the direct interest of everyone's good manner, everyone's pity, everyone's really quite generous ideal. It was a conspiracy of silence, as the cliché went, to which no-one had made an exception, the great smudge of mortality across the picture, the shadow of pain and horror, finding in no quarter a surface of spirit or of speech that consented to reflect it. 'The mere aesthetic instinct of mankind – !' our young man had more than once, in the connexion, said to himself; letting the rest of the proposition drop, but touching again thus sufficiently on the outrage even to taste involved in one's having to *see*. So then it had been – a general conscious fool's paradise, from which the specified had been chased like a dangerous animal. What therefore had at present befallen was that the specified, standing all the while at the gate, had now crossed the threshold in Sir Luke Strett's person and quite on such a scale as to fill out the whole precinct. (*W* 440)

To what extent this partakes of Densher's often desperate sophistries and self-deceptions which he invokes to himself to mask his lying and duplicitous dissimulations, and how much James himself might have esteemed the idea of a society in part made up of 'smiles and silences and beautiful fictions and priceless arrangements', does not matter. What is crucial for the novel is this intimation of the destructive (and perhaps salvatory) arrival – infiltration, invasion – of the *specified*, in more than the form of Sir Luke Strett. Venice becomes the place where finally – finally – one has to *see*. It is where Kate says to Densher, '"If you want things named you must name them"', and he does: '"Since she's to die I'm to marry her. . . . So that when her death has taken place I shall in the natural course have money?"' (*W* 394). It is the place where he makes an unambiguous sexual deal with her. The city, pre-eminently, of art – and artifice – it becomes in the novel a place of deceptions behind deceptions, where beautiful words, 'dignity', 'honour', 'fidelity', 'ideal', 'sublime', 'transcendent', 'loyalty', like the beautiful paintings invoked (Milly is said to be 'lodged' in a Veronese painting; *W* 381), are pressed into service to conceal or mask the 'shabby' realities of motive and manoeuvre which are at work. City of masks, here even apparent 'unmasking' can be but another form of masquerade, as when Milly and Kate, after a social evening, 'wearily put off the mask' only to move into even deeper dissimulation. 'It was when they called each other's attention to their ceasing to pretend, it was then that what they were keeping back was most in the air' (*W* 339). But it is also a place where the masks come off in good earnest, as when Densher unmasks his sexual demands to Kate and she lays bare her plot to deceive Milly to secure her money. These sexual and financial hungers can be dressed up and aesthetized with the highest and finest art, and where better than in Venice, where the costumed deception is consummated; but to rename is not to transform and mystification is not sanitization. And when Lord Mark 'unmasks' (*W* 435) and tells Milly the brutal truth about Densher and Kate – he is 'brutally brutal' (*W* 419–20) to use a phrase from a novel in which the words 'brute' and 'brutal' increasingly recur – she 'turns her face to the wall' (*W* 394). The city which, like Milly's Palace Leporelli seems a compound of 'romance and art and history', (*W* 361), an endless succession of beautiful surfaces, becomes the place for the exposure of the most 'brutal' truths. 'The specified' – endlessly delayed, deferred, silently chased away – in Venice inevitably and finally emerges. And it kills.

In *The Wings of the Dove* Venice is indeed a place of death – actual physical deterioration, pain, decay and collapse; and also more subtle forms of spiritual death and decline (Merton Densher also announces his own death while he is there, and it is both the life and death of his relationship with Kate Croy). It is a place of carnality – not only Milly's physical wasting away, but the very frank, even perhaps rank, sexual embraces of Densher and Kate (surely the most explicit sexual rendezvous in James). But it is also the place of a rather mysterious sense of forgiveness, beneficence, 'mercy'. Sacred as well as Profane Love (Titian's painting is in Rome, but James associated Titian, and the painting, with Venice). To catch this double presence we can use Shakespeare's words in *Measure for Measure*, when Duke Vincentio says to his deputy Angelo:

> In our remove be thou at full ourself;
> Mortality and mercy in Vienna
> Live in thy tongue and heart.
> (I. i. 44–6)

Only it is a matter of mortality and mercy in Venice. Indeed it is a rather Shakespearean Venice (with echoes of the Venice of *Othello; The Moor of Venice*) – not only because of the atmosphere of released carnality, the sense of primal struggles taking place, the hint of a spiritual redemptive drama being played out; but also in the way the climatic and environmental changes reflect, adumbrate and participate in the changing human conditions. The cosmic mood amplifies and extends the individual state. There is a reciprocation of inner and outer weather: calm and turbulence, hope and despair, are both in the body and the soul, and in the air, in the shifting nuances and emphases of the changing seasons. Here again we can note that James must have made a very deliberate choice of Venice for the setting of the climatic scenes of books 8 and 9, for in his long notebook entry (November 1894) in which he muses on the idea for the novel he writes: 'I seem to see Nice or Mentone – or Cairo – or Corfu – designated as the scene of the action' (*N* 107). Clearly, at first he merely thought of a vaguely, randomly exotic, cosmopolitan setting (a James novel in Cairo!). To shift so definitely to Venice he must have had very clear reasons, and I believe it was because for James it was pre-eminently the city or two cities of the great extremes – of all the hope and beauty of life, of the possibilities of art and passion; and all the sense of loss and despair, waste and belatedness. The city of ambiguous transformations, and degenerations, of the physical and the moral and spiritual world: of mortality – and mercy.

When Milly Theale first arrives there – already aware of her mortality, but desperately eager to live (she brings both her death and her desire) – it is summer, and Venice is at its most benign and gracious. There she takes up residence in her 'inodorous' palace, which is, among other things, quite a palace of art. Palazzo Leporelli, full of 'servants frescoes, tapestries, antiques', the 'make-believe of a settlement' (*W* 336), is also a palace of larger 'make-believe' – the made, willed belief that Milly can live. But it is also, from the start, an atmosphere marked by 'common duplicity' and 'suppressions' (*W* 340); at one level to do with Milly's health, but of course at another to do with the hidden relationship between Kate and Densher. There is an indeterminable amount of 'masking'. It is ubiquitous.

As a 'princess in a palace' Milly now has the yearning to sit there for ever, 'remaining aloft in the divine, dustless air', not to 'go down' – 'never, never to go down!' (*W* 345). Down to where the air is indeed 'dusty', and much more ambiguously human than divine. This is the lower air breathed, most notably, by Kate and Densher. From the start Milly announces – actually to the intrusive, and finally fatal Lord Mark – her desire, perhaps her intention, 'to die here'. And until then to live in her 'great gilded shell', her 'caged freedom' (*W* 347–8). Being infinitely rich, she can 'pay for everything' (*W* 342) and is willing to 'pay too much'. Quite what is bought and sold, acquired and exchanged, invested and lost in Venice, is indeed of the essence of the book. Whatever else, Milly claims, 'I give and give and give' (*W* 353) – just what she gives and what she gets, and the nature of her bequests, the results of her bequeathing, are questions which dominate and determine the last part of the book. In the lower part of Venice, Densher is making his own plans from the beginning of book 8 when he considers renting 'a small independent *quartière*, far down the Grand Canal' (*W* 354). Just after his arrival there is a 'turn of bad weather' and indeed he brings with him a change of climate. For what Densher brings to Venice and releases there is 'the very impatience of desire', 'a kind of rage for what he was not having' (*W* 362). And James makes it as clear as he ever could that his impatient desire is unambiguously carnal. What he is 'not having' is sexual relations with Kate. And if he is to go through with *her* plan – to court and deceive Milly for money and subsequent freedom – he is now, in Venice, determined that she shall go through with *his*. Hence the rented, sequestered, secret, rooms – the obverse of the palace in their 'shabbiness and decay'. Note that whatever else the rooms are for, they are not 'to receive Milly Theale'. They are the site of both sexuality and deceit. When Milly intimates her inclination, intention, to visit them, he instinctively averts and thwarts her desire. It would not only be 'the last incongruity': it would 'spoil . . . his game' (*W* 365). In playing and pursuing his 'game', the double plot with Milly and Kate, Densher feels that 'the law was not to be a brute – in return for amiabilities' (*W* 368). Just who is the brute, and what is 'brutal', are other matters explored in this Venice. Densher's first assault on Kate takes place in St Mark's Place (and we know what Ruskin would have said about that): 'the splendid Square, which had so notoriously, in all the years, witnessed more of the joy of life than any equal area in Europe, furnished them in their remoteness from earshot, with solitude and security' (*W* 373). A tense struggle ensues between them as Densher presses demands for 'proof' of her love. 'Come to me,' he demands, and Kate can hardly mistake his 'admirable, merciless meaning' (*W* 378). Meanwhile, the 'only' other sign for their ears was the flutter of doves 'in the bright, historic air' of this 'matchless place' (*W* 373).

That Milly is a 'dove' may be in part due to Ruskin's Venice, where 'the St Mark's porches are full of doves, that nestle among the marble foliage, and mingle the soft iridescence of their living plumes, changing at every notion, with the tints hardly less lovely, that have stood unchanged for seven hundred years.'[24] But Ruskin's writing surely determines the place where Densher first proposes what must be seen as a squalid and treacherous deal with Kate – '"I'll tell any lie you want, any your idea requires, if you'll only come to me"' (*W* 378). It is in Piazza San Marco and at the conclusion of their conspiratorial conversation that Densher 'made her turn so that they faced afresh to Saint Mark's, over the great presence of which his eyes moved while she twiddled her parasol' (*W* 379). For Ruskin St Mark's was not so much a 'Temple' as 'a Book of Common Prayer, a vast illuminated missal', a great 'stone manuscript', and at the end of his chapter on St Mark's he wrote (to quote it again):

> Never had city a more glorious Bible. Among the nations of the North, a rude and shadowy sculpture filled their temples with confused and hardly legible imagery; but, for her, the skill and the treasures of the East had gilded every letter, and illuminated every page, till the Book-Temple shone from afar off like the star of Magi. . . . the sins of Venice . . . were done with the Bible at her right hand. . . . And when in her last hours she threw off all shame and all restraint, and the great square of the city became filled with the madness of the whole earth, be it remembered how much her sin was greater, because it was done in the face of the House of God, burning with the letter of His Law.[25]

Densher and Kate are indeed 'facing' St Mark's as they are planning to 'throw off all shame and restraint'. The fact that Densher moves his eyes over the 'great presence' of the Book-Temple while Kate merely twiddles her parasol is perhaps the first hint that he will in due course respond to the appeal of higher, spiritual values and perhaps be mysteriously 'saved' while Kate, having no eyes for the 'vast illuminated missal', will remain remorselessly materialistic and mercenary. James lacks Ruskin's fierce religious fervour, but in this novel he deploys a Ruskinian sense of Venice as a possible appropriate site for achievements of the highest spirituality and grace, and enactments of particularly culpable evil.

After the open space of the square, Densher moves to the 'court life' of Milly – 'the courts of heaven, the court of an angel' (*W* 384). It is a move from 'prose' to 'poetry'; from a surreptitious contact with a woman out shopping, to a performance for 'ladies housed in Veronese pictures' where Milly, in white, dazzlingly presides, diffusing a spell of 'beatific mildness' while Kate takes second place 'in her accepted effacement' (*W* 388). Nevertheless the conversation, the contest, between Kate and Densher continues. They talk of Milly as a dove, of her 'wealth which was a power', though even here Densher feels that it is her 'spirit' which is the supreme power, while Kate thinks more of her money. The 'wings', thinks Densher, could 'spread themselves for protection' (*W* 389), but what form that protection will take remains, of course, to be seen. But again we may say that around their conversation there is another 'sign' – metaphoric, as befits an abode of 'embodied poetry' – of the 'flutter of doves', or a dove. In this exalted atmosphere, Densher and Kate are tolerably explicit about the plan to have Densher effectively make love, or pay court to, Milly, and their reasons. Here Densher issues his ultimatum, brings his 'test' of Kate to the crisis point. '"I'll stay, on my honour, if you'll come to me. On *your* honour"' (*W* 397). Otherwise he will 'do nothing' – and simply leave Venice, Milly, the whole plot and ensemble. It is the passive, plastic, Densher's moment of feeling 'master in the conflict', and Kate of course capitulates, and ends book 8 with the conclusive, concluding words – 'I'll come'. On her honour. Though what exactly happens to 'honour', his as well as hers, is part of the ensuing drama. When Densher later says, '"I don't know, upon my honour, what I am doing"' (*W* 408), he speaks very exactly. He doesn't know what he is doing on, and to, his 'honour'.

Book 9 finds Densher alone in Venice 'in his faded old rooms', feeling 'the difference' made by Kate's absence. He is obsessed with the memory of her having come to his rooms ('she had come, that once, to stay, as people called it'). His sense of their bodily intimacy – 'the renewed act' – is clearly still very much with him. It gives him a sense of 'renewed engagement to fidelity' and 'the special solidity of the contract'. The words are necessarily becoming ambiguous, problematized. He can only show his 'fidelity' to Kate, honour the 'contact', by immediately beginning to be, or act as if he was, unfaithful to her. He has to disengage himself from her arms, from the place of their embraces, and make for 'the palace'. He is indeed, like Claudius in *Hamlet*, 'to double business bound'. Maintaining mendacity to prove his honour; breaking his word to keep his word. And yet he feels that somehow Milly is doing 'everything'. His own rooms are now filled with Kate, and 'Kate was *all* in his poor rooms', but somewhere above that cloistered, and perhaps claustrophobic, sexual intimacy 'something incalculable wrought for them – for him and Kate; something outside, beyond, above themselves, and doubtless ever so much better than they' (*W* 399–402). Densher's days with Milly that follow Kate's departure are calm, suspended; in one aspect duplicitous, in another brushed with intimations of something divine. Now that Densher feels suddenly able and willing to let Milly come to visit in his rooms, she refuses. '"You mean you won't come to me?" "No – never now. It's over. But it's all right"' (*W* 407). The anti-echo of his exchange with Kate is clearly audible. In trying to keep faith with Kate and yet somehow salvage and assuage his conscience, Densher engages in some tolerably casuistical internal debates. He opts for 'tact', and decides he must and will be 'kind', be 'nice', above all be 'still'. It is the debatable resolution of just not moving, of deciding 'to let himself go – go in the direction, that is to say, of staying' (*W* 411).

But then he is suddenly, inexplicably, debarred from entry to the palace – and the weather changes and 'turns to storm, the first sea-storm of the autumn'. And now we are in the other Venice:

> It was a Venice all of evil that had broken out for them . . . a Venice of cold lashing rain from a low black sky, of wicked wind raging through the narrow passes, of general arrest and interruption, which the people engaged in all the water-life huddled, stranded and wageless, bored and cynical, under archways and bridges. . . . the wet and cold were now to reckon with. . . . he dropped his eyes on the rubbish in the shops. There were stretches of the gallery paved with red marble, greasy now with the salt spray; and the whole place, in its huge elegance, the grace of its conception and the beauty of its detail, was more than ever like a great drawing-room of Europe, profaned and bewildered by some reverse of fortune. He brushed shoulders with brown men whose hats askew, and the loose sleeves of whose pendent jackets, made them resemble melancholy maskers. (*W* 415)

The palace is closed, the shops seems full of rubbish, the 'drawing-room of Europe' is profaned and bewildered; there is 'vice in the air' as indeed there is in the word – vice in V(en)ice. 'The broken charm of the world about was broken into smaller pieces' (*W* 418–19). Lord Mark is in Venice, and somewhere, someone or something has somehow been a 'brute' to Milly, so there is brutality in the cold, wet air as well. After a long exchange between Densher and Mrs Stringham – in the rooms of sexuality and planned deception – Densher seems to have arrived at some ambiguous and unarticulated clarifications and resolves. And with the arrival of the mysteriously benign and apostolic, if not positively deific, Sir Luke, the weather changes to 'autumn sunshine', and a cleansed and rebeautified Venice emerges (the mood is quite that of Shakespeare's last plays). 'Venice glowed and plashed and called and chimed again; the air was like a clap of hands, and the scattered pinks, yellows, blues, sea-greens, were like the hanging-out of vivid stuffs, a laying-down of fine carpets' (*W* 437). It is once again a Veronese painting, but with 'the great smudge of mortality across the pictures'. 'The facts of physical suffering, of incurable pain' (*W* 440–1) are now part of the picture of life in the palace, though Densher can no longer go there. Still, it is as if Sir Luke brings relief at many levels. Densher feels 'a blessed calm after a storm', indeed he feels he is being mysteriously forgiven, exculpated, 'let off' (*W* 444). As though the great doctor had brought, not only balm for Milly, but 'mercy' for him. Milly has indeed 'turned her face to the wall' and we are not to see her again. Her death in Venice is undeniably terrible, a tragic waste, an unspeakable horror, given her absolute desire to live, live and love. But the death is not, we are to feel, in vain.

And, as we learn in the final book, Densher did see her once before he left Venice. By the end there is more than a trace of ambiguous redemption and healing in the air. The seemingly too obviously auspicious phrase 'the third' occurs three times in connection with Densher's penitential, abject and abandoned waiting in Venice after his exclusion from the palace, but hardly with resurrectionary optimism: 'on the third day, when still nothing had come'; 'on the afternoon of his third day, in gathering dusk and renewed rain, with his shabby rooms . . . at their worst', Mrs Stringham arrives, not with good tidings of great joy, but the news that Milly '"has turned her face to the wall"'; after Sir Luke arrives 'when the third day came without a sign he knew what to think'. These last three days are said to be his 'worst' – 'He had never been, as he judged it, so down. In mean conditions, without books, without society, almost without money, he had nothing to do but wait' (*W* 420–2). He is scarcely harrowing hell, but these days of near-absolute deprivation and hopelessness perhaps constitute his purgatory. Shortly thereafter Sir Luke does give him a sign and announces a seeming miracle: '"She can receive you." . . . Sir Luke's face was wonderful. "Yes, she's better"' (*W* 446–7). At which point the novel falls silent, refusing (or unable) to follow Densher back into the palace for his last, transforming meeting with Milly in or through which he is perhaps absolved, perhaps saved. Book 9 ends here, and with the start of the next and final book we are back in London and, indeed back in 'fog', and it is three weeks later. The 'brutality' of (Lord) Mark has been ameliorated and distanced by the benignity and 'mercy' of (Sir) Luke. The deception and moral confusion have been somehow purged and clarified by the generosity (financial and spiritual) of Milly. Densher effectively 'repudiates' what 'in Venice, had passed between' himself and Kate. He has learned 'scruple' as the unscrupulous Kate can see: '"you have fallen in love with her"' she says to Densher (*W* 458). This may or may not be true; but it is clear that he is now concerned to 'save his conscience'. He renounces whatever may have been his 'brutality' and, in the end, he effectively renounces Kate, who still has her mind on the 'money' and the freedom, the carnal freedom, which it could buy. Whatever took place in his final meeting with Milly in Venice, 'the essence was that something has happened to him too beautiful and too sacred to describe. He had been, to his recovered sense, forgiven, dedicated, blessed' (*W* 469). His passion for Kate turns into a 'wasted passion', since she will not accept his new terms of the contract. Milly dies, and Kate refuses him in his new 'dedicated' condition. He loses everything, the whole world. To save his soul. By the end, his relationships have changed, changed utterly. 'We shall never be again as we were' (*W* 509). The intimation is that out of all the waste and mortality something unspeakably precious is saved. We must think, then, not only of death in Venice, but of transfiguration and salvation in Venice as well.

James, thus, for all his return to Venice in travel-writing, reserves the city for a drama which involves the life and death of the soul as well as the brilliant life and terrible death of the body. I feel that there is more at stake in *The Wings of the Dove*, more avidity of released desire – desire to live, desire to love and be loved – than in any other of his novels: the bodies are more carnal, the duplicities and deceptions deeper and more devious, the death more terrible, and the forgiveness, perhaps, more divine. And it was a continuation, with James's own modifications and amplifications, of Ruskin's, and perhaps Browning's, Venice. It consisted of the most beautiful, most gratifying, most uplifting surfaces and images in the world – from one point of view it was a city in a state of perpetual self-transcendence. From another, of course, it was all sadness and decline and ruin and spiritual declension. It also, I think, remained for James the site of a certain inscrutability and impenetrability, rather like, perhaps, the face of the gondolier who will not give Densher precise information about the ladies, indeed will not really tell him anything at all – 'he would have been blank, Densher mentally noted, if the terms could ever apply to members of a race in whom vacancy was but a nest of darkness – not a vain surface, but a place of withdrawal in which something obscure, something always ominous, indistinguishably lived' (*W* 413).

5

Hugo von Hofmannsthal: Because the People There Were Always Masked

HUGO von Hofmannsthal set his first work in Venice. It was a short play-fragment written in 1892 when he was eighteen and entitled *The Death of Titian* (*Der Tod des Tizian*). In his attic, Titian's disciples praise and celebrate the aesthetic vision of life which Titian has created, transforming meaningless real life into meaningful sanctifying art. However, one young disciple, Gianino, has wandered to the very edge of this sanctuary of art and, gazing at the sleeping city of Venice, he experiences an intimation of all the seething, sensual, violent, intoxicating life which lies down there – outside of art, ignored or rather concealed by art; but perhaps more powerful, more rich, more *real* than art. The other disciples rush to explain to Gianino that the life out there is gross, ugly, dull and unredeemable; hence the need for Titian's art at once to transfigure and keep out – extrude, occlude – the merely material world in all its hideousness (and, perhaps, danger). The dying Titian seeks to offer a final opposition by crying "'The God Pan lives!'", and by painting a sort of allegory of the unity of life with the figure of Pan as a veiled puppet in the arms of a young girl (a projection of the androgynous Gianino). But this is only an aesthetic, symbolic – *painted* – image of the reconciliation of life (Pan) and appreciative art (the girl/Gianino). Art thus remains hermetically self-sealing, self-protecting, with the real, *qua* real, still kept at bay, kept out. Gianino feels this and yearns for some fuller participation in, involvement with and relationship to that real life outside of art.

Thus summarized, we can see that this is simply one of the many later nineteenth-century works which depict or dramatize the problematical relationship – or non-relationship – between two realms or worlds. One is the world of art which may be happily and blessedly secluded and protected, beautiful and orderly, sumptuous and self-gratifying; but it may turn out to be estranged, cut off, enfeebled and innutrient – shamefully impotent, guiltily solipsistic, culpably non-social. This world may be variously figured as a palace (which may become haunted); a garden (which may wither to a waste-land); a monastic, meditative retreat (which may become a site of tormented sexual deprivation); or a moated grange in which the feminine principle of beauty languishes in arid exile. The other world is seldom presented or figured but, rather, fantasized or abstracted, idealized or hypostatized – a creation of desire, dream, and perhaps dread. It is the generic realm of the perhaps enviable, perhaps threatening, Other: the world of action, fecund sexuality, politics, the people, the – somehow – *really* real. This world perhaps also represents a devious gesture of the unconscious trying to find and project itself in some movement of the excluded social masses. Of course, this world is no more 'real' than the art world. As in Titian's painting of life in the arms of art, we never get off the canvas. It is perhaps both the simplicity and starkness of this decadent art/life dualism – at once facile and desperate – which strikes us now. What it reveals – or is a symptom of – is the increasing struggle to find a way of using art to break out of what were felt to be the stifling limitations and deleterious exclusions of art. Art somehow to reach the beyond, the beneath, the behind of art. Art for non-art's sake. In this European-wide struggle, there is no more exemplary writer than Hugo von Hofmannsthal.

It is perhaps not suprising that Hofmannsthal should have chosen to situate his little art/life drama in Venice. Venice is at once the heaven-haven of art (Titian's attic) *and* the site of that suppressed, seething, sensual life which potentially both subverts and attracts away from the aesthetic enclave. As a topos and figure, Venice proves to be notoriously and unarrestably double, constantly turning into its opposite and yielding or precipitating exactly contrary moods – fulfilment and loss; illumination and desolation; a sense of glory, plenitude and apotheosis giving way to feelings of dereliction, absence and diminution; the spiritual yielding to the sensual and the splendours turning to miseries. It was so for Byron and Ruskin and for Henry James', and will be for Proust. And in a particularly complicated way it was so for Hofmannsthal.

After the age of twenty-five, Hofmannsthal abandoned lyric poetry completely. In his important book, *Hugo von Hofmannsthal and his Time*, Hermann Broch sees this move as part of Hofmannsthal's ongoing attempts to excise, inhibit and occlude all traces of subjectivity from his writing – his 'Ich-Verschweigung', 'Selbst-Verschweigung', 'Ich-Verschwiegenheit', which Broch translates as 'ego-suppression' and 'ego-concealment'.[1] Hofmannsthal's attempts to break free from the impoverishments, etiolations and attenuations which were the results of the self-regarding cultivation of aestheticism and subjectivity, came to a head in the remarkable 'The Letter of Lord Chandos'. This is a letter addressed to Francis Bacon which purports to come from a young Elizabethan nobleman, Lord Chandos, who is the same age (twenty-six), has the same sort of cultivated family pedigree and has written the same kind of early work as Hofmannsthal himself. It clearly describes some sort of personal crisis, and, published in 1901, it can be seen as a curiously apt document to mark that turbulent period when late Romantic decadence is straining at once both to annihilate itself and to transform itself into those new modes of seeing and depicting which will come to be known as modernism.

What Lord Chandos confesses to, and essays to describe, is a complete breakdown in his relations to language, to other people, to the world of objects, to literature and art, to his own mental coherence. 'But it is my inner self that I feel bound to reveal to you – a peculiarity, a vice, a disease of my mind if you like – if you are to understand that an abyss equally unbridgeable separates me from the literary works lying seemingly ahead of me as from those behind me.'[2] He describes his previous state of joyous integration of being in terms which suggest some fantasy golden age, prior to any dissociation of sensibility.

> In those days, I, in a state of continuous intoxication, conceived the whole of existence as one great unit: the spiritual and physical worlds seemed to form no contrast, as little did courtly and bestial conduct, art and barbarism, solitude and society; in everything I felt the presence of Nature, in the aberrations of insanity as much as in the utmost refinement of the Spanish ceremonial; in the boorishness of young peasants no less than in the most delicate of allegories; and in all expressions of Nature I felt myself. (*H* 132)

If we note something deeply regressive in this nostalgia for such a state of seamless indifferentiation and identity – everything was one, and everything was me – we should also note that Hofmannsthal is here articulating a nostalgia for some impossible lost wholeness and unity of being which is to pervade modernist thinking – and dreaming.

But now he no longer has access to the world around him: the fruit branches recede from his grasp – words and things alike have withdrawn into meaninglessness and unreachability. And the result is a nausea verging on madness. 'My case, in short, is this: I have lost completely the ability to think or to speak of anything coherently. . . . I experienced an inexplicable distaste for so much as uttering the words *spirit, soul* or *body* . . . abstract terms crumbled in my mouth like mouldy fungi' (*H* 133–4). He can no longer look on people and the world around him with what he calls 'the simplifying eye of habit'. 'For me everything disintegrated into parts, those parts again into parts; no longer would anything let itself be encompassed by one single idea. Single words floated round me; they congealed into eyes which stared at me and into which I was forced to stare back – whirlpools which gave me vertigo and, reeling incessantly, led into the void.' He tries to find refuge in 'the spiritual world of the ancients' – but 'in their company I was overcome by a terrible sense of loneliness; I felt like someone locked in a garden surrounded by eyeless statues. So once more I escaped into the open' (*H* 134–5). And then he describes a series of epiphanic moments; moments when fragments of Being suddenly seem radiant with deeply moving but inarticulable revelations. At such moments he sounds like a symbolist working between, say, Emerson and Joyce.

> A pitcher, a harrow abandoned in a field, a dog in the sun, a neglected cemetery, a cripple, a peasant's hut – all these can become the vessel of my revelation. Each of these objects and a thousand others similar, can suddenly, at any moment (which I am utterly powerless to evoke), assume for me a character so exalted and moving that words seem too poor to describe it.

His description of how a 'combination of trifles sent through me such a shudder at the presence of the Infinite' (*H* 135–7) could readily be matched by descriptions from other symbolists – or mystics.

But there is a particular cast or twist to some of Hofmannsthal's visionary moments which turns them into imponderably perverse epiphanies. As, for instance, when he describes how, on an evening walk, he suddenly remembers an order he had given that morning for rat-poison to be spread in his milk-cellar – and 'there suddenly loomed before me a vision of that cellar, resounding with the death-struggle of a mob of rats.' He compares it to a vision of the burning of Carthage, but 'there was something more, something more divine, more bestial; and it was the Present, the fullest, most exalted Present.' It has nothing to do with pity; rather, 'an immense sympathy, a flowing over into these creatures, or a feeling that an aura of life and death, of dream and wakefulness, had flowed for a moment into them – but whence?' (*H* 136–7). And we may notice that while there are some what we might call aesthetically neutral objects, which afford him his shuddering epiphanic moments – a pitcher, a hut – it is more likely to be the lowly, the crippled, the abandoned or even the conventionally ugly and loathsome thing which precipitates the experience. He is drawn to the despised and the neglected; almost, we might say, to the insulted and the injured. An 'insignificant creature' – like a beetle or a rat – can now 'mean more to me than the most beautiful, abandoned mistress of the happiest night'. Obviously some very radical inversion, or convulsion, of values is taking place in his disoriented – or reoriented – mind. At the door of one of his peasant's huts, 'my eye lingers long among the ugly puppies or upon a cat stealing stealthily among the flower-pots; and it seeks among all the poor and clumsy objects of a peasant's life for the one whose insignificant form, whose unnoticed being, whose mute existence, can become the source of that mysterious, wordless, and boundless ecstasy' (*H* 139).

I believe we can find here a sort of inchoate new aesthetic – disturbing, challenging, negating established hierarchies of value, beauty, worth; looking for *fleurs du mal* – which in various forms will be seen at work in much subsequent twentieth-century art. But we must also note in the 'Letter' a trembling instability, a move towards some sort of inner vertiginous disintegration. As when, near the end, he describes how he identifies with the figure of the ancient Crassus who became enamoured of his tame lamprey fish – another move towards the abject, since Crassus was mocked as a 'ridiculous and contemptible' figure.

> Now and then at night the image of this Crassus is in my brain, like a splinter round which everything festers, throbs, and boils. It is then that I feel as though I myself were about to ferment, to effervesce, to foam, and to sparkle. And the whole thing is a kind of feverish thinking, but thinking in a medium more immediate, more liquid, more glowing than words. It, too, forms whirlpools, but of a sort that do not seem to lead, as with the whirlpools of language, into the abyss, but into myself and into the deepest womb of peace. (*H* 140)

But does it always lead to the 'deepest womb of peace' or may it find itself flowing, or foaming, into 'the death struggle of a mob of rats'? Or is there, perhaps, finally no difference? In the critical state of finding the self entirely alienated from all the known anchorings of language, Hofmannsthal depicts the self in a condition of extreme precariousness in which some sort of neo-religious ecstasy is indistinguishable from nightmare – Conrad's 'the horror'; Orwell's worst thing in the world. As we shall see, he found no more fitting site than Venice where he might explore this possible fusion, or confusion, of realms.

Hofmannsthal's own 'escape into the open' took him next to drama, and it is notable – for my purposes – that a particular influence which prompted him in that direction was Thomas Otway's *Venice Preserved*, which he apparently read while doing his military service in Galicia in 1896. Otway's play displaces away from seventeenth-century England on to a much earlier Venice a theme of political decadence, and extreme sexual corruption and lasciviousness (with a brothel scene involving the most degrading kind of sado-masochism): 'Bankrupt Nobility, a harrast Commonalty / A Factious, giddy, and divided Senate', and a treasonable plot of justifiably angry nobles and patriots who threaten to turn into an insurrectionary mob. The plot is betrayed by vacillation on the part of the most sympathetic character; but the dominant image is of a state in extreme political and passional disarray, deep into decadence. Hofmannsthal translated and reworked the play and it was published in 1905 as *Das Gerettete Venedig.* Whether or not he intended a comment on his own contemporary Vienna we can hardly decide. He insisted that the production should suggest 'a conservative-reactionary period rotten at the roots . . . like pre-March [1848] Austria'. Carl Schorske sees the play – a translation of a displacement – as representing a mixture of involvement and evasion on Hofmannsthal's part.

> Both in the play and in the form of its production, then, Hofmannsthal approached contemporary social reality cautiously and evasively. He wishes neither an escape into history and myth nor a direct representation of modern society and its problems. By using a suggestive, rather than a literal, milieu, he realized in this frightening drama of social disintegration the promise he had seen in drama as a literary form when he wrote Andrian from squalid Galacia. Drama, he said, would both connect one to life and free one from it.[3]

Hofmannsthal continued writing drama until the end of his life, and, perhaps because of his work with Richard Strauss, it is that for which he is now principally remembered. But he also turned to narrative work and produced one of the most interesting (and most neglected) prose works of the early years of modernism, rightly spoken of by Hermann Broch in the same breath as Joyce, Proust and Mann – the unfinished and unfinishable *Andreas* (there is a fragment from 1907; it was taken up again in 1911, worked on throughout the First World War and then abandoned). Here the setting of Venice is absolutely crucial in enabling Hofmannsthal to explore and extend the states of consciousness, and perception which are adumbrated in 'The Letter of Lord Chandos'. (I note in parenthesis that, just before returning to this work in 1909, Hofmannsthal wrote a less ambitious novel, *Christinas Heimreise* (1910), which is also set in Venice and which narrates, as comedy, one of the seduction incidents from Casanova's Memoirs. Around this time, another Viennese novelist, Arthur Schnitzler, also took up the figure of Casanova. But this work, *Casanovas Heimfahrt (Casanova's Homecoming)*, concentrates on the melancholy and humiliating return of the ageing, ravaged and exhausted Casanova to a cold, unwelcoming Venice. Published in 1918, it hits perhaps the right elegiac note – given the time and place.)

Before looking at *Andreas* I want to say a word about Hofmannsthal's essays, or rather, at this point, quote some eloquent words of Hermann Broch concerning the general topography and concern of these essays.

> In their entirety these essays describe the great ellipse of landscape stretching from northern Italy to southern Bohemia, with the Austrian Alps as its nucleus, a region full of heroic culture and heroic nature;

> with its focal points in Venice and Vienna it provides the mirror, so to speak, for Hofmannsthal's 'Austrianhood' . . . deeply entangled in Austrian culture . . . Hofmannsthal unceasingly experienced the anonymity of culture-forming powers . . . the more involved in such development he became, the more this unfurling of culture appeared to him as a natural process; is not poetry also a product of nature, like the language in which it has its place? Is the creation of culture not the innermost nature of man? . . . Who can still draw the line that separates the two? The Hapsburg empire was the product of wars and acts of state; nevertheless it seems (independent of those auxiliary political mechanisms) to have emerged from a preexistence rooted in its soil, providing it with an eternal, postexistential being. And it is just as incomprehensible that Venice was once upon a time actually built by pile sinkers, masons, and roofers; does not Venice likewise possess a spiritual existence created and protected by nature? The artificial flows into the natural, the natural in turn into the artificial, and whether on the stage or in so-called life, the planes of reality cut across one another, with the result that man constantly wanders between changing dream sceneries, whose origins are in an anonymous Somewhere but are nevertheless created by man himself. His ego has been discarded, yet he recognizes it everywhere, man's reality lies in the anonymous, and whatever he creates only becomes real when he, like the folk artist, has been submerged in anonymity, returned to the natural, stripped of everything homunculoid and led to the rediscovery of his shadow.[4]

The 'naturalization' of culture is an old theme, and, as we have seen and will see, this, and what we might reciprocally call the 'culturization' of nature, are themes constantly provoked by Venice – the 'naturalization' of Venice is always a seductive conceit, witness Melville's 'reefs of palaces'. The seemingly increasing interchangeability of the nature/culture terms, even to the sense of imminent identity, which the city seems to foster, merits a reapplication of the famous speech by Polixenes:

> Yet nature is made better by no mean
> But nature makes that mean. So, over that art
> Which you say adds to nature, is an art
> That nature makes. . . .
> This is an art
> Which does mend nature – change it rather; but
> The art itself is nature.
>
> (*The Winter's Tale* IV. iv. 89–97)

One way or another, *everything* – reefs and palaces alike – stems from 'great creating nature'. In Emerson's succinct words, 'Nature who made the mason, made the house.' It is a salutary, indeed an exhilarating reminder; even if we may want to go on to say that, for our purposes, it is often more helpful, more interesting to *classify* reefs and palaces differently – bearing well in mind the relative provisionality and arbitrariness of our classifications.

The 'naturalization' of empire – the Habsburg empire springing from the soil – is perhaps another matter. I detect a Heideggerian note in Broch's gloss on Hofmannsthal. The (literal) 'bracketing out' of the political – '(independent of those auxiliary political mechanisms)' – not to mention the marginalizing of all those pile sinkers, masons and roofers, the actual anonymous labour forces which build history, points to one of the central problems of modernism which, taking my clue from Broch, I will simply call the 'auxiliarization' of the political. I do not want to lean too hard on this point: one can appreciate the feeling that Broch is trying to convey, and anyway Venice has a way of depoliticizing writers as no other city does. But if history is made a matter of spirit working independently of merely 'auxiliary' political mechanisms – for which read secondary, incidental, inessential, and so on – then many problems can be glossed, responsibilities occluded, awkward questions eluded or unasked. And the unimpeded reciprocal flow of the natural into the artificial, reality into dream, and so forth, causes problems, perhaps insuperable problems, of identity and narrative, which Hofmannsthal particularly associates with – and chooses to locate, pursue and abandon in – Venice, or his vision of Venice. As we shall see in the *Andreas* fragments.

One essay which Hofmannsthal wrote in 1908 is worth mentioning before turning to those fragments – 'A Memory of Beautiful Days'. It is offered as a memory concerning a late-afternoon arrival in Venice with, perhaps, a girlfriend and her brother; the sensations of gliding and walking through the city; and the author's dreams, thoughts and desires as he returns to his inn and lies on his bed in a reverie. The city is fabulous and 'dreamlike', and everywhere girls brush past him; there are glances and glimpses – the gleam of a tender neck as a black shawl briefly slips – and there is something apparitional about the women: they are briefly there and then they disappear 'like bats in the crack of a wall'. Passing and pausing at booths of antiques, jewels, silks, shells, he is filled with a creative desire to 'fashion something like them with my own hands', 'to produce something out of the fermenting bliss in me'. Cryptically, he says: 'although aware of the dark powers, I still did not know what it was that I should create' (*H* 198–201) – so he returns to his inn. As he mounts the stairs, another beautiful woman passes him. There is no contact between them, but when he is lying on his bed he later hears her laughing and talking in the next room to, perhaps, her lover – giving herself? refusing herself? It is the start of an erotic reverie or fantasy. When he hears her lover (?) leave he can possess the woman in his own way.

> So she was alone. At the moment it seemed more wonderful to be wrapped about by solitude, alone and next to her, than with her. It was like a domination of her out of the darkness. It was Zeus to whom it had not yet occurred that he could throw Amphitryon's body round his divine limbs and appear to her, who would be doubtful and doubt her doubts and with these doubts transform her face like a wave. But the darkness tried to pull me into it, into a black boat that glided along over black water. Light no longer existed anywhere but near this woman. My thinking must not fall entirely into darkness, else I too shall sleep; like a sparrow-hawk it had to circle about the Luminous, above reality, above myself and this sleeping woman. Rapture of the stranger who comes and goes . . . (thus my thinking nourished itself on the Luminous and continued to circle). . . . Thus he must feel who today is not allowed to sleep next to his beloved. So it has to be. Coming and going. Abroad and at home. To return. At times Zeus returned to Alcmene. Our deepest desire aims at transformation. (*H* 203)

Transformation (Zeus into Amphitryon); merging (Zeus with Alcmene); oscillations (master–stranger, coming–going, home–abroad); circling (trying to circle about the light and resist the darkness which is drawing him); reality located in the body of the unknown woman with whom he is and is not sleeping. This is the very distillation of Hofmannsthal's Venetian reverie.

His dream then drags him 'mountainwards', which is also towards his childhood – which, in turn, is at once like a distant lake and a nearby house he can walk into. 'It was a self-possessing and a self-not-possessing, a having-all and a having-naught. Morning air of childhood mingling with premonition of being dead.' His dreams draw together and dissolve all opposites, while some slightly rustling paper awaits the sleeping writer. He wakes. 'The white pages gleamed in full morning light, they were asking to be covered with words, they wanted my secret in order to give me back a thousand secrets in return.' And – this is the critical moment – he can bring nothing back from his rapturous reveries and dream dissolutions. 'A magic formula pressed and quivered in me, but I could not remember the first word. I possessed nothing but the transparent colourful shadows of my dreams and half-dreams.' Impatiently, he tries to pull the shadows towards him, but they retreat as if into the walls and furniture. The room looks 'knowing, but mocking and void'. Effectively he is at the edge of the Lord

Chandos experience. As he relaxes, the shadows reappear, and this tremulous, fugitive ebb-and-flow of the phantasmal, the transparent, the insubstantial traces of his dreams, gives him a kind of provisional, precarious confidence in his creative potentialities.

> I felt how I could draw forth from the naked floor real characters, and how they shone and cast physical shadows, how my wish moved them against one another, how they were actually there for my sake and still took notice only of one another, how my wish had formed for them youth and age and all masks and fulfilled itself in them, and how they were yet detached from me and lusted one for the other and each for itself. I could love away from them, and could let a curtain fall in front of their existence. (*H* 205)

Vividly and succinctly, this surely describes the dream or aspiration of a particular form of modernist writing: to create characters who, as it were, are autonomous and who (somehow) escape the manipulations of the omniscient, omnipotent and indeed potentially omnivorous author. The author releases and realizes all his desire in creating the characters and their destinies – they *are* his desire – yet this imperial and imperious subjectivity is, magically, transcended, eluded, defied. (Hofmannsthal knew about magic and desire: 'I let my wish – which was directed towards fidelity and infidelity, towards departure and remaining, towards here and there – play against them like a magic wand.') But there is one more stage to Hofmannsthal's waking experience in his room in Venice.

> Yet all the time, as the slanting rays of the sun beyond a voluptuous thunder-cloud fall on a livid-green garden landscape, I saw how the splendour of the air, of the water and of the fire, streamed into them as it were from above in slanting, spectral rays, so that they were, for my mysteriously favoured eye, simultaneously human beings and sparkling incarnations of the elements. (*H* 205–6)

Hofmannsthal's waking dream of creating or summoning 'real characters' (who cast 'physical shadows') seems to evaporate or dissolve, and the fantasized 'human beings' are disembodied by the inrush of the elements even as they tremble in his mind on the edge of incarnation. Hofmannsthal here writes about the writing he dreamed towards *but did not do*, in a past Venetian interlude. Venice as the site of a writing which is both desired and unaccomplished – ecstatically impossible – makes a fitting introduction to *Andreas*.[5]

The first fragment of the novel seems to date from 1907 when the novel was first planned or considered. It is entitled 'Journal of Herr von N's Tour to Venice, 1779' and is a mere couple of pages. (The date is worth noting. Broch states that Hofmannsthal deliberately set the novel in Austrian Venice, but the dates mentioned in the other fragment make it take place in 1778. Venice was not handed over to the Austrians by the French until 1814 – perhaps the low point of its humiliation. In 1778–9 it was certainly in decadence and decline but it was still, as it were, Casanova's Venice.) The fragment opens in the first person. 'I remember things very exactly – always had a good memory, won the Grand Cross of Excellence at school because I could recite the rulers of Austria backwards and forwards.' And then: 'Reasons for the tour of Venice: Artists, great names. Palaces, behaviour in drawing rooms, starting a conversation. To make an appearance, to please.' This sounds like the beginning of the memoirs of a confident young nobleman, or youth, recalling something like an eighteenth-century Grand Tour. It continues: 'Arrival. Starts to look for lodgings. Troops of actors waiting on canal bank. An actress ogles him from the lap of a fellow-actor.' The oscillation between 'I' and 'he' continues throughout the fragment, but the repertoire of figures and types mentioned constitutes a fairly standard Venetian cast. Actors ('Everybody is connected with the theatre'), ladies of fashion, courtesans, a dishevelled nobleman who has gambled away his clothes, a patrician putting on a harlequin costume, artists (portraits and copies), masked ladies: less usual are the figures of a grave and dignified knight (Sacramoza) and a violent and intemperate duke (Camposagrado). The only unusual incidents sketched out involve the violent duke. On a visit to a lovely courtesan who keeps a bird in a cage, 'Camposagrado very angry, devours the bird and goes.' The fragment concludes: 'In the church, Camposagrado with servants to light him; returns alone, is attacked by a dog. He masters the dog with his teeth' (*H* 74–6). To the extent that Herr von N. came to Venice to study 'behaviour in drawing rooms', he was doubtlessly scheduled to be in for a series of barbaric shocks.

In the later fragments, the plan for the novel has changed radically. The visitor to Venice is now a very uncertain, passive and susceptible young man named Andreas; he is *sent* on the Grand Tour, and the reasons for this have changed – and proliferated. 'Tour due to the calculating *snobisme* of his father.' or: 'ANDREAS. – Reason for sending him on the tour: difficult, protracted convalescence after a mental crisis, some listlessness, loss of a sense of values, confusion of ideas.' Or again: 'Andreas (at bottom) goes to Venice chiefly because the people there are always masked.' There is no more of the confident 'I' ('The ordinary "I" an insignificant construction, a scarecrow'), and as a confused, disoriented and questing young sensibility Andreas may be seen to be related to such near contemporaries as Musil's Ulrich, Proust's narrator, Joyce's Stephen Hero. He carries the splits and splittings of his time. 'Andreas: two halves which gape assunder. – Andreas's character not yet formed: he must first find himself in these vicissitudes. His shyness, his pride – all untested till now. – Not clear about his own states of mind – always too much, too little' (*H* 77). A late fragment, dated 1912, is subtitled 'The United' ('Die Vereinigenten'), and one note reads: 'we live only by differentiation . . . but to unite is as indispensable as to differentiate – the *aurea catena* of Homer' (*H* 96). The fragments are full of opposites, antinomies, doubles, splittings, divisions, dualities, partializations. Some great synthesis and integration; a gathering in; a bringing together (psychological, cultural, metaphysical) – this is the manifest aspiration of both Andreas and the writing, and clearly Venice is viewed as a site or locus of possible fusions. Thus: 'THE KNIGHT OF MALTA. – He moves in a time which is not quite the present, and in a place which is not completely here. – For him, Venice is the fusion of the classical world and the Orient, impossibility, in Venice, of relapsing into the trivial, the unmeaning' (*H* 114).

But the Chandos vertigo is even more intensely experienced. People and places tend to divide, double ('Everything has two meanings'), fragment, turn into someone or something else, or simply disappear. Venice becomes instead a place of accelerating disintegrations, or bewildering and unstable transformations. The last note of a 1912 fragment reads: 'Andreas's return. – He was what he might be, yet never, hardly ever, was. – He sees the sky, cloudlets over a forest, sees the beauty, is moved – but without that self-confidence on which the whole world must rest as on an emerald; – with Romana, he says to himself, it might be heaven' (*H* 125). This perhaps marks the hope or aspiration, but it is tentative, insecure, provisional in the extreme. It moves in the subjunctive realm of 'might be' and involves a tremulous return to a dreamed-of landscape of the past. By contrast, the conclusion to the fragment almost certainly written after this (and certainly the most completely written piece: 'The Wonderful Mistress' has unusual narrative amplitude and continuity) leaves Andreas lost – in the past perfect tense, in Venice. 'He entered the church – it was empty. He returned to the square, stood on the bridge, and looked in every house, and found nobody. He went away, wandered through some streets, then after some time returned to the square and entered the church through the side door, went back through the archway, and found nobody' (*H* 72–3). There is one other sketch for an ending, to which I will return. But effectively Hofmannsthal's *narrative* ends – halts, falters and falls into darkness – exactly *here*; in silence, isolation, emptiness, absence. Venice has turned her other face and become a site of pure vacancy. Where the writing has to stop.

From what we have, and what we can infer, *Andreas* was intended to be a sort of *Bildungsroman*: the story of the young Herr von Ferschengelder sent by his parents to Venice for purposes of education – whether he would there broaden his mind or lose it altogether is hardly decidable. The work establishes a clear contrasting topography. His journey leads him first to the Carinthian Alps where he encounters the noble peasant family of Finnazer, and their lovely daughter Romana. All is simple, pure, innocent, so ideal and clear as to seem more like a dream, and the possibility of union with Romana affords him intimations of ecstasy. But he has to move on to Venice, and on means down; down from nature to culture, from mountain clarity to Venetian complexity; from innocence to experience, trust to scepticism, true faces to masks, chaste love to lubricious sexuality. It is perhaps a descent from dream to reality, though Venice becomes very dreamlike, and, in intermittent recollections, the mountain life seems more real. But in this world such stable distinctions are never going to hold. The enchantments, distractions and bewilderments of Venice at first serve to obliterate thoughts of Romana and her world. Hermann Broch evokes Andreas's experience of Venice.

> Here in the never-ending maze of alleys and canals, a reflected image of every intrigue, every possible human entanglement, he gets caught in a net of reflections and counter-reflections, in a thicket of psychic identifications and antagonisms, in a spiritual masquerade packed with erotic depths and superficialities. Into what kind of watertown filled with beauty and mud had fate brought him? It is salt water, yet not sea – could the life voyage, youth and age seemingly blended, be coming so soon to an end in this glitter of threatening ambiguity? [5]

But the two realms suggested by the mountains and Venice are not so separate and mutually uninfluencing – or uncontaminating. A brutish murderer-on-the-run, Gotthilf, forces himself as a manservant on to the too feebly resistant Andreas (he is hopelessly porous to influence, suggestion, the will and force of others, as becomes clear in Venice). Gotthilf's diabolical behaviour hideously lacerates the mountain idyll – he seduces a servant girl at the Finazzer farm, then ties her to a bed and sets fire to her. Gotthilf is a nightmare figure of gross and bestial profanations and violations – and Andreas cannot keep nightmares out. This is literally the case. While sleeping in the serene bosom of the farm, he dreams of a cat whose back he had broken when he was a child. The cat took a long time to die. 'Creeping like a snake with its broken back, it came towards him, and panic seized him as it looked at him' (*H* 40). The nightmare ends with him desperately trying to struggle his way out of a wardrobe full of his parents' worn-out clothes – suggestive enough to obviate need for comment. The point is, there is a constant seepage, if not invasion, of the bestial, the deformed, the perverse, the vile into Andreas's consciousness – from both within and without. The aspiration – the dream – is to discover, experience, and prolong some all-subsuming, all-unifying, all-integrating ecstasy; but always the Chandos experience – everything keeps 'falling apart', with always the possibility of a leering, looming Gotthilf, the snake-like approach of the broken-backed creature. There are *moments* – epiphanic moments – of an intense, suffusing joy and sense of certainty, as when from the mountains he looks back at the farm and imagines Romana praying, praying within his heart. But such moments of solitary bliss cannot be translated into a mode of living: the lyric instant will not yield a narrative extension. The other note for a possible ending to the novel, which I mentioned, has the following scenario.

> LAST CHAPTER. As Andreas takes flight and travels up the mountain, he feels as if the two halves of his being, which has been torn asunder, were coming together again. . . . when he reaches Castle Finazzer the next day, Romana is not there. Gradually it comes out that she has fled to the alp on his account; then that she has had a terrible fever, has constantly spoken of him, then taken a vow never to see him again unless he comes from Vienna to make her his wife (prudery now as infinitely exaggerated as previous candour). He leaves a decisive letter for Romana. Last chapter. He leaves at daybreak. They arrive at sunrise. Up to the mountain pasture with the mother. Romana creeps into the farthest cleft and finally threatens to throw herself down from there. (*H* 100)

'Last chapter' is repeated in the notes and we may fairly say that Hofmannsthal is always finishing just as he is always starting – over and over again. This conclusion simply ends on an extreme point or edge of unresolved antinomy, or sunderedness, with no intimations of unity or unification inscribed.

Andreas could never have become a completed novel. Andreas himself is more of an area of susceptibility than a character. He is described as 'the geometrical locus of the destinies of others' and his 'soul' is perpetually 'quivering' so that he is at once 'empty and overburdened'. There is no principle of intention, no directed or desiring energy in him. His 'mania of self-abasement' is referred to, and his main aspiration is somehow to be rid of 'the burden of myself'. But he has no real projects. 'Andreas roaming sadly about: these quite small details: picking up a twig, throwing it away with love' (*H* 104). Now, we can certainly find passive characters roaming sadly about, astray in the small details of randomness and contingency, in the history of the novel – sentimental voyagers, superfluous men, men without qualities, outsiders, ambassadors, underground note-takers, Dublin night-walkers, and so on. But Andreas is so completely discontinuous, such an unrelated series of vivid, cryptic instances, that notes and jottings, hints and suggestions, glimpses and mutterings – that is, a constant aspiration towards, and a constant failure to achieve, narrative incrementality – are the very image of the mode of his existence. In this case, the fragment is, exactly, the appropriate form.

One note refers to the 'mysteriousness' of the connection between one time and another. Elsewhere, there is the single word, 'Relatedness', followed by this: 'Alone with the child, the child looks up: "Out of the substance, which I may not seek – for I have that substance – all the heavens and hells of all religions have risen – to cast them away would be gross darkness – The child's look: links me, the words in my mouth, to these walls, to their protection, to what is simply there"' (*H* 114). The words are unpositioned, unascribed, unsituated. They drift, they float – as Venice in its own mysterious way seems to float – and, rather than connecting and relating things, they move always towards dissolution. That is, indeed, a key word. In notes for the death of Sacramoza, the Knight of Malta, we read: 'Ecstasy of dissolution. . . . Before death: hears water flowing, desire to conjure up all water he has ever heard flow' (*H* 98) – desire for 'the universal solvent' recurs throughout the fragments. Now, certainly, principles and problems of consistency, connectedness, continuity both of individual identity and of perceptible reality, are matters which were being explored in quite radical ways by the great novelists of the period – James and Conrad, and a very little later Joyce, Proust and Musil. But, unlike these writers, Hofmannsthal finds no new principle of narrative reintegration. Rather, he takes the experience of disintegration to the extreme point at which writing itself dissolves – or, rather, fragments back into silence. And it is not accidental that Hofmannsthal locates or discovers this termination or impossibility of the novel (he never attempted another, turning to fairy tale and the stage) in Venice. Venice was to have been 'the real' of initiation and experience – and degradation – for the young Andreas. Once he has entered the city, 'his thoughts become more disorderly and impure.' But it turns out to be the place where the very ground of meaning dissolves. A late – possibly the last – note contains this outline:

> Andreas: Outcome of tour to Venice: he feels with horror that he can never return to the narrow life of Vienna, he has grown out of it. But the state of mind he has attained brings him more distress than joy, it seems to him a state in which nothing is conditioned, nothing made difficult, and therefore nothing exists. All only brings to mind relationships without being so. Everything is stale, there is nothing to seek, but for that reason, nothing can be found. – Question: whether these fragments in the kaleidoscope could arrange themselves. (*H* 125)

Question for Andreas: question for Hofmannsthal. We have seen the answer.

Given his essentially disintegrative vision, it is not surprising that Hofmannsthal cannot evoke those real, independent characters with their own physical shadows he dreamed about. If you gather together the hints and outlines for the figure of the Knight of Malta, his beliefs, aspirations, devotions, dedications and disillusions, you are confronted with a bewildering medley of enigma, asceticism, nobility, mysticism and collapse. The women figures decompose into aspects of the ethereal and the erotic: 'The Lady (Maria) and the cocotte (Marquita) are both Spanish: they are dissociated aspects of one and the same personality, which play tricks on each other.' And Nina – the courtesan whom Andreas visits in the one fragment which aspires to continuous narrative – looms, recedes and dissolves as in a dream. In fact, his whole experience in Venice has the quality and texture of a dream, and at times Hofmannsthal creates an atmosphere of eerie incomprehensibility – seductive, threatening, vertiginous – which in some respects anticipates the atmosphere to be definitively charted and figured only a few years later in Kafka's *The Trial.* But, while Kafka's nightmares relentlessly, claustrophobically, appallingly, hold, Hofmansthal's dream world dissolves, and the writing gives up. There is no sense of historical time in the work, and thus, *a fortiori*, no sense of history, no sense of the social and political, not to mention the economic. 'The real doers are elsewhere' reads one revealing note. As a result there is nothing for the writing to hold on to in Hofmannsthal's Venice, which may be said alternatively to elude and defy – defeat, even – writing.

In the final episode of the narrative fragment, Andreas makes his way through Venice to visit Nina. He loses his way, misrecognizes houses, or mislays them. He approaches a church. Suddenly there is a woman. 'He could not quite make out where she had come from. . . . He had heard no step approaching or crossing the square, and he found himself wondering whether, with her respectable, plain dress, she wore house shoes which muffled her steps, then wondered at himself for wondering.' Is she startled: is she staring at him anxiously? He enters the church, and so does she. She seems to be in mourning, and he tries to avoid intruding on her privacy by not looking at her, though he has a sense that she turns to him in entreaty. Then 'the next moment he could not but regard, if not the movement, then any reference to himself as his imagination, for the stranger had shrunk back into the prie-dieu and was motionless.' He starts to leave quietly, turns for one last look – and is amazed to see another woman in her place. 'In her dress the woman did not greatly differ from the other, who must have departed with an almost incredible swiftness and stealth.' Her bearing is quite different, and she gives him an impudent – or is it an angry? or is it a childish? – look. Standing outside in the square, he feels someone brush past him. This seems to be yet a third woman.

> The swift, almost running steps, the abruptly averted face as she brushed past him – all this was too violent not to be intentional. . . . the audacious freedom of the body was so strange, as she ran towards the bridge in front of Andreas, flinging her slender legs till her skirts flew,

> that for a moment Andreas thought it might be some youth in disguise playing a prank on the foreigner he obviously was. And yet again, something told him without possibility of doubt that the being before him was a girl or woman, as she herself came to a standstill on the little bridge as if waiting for him. In the face, which he thought pretty enough, there was a dash of impudence; her whole behaviour looked absolutely wanton, yet there was something about it which attracted rather than repelled him. (*H* 62)

Wishing to avoid this boldly propositioning woman, he turns back into the church. The other woman has gone. Indeed, 'It was as if the stone floor had opened and swallowed up the mourner, casting up in her place that other strange creature' (*H* 63). I have given this brief episode in detail to convey the sense of uncanny metamorphosis which is characteristic of the unstable ontology of the work.

Andreas then finds his way into a strange garden-courtyard with a vine-leaf roof. He sees a face looking down at him through an opening in the roof, and a hand with bleeding fingertips reaches down towards him. Then the mouth calls 'I'm falling', and the body seems to jerk back and slide down over the wall. Andreas dashes out to cut off the retreat of the mysterious being who, he feels, has sought him out. As he runs down a passage which he is sure must lead to the courtyard, his companion Zorzi, who has somewhat mysteriously reappeared, tells him: "'The house has no courtyard: there's a blank wall there."' By now, Andreas has 'lost all sense of direction': he both 'understands nothing' and 'rejected any explanation'. That is, he is sinking deeper into a vortex where things are increasingly taking on wild, expressionistic, phantasmal features. When he finally confronts the courtesan, Nina, he is 'utterly dazed' by what seems to be her yielding to him. Images and phantoms seem suddenly to proliferate and beset him – pouring into him, pouring out from him, it is impossible to say which.

> In a lightning flash he saw her mother, her father, her sister, her brothers, he saw the choleric duke rise from the space round the sofa, the bleeding head of a parrot in his hand; the head of a jewish admirer rose noiselessly beside him – he looked like the servant, but wore no wig; and the Hungarian captain, whose hair was in plaits, ferociously brandished a curved knife. (*H* 71)

This surely is delirium enough, and sure enough, at the height of it, suddenly 'Gotthilf's face grinned up at him; the beauty of the moment dissolved.'

He finds himself outside. 'The square lay deserted as before: the empty boat hung motionless below the bridge.' He returns to the church and finds that empty too. He walks through the streets and, as I have already quoted, 'found nobody'. In this Venice, visions turn to blanks; searching turns to losing; an enchanting and imminently yielding beauty turns to nightmare and rejection; the feverish quest for some plenitude, some fullness of being, suddenly leaves the quester desolate, disoriented – we might say disoriginated, for there is no way back – and abandoned. Suddenly the churches, like the streets, like the squares, like the boats, are 'empty'. Such a Medusa-faced Venice is adumbrated by other writers, but never taken to such a terminal and terminating sense of utter vacancy as in this fragment by Hofmannsthal. He never tried to write of, or from, Venice again.

One final passage which gives us, perhaps, a vital insight into Hofmannsthal's vision. He describes a childhood memory of a local theatre, and how he loved to watch the actors and musicians assembling their equipment. 'Between the neck of a brass fiddle and the head of a fiddler, he once saw a sky-blue shoe, embroidered with tinsel. The sky-blue shoe was more wonderful than all the rest.' Later he sees the shoe on the singing princess. 'All that was beautiful, but it was not the two-edged sword which had pierced his soul, from tenderest delight and unutterable longing to tears, awe, and ecstasy, when the blue shoe stood empty beneath the curtain' (*H* 10). Here the epiphanic moment is indistinguishable from fetishism, and is perhaps the extreme result of the sort of fragmenting, disintegrative vision which Hofmannsthal explores, one might say, even to obliteration. One might also say that the other great modernists had disintegrative visions, or visions of disintegration. But they worked out new modes of integration, even if only by writing about the search for them. And a sense of place, *some* sense of place, is invariably there in their writing, even if it is under threat. Joyce once maintained that the Dublin of 1904 could be reconstructed from *Ulysses*. This is exactly what you could *not* say about Hofmannsthal's Venice, which is the very site of self-abolition – of both city and character. Whether, finally in horror or ecstasy, there is no knowing. Or, rather, no writing.

6

Marcel Proust: Threefold and Unique

> What marvellous and inexhaustible lessons Venice can give us, now that Ruskin has made its stones speak, and, thanks to the superb translation of Madame Crémieux, can now address himself to us in our own language, like one of those apostles endowed with the gift of glossolalia who are figured in St Mark's baptistery!

This is from a review, written by Proust in 1906, of a translation of *The Stones of Venice.* He goes on to say how the great beauty and happiness which Venice seems to promise can vanish into a 'dismal ennui' as one relentlessly pursues them in the city itself.

> But now, on our return from our Ruskinian pilgrimages, full of painstaking activity, now that we will seek truth rather than pleasure [*jouissance*], the pleasure will be all the deeper, and Venice will pour forth the greater enchantment for having been for us a place of study and for offering bliss as a supplement [*la volupté par surcroît*]. Passionate pilgrims of stones which were first of all thoughts for us, and then became thoughts again, what admirable sermons we heard the Master give beside the waters! To the colours of the skies of Venice, of the mosaics of St Mark's, new colours will add themselves, still more prestigious because they are the very shades of a marvellous imagination, the colours of Ruskin, which his prose, like an enchanted ship, carries across the world.[1]

Ruskin made the stones of Venice speak, and now – through translation – the stones of Venice can speak through *The Stones of Venice* to us in our own language. Working away in the actual city can be both dispiriting and disappointing (though sensual bliss might come in), but in retrospect, as in prospect and anticipation, the stones, skies and mosaics of Venice take on an extra value and beauty because they have been refracted through Ruskin's marvellous writing. One kind of *jouissance* gives way to, or perhaps leads to, another, deeper one. The pleasures of pleasure begin to refine themselves into the pleasures of truth, the more so as the actual Venice recedes *and becomes more beautiful.* Proust had already written:

> Undoubtedly, if Ruskin's books had at first created in us a kind of fever and desire that, in our imagination, gave to Venice and to Amiens a beauty which, once in their presence, we did not find in them at first, the shimmering sun of the canal or the golden cold of a French autumn on which they were first read has given these pages a charm we feel only later, less fascinating than that when they were first read, but deeper perhaps, and which they will keep as indelibly as if they had been dipped in some chemical preparation which leaves beautiful, verdant reflections on the pages, and which, here, is nothing but the special colour of the past.[2]

The deeper charm will only be felt and appreciated later, in pages which seem to have been dipped in the special colour of the past, pages in which – on which? – memories of the now-dead Ruskin and the never-to-be-revisited Venice coexist and coalesce, at once consubstantial and dematerialized. Quite a lot of Proust's relation to Ruskin and Venice is adumbrated, embryonically, in the short book review and this earlier comment. It is very apt that the remarks should occur in a review of a *translation.* 'So that the essential, the only true book, though in the ordinary sense of the word it does not have to be "invented" by a great writer – for it exists already in each one of us – has to be translated by him. The function and task of a writer are those of a translator [*un traducteur*].[3] This comes near the end of the great labour to 'translate' the past of living into the present of writing – a past which had itself, to a substantial degree, been composed of acts of reading and translation, including translation in the most literal sense.

Ruskin 'translated' Venice; Proust translated Ruskin. Here, some dates and biographical details are in order. Proust's first interest in Ruskin seems to date from 1899 when he asked his mother to send him his copy of Robert de la Sizeranne's *Ruskin et la religion de la beauté.* Thereafter, it could be fairly said that he was obsessed with Ruskin, and certainly immersed himself in his writings to the point of saturation, at least until 1906. The details of his involvement with Ruskin's work after that – letters, essays translations – perforce comprise another story. But some salient details are helpful. Ruskin died in January 1900. Perhaps coincidentally and perhaps not, Proust arrived in Venice for the first time in April of the same year, accompanied by his mother. (Apart from a rather furtive visit to Venice on his own in October of the same year, this was also his *last* visit to Venice – at least in the flesh, as it were.) It was his mother who, incidentally but not irrelevantly, often translated passages of Ruskin for Proust, whose English was apparently never very good. While he was in Venice he met Marie Nordlinger for the first time (it is suggested she is a part-source for Albertine), and she read and translated passages from *The Stones of Venice* as they toured the city – once, during a storm, actually in the baptistery of St Mark's. I shall come back to this important moment. It was after this visit that he added a crucial postscript to his essay on Ruskin which was to be the introduction to his translation, *La Bible d'Amiens.* Most of the essay was written before his visit to Venice: the added part has to be at least from 1903.

The importance of this postscript is that it seems to be a Declaration of Independence from Ruskin – a critical and crucial distancing by Proust from the dominant, and dominating, authority to whom he had surrendered. This disagreement with, or disaffiliation from, or challenge to, Ruskin was continued in Proust's important essay 'Sur la lecture', which was written as a preface to his translation of Ruskin's *Sesame and Lilies* in 1905 (published the following year). It was in the same year that Proust wrote to Madame Catusse: 'Venice is too much a graveyard of happiness for me to feel strong enough to go back there.'[4] He never did. What was to become for his narrator-character Marcel the matter of an endlessly prolonged anticipation and deferral – the image of the unreachable, the unpossessable (between meeting the Name of Venice and actually visiting the place, there intervene, in the English translation, 2278 pages) – became for Proust himself an interminable nostalgia, the very essence of the unrepeatable, the unrecapturable (or, rather, the recapturable in another medium – not visiting, but writing). Either way, the actual city, Venice, becomes a dream – of the not-yet or the never-again.

On more than one occasion and in different ways, Proust affirms quite simply that 'Ruskin made the world beautiful for me'. Above all, perhaps, he made Venice not just beautiful (it needs that less than any city in the world) but, effectively, *the* site of the Beautiful – the essence realized, the absolute achieved. As such, it is almost impossible, unbearable to contemplate – it makes young Marcel physically sick. It is a beauty that both awakens *and* – should it turn its Medusa face – devastates all desire. For, as well as making Venice the City Beautiful, Ruskin made it a place – *the* place – of appalling warnings, unspeakable degradations and degenerations, chillingly admonitory warnings; a site of irreversible human decline, irredeemable moral collapse. The Earthly Paradise – and Gomorrah. Proust has to confront and contain – *re*contain – both these Venices.

Ruskin 'during the whole of his life knew but one religion: that of beauty'.

Thus Proust in his Preface to his translation, *La Bible d'Amiens* (*ORR* 32). This would seem to make of the impassioned moralist some sort of nineties aesthete. But Proust is far subtler in his deployment and interchanging identification of terms than that. 'It was in Beauty that his nature led him to seek reality, and his entirely religious life received from it an entirely aesthetic use. But this Beauty to which he thus happened to dedicate his life was not conceived of by him as an object of enjoyment made to charm, but as a reality infinitely more important than life' (*ORR* 33). For Ruskin, then, in beauty lay the real, the really Real. Of course he was religious, but instead of making Beauty into a religion, as the aesthetes did, he made religion into a Beauty. The point, put crudely, is that, while Ruskin believed in God (or certainly did in the writing of *The Stones of Venice*), Proust, at this period, effectively believed in Ruskin. But Proust's instinct to relocate the sacred in the aesthetic, to equate and identify religion and art, was an example of just that misplaced secularization of the sacred which Ruskin had seen as being at once symptom and cause of Venice's horrendous degeneration. Proust must either somehow appropriate Ruskin and, ever so tactfully, reword ('translate') him on and in his, Proust's, own terms – or he must, all respectfully, find Ruskin guilty of succumbing to his, Proust's, own temptations. He did both.

> It is thus that his religious feeling directed his aesthetic feeling. . . . That something of the divine which Ruskin felt was the basis of the feeling which works of art inspired in him was precisely what was profound and original in this feeling and which imposed itself on his taste without being susceptible to modification. And the religious veneration with which he expressed this feeling, his fear of distorting it in the slightest degree when *translating* it, prevented him, contrary to what has often been thought, from ever mixing any artifice of reasoning that would be foreign to his impression when faced with works of art. So that those who see in him a moralist and an apostle enjoying in art what is not art are as mistaken as those who, neglecting the profound essence of his aesthetic feeling, confuse it with a voluptuous dilettantism. So that, in short, his religious fervour, which had been the sign of his aesthetic sincerity, strengthened it further and protected him from any foreign encroachment. Whether some of these conceptions of his supernatural aesthetics be false is a matter which, in our opinion, is of no importance. All those who have any understanding of the laws governing the development of genius know that its force is measured more by the force of its beliefs than what may be satisfying to common sense in the object of those beliefs. (*ORR* 36)

To the extent that this *is* Ruskin – and it is a wonderfully delicate, sensitive and persuasive summarizing portrait – Ruskin is now almost indistinguishable from Proust, who would develop his own form of 'supernatural aesthetics'. Genius, art, religion, everything – all depend on the force of the force. And when Proust writes, 'It was the charming play of his inexhaustible richness to pull out from the marvellous jewel case of his memory treasures that were always new: one day the precious rose window of Amiens, the next the golden lacework of the porch of Abbeville, to join them with the dazzling jewels Italy' (*ORR* 38), one hardly knows whether he is writing about Ruskin's writing, or – proleptically – his own.

'But in him everything was love, and iconography, as he understood it, would better have been called iconolatry' (*ORR* 40), Proust wrote about Ruskin shortly *before* his first visit to Venice. Between 'icon' and 'idol' the distinction can easily become blurred, just as 'graphy' can merge into 'latry' as writing becomes worshipping. Some time after his return from Venice (in fact in 1904, in the 'Post-Scriptum' added to the Preface), Proust addressed himself directly to the difficult and potentially threatening problem of Ruskin and idolatry. He had had a particularly important experience in Venice, as he describes in the added postscript. One day, Marie Nordlinger helped him to read some passages from *The Stones of Venice* while they were actually in the baptistery of St Mark's. The passages included the famous denunciation of Venice containing the sentence: 'But the sins of Venice, whether in her palace or in her piazza, were done with the Bible at her right hand.' Proust made the reasonable protest that a sin could hardly be more or less of a sin according to the distance from, or proximity to, St Mark's when it was committed. But it was clearly a troubling moment for Proust. He describes the hour as 'dark and tempestuous', which could refer to both inner and outer climatic conditions. For, inevitably, Ruskin's denunciations could be all too easily applied to Proust himself – unbeliever, aesthete, snob, sodomite, and so on – with indeed the 'Book-Temple' very exactly at his right hand, just like the erring Venetians. What he does is both to elude the implication, and then to turn the tables on Ruskin – here as so often, attack, albeit of the most reverential kind, being the best form of defence.

He quotes in full the long passage of denunciation, which is of course the crescendoing conclusion to Ruskin's chapter on St Mark's, and then proceeds, not exactly to out-write Ruskin (an impossible task), but, as it were, to *over*-write him. He stands to one side of the passage, avoiding any personal implications it might have for him, and says – well, it is undeniably a passage of 'great beauty' but it is 'rather difficult . . . to give an account of the reasons for this beauty'. Isn't there 'something false' in it?

> And yet there must be some truth in it. Properly speaking, there is no beauty that is entirely deceitful, for aesthetic pleasure is precisely what accompanies the discovery of a truth. To what kind of truth may correspond the very vivid aesthetic pleasure we experience when reading

> such a page is rather difficult to say. The page itself is mysterious, full of images both of beauty and of religion, like this same church of St Mark where all the figures of the Old and New Testaments appear against the background of a sort of splendid obscurity and scintillating brilliance . . . the emotion I felt, as I was reading this page, among all those angels which shone forth from the surrounding darkness, was great, and yet perhaps not very pure. In the same manner as the joy of seeing the beautiful, mysterious figures increased, but was altered in some way by the pleasure of erudition that I experienced upon understanding the text that had appeared in Byzantine letters around their haloed brows, so in the same way the beauty of Ruskin's images was intensified and corrupted by the pride of referring to the sacred text. A sort of egotistical self-evaluation is unavoidable in those joys in which erudition and art mingle and in which aesthetic pleasure may become more acute, but not remain as pure. And perhaps this page of *The Stones of Venice* was more beautiful chiefly because it gave me precisely those mixed joys I experienced in St Mark's, this page which, like the Byzantine church, also had in the mosaics of its style that dazzling in the shadows, next to its images, its biblical quotation inscribed nearby. Furthermore, was this page not like those mosaics of St Mark's which professed to teach and cared little about their artistic beauty? Today they give us pleasure only. Yet the pleasure their didacticism gives the scholar is selfish, and the most disinterested is still that given the artist by this beauty little thought of, or even unknown, by those who merely intended to teach the masses and who in addition gave them beauty. (*ORR* 53–4)

I quote the passage at length because I regard it as a great moment – one might call it a paradigm moment – of modernism. An unbelieving modern writer is recuperating a moralizing predecessor who was in turn recuperating the didactic religious art of an earlier age. Proust retrieves and reclaims the beauty of the religion, the morality and the art – in and on his own terms. The emotion and the pleasure are, alike, 'great' but perhaps not 'very pure'. This is the 'mixed joy' of a modern, reading – translating? – an earlier writer who was in turn reading an earlier past. It is, surely, an exemplary example of how we – we moderns – *re*possess our past. It is always '*re*', as I shall try to explain later. Proust notes that there is a kind of pleasure and pride – and beauty – in the way in which Ruskin refers to, and deploys, his erudition, references, images. The message is ostensibly religious and moral but there is a manifest sort of self-reflexive egoism ('retour égoïste sur soi-même') in the sheer pleasure and referential range of the writing itself. Rather like, says Proust, the mixed feelings and pleasures he gets from St Mark's itself – the sombre gloom and the serious biblical message; but then the glow of the precious materials and the radiance of the artistic skill. Mixed, mixed. The mosaics of the page are like the mosaics of the cathedral. Thus Proust effectively equates, merges, identifies, Ruskin's book with the Venetian 'Book-Temple' – both move and engage him by their style which dazzles in darkness ('style éblouissant dans l'ombre'). Ruskin textualizes Venice; Proust now retextualizes Ruskin by, as it were, reabsorbing or subsuming his writing into the very place he wrote about. It is effectively a case of reciprocal textualization, and Proust can now experience and extract an equal, mixed, pleasure from the book-Venice which he was now actually seeing, and the Venice-book which Ruskin had written about it. The implication is that they are inseparable, even indistinguishable. Ruskin's dark moralizing becomes another tone, a colour value, and aesthetic increment, to the stones of Venice themselves.

We have seen the problems Ruskin had with the notion of 'idolatry', struggling to extricate – exculpate – himself from its indicting entanglements. Proust firmly resituates him at the heart of them. 'It seems to me that at the very basis of Ruskin's work, at the root of his talent, is found this idolatry.' It is not a matter of a lapse now and then, a failing here and there:

> the true conflict between his idolatry and his sincerity took place not at certain hours of his life, not in certain pages of his books, but at every moment, in those profound, secret regions almost unknown to us, where our personality receives images from imagination, ideas from intelligence, words from memory, asserts itself in the continual choices it must make, and in some way without respite decides the fate of our spiritual and moral life. In those regions, it seems that Ruskin never ceased to commit the sin of idolatry. At the very moment he was preaching sincerity, he was himself lacking in it, not by what he said, but by the way in which he said it. The doctrines he professed were moral doctrines and not aesthetic doctrines, and yet he chose them for their beauty. And since he did not wish to present them as beautiful but as true, he was forced to deceive himself about the nature of the reasons that made him adopt them. (*ORR* 50–1)

Proust is, of course, examining his own idolatrous proclivities even as he is exploring those profound, secret regions which decide the fate of our moral and spiritual life. 'I am today so accustomed to Ruskin that I have to search my innermost self to understand the source and understand the nature of this idolatry' (*ORR* 58). Exactly so. He is, understandably, the reverse of censorious – indeed decreeing 'idolatry' to be 'an infirmity essential to the human mind' (*ORR* 54). There is no 'infirmity' of his own mind which he tracked more assiduously. There is a rather strange moment in *A la recherche du temps perdu* when Marcel, uncharacteristically, recalls making quite a long speech of rebuke to Charlus (he is usually the silent listener). It is wartime and Charlus wonders whether the statue of St Firmin in Amiens has been destroyed as well as the church at Combray – 'if so, the loftiest affirmation of faith and energy ever made has disappeared from this world.' Wondrously, Marcel takes spirited issue with him.

> 'You mean its symbol Monsieur. . . . And I adore certain symbols no less than you do. But it would be absurd to sacrifice to the symbol the reality that it symbolises. Cathedrals are to be adored until the day when, to preserve them, it would be necessary to deny the truths which they teach. The raised arm of St Firmin said, with an almost military gesture of command: "Let us be broken if honour requires." Do not sacrifice men to stones whose beauty comes precisely from their having for a moment given fixed form to human truths.' (III, 822–3)

This categorical refutation of idolatry comes a little awkwardly in the texture of the novel. It is strident, didactic, by Proust's standards even crude. It may be seen as continuing his challenging of Ruskinian idolatry, but more obviously it is part of his struggle with his own all too manifest idolatry – social and aesthetic – which makes up a major theme of the novel. We might suggest that the struggle with Ruskin in St Mark's becomes a constitutive force in the novel in which Proust has to become a systematic, subtle and relentless iconoclast of his own most cherished idols – objects, people, places. Among other things, Venice must fall again.

The closing paragraphs of the postscript return to an encomium of Ruskin; how his writing 'roused in me that longing without which there is never true knowledge' – an adumbration of the role of desire in the novel to come; how, reading Ruskin, 'all at once the universe regained an infinite value in my eyes' (*ORR* 57–8). Proust will have to find his own mode of *re*gaining. He goes on to say:

> I left for Venice in order to be able before dying to approach, touch, and see incarnated in decaying but still-erect and rosy palaces, Ruskin's ideas on domestic architecture of the Middle Ages. What importance, what reality in the eyes of one who must soon leave the earth, can be possessed by a city so special, so fixed in time, so specific in space as Venice, and how could the theories on domestic architecture which I could study and verify there on living examples be those 'truths which are more powerful than death, which prevent us from fearing it, and which almost make us love it'? (*ORR* 59)

Taking this as a generic question – what might be the timeless reality and truth to be found in time-bound Venice? – we may say that *A la recherche du temps perdu* is devoted to answering it.

Speaking of the passion he once had for Ruskin's work – he talks exactly of a love and infatuation which, implicitly, was bound to fade, though never disappear – Proust says that he is employing the sort of 'cold memory' which, 'lacking a resurrection we can no longer bring about', only recalls facts and tells you 'you were thus', that kind of memory 'affirming to us the reality of a lost paradise instead of giving it back to us through recollection' (*ORR* 61). Proust is drawing away from Ruskin and moving towards formulating the re-creative – the re-collective, 'resurrective' – operations of another kind of memory. And Ruskin at a distance is, in a way, Ruskin most appreciated. 'It is when Ruskin is far away from us [*bien loin de nous*] that we translate his books and try to create a fair likeness of the characteristics of his thought' (*ORR* 61). *Trans*-late in every sense: what is important is just the distance, the space (and/or time) across which. In some crucial way, it is better if the loved one, or object, or place – here Ruskin and his writings – is away, absent, far. In his novel, Proust was to assert 'an inevitable law which arranges things so that one can imagine only what is absent'. Albertine, Venice, Ruskin – all in their different ways are loved and desired in relation to their absence – when they are away, afar. *Bien loin.*

In 'Sur la lecture', which he wrote as an introduction to his translation of *Sesame and Lilies* (1906), Proust continues to establish a kind of distance from Ruskin. He takes issue with the supreme importance attached to the act of reading in 'Of Kings' Treasuries': 'Reading should not play the preponderant role in life that Ruskin assigns to it' (*ORR* 110). Why not? Because 'we feel quite truly that our wisdom begins where that of the author ends, and we would like to have him give us answers, when all he can do is give us desires' (*ORR* 114). As Ruskin had given him desires, but answers which he had had to reject. What Proust wanted to avoid was the paralysed passivity of one kind of reading, being engulfed and literally enthralled by the irresistible power of a majestically authoritative text. As Ruskin had enthralled him. He had to break free to embark on his own creative activity, so that reading, while it can of course nourish quite indispensably, must be left, as it were, behind. Assimilate the desires and shed and forget the 'answers'. He is responding, as he sees it, to a law 'which perhaps signifies that we can receive the truth from nobody, and that we must create it ourselves . . . that which is the end of their wisdom appears to us but the beginning of ours, so that it is at the moment when they have told us all they could tell us that they create in us the feeling that they have told us nothing yet' (*ORR* 114–15). And again: 'Reading is at the threshold of spiritual life; it can introduce us to it; it does not constitute it'

(*ORR* 116). Proust was approaching his own 'threshold' between criticism and creation; or between one form of 'translation' and another, more far-reaching, one.

He is against what he calls the 'fetishistic respect for books', the kind of reader who treats the book as 'a motionless idol, which he adores for itself' (*ORR* 120). He is against the kind of reading which elicits or encourages 'a kind of laziness' which prevents or discourages the reader 'from descending into the deep regions of the self where the true life of the mind begins'(*ORR* 117). This would seem to be a continuation of his ongoing struggle against his own strong tendencies to fetishism and idolatry. As if, in writing about reading, he is, among other things, telling himself to stop *simply* reading (and 'idolizing' in general) and start writing in good earnest. It is notable that he concludes this essay in Venice. He makes a final point that it is not just the sentences of a text which may contain its life and value, but the gaps and silences as well. 'Between the sentences . . . in the interval separating them, there still remains today as in an inviolate burial chamber, filling the interstices, a silence centuries old' (*ORR* 128). The final paragraph is as good an introduction to his novel as one could find.

> How many times, in *The Divine Comedy*, in Shakespeare, have I known that impression of having before me, inserted into the present actual hour, a little of the past, that dreamlike impression which one experiences in Venice on the Piazzetta, before its two columns of gray and pink granite that support on their Greek capitals, one the lion of Saint Mark, the other Saint Theodore trampling the crocodile under his feet . . . keep on prolonging in our midst their days of the twelfth century, which they interpose in our today [*qu'elles intercalent dans notre au-jourd'hui*]. . . . All around, the actual days, the days we are living, circulate, rush buzzing around the columns, but suddenly stop there, flee like repelled bees; for those high and slender enclaves of the past are not in the present, but in another time where the present is forbidden to penetrate. Around the pink columns, surging up toward their wide capitals, the days of the present crowd and buzz. But, interposed between them, the columns push them aside, reserving with all their slender impenetrability the inviolate place of the Past [*la place inviolable du Passé*]: *of the Past familiarly risen in the midst of the present*, with that rather unreal complexion of things which a kind of illusion makes us see a few steps ahead, and which are actually situated back many centuries; appealing in its aspect a little too positively to the mind, overexciting it a little, as should not be surprising on the part of a ghost from a buried past; yet there, in our midst, approached, pressed against, touched, motionless, in the sun. (*ORR* 128–9; my italics)

This is the very architecture and terrain of his novel to come; and the italicized words its plot and climax. Venice has become the site and structure of his book. His novel will be another experience of Venice – a Venetian experience. Remember that, *in* the novel, the final precipitant *of* the novel which he ends by starting to write – the creatively generative and originating, or *re*originating, epiphanic moment – is a *kinetic* experience which activates a memory, and releases a 'dazzling and indistinct vision' ('la vision ébloissante et indistincte'). That vision seems to say to him: '"Seize me if you can, and try to solve the riddle of happiness which I set you [*résoudre l'énigme de bonheur*]". And almost at once I recognized the vision: it was Venice.' The crucial kinetic experience is, of course, his tripping or staggering on some uneven paving stones, and it is while he is prolonging his wobble that time is suddenly annihilated and he also experiences/re-experiences the sensation of standing/standing-again on 'two uneven stones in the baptistry of St Mark's'. This is the point at which he starts to become certain of the clue, the key, the secret, the mystery, the magic, which will enable him to embark on his vast work. We may fairly say that the stones of Venice finally, literally, rocked him into writing.

But not quite immediately: he was still, as it were, standing on the threshold of his great work. It is difficult to say exactly when he finally started on the novel as we know it today, though he was certainly at work on it by the summer of 1909. Prior to that, he had written a work, never published in his own lifetime, known as *Contre Sainte-Beuve*. He also wrote many miscellaneous essays, some of them clearly being tentative approaches to the autobiographical fiction which emerged out of them and which, indeed, would be reincorporated into the novel.[5]

In the Prologue or Preface to this work, Proust uses the following words within the first three pages: *ressaisir* (repossess), *rencontrer* (encounter), *ressusciteront* (resuscitate), *résurrection* (resurrection), *refis* (retraced) – as he will later use *reconstruire* (reconstruct, re-establish) and, most famously of course, *recherche*. He is, indeed, recruiting 'fresh energies for my pursuit of the past' ('ma poursuite du passé'), as he puts it (*BWSB* 20), and 'resurrection' was to be his theme. He associates this particularly with Venice, and indeed gives an account of the episode which, rewritten, is to be the climactic point of his novel.

> In the same way, many days in Venice which intellect had not been able to give back, were dead for me until last year, when crossing a courtyard I came to a standstill among the glittering uneven paving-stones. . . . I felt an invading happiness, I knew that I was going to be enriched by that purely personal thing, a past impression, a fragment

> of life in unsullied preservation (something we can only know in preservation, for while we live in it, it is not present in the memory, since other sensations accompany and smother it) which asked of it that it might be set free, that it might come and augment my stores of life and poetry. But I did not feel that I had the power to free it. No, intellect could have done nothing for me at such a moment! Trying to put myself back into the same state, I retraced my steps a little so that I might come afresh to those uneven shining paving-stones. It was the same sensation underfoot that I had felt on the smooth, slightly uneven pavement of the baptistry of Saint Mark's. The shadow which had lain that day on the canal, where a gondola waited for me, and all the happiness, all the wealth of those hours – this recognised sensation brought them hurrying after it, and that very day came alive for me. (*BWSB* 18–19)

Captivity and liberation were to figure on many levels in the novel to come.

One very important person is absent from that passage, his mother. But she is restored in another piece which is entitled 'Talking to Mama'. While she is talking, he sees the sunlight 'enamelling' the weathercock on the house opposite. One 'enamel' releases another – and, as he recalls that *then*, Venetian memories of later days flood the *now* of his writing:

> the golden angel on the campanile of Saint Mark's, when my window-shutters above the alley alongside the Palazzo X . . . in Venice were opened And from my bed I could see one thing only, the sun – not face to face but in an enamel of flame on the golden angel of the campanile of Saint Mark's, who in an instant exactly informed me of the hour and permeating light of that Venetian day, bringing to me on his dazzling wings a promise of beauty and of greater joy than ever he brought to Christian hearts when he came heralding: 'Glory to God in the highest, and on earth peace, good will toward men.' (*BWSB* 64–5)

It is a bold claim: Proust is effectively appropriating the religion of orthodox believers as he lays claim to a more than Christian joy. It is in Venice, as we shall see, that he redefines piety for his private purposes. And, crucially, the visit to Venice was made with his mother.

> and before we reached Venice, Mamma read me that dazzling passage in which Ruskin successfully compares it to a coral reef in the Indian-seas and to an opal. . . . at noon-day, when my gondola brought me back in time for lunch, from far away I often caught sight of Mamma's shawl, with a book weighting it down against the wind, lying on the alabaster balustrade. . . . Mamma sat behind its balustrade of various-

> coloured marbles, waiting for me and reading the while, wearing the pretty hat that netted her face in a white veil. . . . she wafted me a tenderness that rose from the depth of her heart. (*BWSB* 66)

The shawl, the book, the mother, all 'chime' together in a memory of Venice, a crucial configuration which is to recur in the novel. In a very deep sense his mother is indeed 'behind' that novel. 'I felt how impossible it would be to set out for Venice, for any place on earth, where I should be without her' (*BWSB* 67). And his grandmother made a visit to Venice when she knew she was dying, simply to see the Doges' Palace. Proust believed that 'she would not have attached so much importance to that joy she got from the Doges' Palace if she had not felt it to be one of those joys which, in a way we but imperfectly understand, outlive the act of dying, and appeal to some portion of us which is not, at the least, under the dominion of death' (*BWSB* 185). Venice was indeed to become the site where Proust was to find his own way of pronouncing that death shall, after all, have no dominion.

Another connection is establishing itself in Proust's mind – between desire and distance, which will in turn relate desire and Venice. Warner uses the phrase. 'Fair Unknown' to translate what in the French is both 'un bel inconnu' and 'cet inconnu désiré' (*CSB* 97, 130). The point, of course, is the 'inconnu', the unknown- or not-yet-known-ness. 'We must admit that, for all of us, there was once a Fair Unknown . . . who vanished as soon as we met him' (*BWSB* 51). Him, or her, or them, or it. 'So it has to be, apparently, in the case of things, and places, and griefs, and loves; those in possession of them do not see the poetry; it only shines at a distance' (*BWSB* 41). He has learned that, and appetite is 'all the sharper because it could not be gratified' (*BWSB* 33). Or, to put it another way, 'the state of being unsatisified is essentially part of the desire' (*BWSB* 62). Which is why, as he perhaps rather self-exculpatingly puts it, 'one must live among desirable desires' (*BWSB* 62) (the French is perhaps more explicit: 'vivre où le désir est délicieux'; *CSB* 132). The desire for Venice was a particularly desirable desire, as we shall see – 'the whole world is summed up in that sunlight on a palace in Venice which makes us determine on our journey' (*BWSB* 63). Determine on it, then deferring, and deferring, and deferring it. Because distance is required to keep the desire desirable – delicious. Proust is learning about what we might call the long-circuiting of desire. And he is learning something else: 'often two desires coalesce, as for two years past I have wanted to revisit Chartres, where after I had looked at the porch I would go up the tower with the sexton's daughter' (*BWSB* 53). The 'coalescence of desires' is a major motif in the novel to come or, more likely, already being written. There, he describes 'the habit that I had acquired of nursing within me certain desires, the desire for a young girl of

14 John Ruskin, 'Quivi Trovammo' from *Modern Painters V*, plate LXXVIII. See p. 135.

15 John Ruskin, 'Study of Carpaccio's St Ursula'. See p. 151. This was Ruskin's final 'Myth of Venice'. 'There she lies, so real, that when the room's quite quiet – I get afraid of waking her. How little one believes things, really! Suppose there *is* a real St Ursula, di ma – taking care of somebody else, asleep, for me?' (Letter to Joan Severn 19 September 1876.) (The Principal and Fellows of Somerville College, Oxford)

16 Sebastian del Piombo, 'S. Giovanni Crisostomo'. The Venetian painting which had a special appeal for Henry James – see p. 172. (Pala di S. Giovanni Crisostomo, Venice: Photo: Scala, Florence)

17 'The Baptism', mosaic, San Marco, Venice – a crucial work for Proust, see p. 259. (Scala, Florence)

18 John Ruskin, 'Capitals, Concave Group' from *Stones of Venice I*, plate 17. This was the 'signed column' so important for Ezra Pound – see p. 272.

19 The Malatesta Temple, Rimini. See p. 314. (Scala, Florence)

20 Piero della Francesca, 'Malatesta'. See p. 315. (Sigismondo Malatesta davanti a S. Sigismondo, Rimini: Photo: Scala, Florence)

21 Agostino di Duccio, 'The Moon'. See p. 317. (The Malatesta Temple, Rimini)

22 Agostino di Duccio, 'Angel Holding a Curtain'. See p. 317.
(The Malatesta Temple, Rimini)

23 Interior column of Santa Maria dei Miracoli – Pound's 'jewel box' see p. 340. (Kindly provided by Rosella Zorzi)

24 Exterior of Santa Maria dei Miracoli.

good family . . . the desire for handsome lady's-maids, and especially for Mme Putbus's . . . the desire for Venice, the desire to settle down to work . . . the habit of storing up all these desires, without assuaging any of them' (III, 81). It is notable that, grammatically at least, erotic and creative desire are equated, and both, if not identified with, certainly aligned – coalesced – with the desire for Venice. As Peter Collier rightly notes, 'the metonymic contagion is indicative of psychological relationships.[6] Venice promises both sexual and cultural fulfilment, *and* the stimulus to creative work. All very desirable desires.

In his notes to his translation of *Sesame and Lilies*, Proust draws admiring attention to how Ruskin plays on and deploys and develops 'the three meanings of the word *Sesame*, reading which opens the doors of wisdom, Ali Baba's magic word, and the enchanted grain' (*ORR* 144). Ruskin, he says, 'delighted in worshipping a word' (more evidence of idolatry), 'he reveres it', 'he is amazed at the secret virtue there is in a word': 'A word is for him the flask full of memory, of which Baudelaire speaks' (*ORR* 157). As so often, it is hard to see where Proust writing about Ruskin shades into Proust writing about himself. Hard for Proust too, no doubt. There is a moment in the Venetian section of the novel – to which I shall return – when a few words from a stockbroker remind him of some words of a bath attendant, which in turn bring back to mind the now dead Albertine. 'And these words which had never recurred to my mind acted like an "Open Sesame!" upon the hinges of the prison door' (III, 655). The prison is a prison in the memory, 'the *Piombi* of an inner Venice' ('Piombi' – the famous leaded cells in the Ducal Palace) in which 'Albertine dwelt within me, alive, but so remote, so profoundly buried that she remained inaccessible to me' (III, 654). In this episode, the glimpse of Albertine is so fleeting that she can hardly be said to have made her escape. But the overall concern remains – what will release the prisoners? Proust himself knew *The Arabian Nights*, but he must also have had somewhere in mind the words of Ruskin he had so recently translated – concerning 'that old enchanted Arabian grain, the Sesame, which opens doors, not of robbers', but of Kings' Treasuries'. And of Memory's Prisons.

The magic of words is intimately aligned with the magic of Names, indeed one might have thought inseparably so, though I shall in due course attempt to draw a distinction as Proust himself was to do. In a fragment entitled 'Names', or 'Noms de personnes', which would evolve into the opening of *The Guermantes Way*, Proust writes of 'that mysterious current which the Name, that prior existence to the known, sets flowing, and which is incompatible, as now and then our dreams are, with anything we could have experienced' (*BWSB* 175). It is the previousness, literally the priority, of the Name to the known which gives it its superior power: 'the inevitable disappointment of our encounter with things that we knew as names' becomes an article of faith for Proust (*BWSB* 177). What this inevitable disappointment demonstrates, as far as Proust is concerned, is that that inner inrush of a sense of possible magic and beauty, that current of desire, set flowing by the Name, is evidence of and is concerned with 'a far more living reality, which tends perpetually to reshape itself within us, and which, while forsaking the countries we have visited, spreads out over all the others and flows back over those we have known, as soon as we have begun to forget them, as soon as they have once again becomes *names* to us' (*BWSB* 177).

First, Names conjure dreams and arouse desire; then the encounter with the things, places, persons named dissolves the dreams and thwarts or deadens the desire; but later again, as we forget the actual physical encounter, the material proximity and impingement, we may experience a new and more intense kind of bliss, a sense of circumambiently flowing felicity, when, with the inevitable attenuations of amnesia, these bodies and places thin out once more into merely, but magically, Names. If, that is, we stumble on, stumble over, the – utterly unpredictable – right 'Open Sesame!' It is precisely the *pre*-materiality and *post*-materiality of the Name which is crucial. Referring to the titles and names of noble families which may set us dreaming, Proust describes the names as 'vivid, and yet transparent, since no base matter [*matière vile*] clings to them. . . . In our minds the people take on the purity of their immaterial nomenclature' (*BWSB* 178). The French is 'cette pureté de leurs noms qui sont tous imaginatifs' (*CSB* 332), which is another way of saying that matter is vile and imagination pure. Blessed be Names in their radiant non-corporeality! 'Perhaps in such names I shall find something so different from myself that in truth it will be almost consubstantial with the stuff that Names are made of' (*BWSB* 180). I am – I wish to become – such stuff as *Names* are made on. That is another way of writing Proust's ambition, and his ambition in writing.

In the onomastic theophany which is so central to Proust's work, no name carried more resonance than 'Venice'. For Proust that word-name was a site of semantic excess, overfilled with desires, anticipations, dreams, expectations, vast hoped-for experiential appropriations. At the same time, it became a site of semantic evacuation, disillusion and loss – in effect, experiential expropriations. In the novel, Marcel certainly finds it easier to visit 'Venice' than to go there. Indeed 'visiting' and not-getting to Venice is one of the recurring preoccupations and themes for over five-sixths of the book. (He meets and 'visits' the name on page 45 and finally goes to the place on page 2823.) More to the point, perhaps, he finds that not-going there is, precisely, a necessary condition of 'visiting' it: when he *does* go there it soon becomes effectively a place un-visited, un-visitable. Or more simply, when he finally reaches Venice, enters, penetrates, holds and embraces it, he soon loses it. It becomes a place of dissolution, divestment and de-creation. In this, Venice is the paradigmatic word and object (name and place) in the book. Venice *written* is Venice absent, and its value – its over-value – is precisely dependent on its almost endlessly prolonged and perpetuated absence. Farness is all. In terms of Proust's novel, Venice (the word-name) both represents and *is* the indefinable and unconfinable pleasure of absence, a pleasure which is indistinguishable from pleasure deferred, or that deferral which is pleasure. Venice present is Venice lost. The pleasure of 'writing' Venice is incompatible with the pleasure of seeing Venice The pleasure of the word predcludes the pleasure of the place. And, of course, vice versa. The proposition is reversible, symptomatic of the inescapable chiasmus of the dialectic of pleasure. Consummation is frustration; acquisition is depletion; ownership is disaccommodation; possession is deprivation. Finding is losing. But perhaps that losing is a prelude to another finding – a finding *again* – in another mode. This is of course the very theme of the book. Venice. Venice and the word 'Venice'. Places and Names. 'Noms de Pays: Le Nom'; 'Noms de Pays: Le Pays'. The pleasure of Venice is no unambiguous matter.

Venice, then, is a dominant, recurring entity in the novel – locus, topos, topic. 'Le désir de Venise' is the desire that runs through the book. Desire for Venice of course, but also desire *of* Venice, or, as we may say (stressing the genetive, the partitive possessive), the desire which is part of Venice, which emanates from Venice – Venetian desire. 'De' signals two exactly contrary directions – a desire flowing from Marcel to Venice, and a desire flowing from Venice to Marcel. Thus he can speak not only of his 'désir de Venise' but also of his 'imaginations vénitiennes' – what moves towards Venice as a lack, a need, a desire, returns from Venice-imagined as a quality which both colours and constitutes that lack, need, desire. The process is, of course, endlessly circular with no very clear beginning. For Marcel, to know about Venice was at once to desire it; and, inextricably, to know and experience desire was at once to desire Venice. It may be objected that Marcel's first and constitutive experience of loss, lack and desire was of his mother. I shall suggest that, by a process of identification, extension, transference and displacement which is not hard to understand, Venice and the mother (who *read* him Ruskin, and *took* him to the city) are both metaphorically and metonymically related – if not exactly interchangeable, then susceptible of indefinite substitutability.

The young Marcel is familiar with 'Venice' – like everybody else – through reproductions and representations; it is the already-written (Ruskin), the already-painted (Carpaccio). It is also, from the start, associated with a desired but prohibited woman – the actress Berma, attendance at whose performances the doctor has advised against, as he has advised against travel, on the grounds of Marcel's over-excitability. 'A Carpaccio in Venice, Berma in Phédre' are, alike, 'the unique and inconceivable object of so many thousand dreams' (I, 475–6) and, like Nietzsche's figure of Truth, seductive because veiled –

'concealed, like the Holy of Holies, beneath the veil that screened her from my gaze' (I, 478). This is the early manifestation of a yearning which will reach a climax in the actual Holy of Holies in St Mark's. 'But,' insists Proust, 'what I demanded from this performance – as from . . . the visit to Venice for which I had so intensely longed – was something quite different from pleasure: verities pertaining to a world more real than that in which I lived, which, once acquired, could never be taken from me again' (I, 477). As we shall see, Venice is to afford him both venery ***and*** verity.

When his father promises him, as a young boy, a visit to Venice, which as a 'name' had 'magnetised my desires' (I, 422), the prospect of actually walking in his 'supernatural city' – the idea that Venice might emerge from 'ideal time' so that his world would interpenetrate with that supernatural, 'imaginary' dream of his desires – makes him physically sick. The imagined effort of 'penetrating' that desired place – and the description is sufficiently orgasmic – almost literally un-mans, un-bodies him. It is a prosaic remark by his father that precipitates the attack. 'At these words' – his father simply observes that it must still be pretty cold on the Grand Canal, better take an overcoat –

> I was raised to a sort of ecstasy; I felt myself – something I had until then deemed impossible – to be penetrating indeed between those rocks of amethyst, like a reef in the Indian Ocean; by a supreme muscular effort, far in excess of my real strength, divesting myself, as of a shell that served no purpose, of the air in my own room which surrounded me, I replaced it by an equal quantity of Venetian air, that marine atmosphere, indescribable and peculiar as the atmosphere of dreams, which my imagination had secreted in the name of Venice; I felt myself undergoing a miraculous disincarnation, which was at once accompanied by that vague desire to vomit which one feels when one has developed a very sore throat; and I had to be put to bed with a fever so persistent that the doctor declared not only that a visit to Florence and Venice was absolutely out of the question, but that, even when I had completely recovered, I must for at least a year give up all idea of travelling and be kept from anything that was liable to excite me.
>
> And alas, he also imposed a formal ban on my being allowed to go to the theatre to hear Berma. (I, 426–7)

This is one of the most sexual descriptions in the book. With a supreme physical effort he 'penetrates' Ruskin's description of Venice. It leaves him with a feeling of 'miraculous disincarnation', as orgasm has been said to do. One might say that, at this moment, Marcel effectively loses his virginity. And Venice, at the moment of imminent taking and possession, suddenly recedes into indefinite distance and deferral. It, or she, is banned, banished, forbidden, taboo. He is punished for his transgression – what one might call his premature ejaculation. At the same time, he is forbidden to go to see Berma – that other desired and veiled body and place, that linked mysterious object of desire. It is his father' power to grant access to, and to withhold and forbid, both Venice and Berma. As he can the mother's goodnight kiss.

Writing of the time when he was in love with the Duchesse de Guermantes, Marcel includes a delicate description of those hypnagogic moments between waking thought and sleep; while going to sleep you can be thinking about not being able to go to sleep, and so when asleep a 'glimmer' of thought can remain in 'almost total darkness'. This in turn can become a 'reflexion' during sleep on the thought that one cannot sleep, which can in turn generate 'a reflexion of this reflexion' which can lead to a 'further refraction', and so on.

> These shadows were barely distinguishable; it would have required a keen – and quite useless – delicacy of perception to seize them. Similarly, in later years, in Venice, long after the sun had set, when it seemed to be quite dark, I have seen, thanks to the echo, itself imperceptible, of a last note of light held indefinitely on the surface of the canals as though by the effect of some optical pedal, the reflexions of the palaces displayed as though for all time in a darker velvet on the crepuscular greyness of the water. (II, 147)

The last reflections of the Venetian waters become the final faint reflections of the mind at the very edge, and just beyond the edge, of sleep (Proust elsewhere describes himself as one of those 'who love to stroll on the edges of the waters of thought'; *ORR* 88); and light, audaciously, turns to a music in the memory – which will, indeed, be the music of time. Venice reflected and reflecting in and on its waters is becoming the very image of that mysterious terrain of the mind where the conscious and the unconscious meet and, albeit faintly and fleetingly, make strange incursions – tentative or vestigial forays – into each other's realm. The passage continues:

> One of my dreams was the synthesis of what my imagination had often sought to depict, in my waking hour, of a certain seagirt place and its mediaeval past. In my sleep I saw a Gothic city rising from a sea whose waves were stilled as in a stained-glass window. An arm of the sea divided the town in two; the green water stretched to my feet; on the opposite shore it washed round the base of an oriental church, and beyond it houses which existed already in the fourteenth century, so that to go across to them would have been to ascend the stream of time. This dream in which nature had learned from art, in which

> the sea had turned Gothic, this dream in which I longed to attain, in which I believed that I was attaining to the impossible, was one that I felt I had often dreamed before. (II, 147–8)

'In which nature had learned from art': Venice as a site where the usual distinguishing categories of nature and culture no longer hold – where nature and art might seem to work together, change places, merge, become indistinguishable – is a theme constantly sounded in this study. Here the sea can turn Gothic, while the Gothic city rises from the sea like a coral reef (to use an image employed by both Ruskin and Melville). When, earlier, Elstir is discussing the 'massive' ships in Carpaccio's Venetian paintings – ships 'like lesser Venices set in the heart of the greater' – he says: '"You can't tell where the land finished and the water began, what was still the palace or already the ship, the caravel, the galley, the Bucintoro"' (I, 959). Not being able to tell where the land finishes and the water begins is of a piece with larger epistemological, even metaphysical, uncertainties and doubts about boundaries. Venice becomes supremely the place where seemingly distinct categories can leak, or indeed soak, into each other – carnival again, but this time a carnival of the mind and senses. For Proust, it will become the place where he can't tell where Time finishes and Eternity begins.

It is in his account of his relationship with Albertine – which may be seen as *the* central relationship – that the references to Venice begin to proliferate. He (often) does not want to marry Albertine because if he did he would not, so he feels, be able to go to Venice. Yet he does not want to go to Venice because that would, as he sees it, mean letting go of, and losing, Albertine. They appear, always, as mutually exclusive alternatives, or, we might say, as interchangeable desires and obstacles to desire; the one always (happily?) preventing the other. Frustration is thus assured – and longing prolonged. The end of the second volume sees Marcel 'only waiting for an opportunity for a final rupture . . . in order to remain free, not to have to marry her if I did not wish to do so, to be able to go to Venice' (II, 1150). But why can he not go to Venice *with* Albertine – have both, as we say? 'I should have liked, as soon as I was cured, to set off for Venice, but how was I to manage it, if I married Albertine, I who was so jealous of her that even in Paris whenever I decided to stir from my room it was to go out with her?' (III, 21). Again: 'I could not even go to Venice, where, while I lay in bed, I should be too tormented by the fear of the advances that might be made to her by the gondolier, the people in the hotel, the Venetian women' (III, 399). As he elsewhere observes with that Proustian acuteness of insight into the contradictions in his own malady: 'We consider it innocent to desire, and heinous that the other person should do so' (III, 168). Since there is such a thing as 'retrospective jealousy', 'jealousy is thus endless' (III, 81). And thus, also, is the perpetuation of blocked desire. Hence the recurrence of such observations as 'had it not been for Albertine . . . I might at that moment be dining in Venice' (III, 174). Dining, or more. 'If Albertine had not been up there, and indeed if I had merely been in search of pleasure, I would have gone to demand it of unknown women, into whose life I should have atempted to penetrate, in Venice perhaps' (III, 336). If, perhaps, might have, would have: by keeping Albertine firmly in place, in the way (she is *his* 'captive' after all), Marcel enables himself to range freely in the conditional tenses, the fantasized terrain of desires imagined and unrealized – to which he has given the name 'Venice'.

'If my life with Albertine were to prevent me from going to Venice, from travelling'(III, 167) – Marcel comes to understand how interwoven and interdependent his desires are.

> But these very similarities between desire and travel made me vow to myself that one day I would grasp a little more closely the nature of this force, invisible but as powerful as any belief or, in the world of physics, as atmospheric pressure, which exalted cities and women to such a height so long as I did not know them, and, slipping away from beneath them, made them at once collapse and fall flat on the dead level of the most commonplace reality. (III, 170)

Marcel will finally transcend the impossible double bind of either/or – Albertine/Venice – not by the satisfaction of 'both', but by the relinquishment of 'Neither'. He will attain to the beyond of desire by grasping, a little more closely, the nature of its force. But not yet.

Lying in bed one day, he catches a smell of petrol from the street. It immediately revives a desire 'to make love in new places with a woman unknown'. Tracing out the how and the why of the evocative and arousing power the 'scent' was having on him, he finds himself among the memories of old desires, and the old magic of a favourite Name.

> But all of a sudden the scene changed; it was the memory, no longer of old impressions but of an old desire, only recently reawakened by the Fortuny gown in blue and gold, that spread before me another spring, a spring not leafy at all but on the contrary suddenly stripped of its trees and flowers by the name that I had just murmured to myself: 'Venice'; a decanted springtime, which is reduced to its essence and expresses the lengthening, the warming, the gradual unfolding of its days in the progressive fermentation, no longer, now, of an impure soil, but of a blue and virginal water, springlike without bud or blossom, which could answer the call of May only by gleaming facets fashioned

> and polished by May, harmonising exactly with it in the radiant, unaltered nakedness of its dusky sapphire. Likewise, too, no more than the season to its flowerless creeks, do modern times bring any change to the Gothic city; I knew it, even if I could not imagine it, or rather, imagining it, this was what I longed for with the same desire which long ago, when I was a boy, in the very ardour of departure, had broken and robbed me of the strength to make the journey: to find myself face to face with my Venetian imaginings, to observe how that divided sea enclosed in its meanderings, like the sinuosities of the ocean stream, an urbane and refined civilisation, but one that, isolated by their azure girdle, had evolved independently, had had its own schools of painting and architecture, to admire that fabulous garden of fruits and birds in coloured stone, flowering in the midst of the sea which kept it refreshed, lapped the base of its columns with its tide, and, like a sombre azure gaze watching in the shadows, kept patches of light perpetually flickering on the bold relief of the capitals.
>
> Yes, I must go, the time had come. (III, 421)

How things bind and blend themselves together! Well might Proust have echoed his Master as desire calls out to desire across a chain of associations and a smell of petrol takes him back to a remembered imagination of 'Venice'. And he is ***determined***, this time, to ***go***. 'Yes, this was the moment . . . choose a fine day like this . . . when she [Albertine] had ceased to matter to me, when I was tempted by countless desires . . . and without seeing her again, set off for Venice.' He sets about the practicalities.

> I rang for Françoise to ask her to buy me a guide-book and a time-table, as I had done as a boy when already I wanted to prepare in advance a journey to Venice, the fulfilment of a desire as violent as that which I felt at this moment. I forget that, in the meantime, there was a desire which I had attained without any satisfaction – the desire for Balbec – and that Venice, being also a visible phenomenon, was probably no more able than Balbec to fulfil an ineffable dream, that of the Gothic age made actual by a springtime sea, that now teased my mind from moment to moment with an enchanted, caressing, elusive, mysterious, confused image. (III, 421)

But of course, just at this (the second) moment when he thinks he is about to actually depart for Venice, because convinced of his necessary 'indifference' to Albertine, he is told that she has left – and the prospect, the proximity, the imminence of Venice once again totally disappears. It is replaced by the more immediate, more immanent loss and disappearance of Albertine – and, once again, physical upset supervenes ('I gripped my heart in my hands, which were suddenly moistened by a perspiration' – not, this time, premature proto-sexual excitement, but somatic anxiety, though the two can be nearly enough allied). As he only desires one presence – Venice *or* Albertine (or Berma or, I suggest, mother) – so he only requires one absence. The lack of Albertine is all he needs. 'La Prisonnière' immediately gives way to 'La Fugitive'. The captured becomes the flown.

The smell of petrol took him to Venice by way of a Fortuny gown, and I wish to digress on this a little. In an early conversation involving Albertine and Elstir, the subject of Venetian lace comes up. Albertine expresses immediate interest and, in her own coalescence of desires, conflates lace and place. '"Oh, I should so like to see that lace you speak of; it's so pretty, Venetian lace . . . and I should so like to see Venice."' The second desire will not be gratified – not if Marcel can help it; but Elstir holds out an interesting hope in connection with the first.

> 'You may, perhaps before very long,' Elstir informed her, 'be able to gaze at the marvellous stuffs they used to wear. One used only to be able to see them in the works of the Venetian painters. . . . But I hear that a Venetian artist, called Fortuny, has rediscovered the secret of the craft, and that in a few years' time women will be able to parade around, and better still to sit at home, in brocades as sumptuous as those that Venice adorned for her patrician daughters with patterns brought from the Orient. But I don't know whether I would much care for that, whether it wouldn't be too much of an anachronism for the women of to-day, even when they parade at regattas, for, to return to our modern pleasure-craft, the times have completely changed since "Venice, Queen of the Adriatic".' (I, 960)

Fortuny started to produce such gowns in 1910 – Collier gives the historical details.[7] For Proust the important sequence would go something like this: *original* oriental patterns were *transported* to historical Venice for the purposes of adornment; dresses *incorporating* these patterns were then *represented* in contemporary paintings (primarily by Carpaccio); historical Venice *fades* and the dresses *disappear*; a later artist, working from the *preserved images* of the dresses, *re-creates* them in another mode, and thus *revives* or *resurrects* that earlier Venice in which the *original* dresses (themselves in a sense *copies* or *adaptations*) moved, and glowed, and had their day of triumph and joy. The words which I have somewhat laboriously italicized offer a descriptive account of what Proust took to be the procedures and processes of the resuscitatory and preservative powers and provenances of art.

Much later, in the novel, the gowns anticipated by Elstir become available.

> These Fortuny gowns . . . were those of which Elstir, when he told us about the magnificent garments of the women of Carpaccio's and Titian's day, had prophesied the imminent return, rising from their ashes, as magnificent as of old, for everything must return in time, as it is written beneath the vaults of St Mark's, and proclaimed, as they drink from the urns of marble and jasper of the Byzantine capitals, by the birds which symbolise at once death and resurrection. As soon as women had begun to wear them, Albertine had remembered Elstir's prophecy, had coveted them, and we were shortly to go and choose one. . . . these Fortuny gowns, faithfully antique but markedly original, brought before the eye like a stage decor, and with an even greater evocative power since the decor was left to the imagination, the Venice saturated with oriental splendour where they would have been worn and of which they constituted, even more than a relic in the shrine of St Mark, evocative as they were of the sunlight and the surrounding turbans, the fragmented, mysterious and complementary colour. *Everything of those days had perished but everything was being reborn*, evoked and linked together by the splendour and swarming life of the city, in the piecemeal reappearance of the still-surviving fabrics worn by the Doges' ladies. (III, 376; my italics)

As Collier points out, 'everything must return in time' – or any equivalent phrase – is nowhere written on or beneath the arches of St Mark's, and he is surely correct in surmising that Proust is recalling a passage in Ruskin's *The Stones of Venice* in which he infers an implicit or metaphoric message 'written' in the arches: 'There is a message written in the dyes of them, that once was written in blood; and a sound that echoes in their vaults, that one day shall fill the vault of heaven; – "He shall return to do judgment and justice."'[8] Proust has made a significant modification to the 'message' in his transposition. He is interested in notions of return: less so, or not at all, in concerns of 'judgment and justice'. That a dress derived from a painting should have ascribed to it more 'evocative power' than a relic in a shrine might seem a bold, even blasphemous, claim. But clearly Proust wants to move the whole vocabulary of 'resurrection' into – or appropriate it for – the secular realm, and his own purposes. And we should recall that, in time, he will compare his own writing not only to the labour of building a cathedral but to the work of a dressmaker. What a Fortuny gown can do, he, he hopes, can do even better.

As regards the Fortuny gowns now on sale in Paris, they decide on buying one (and Marcel orders five more). Albertine first wears it on an evening which turns out to be less than auspicious, even ominous.

> It was the very evening on which Albertine had put on for the first time the indoor gown in gold and blue by Fortuny which, by re-

> minding me of Venice, made me feel all the more strongly what I was sacrificing for her, who showed no corresponding gratitude towards me. If I had never seen Venice, I had dreamed of it incessantly since those Easter holidays which, when still a boy, I had been going to spend there, and earlier still, since the Titian prints and Giotto photographs which Swann had given me long ago at Combray. The Fortuny gown which Albertine was wearing that evening seemed to me the tempting phantom of that invisible Venice. It was covered with Arab ornamentation, like the Venetian palaces hidden like sultan's wives behind a screen of pierced stone, like the bindings in the Ambrosian library, like the columns from which the oriental birds that symbolised alternatively life and death were repeated in the shimmering fabric, of an intense blue which, as my eyes drew nearer, turned into a malleable gold by those same transmutations which, before an advancing gondola, change into gleaming metal the azure of the Grand Canal. And the sleeves were lined with a cherry pink which is so peculiarly Venetian that it is called Tiepolo pink. (III, 401)

The Fortuny gown brings together the exotically erotic (sultan's wives) and the exotically literary (bindings from a library of oriental books); columns and canals; mysterious transmutations (blue fabric into malleable gold, water into metal); and – life and death. All in the evocative imagery *of* Venice worn *on* Albertine's body. This is, indeed, a sumptuous coalescence.

Sumptuous, yet vaguely mortuary – it is *all* art, adornment and artefact, with the living woman completely submerged. Albertine seems to sense this. After their quarrel – as so often, about her supposed infidelities with other women – Marcel attempts a reconciling kiss. 'I kissed her then a second time, pressing to my heart the shimmering golden azure of the Grand Canal and the mating birds, symbols of death and resurrection. But for the second time, instead of returning my kiss, she drew away with that sort of instinctive and baleful obstinacy of animals that fear the hand of death' (III, 406). And she is right in her instinct. Marcel wants to 'embrace' Venice rather than Albertine. She is here being deployed as the living vehicle of his cherished symbols of 'death and resurrection' and, while the pursuit of Venice and those symbols might lead to a vision of resurrection for Marcel, she seems to feel that, in one sense or another, it means death for her. The Fortuny gown is, of course, intended to heighten the erotic excitement, but in the event it impedes physical contact. '"I dare not approach you for fear of crumpling that fine stuff, and there are those fateful birds between us. Undress, my darling."' But Albertine has felt 'the hand of death'. '"No, I couldn't possibly take off this dress here. I shall undress in my own room presently"' (III, 407). Images of Venice, Venetian symbols, literally come between them, and Albertine seems to apprehend that Marcel is using her, in some complex way, to inflame and maintain his desire and aspiration for Venice and all it connotes, by keeping her body (she is after all 'the captive') interposed between him and his prime desire. And that body knows that what is life to him means death for her. Understandably, the body refuses to yield. In the event, she is shortly to die in good earnest and, predictably enough, Venice again recedes. 'Venice, where I had thought that her company would be irksome (doubtless because I had felt in a confused way that it would be necessary to me), no longer attracted me now that Albertine was no more' (III, 492). With the removal of the obstacle comes the extinction of the desire.

'As for the third occasion on which I remember being conscious of nearing total indifference with regard to Albertine (and this time to the extent of feeling that I had finally arrived at it), it was . . . in Venice' (III, 637). So he has finally got there. 'My mother had taken me to spend a few weeks there.' The coast is finally clear. There is now just Marcel, and his mother, and – and in – Venice. The part of the novel which actually takes place in Venice is some thirty pages, the merest fraction of the work as a whole; and yet it is not only the crucial preparation for the narrator's final epiphany and vision. It also contains, in little, many of the most important themes of the book. There is a false resurrection – involving Albertine: and intimations of a true one – due to the presence of the mother in Venice. There is a reprise of the importance of Carpaccio and Fortuny, makers and preservers of images of Venice. There is one, and only one, society scene, but it anticipates the crucial final social gatherings of the book. There is the gratification of the lowest sexual desires, and intimations of a higher satisfaction – venery and verity, as I have said. There is the most serious and important reference to the name of Ruskin in the whole work (there is an earlier bantering one). There are insights into the different modes of the operations of memory. And there is the great theme of Venice found and Venice lost – or desire gratified which becomes desire dead; or that possession which is deprivation. The whole episode is of course seamlessly continuous, but it can be roughly divided into ten scenes for separate consideration.

The sequence starts, as the whole novel does, with Marcel in bed. His eyes open to a new promise.

> When, at ten o'clock in the morning, my shutters were thrown open, I saw blazing there, instead of the gleaming black marble into which the slates of Saint-Hilaire used to turn, the golden angel on the campanile of St Mark's. Glittering in a sunlight which made it almost impossible to keep one's eyes upon it, this angel promised me, with its outstretched arms, for the moment when I appeared on the Piazzetta

> half an hour later, a joy more certain than any that it could ever in the past have been bidden to announce to men of good will. (III, 637–8)

Going out for a stroll 'in Venice where everyday life was no less real than in Combray' (we shall see what 'everyday life' in Venice means to him), he finds that the street is 'entirely paved with sapphire-blue water'. Water into sapphire – flowing into fixed, nature into art: an early intimation of things to come. He accumulates many 'impressions', not least of the Gothic windows.

> Of this sort was the window in our hotel behind the clusters of which my mother sat waiting for me, gazing at the canal with a patience which she would not have displayed in the old days at Combray, at a time when, cherishing hopes for my future which had never been realised, she was unwilling to let me see how much she loved me. Nowadays she was well aware that an apparent coldness on her part would alter nothing, and the affection she lavished upon me was like those forbidden foods which are no longer withheld from invalids when it is certain that they are past recovery. (III, 638–9)

There is no longer any obstacle to a direct recognition and exchange of love for the mother and mother-love. But '*forbidden* foods'? Presumably the love of a mother is only 'forbidden' to the extent that it threatens – or promises – to become incestuous. Which it very nearly does in a remarkable, and remarkably important, passage.

> And because, behind its multi-coloured marble balusters, Mamma was sitting reading while she waited for me to return, her face shrouded in a tulle veil as heart-rending in its whiteness as her hair to me.

The mother is often seen sitting 'behind' and, in truth, she is behind everything in the book, behind the book itself, as she sits waiting for Marcel's 'return' in every sense. He has been on a very extensive detour. Mother, book and veil. It is, as it were, an opposite triad to bell, book and candle; for, whereas the latter spells excommunication, the former promises, let's call it, a kind of *re*communication, a communing with something other and higher.

> as soon as I called her from the gondola, she sent out to me, from the bottom of her heart, a love which stopped only where there was no longer any corporeal matter to sustain it, on the surface of her impassioned gaze which she brought as close to me as possible, which she

> tried to thrust forward to the advanced post of her lips, in a smile which seemed to be kissing me. (III, 639–40)

This, surely, is the language of a lovers' rendezvous. But the description of a love which stops short only for lack of 'corporeal matter to sustain it' suggests a love – a something – which can transcend these merely corporeal limitations, like those Names which float free of gross maculate contamination. With incest and transcendence coming so close together, it is a matter – that peculiarly Venetian problem – of where one sort of desire stops and another starts. As the immediately following paragraphs reveal, there is a Venice of art, and a Venice of sex (of the most anonymous, exploitative kind). Which is more 'real' – and where to go in pursuit of that elusive entity?

From the smile of the mother to the benedictions of art.

> And since, in Venice, it is works of art, things of priceless beauty, that are entrusted with the task of giving us our impressions of everyday life, it is to falsify the character of that city, on the grounds that the Venice of certain painters is coldly aesthetic in its most celebrated parts . . . to represent only its poverty-stricken aspects, in the districts where nothing of its splendour is to be seen. . . . It has been the mistake of some very great artists, from a quite natural reaction against the artifical Venice of bad painters, to concentrate exclusively on the Venice of the more humble campi, the little deserted rii, which they found more real. (III, 640)

No less than Ezra Pound, Proust wants something to 'lead back' – or lead on – 'to splendour'. And, as also with Pound, the high art of Venice, and that Venice which is art, is a crucial way. It is an art which deliberately ignores, or omits, the splendour-free 'poverty-stricken aspects' of the city, the 'humble' and 'deserted' parts (or, we might say, the domain of the humble and deserted in general – the great realm of the overlooked). It is a mistake, one feels he implies it is a kind of affectation or reverse snobbery, to suggest such parts of the city are 'more real'. Nevertheless, Marcel *immediately* heads straight for them.

> It was this Venice that I used often to explore in the afternoon, when I did not go out with my mother. The fact was that it was easier to find there women of the people, match-sellers, pearl-stringers, glass or lace makers, young seamstresses in black shawls with long fringes. (III, 641)

He is probably unaware that that sentence could almost have been written by Casanova, whose pursuit of what can only be called street-sex with the daughters of the poor he is unconsciously emulating; though perhaps the choice of occupations – fire, pearls, glass, lace are involved – is not entirely adventitious and random, coming from a man who was interested in flares of insight, precious works of beauty, reflections, and who would, in time, himself aspire to be a kind of seamstress in writing. With all these women, he is trying to work out, or work through, problems connected with desire. Was he looking for Albertine replicas, Albertine substitutes, or what?

> Who, in any case, could have told me precisely, in this passionate quest of mine for Venetian women, how much there was of themselves, how much of Albertine, how much of my old, long-cherished desire to visit Venice? Our slightest desire, though unique as a chord, nevertheless includes the fundamental notes on which the whole of our life is built. . . . There were many things that I made no attempt to identify in the excitement I felt as I went in search of Venetian women. (III, 641)

His entrance into the 'poor and populous districts' in quest of 'plebeian girls' – like and unlike Albertine – is an almost explicitly sexual penetration, presided over by oriental magic.

> My gondola followed the course of the small canals; like the mysterious hand of a genie leading me through the maze of this oriental city, they seemed, as I advanced, to be cutting a path for me through the heart of a crowded quarter which they bisected, barely parting, with a slender furrow arbitrarily traced, the tall houses with their tiny Moorish windows. (III, 641)

He is back with – and perhaps delibertely, excitingly, mingling – his childhood delight in the *Arabian Nights* and his later pleasure in sexual promiscuity. He simply – I'll say it once – wants to fuck Venice, and all that it has accumulatively meant to him. Regressive is perhaps not quite the word: but this is something he will have to pass beyond. From these outings, he learns at least one important lesson – 'I had to consent to a further departure from the principle of the individuality of desire' (III, 642). Object-choice, as Freud called it, and the vicissitudes and arbitrariness thereof. Desire for this or that, here or there, him or her – this is not, finally, so important. What matters is simply desire itself. But more of that later.

He returns – as of course he always will – to his mother and recalls a ride with her in a gondola. As they glide along the Grand Canal, the great historic buildings appear as a 'chain of marble cliffs' – an image found in Ruskin which will reappear in Pound.

> Seen thus, the buildings arranged along either bank of the canal made one think of objects of nature, but of a nature which seemed to have

> created its works with a human imagination. But at the same time (because of the always urban character of the impressions which Venice gives almost in the open sea on those waters whose ebb and flow makes itself felt twice daily, and which alternately cover at high tide and uncover at low tide the splendid outside stairs of the palaces) . . . we passed the most elegant women in the hazy evening light . . . languidly reclining against the cushions of their floating carriages . . . thus any outing, even when it was only to pay calls or to leave visiting-cards, was threefold and unique in this Venice where the simplest social coming and going assumed at the same time the form and the charm of a visit to a museum and a trip on the sea. (III, 644)

What does *not* come together, conflate, in this Venice? Buildings like objects of nature, but nature working like culture; a high urbanism and urbanity in (almost) the open sea; waters that cover and uncover, bury and reprieve, the work of man each day; an outing which is at once a sea trip, a matter of etiquette and a visit to a museum – dealings with nature, society and art converge into one, 'threefold and unique'. Venice, the place where the Trinity – this trinity – becomes also a Unity. Three and One. The religious suggestions are inescapable.

The next scene is the one 'social' scene I mentioned. It might seem like a strange interpolation. Why interrupt what otherwise seems the constant preoccupation with Venice and the mother, Venice and Albertine, Venice and the 'plebeian women', Venice and art? But in an important sense it is a prefiguration: one might call it a John-the-Baptist of a scene foreshadowing the advent of a greater scene, the scene which will be the salvation of Marcel, affording him a vision of the redemptive possibilities of art. It concerns a surprise encounter – or, rather, a hidden overseeing and overhearing – with Madame de Villeparsis and her lover of old, Monsieur de Norpois, having dinner in another hotel. Marcel and his mother – at another table – are joined by a friend, Madame Sazerat, and Marcel mentions that he has just seen Madame de Villeparsis. Madame Sazerat turns pale on hearing the name. Because this was the woman '"who drove my father to distraction, ruined him and then abandoned him immediately. Well, she may have behaved to him like the lowest prostitute . . . but now that my father is dead, my consolation is to think that he loved the most beautiful woman of his generation, and as I've never set eyes on her, it will be a sort of solace in spite of everything"' (III, 648). Marcel conducts her to a suitable spot, and points out Madame de Villeparsis.

> But, like a blind person who looks everywhere but in the right direction, Mme Sazerat did not bring her eyes to rest upon the table at which Mme de Villeparsis was dining, but, looking towards another part of the room, said:

> 'But she must have gone, I don't see her where you say she is.'
> And she continued to gaze round the room in quest of the loathed, adored vision that had haunted her imagination for so long.
> 'Yes, there she is, at the second table.'
> 'Then we can't be counting from the same point. At what I count as the second table there's only an old gentleman and a little hunch-backed, red-faced, hideous woman.'
> 'That's her!'

If any one little scene encapsulates the shock of *non*-recognition, recognition refused, at the heart of this extraordinary work, it is this. It exactly adumbrates Marcel's experience at the climactic party given by the Princesse de Guermantes, on the way to which he has the crucial epiphanic experience on the uneven paving-stones. He sees many of his earlier acquaintances, but seemingly they are all engaged in some sort of 'masquerade' – strange masks for familiar faces; weird attire unrecognizable hair, or hairless, styles; incredible bodily postures. What kind of mad fancy-dress party is this? Then he realizes. They have simply grown old.

> Some men walked with a limp, and one was aware that this was the result not of a motor accident but of a first stroke: they had already, as the saying is, one foot in the grave. There were women too whose graves were waiting open to receive them: half paralysed, they could not quite disentangle their dress from the tomb-stone in which it had got stuck, so that they were unable to stand up straight but remained bent towards the ground, with their head lowered, in a curve which seemed an apt symbol of their own position on the trajectory from life to death, with the final vertical plunge not far away. (III, 980)

Distressing. 'I had made the discovery of this destructive action of Time at the very moment when I had conceived the ambition to make visible, to intellectualise in a work of art, realities that were outside Time' (III, 971). In a more intense way, Marcel at this party experiences what Madame Sazerat experienced in the dining-room in Venice – the loss of a 'vision that had haunted her imagination'. Were *these* the towering figures who had loomed so awe-inspiringly, whether 'loathed' or 'adored', in his younger years? Then, if anything is to be saved, while Time does its inexorable work of downward, degenerative metamorphosis, Marcel must embark on another kind of work which will 'transpose' all his garnered and remembered impressions into, using another phrase from the Venetian interlude, 'a wholly different and far richer key' (III, 637).

The third episode involves what I have called the 'false resurrection' of Albertine. At first she nearly escapes from the prison of his 'inner Venice', because of some chance words from his stockbroker, and then she seems to have escaped from the grave when Marcel receives a letter which he misreads as coming from her and expressing a desire to discuss marriage. He then realizes that though he intermittently grieved for her 'when certain involuntary memories had brought her alive again for me' – and thus she 'survived her physical death' – now that those *thoughts* are dead, her apparent return to *physical* life still leaves her in obliteration: 'Albertine did not rise again for me with the resurrection of her body' (III, 656). At this stage, Marcel thinks that this is because he has changed and cannot recapture his former self – the self that was obsessed with Albertine. 'I should have been incapable of resuscitating Albertine because I was incapable of resuscitating myself, of resuscitating the self of those days' (III, 657). We might think that, at this point, he is misreading notions of 'resuscitation' just as he has misread the letter. That there is a good deal of his former self still alive is indicated by a detail included in this section. His 'Venetian interests' had been 'concentrated for some little time past on a young vendor of glass-ware' – glass again, to see his own reflection? to drink from? – whom he wishes almost literally to buy (some worry about money at this point) and take back to Paris where he would keep her 'for my sole convenience'. Another 'Captive'? The young girl is so beautiful, it would, he says, be 'like acquiring a Titian before leaving the place' (III, 655). The conflation of art and girl – the aestheticization of her body – into a single object of Venetian desire is the recurrence of an old form of desire. (At this point Marcel is something of a prisoner of his 'inner Venice' as well.) Perhaps not surprisingly, with the death of his love for Albertine, now conclusively proved as he feels, Marcel is more than a little overwhelmed by what he takes to be 'the general law of oblivion' (III, 659). Though he still nurses a 'desire not to be parted from myself by death, to rise again after my death' (III, 660). Thus, appropriately, this section concludes with the phrase 'desire for immortality' – of which he says death will 'cure us'.

Appropriately, because he immediately moves to a second episode involving his mother, in which he has important intimations of a different mode of 'resuscitation' – or preservation – and also, we might note, a different and a better way of conjoining art and the female. It starts with him collecting his notebooks 'for some work I was doing on Ruskin' (III, 660). Then he joins his mother and together they go to St Mark's. It is a pregnant foregathering – Ruskin for the one occasion present as a tutelary figure; together *with* the mother *in* St Mark's; and Marcel, now under the guidance and with the benediction of the two crucial 'parental' presences, as it were, is beginning to write. The following long passage is one of the most important in the whole work.

> we would set off for St Mark's, with all the more pleasure because, since one had to take a gondola to go there, the church represented

> for me not simply a monument but the terminus of a voyage on these vernal, maritime waters, with which, I felt, St Mark's formed an indivisible and living whole. My mother and I would enter the baptistery, treading underfoot the glass mosaics of the paving, in front of us the wide arcades whose curved pink surfaces have been slightly warped by time, thus giving the church, wherever the freshness of this colouring has been preserved, the appearance of having been built of a soft and malleable substance like the wax in a giant honeycomb, and, where time has shrivelled and hardened the material and artists have embellished it with gold tracery, of being the precious binding, in the finest Cordoba leather, of the colossal Gospel of Venice. Seeing that I needed to spend some time in front of the mosaics representing the Baptism of Christ, and feeling the icy coolness that pervaded the baptistery, my mother threw a shawl over my shoulders. . . . A time has now come when, remembering the baptistery of St Mark's – contemplating the waters of the Jordan in which St John immerses Christ, while the gondola awaited us at the landing-stage of the Piazzetta – it is no longer a matter of indifference to me that, beside me in that cool penumbra, there should have been a woman draped in her mourning with the respectful and enthusiastic fervour of the old woman in Carpaccio's *St Ursula* in the Academia, and that that woman, with her red cheeks and sad eyes and in her black veils, whom nothing can ever remove from that softly lit sanctuary of St Mark's where I am always sure to find her because she has her place reserved there as immutably as a mosaic, should be my mother. (III, 660–1)

Then: now. Then – the vernal waters, and a voyage which concludes with Marcel working in St Mark's under the benevolent gaze and protective shawl of the Madonna-like mother – a 'terminus' in every sense. He is beginning to work like Ruskin, seeing, as Ruskin did, St Mark's as a magnificent, sacred volume. The work involves a close study of mosaics, mosaics of the supreme Baptism which, for believers, was the baptism of the figure who would ensure eternal life for us. Now – the waters of the Grand Canal have blended with the waters of Jordan, and the waiting gondola linked to St John, the mother of the black veils has been transmuted into art and thereby eternized. The whole passage starts on those ebbing and flowing waters of Venice and ends in the radiant and fixed immutability of a mosaic. It is surely a far, far better thing to see your mother as a Carpaccio than to try to lure and secrete a young girl into your bachelor prison as a Titian. Marcel is being baptized, immersed, in the rivers of Venice-Jordan, to arise into a newly appreciated realm and life of memory and art. For if his great work is going to be like a dress, it will also, itself, be a mosaic.

The reference to Carpaccio leads on to the next episode, in which Marcel recalls experiencing a strange moment of recognition in front of one of Carpaccio's Venetian paintings. On one of the figures in the painting

> I had recognised the cloak Albertine had put on to come with me to Versailles . . . she had flung over her shoulders a Fortuny cloak which she had taken away with her next day and which I had never thought of since. It was from this Carpaccio picture that the inspired son of Venice had taken it, it was from the shoulders of this *compagna della Calza* that he had removed it in order to drape it over the shoulders of so many Parisian women. (III, 662)

From painting to gown to female shoulders – three 'textures' which are indeed crucial in the many-layered text of the book. The moment 'almost succeeded . . . in reviving my love for Albertine' (III, 661). But only 'almost'. That particular resurrection is not to be – although the next two episodes record an oscillation between new and old desires. He goes, with his mother, to Padua, where they look at the Giotto frescoes and the 'flights of angels' which seem to 'defy the laws of gravity' (III, 663). Again, a celestial art which leaves mortal matter below and behind. But back in Venice, on the prowl without his mother, he meets a young Austrian woman who in some ways reminds him of Albertine. He wonders whether she, too, loves other women – a speculation which clearly excites him though he tries to mask it by representing it to himself as 'intellectual curiosity' (III, 665). However, she obdurately deflects or denies his importuning and prurient enquiries, and he never sees her again. Yet clearly he is not entirely free of a particular type of enthralling carnality.

The next two episodes record a more disturbing oscillation. In the first he both finds and loses a magic night-time Venice.

> After dinner, I went out alone, into the heart of the enchanted city where I found myself in the middle of strange purlieus like a character in the *Arabian Nights*. It was very seldom that, in the course of my wanderings, I did not come across some strange and spacious *piazza* of which no guide-book, no tourist had ever told me.

He speaks of this other Venice as 'crystallising'. (Ruskin too, remember, had spoken of 'the Arabian nights of Venice', and he too longed for a 'pure crystalline structure'.) This is, indeed, a Venice all of art and dream.

> A vast and splendid *campo* of which, in this network of little streets, I should never have guessed the scale, or even found room for it, spread out before me surrounded by charming palaces silvery in the moonlight. It was one of those architectural ensembles towards which,

> in any other town, the streets converge, lead you and point the way. Here it seemed to be deliberately concealed in a labyrinth of alleys, like those palaces in oriental tales whither mysterious agents convey by night a person who, brought back home before daybreak, can never find his way back to the magic dwelling which he ends by believing that he visited only in a dream. (III, 665)

Venice, of course, is not 'any other town', and it conceals as much as it leads and points the way. It can give you more than you had dreamt. But it can then take away what you can ill afford to lose. Marcel sets out to find by day what had been magically afforded him by night – 'my beautiful nocturnal *piazza*'. He turns this way and that, feeling always *about* to see 'the beautiful exiled *piazza*' appear. But:

> At that moment, some evil genie which had assumed the form of a new *calle* made me unwittingly retrace my steps, and I found myself brought back to the Grand Canal. And as there is no great difference between the memory of a dream and the memory of a reality, I finally wondered whether it was not during my sleep that there had occurred, in a dark patch of Venetian crystallisation, that strange mirage which offered a vast *piazza* surrounded by romantic palaces to the meditative eye of the moon. (III, 665–6)

The 'mysterious agents' at work in Venice include evil genies as well as wizard guides. For Marcel to run up against a blank while pursuing a visionary Venice is to run into a 'dark patch of Venetian crystallisation' in more senses than one. There is, thus, a Venice that seems to withhold what it had seemed to offer. Here Marcel contents himself with a kind of reversible proposition – that there is little to choose between a dream of reality and a real dream. But there is worse to come.

His persisting 'venery', still coexisting with the 'verities' he had glimpsed in St Mark's, makes him resolve to stay on in Venice when his mother decides to leave: 'it was the desire for certain women that kept me' (II, 666) – kept him 'in a state of agitation', and kept him in Venice. Particularly when he sees that Madame Putbus and her attendants are expected at the hotel, since this promises 'hours of casual pleasure'. To pursue this sort of 'casual pleasure' he has, as it were, to let the mother go, and when she sets out for the railway station he resolutely sits on the hotel terrace with a drink, watching the sunset and listening to someone singing *O sole mio*. Then occurs that great negative epiphany which almost all writers of Venice seem to experience.

> The sun continued to sink. My mother must be nearing the station. Soon she would be gone, and I should be alone in Venice. . . . I felt

> myself to be alone; things had become alien to me. . . . The town that I saw before me had ceased to be Venice. Its personality, its name, seemed to me to be mendacious fictions which I no longer had the will to impress upon its stones. I saw the palaces reduced to their basic elements, lifeless heaps of marble with nothing to choose between them, and the water as a combination of hydrogen and oxygen, eternal, blind, anterior and exterior to Venice, oblivious of the Doges or of Turner. And yet this unremarkable place was as strange as a place at which one has just arrived, which does not yet know one, or a place which one has left and which has forgotten one already. I could no longer tell it anything about myself, I could leave nothing of myself imprinted on it; it contracted me into myself until I was no more than a throbbing heart and an attention strained to follow the development of *O sole mio.* In vain might I fix my mind despairingly upon the beautiful and distinctive curve of the Rialto, it seemed to me, with the mediocrity of the obvious, a bridge not merely inferior to but as alien to the notion I had of it as an actor of whom, in spite of his blond wig and black garments, we know quite well that in his essence he is not Hamlet. So it was with the palaces, the canal, the Rialto, divested of the idea that constituted their reality and dissolved into their vulgar material elements. (III, 667)

Venice has turned into a site of contraction, divestment, extinction. The place where meanings and values drain away; a place of disassociation and alienation. Venice is the place where he loses the *idea* of Venice, and all he is left with is the mute unmeaning 'material elements' – the stones. The stones of Venice without *The Stones of Venice.* Venice thus unbooked is just exactly no place at all. It gets worse.

> in this lonely, unreal, icy, unfriendly setting in which I was going to be left alone, the strains of *O sole mio*, rising like a dirge for the Venice I had known, seemed to bear witness to my misery. . . . I ought to have made up my mind to leave without losing another second. But this is precisely what I was powerless to do; I remained motionless, incapable not merely of rising, but even of deciding that I would rise from my chair. (III, 668)

Venice has turned her Medusa face on him with a vengeance. He is paralysed – 'petrified'.

The soul of the city has 'contracted', mockingly, into the '*sole*' of a popular song, and somehow the absence of the mother is – once again – behind all this.

> My mother must by now have reached the station. In a little while she would be gone. I was gripped by the anguish that was caused me by

> the sight of the Canal which had become diminutive now that the soul of Venice had fled from it, of that commonplace Rialto which was no longer the Rialto, and by the song of despair which *O sole mio* had become and which, bellowed thus beside the insubstantial palaces, finally reduced them to dust and ashes and completed the ruin of Venice. (III, 669)

Venice has fallen – *again*. And Marcel, without the maintaining presence of the mother, is approaching terminal depletion, as ruined as the vacated and vacant Venice – a very different 'terminus' from the earlier one, in the presence of his mother. 'I remained motionless, my will dissolved' (III, 668). What of '*sole*' is left?

The last scene in the Venetian sequence is simply his departure. It is the 'unsuspected defensive power of inveterate habit' (III, 670) which prompts, or drags, him into action. He is just in time to catch up with his mother, and they leave Venice together on the train. She is his primal, primary attachment, the originating Venice behind all the subsequent and supplementary Venices of his desires. And it is a definitive departure. Not only does he never visit Venice again in the course of the book. It never again serves as a figure of yearning or loss. Though of course it still has a crucial role to play in the final vision and discovery of the way in which memory can triumph over time.

After the uneven paving stones have transported him back to St Mark's baptistery in Venice, Marcel ponders why the moment, and the 'image' of Venice, should have 'given me a joy which was like a certainty which sufficed, without any other proof, to make death a matter of indifference to me?' (III, 900). The answer to that question is nothing less, finally, than the whole work. But, in briefer terms, the experience of being – existing – simultaneously in two different times, brings to life, makes him aware of the existence of, a 'being' within, who/which must be 'extra-temporal'.

> The truth surely was that the being within me which had enjoyed these impressions had enjoyed them because they had in them something that was common to a day long past and to the present, because in some way they were extra-temporal, and this being made its appearance only when, through one of these identifications of the present with the past, it was likely to find itself in the one and only medium in which it could exist and enjoy the essence of things, that is to say: outside time. (III, 904)

This 'being' who has been 'reborn in me' is 'nourished only by the essences of things', and what the paving-stone experience afforded him was a rare apprehension of 'a fragment of time in the pure state' (III, 905).

This idea that the 'true self' is, as it were, buried or imprisoned deep within while the appetitive and instrumental self ranges through the delusive contaminations and distractions of daily modern life; and that this 'true self' which may for years seem to be 'dead' is in fact 'not altogether dead' and may, in some entirely unanticipated, unsought moment, be miraculously 'awakened and reanimated as it receives the celestial nourishment that is brought to it' (III, 906) – this idea is an increasingly common one in later nineteenth-century literature. One definitive version may be found in Matthew Arnold's poem 'The Buried Life'. For Proust, this sudden exhumation of the buried self is the only resurrection that matters, a resurrection intimately involved with his momentary experiences of the resurrection of the past – Venetian stones in Parisian pavements.

> Always, when these resurrections took place, the distant scene engendered around the common sensation had for a moment grappled, like a wrestler, with the present scene. Always the present scene had come off victorious, and always the vanquished one had appeared to me the more beautiful of the two, so beautiful that I had remained in a state of ecstasy on the uneven paving-stones . . . endeavouring to prolong or to reproduce the momentary appearances of the Combray or the Balbec or the Venice which invaded only to be driven back, which rose up only to abandon me in the midst of the new scene which somehow, nevertheless, the past had been able to penetrate. (III, 908)

Grapple, wrestle, invade, penetrate – there is something distinctly erotic in the way Proust conceived of the past suddenly seeming to seduce and insinuate, even thrust, itself into the present. Always to be vanquished, but, in being so, always more beautiful. Fairer through fading, indeed. All Proust's desire is now for those 'fragments of existence withdrawn from Time' (III, 908). But, as he notes, the contemplation of these fragments, 'though it was of eternity, had been fugitive. And yet I was vaguely aware that the pleasure which this contemplation had, at rare intervals, given me in my life, was the only genuine and fruitful pleasure that I had known' (III, 908). His quest now will be for this very different kind of 'fugitive'. Not the carnal Albertine, but the past transported into the purity of extra-temporality – 'real without being actual, ideal without being abstract' (III, 906).

This leads to what is effectively his farewell to Venice: Venice the place, Venice the name, but not – not quite – Venice the word.

> To this contemplation of the essence of things I had decided therefore that in future I must attach myself, so as somehow to immobilise it; but how, by what means, was I to do this? Naturally . . . at the moment when the unevenness of the two paving-stones had extended in

every direction and dimension, the desiccated and insubstantial images which I normally had of Venice and St Mark's and of all the sensations which I had felt there, reuniting the piazza to the cathedral, the landing-stage to the piazza, the canal to the landing-stage, and to all that the eyes see the world of desires which is seen only by the mind – naturally at those moments I had been tempted, if not, because of the time of the year, to go and walk once more through the watery streets of Venice which for me were above all associated with the spring, at least to return to Balbec. But this thought did not for an instant detain me. I knew for one thing that countries were not such as their names painted them to my imagination, so that now it was scarcely ever except in my dreams, while I was asleep, that a place could lie spread before me wrought in that pure matter which is entirely distinct from the matter of the common things that we see and touch but of which, when I had imagined these common things without ever having seen them, they too had seemed to me to be composed: and I knew also that the same was true of that other species of image which is formed by the memory, so that not only had I failed to discover the beauty of Balbec as I had imagined it when I had gone there for the first time, I had failed also when I went back the second time to rediscover the remembered beauty which that first visit had left me. Experience had taught me only too well the impossibility of attaining in the real world to what lay deep within myself; I knew that Lost Time was not to be found again on the piazza of St Mark's any more than I had found it again on my second visit to Balbec or on my return to Tansonville to see Gilberte, and that travel, which merely dangled once more before me the illusion that these vanished impressions existed outside myself, could not be the means I sought. (III, 910)

The 'matter of common things', even the matter of Venetian stones, is being abjured, relinquished, for that 'pure matter' which can only exist in the absence of sight and touch and which, indeed, cannot survive such sensory knowledge. Venice seen is 'Venice' lost. While it had only been a name, for Marcel it served to release 'that mysterious current which the Name, that prior existence to the known, sets flowing, and which is incompatible, as now and then our dreams are, with anything we could have experienced' (*BWSB* 175). But after the actual visit – material, corporeal – to the place itself, the name loses that magic power. As a potent provoker of desire, even the name of 'Venice' all but disappears from the remainder of the book. There are two or three further references and they seem to concern Venice read in books, books read in Venice: 'the fashion in which I once imagined Venice and of the desire I had to go there as the actual phrases of a book' (III, 921). He considers the temptation to become a bibliophile, saying that if he did become a collector he would seek out first editions, by which he means 'the edition in which I read it for the first time'.

> The library which I should thus assemble would contain volumes of an even greater value; for the books which I read in the past at Combray or in Venice, enriched now by my memory with vast illuminations representing Saint-Hilaire or the gondola moored at the foot of San Giorgio Maggiore and the Grand Canal incrusted with sparkling sapphires, would have become the equals of those ancient 'picture books' – illustrated bibles or books of hours – which the collector nowadays opens not to read their text but to savour once more the enchantment of the colours. (III, 923)

The place Venice would become a sort of supplementary private illustration in a book. But Marcel decides against becoming such a collector. 'I know very well how easily these images, deposited by the mind, can be effaced by the mind. For the old images it substitutes new ones which no longer have the same power of resurrection' (III, 924). Venice necessarily includes the books he read in Venice, and Marcel is turning away from both. He wants, somehow, to find his way back to the 'old images' – the primal, primary ones, we might say. 'The only way to savour them more fully was to try to get to know them more completely in the medium in which they existed, that is to say within myself, to try to make them translucid even to their very depths' (III, 911). The only Venice he will revisit will be the Venice within, that old Venice of anticipation and desire.

This resiting and reconstitution of Venice are at the same time, then, the relocation and redirection – effectively the redefinition – of desire. In this connection there is one late reference to Venice which seems almost scandalous in context. This context is Marcel's discovery of the extreme of Monsieur de Charlus's degradation and sexual perversion, when he has seen him pursuing and purchasing his grotesque sado-masochistic pleasures in Jupin's establishment. Marcel almost offhandedly offers this explanatory comparison: 'In short his desire to be bound in chains and beaten, with all its ugliness, betrayed a dream as poetical as, in other men, the longing to go to Venice or to keep ballet-dancers' (III, 870). Marcel is thus suggesting that his own lifelong desire and that of Monsieur de Charlus have a similar origin, morphology and effect. Thus to conjoin what seems like an ultimate of aesthetic aspiration, a dream of beauty, of life-transformed-into-art, with an extreme of degradation, a dream of ugliness, of life-deformed-into abjection, is to suggest a worrying equivalence, if not identity, of desires. This is not, of course, a matter of solidarity with deviance, an attempt to defend and justify the strange swervings and destinations of homosexual desire. It is, rather, to suggest that what these desires and yearnings have in common is the fact that, as Marcel remarkably says of Monsieur de Charlus's perversions, they force men to take life seriously. Just that. But, as Proust makes us realize, it is a very great deal. Not *what* we desire, but *that* we desire – that, finally, is the crucial thing. The different termini to which desire may drive, the different products of desire – this is what the book is all about, a book which is itself a supreme product of desire.

Venice is allowed to dematerialize into a pure, inner residue; and the name 'Venice' is allowed to fade. Marcel is moving beyond.

> For if names had lost most of their individuality for me, words on the other hand now began to reveal their full significance. The beauty of images is situated in front of things, that of ideas behind them. So that the first sort of beauty ceases to astonish us as soon as we have reached the things themselves, the second is something that we understand only when we have passed beyond them. (III, 974)

First, the name. Then, the place. Finally, when the place has lost its materiality and the name its individuality, there remain – words. Ruskin, said Proust, 'delighted in worshiping a word' (*ORR*, 145) – it was an aspect of his idolatry.

> A word is for him the flask full of memory, of which Baudelaire speaks. Apart even from the beauty of the sentence where it is placed (and here is where danger could commence), he reveres it. . . . He is amazed at the secret virtue there is in a word, he marvels at it; pronouncing this word in the most informal conversation, he points it out, draws attention to it, exclaims in admiration. Thus he gives the simplest things a dignity, a grace, an interest, a life, the result being that those who have approached him prefer his conversation to almost all others. But from the viewpoint of art one sees what the danger would be for a writer less gifted then he; words are in fact beautiful in themselves, but we are not for nothing in their beauty.

That last clause is a mistranslation of the French, which reads 'mais nous ne sommes pour rien dans leur beauté',[9] meaning 'but we have no part in their beauty', the beauty of words is not the result of our agency. The quotation continues:

> For a musician there is no more merit in using a mi than a sol; but when we write we have to consider the words at the same time as works of art, whose profound meaning we should understand and whose glorious past we should respect, and as simple notes which will

> have value (in respect to us) only by the place we will give them and by the relations of feeling we will establish between them. (*ORR*, 157–8)

When writing, we should consider and treat words at once as both 'œuvres d'art' and 'simples notes'. He is not making the obvious, though important, point that language is both referential and reflexive – it talks about things and talks about itself equally happily and often simultaneously. Proust is making a subtler distinction which is extremely important to himself as a writer. Words are already works of art; they bring the beauty of their resonances and associations with them. No credit to the writer there. The 'danger' he twice refers to, in connection with some hypothetical lesser would-be Ruskin, is that he might just jiggle around with the already-beautiful words, delighting in this or that arrangement and relying on the beauty of the words to carry the day. There are certainly schools of thought and practitioners who would be content to claim just that – writing is, after all, always a more or less felicitous rearranging of pre-existent entities. What else is Proust insisting? Words as 'simple notes' are more like Saussure's arbitrary signifiers which take on meaning according to their place in a chain of other signifiers. Context is all. Here again, what is important is the 'placing' – literally, a writer does not give the word its beauty, he gives it its place. In the handling of words both as art-works, thick and heavy with beauty, and as musical notes, light and empty sounds, either way the writer is the arranger, the orchestrator, the mosaicist. His contribution is, exactly, not the beauty of the words, but 'the relations of reason or of feeling' he may establish between them. Proust, I think, wants to guard against mere word-play, a veneration for words in and for themselves, an aesthetic of pure writing. He does not want to bracket the world out. As he moved further into immateriality, that pure matter which is no matter, beyond name and place into the realm of idea, discovering more significance in words than names – surely a fine, if crucial, distinction at best – Proust does seem to be approaching that state of mind in which 'words alone are certain good'.[10] Almost he seems to move beyond desire, or at least all externally attached and liberated desire: an ultimate emancipation from Albertine, even from Venice, perhaps too from the mother. Henry James had started one essay on 'Venice' with the sentence: 'It is a great pleasure to write the word.' Coming where it does, 'the word' obviously refers to 'Venice'. Yet the sentence could also comprehend a more generic pleasure – writing 'the word' in general. For Proust, it would seem that that became the only pleasure that really mattered. Yet, even as he concludes his account of his odyssey to that state of mind, he has already given us – it is central to the whole work – another 'Venice Preserved'. Preserved, of course, in and on his own terms.

7

Ezra Pound: The White Forest of Marble

PROUST quite avowedly loved Ruskin, or Ruskin's writing, this side, or perhaps the other side, idolatry. 'He will teach me. . . . He will purify me. . . . He will intoxicate me and will give me life.'[1] Pound is reticent to the point of occlusion with respect to Ruskin, but the debt is large and undeniable, as I have already intimated. In fact, *both* Proust's great (unfinished) novel *and* Pound's great (unfinished) poem can be seen as coming out of, and recontaining, Ruskin's Venice. And Ruskin, too, never felt he had finished a work, or his work. ('I care for nothing but my work – and that's always unfinished – *most* unfinished when it's done'[2]). The great unfinished *Praeterita* is his most fitting memorial. Pound had little to say about Proust. In the few, scattered references to him, his name is usually linked with that of Henry James, and the two of them contrasted with Joyce, who went further – in developing the art of the novel – than both of them. He can be nasty about Proust's snobbery, and on one occasion, when he was growing dissatisfied with Paris, spoke of the city as being typified by 'the indisputable enervation of Proust'.[3] This was written in 1922, the year of Proust's death – which is a kind of irony. But although Pound gives little evidence of any enthusiasm for Proust's work, such as he might have read, I shall be suggesting that there is more similarity between their respective works than might at first be apparent. The mediating link is of course Ruskin.

There are very few explicit references to Ruskin in Pound's writing, and when they occur they can be disparaging or condescending ('Ruskin was well-meaning but a goose'[4]). But, as is now being demonstrated and documented, the Ruskinian influence on Pound is absolutely pervasive.[5] There are half a dozen references to Ruskin in Pound's assorted art criticism;[6] none of them much to my immediate purpose, but indicative of the fact that Pound was much more familiar with Ruskin's work than he ever felt it necessary to indicate. This is not to suggest that Pound was concerned to cover his tracks – for Pound, literature came first; it was almost irrelevant who wrote it. The truth of the matter, I think, may be found in a remark made by Pound in 1955, as reported by James Dickey: '"It's not that Ruskin didn't SAY it, it is that the Meyers, Marbles, Sulzbuggers, Belmonts promptly wipe it out of the public mind."'[7] (If the Ruskinian vision had been 'wiped out', then Pound would have to SAY it again – in his own way. Make it new.) It cannot, of course, be demonstrated that Pound's crucial visit to, and sojourn in, Venice in 1908 – where, after all, he collected and published his first book of poetry, *A Lume spento*, and compiled the 'San Trovaso Notebook' – was due to the inspirational and alluring power of Ruskin's Venetian writing (though it must be deemed likely), but he certainly met a direct Ruskinian influence shortly after his arrival in the figure of the Reverend Alexander Robertson, pastor of the Presbyterian Church, who had indeed once seen Ruskin plain and talked to him – on Ruskin's last visit to Venice in 1888 – and published his own Ruskinian book, *The Bible of St Mark's: St Mark's Church, the Altar and Throne of Venice*, in 1989. Pound's Venice is certainly in part Ruskin's Venice, as it is also partly Browning's Venice and perhaps James's Venice, and I will come to that. But I want to approach these matters a little more circuitously.

On a visit to Venice in 1920 Pound wrote an autobiographical essay entitled 'Indiscretions' which starts: 'It is peculiarly fitting that this manuscript should begin in Venice, from a patent Italian inkwell designed to prevent satisfactory immersion of the pen. If the latter symbolism be obscure, the former is so obvious, at least to the writer, that only meticulous honesty and the multitude of affairs prevented him from committing it to paper before leaving London.' Venice is, he goes on to say, 'an excellent place to come to from Crawfordsville, Indiana',[8] and he proceeds to record his visits.

> Let it therefore stand written that I first saw the Queen of the Adriatic under the protection of that portentous person, my great aunt-in-law, in the thirteenth year of my age. . . . Venice struck me as an agreeable place – as, in fact, more agreeable than Wyncote, Pa., or '47th' and Madison Avenue. I announced an intention to return. I have done so. I do not know quite how often. By elimination of possible years: 1898, 1902, 1908, 1910, 1911, 1913, 1920.'[9]

In 1920 he was, he said, there to see whether 'Venice could give one again and once more either the old kick to the senses or any new perception' and whether 'the possible "picturesque" of roof-tiles, sky-tones, mud-green tidal influx, cats perched like miniature stone lions on balconies, etc., is going to afford a possible interest – after all that has been "done" about Venice'.[10] He had written his first canto in 1917; *A Draft of XVI Cantos* would be ready by the autumn of 1923 though not published until January 1925; canto XVII, in which Venice appears as 'the forest of marble', was written in 1924; while the more explicitly Venetian cantos, XXIV–XXVI, were written between 1928 and 1930. In 1920 Venice must have given him more than old kicks and afforded more than a possible interest, for he must have sensed, if he did not know, that his *Cantos*, wherever they might take him, would be laced with references to Venice, would, indeed, in a very important sense, be grounded in Venice – Ruskin's Venice, Browning's Venice, but also – why not? – Pound's Venice. He must have at least speculated that he would 'do' something about Venice, some writing, such as had not been done before. Though he can have had no inkling of how the city would return to his mind, and his writing, in later years, nor in what utterly unanticipatable circumstances.

John Gould Fletcher, a compatriot of Pound, whose own writing never really amounted to very much, wrote of Pound that he was 'a pioneer in the last great wave of American expatriates who, like myself, had turned from the West to the East and had come abroad before the European War, bent on submitting their own rude and untaught native impulses to the task of assimilating and, if possible, surpassing the traditional achievements of Europe.'[11] The cadences of this perhaps sound more like Henry James than Pound himself, but Pound himself felt close to James and greatly revered him – as his frequent eulogies and gestures of homage to the Master attest. Where James saw a Venice already 'Ruskinized', Pound, to some extent, sees the city, sees Europe, necessarily through Jamesian eyes as well. But although Ruskin is named or evoked far less frequently than James by Pound (arguably only once seriously – I'll come back to this) his influence is, I think, more deeply pervasive.

In canto XLV there are these lines:

> Came not by usura Angelico; came not Ambrogio Praedis,
> Came no church of cut stone signed: *Adamo me fecit.*[12]

This 'signed column' is referred to more than once by Pound. In canto LXXVIII:

> So he said, looking at the signed columns in San Zeno
> 'how the hell can we get any architecture
> when we order our columns by the gross?'
> (LXXVIII, 480)

Here at least the church is named – San Zeno – if not the place, which is Verona. Hugh Kenner established the details – of how Pound visited the church and looked at the 'signed columns' in the company of Edgar Williams, a prize student of architecture who is presumed to have said the words quoted in canto LXXVIII. The signed columns represent for Pound, clearly enough, the kind of personal craftsmanship possible in the non-usurious Middle Ages but no longer possible under capitalism and mass production. The interesting, or extra-interesting, thing is that this capital with its twin columns had a particular importance for Ruskin, who both called attention to it and reproduced a drawing of it in *The Stones of Venice*.

He calls the twin columns (one is straight, the other twisted, and together they form the capital) 'among the most interesting pieces of work I know in Italy'. What particularly interests Ruskin is just the fact that one of the columns is straight, the other twisted – 'both shafts have the same section, but one received a half-turn as it ascends, giving it an exquisite spiral contour.'[13] In the chapter entitled 'The Cornice and Capital' Ruskin concentrates upon the signed capital and includes an engraved illustration. 'Its workman was proud of it, as well he might be: he has written his name upon its front (I would that more of his fellows had been as kindly vain), and the goodly stone proclaims for ever, ADAMINUS DE SANCTO GIORGIO ME FECIT.'[14] In San Zeno the column is quite difficult to find and in relative darkness; in other words, you do not come across it, you go looking for it. Pound, I am suggesting, clearly knew Ruskin's *The Stones of Venice* well. Hugh Witemeyer was the first to marshall all the relevant evidence, and he concluded: 'Ruskin established the signed capital as a symbol of civilized craftsmanship in the 1850's. When Pound evokes the signature of Adaminus *contra usura* eighty-five years later (1936), he is working in a venerable Victorian tradition.'[15]

The one unmistakably serious reference to Ruskin in Pound's work occurs in *Hugh Selwyn Mauberley* at the start of the 'Yeux Glauques' poem.

> Gladstone was still respected,
> When John Ruskin produced
> 'King's Treasuries': Swinburne
> And Rossetti still abused.[16]

Hugh Witemeyer is surely correct in seeing this as a positive reference to Ruskin's defence of the Pre-Raphaelites rather than, as some critics have thought, a reference to Ruskin's reactionary attack on Whistler. Indeed, Witemeyer thinks there is more to the reference than that: 'Ruskin's critique of English attitudes toward literature and art in "Of King's Treasuries" parallels Pound's critique in *Hugh Selwyn Mauberley* so closely that the allusion in "Yeux Glauques" can only be taken as an act of homage.'[17] Witemeyer makes the case well and convincingly and here I simply want to enlarge on the possible importance of Ruskin's lecture (the first of two which make up

Sesame and Lilies) to the poet who in time would himself refer to 'that treasure of honesty / which is the treasure of states' (canto LXXVII, 470). – what kingly treasure was for Ruskin we shall see.

Ruskin starts his lecture by announcing 'I want to speak to you about the treasures hidden in books; and about the way we read them, and could, or should read them. A grave subject you will say; and a wide one!'[18] Grave and wide and absolutely central, certainly, for the man who would write his own *ABC of Reading*. This is how a true book comes into being for Ruskin:

> The author has something to say which he perceive to be true and useful, or helpfully beautiful. So far as he knows, no one has yet said it; so far as he knows, no one else can say it. He is bound to say it, clearly and melodiously if he may; clearly, at all events. In the sum of his life he finds this to be the thing, or group of things, manifest to him; – this, the piece of true knowledge, or sight, which his share of sunshine and earth has permitted him to seize. He would fain set it down for ever; engrave it on rock, if he could: saying, 'This is the best of me; for the rest, I ate, and drank, and slept, loved, and hated, like another: my life was as vapour, and is not; but this I saw and knew; this, if anything of mine, is worth your memory.' That is his 'writing'; it is, in his small human way, and with whatever degree of true inspiration, his inscription, or scripture. That is a 'Book'.

It may seem a very simple definition, yet precisely in its pared-down spareness it seems to chime with Pound's own mode of writing which with its clean, chiselled objectivities ('granite next sea wave / is for clarity'; canto CVI, 753) would indeed seem fain to be engraved on rock – rock-drill indeed. For Ruskin all such books comprise an 'eternal court', a great 'aristocracy of companionship' which is permanently 'open to labour and to merit, but to nothing else'.[19] The 'labour' is important and, whether or not the following paragraph particularly struck Pound, it is a passage which any reader of the *Cantos* would do well to keep in mind and take to heart:

> at least be sure that you go to the author to get at *his* meaning, not to find yours . . . be sure also, if the author is worth anything, that you will not get at his meaning all at once; – nay, that at his whole meaning you will not for a long time arrive in any wise. Not that he does not say what he means and in strong words too; but he cannot say it all; and what is more strange, *will* not, but in a hidden way and in parables, in order that he may be sure you want it. I cannot quite see the reason of this, nor analyse that cruel reticence in the breasts of wise men which makes them always hide their deeper thought. They do not give it you by way of help, but of reward, and will make themselves sure that you deserve it before they allow you to

> reach it. But it is the same with the physical type of wisdom, gold. . . . Nature . . . puts it in little fissures in the earth, nobody knows where; you may dig long and find none; you must dig painfully to find any. . . . And your pick-axes are your own care, wit, and learning; your smelting furnace is your own thoughtful soul. Do not hope to get at any good author's meaning without those tools and that fire; often you will need sharpest, finest chiselling, and patientest fusing, before you can gather one grain of the metal.[20]

This is not to justify the undoubted impenetrable obscurities to be found in the *Cantos*, nor to explain the unfollowable privacy of many of its leaps and allusions, the unfathomable arbitrariness of some of its juxtapositions and arrangings. It is to say that true reading involves real work, and that true writing may be unavoidably difficult. 'Obscurities inherent in the thing occur when the author is piercing, or trying to pierce into, unchartered regions; when he is trying to express things not yet current, not yet worn into phrase; when he is ahead of the emotional, or philosophic sense (as a painter might be ahead of the colour-sense) of his contemporaries.'[21] Thus Pound in 1920 – at the very outset of the *Cantos*, we might say. And in canto XCVI there is the following unascribed note in italics: '*If we never write anything save what is already understood, the field of understanding will never be extended. One demands the right, now and again, to write for a few people with special interests and whose curiosity reaches into greater detail*' (XCVI, 659). So sometimes, yes, you need 'those tools and that fire'.

Ruskin and Pound share a passionate concern with the state of the language in general. Here is Ruskin:

> There are masked words droning and skulking about us in Europe just now . . . which nobody understands, but which everybody uses, and most people will also fight for, live for, or even die for, fancying they mean this, or that, or the other, of things dear to them. . . . There were never creatures of prey so mischievous, never diplomatists so cunning, never poisoners so deadly, as those masked words; they are the unjust stewards of all men's ideas: whatever fancy or favourite instinct a man most cherishes, he gives to his favourite masked word to take care of for him; the word at last comes to have an infinite power over him, you cannot get at him by its ministry.[22]

These 'masked words' are, as Witemeyer suggests, the 'old men's lies' Pound rails against in *Hugh Selwyn Mauberley* – and this from a later essay: 'As language becomes the most powerful instrument of perfidy, so language alone can riddle and cut through the meshes. Used to conceal meaning, used to blur meaning, to produce the complete and utter inferno of the past century . . . against which, SOLELY a care for language, for accurate registration by language avails' (*LE* 77). This is one of the things Pound takes from Kung: 'To call people and things by their names, that is by the correct denominations, to see that the terminology was exact',[23] and he waged a lifelong war on what he called 'ungodly indistinctness' (*SP* 91). 'Precision' is the quality Pound invokes more often than any other and he would have found a comparable emphasis in Ruskin: with a 'well-educated gentleman', says Ruskin, 'whatever language he knows, he knows precisely.'[24] More to the point, more to Pound's point, Ruskin insists that you must learn 'to deal with words rightly' – get good dictionaries, learn the Greek alphabet, be aware of roots and derivations, try to recognize Saxon, German, French, Latin words and influences, ('It can't be all in one language'; canto LXXXVI, 563), and read as carefully, patiently, searchingly as possible. If you do, 'the general gain to your character, in power and precision, will be quite incalculable.'[25] Precision and power. Pound never tires of invoking and stressing 'precision' ('In the art of Daniel and Cavalcanti, I have seen that precision which I miss in the Victorians' (*LE* 11); 'all things are here brought to precisions / that we shd/ learn our integrity' (canto LIX, 324); and 'power' was equally important. 'Properly, we shd. read for power. Man reading shd. be man intensely alive. The book shd. be a ball of light in one's hand' (*GTK* 55). Ruskin himself could hardly have expressed a sense of the supreme value of a true 'Book' more beautifully.

There is much in the rest of Ruskin's lecture which exactly anticipates, or fore-echoes, the ever more biting (and, later, ever more desperate, even hysterical) social criticism of Pound. 'Above all, a nation cannot last as a money-making mob: it cannot with impunity, – it cannot with existence, – go on despising literature, despising science, despising art, despising nature, despising compassion, and concentrating its soul on Pence.'[26] ('Rapacity is the main force in our time in the occident'; *GTK* 15.) 'What an absurd idea, it seems, put fairly in words, that the wealth of the capitalists of civilised nations should ever come to support literature instead of war!'[27] ('To be men not destroyers'; notes for canto CXVII, 803). But it is the end of the lecture I wish to look at. Having established that the real treasure is 'Wisdom', just as he continued to stress 'There is no Wealth but Life' in other works, Ruskin concludes by saying that what we really need is 'better bread':

> bread made of that old enchanted Arabian grain, the Sesame, which opens doors; – doors, not of robbers', but of Kings' Treasuries.
>
> Friends, the treasuries of true kings are the streets of their cities; and the gold they gather, which for others is as the mire of the streets, changes itself, for them and their people, into a crystalline pavement for evermore.[28]

Mire into gold – there is a metamorphosis indeed. 'The undeniable tradition of metamorphoses teaches us that things do not always remain the same. They become other things by swift and unanalysable process' (*LE* 431). The notion and tradition of 'metamorphosis' are of course crucial in Pound's work: not only Ovidian – with Baucis and Philemon turning into trees standing somewhere near the centre of the *Cantos* (XC, 605) – but a more pervading sense that things may become other things 'by swift and unanalysable process', may turn into something rich and rare, precious by other than monetary standards; a wealth and treasure undreamed of. Mire into gold. Precious stones and precious metals – as opposed to filthy lucre – play an important role in the *Cantos* – positive, honorific, even ecstatic – when Pound in various ways seeks 'to affirm the gold thread in the pattern'; at times, indeed, they serve 'to lead back to splendour' (CXVI, 797). And in this gleaming and glowing and glittering, this shining and beaming, these dazzling translucencies, there is no word more important to Pound – also beloved of Ruskin – than 'crystalline'.

The Platonists, wrote Pound, 'caused man after man to be suddenly conscious of the reality of the *nous*, of mind, apart from any man's individual mind, of the sea crystalline and enduring, of the bright as it were molten glass that envelops us, full of light' (*GTK* 44). If you can become 'suddenly conscious' of it in nature, so you can in art. 'There is a flood of life caught in this crystal' (*GTK* 287) Pound writes of Hardy's poetry – and how right it is that Pound should have appreciated and esteemed Hardy, like himself essentially a great poet of loss, elegy, memory. There are many occasions in the *Cantos* when the poetry moves, as it were, towards crystal:

> Out of which things seeking an exit
> To the high air, to the stratosphere, to the imperial
> calm, to the empyrean, to the baily of the four towers
> the NOUS, the ineffable crystal
>
> (XL, 201)

But most of the references occur in 'Rock-Drill' and after, when, perhaps, he was intermittently trying to 'write paradise' ('When you get out of the hell of money there remains the undiscussable Paradiso'; *GTK* 292).

In canto XCI there are no fewer than seven invocations of 'crystal':

> The GREAT CRYSTAL
> doubling the pine, and to cloud
>
> Crystal waves weaving together toward the gt/healing

She has entered the protection of crystal [i.e. the Princess Ra-Set]

Light & the flowing crystal
never gin in cut glass had such clarity
That Drake saw the splendour and wreckage
in that clarity
Gods moving in crystal

In the barge of Ra-Set
On river of crystal
[close to the ominous line *'Democracies electing their sewage'*]

& from fire to crystal
via the body of light
[close to the ominous parenthesis '(to the tough guy Musonius: honour)']

'Ghosts dip in the crystal,
adorned'
(XCI, 611, 613, 615, 617)

And in canto XCIV:

Above prana, the light,
past light, the crystal.
Above crystal, the jade!
(XCIV, 634)

While in the concluding canto of 'Rock-Drill':

That the crystal wave mount of flood surge . . .
The light there almost solid.
(XCV, 644)

which looks back to one of the most moving passages in the *Cantos*:

J'ai eu pitié des autres.
Pas assez! Pas assez!
For me nothing. But that the child
walk in peace in her basilica,
The light there almost solid.
(XCIII, 628)

In canto CXVI it is as though he hopes his work is 'crystalline':

I have brought the great ball of crystal;
who can lift it?
(CXVI, 795)

But in a late fragment ('Addendum for C') it is part of a trilogy of things yearned for:

pure Light, we beseech thee
Crystal, we beseech thee
Clarity, we beseech thee
(799)

The appeal is to Dione, according to one tradition a daughter of Earth and mother of Aphrodite. For Pound, the gods were still there to be appealed to. For Ruskin, the streets of nineteenth-century Europe were becoming increasingly fouled with money-making 'mire' just as its skies were darkening with ever-more ominous 'storm clouds'; for contrast – compensation, consolation – he longed to evoke, invoke, the clean, the bright, the pellucid, the effulgent, the Dantesque paradisal: Light, Crystal, Clarity. For Pound it was, I think, the same.

Lo, there are many gods whom we have seen,
Folk of unearthly fashion, places splendid,
Bulwarks of beryl and of chrysoprase.[29]

Of 'places splendid' what place more splendid, more 'berylline' if not crystalline, more 'purifying', perhaps, than Venice?

O Dieu, purifiez nos coeurs!
purifiez nos coeurs!

Yea the lines hast thou laid unto me
in pleasant places,
And the beauty of this thy Venice
hast thou shown unto me
Until is its loveliness become unto me
a thing of tears. . . .

O God of waters,
make clean our hearts within us
And our lips to show forth thy praise,
For I have seen the
shadow of this thy Venice
floating upon the waters.
And thy stars
have seen this thing out of their far courses
have they seen this thing,

O God of waters.
Even as are thy stars
Silent unto us in their far-coursing,
Even so is mine heart
become silent within me.
(*CEP* 60–1)

I am not advancing this ('Night Litany') as a great poem. It is still too much in the shadow – and the liquefactions – of Swinburne, as is a good deal of the writing in *A Quinzaine for this Yule* (1908), where this poem appeared. In 1914 Pound wrote: 'we have had so many other pseudo-glamours and glamourolets and mists and fogs since the nineties that one is about ready for hard light' (*LE* 380). In his next book of poetry, Pound inscribed a 'Revolt' subtitled '*Against the crepuscular Spirit in Modern Poetry*', which starts:

I would shake off the lethargy of this our time,
and give
For shadows – shapes of power
For dreams – men.
(*CEP* 96)

And indeed in his subsequent work Pound can be seen pursuing 'hard light' – crystal – and delineating 'shapes of power' and 'men' – such as Sigismondo Malatesta. But 'Night Litany' is important because it reveals, in what is Pound's first sustained invocation of Venice in poetry, that the city was for him epiphanic. If there was a God – a God of silence, a God of waters – then He was manifest in the 'Beauty' of 'this thy Venice' the 'loveliness' of which is like some stupendous unearned benefaction bestowed on mankind and is a thing of 'wonder' even to the stars. Pound's depiction of Venice would become considerably more complicated in the *Cantos*, but I think it worth emphasizing that if 'places splendid' could be 'gods' then, at least at the time he began writing poetry seriously, no city was more of a god than Venice – of his 'sacred places', then, no place more sacred, or even as sacred.

'Eleusis did not distort truth by exaggerating the individual, neither could it have violated the individual spirit. Only in the high air and the great clarity can there be a just estimation of values. . . . I assert that the Gods exist' (*GTK* 299). It should be added that shortly before that statement, in the same volume, Pound had wondered or queried: 'The truth having been Eleusis? and a modern Eleusis being possible in the wilds of a man's mind only?' (*GTK* 294) – thus opening the possibility that any belief in any mode or apparition of the sacred had become an inexorably and irretrievably private matter. But that it was a vitally important matter Pound has no doubt. 'Without gods, no culture. Without gods, something is missing' (*GTK* 126). He certainly felt there was an intimate and vital relationship between the gods and the arts. Referring to 'the order' – the order presumably of the timeless truths and beauties of the past – Pound asserts: 'The arts alone can transmit this. / They alone cling fast to the gods' (*CEP* 271). What constituted the 'gods' was necessarily no matter of narrow orthodoxy for Pound. In 'The Child's Guide to Knowledge' Pound wrote: 'What is a god? A god is an eternal state of mind. . . . By what characteristic may we know the divine forms? By beauty. . . . In what manner do gods appear? Formed and formlessly. . . . May they when formed appear to anything save the sense of vision? We may gain a sense of their presence as if they were standing behind us.' (*SP* 47–8). However, Pound prefaced his essay on 'Religio' with the assertion, 'To replace the marble goddess on her pedestal at Terracina is worth more than any metaphysical argument' (SP 45), and clearly Pound's sense of the sacred, or the numinous, had a strong inclination to the plastic – granite, marble, ivory; sapphire, jade, emerald, diamond: crystal. And – 'this thy Venice'.

At times, of course, Pound, very much not the first nor the last, felt the modern world to be definitively desacralized, that 'the Gods no longer walked in men's gardens' (*LE* 431). But his deeper convictions and feelings seem to be those articulated in the late efflorescences of the final *Cantos.* As in CXIII:

> And who no longer makes gods out of beauty
> Θρῆνος   this is a dying. . . .
>
> The Gods have not returned. 'They have never left us.'
> They have not returned.
> Cloud's processional and the air moves with their living.
> (CXIII, 786–7)

Compare these lines from Browning's *Sordello*:

> as a God may glide
> Out of the world he fills and leave it mute
> A myriad ages as we men compute,
> Returning into it without a break
> O' the consciousness.[30]

I hope the point of the comparison with Browning will emerge later. Here let me just remark that one of the finest of Pound's early poems is called, indeed, 'The Return' –

See, they return; ah, see the tentative
  Movements, and the slow feet,
  The trouble in the pace and the uncertain
  Wavering!

(*CEP* 198)

– and one could say that it was an abiding concern of Pound's whether the gods, whatever they might be felt to specify or gesture towards, might return into this our world – glidingly, waveringly – or whether the deeper or finer truth is that they never left us; that the air, now as always, 'moves with their living'. (In this matter of the 'gods', Pound has something of Ruskin's sense of the continuity of religion, or, as Proust wishes to define it, 'of the permanence of an aesthetic feeling which Christianity does not interrupt' (*ORR* 95). Proust delights in bringing forward quotations from Ruskin which bear this out, among them the following: 'I am no despiser of profane literature. So far from it that I believe no interpretations of Greek religion have ever been so affectionate, none of Roman religion so reverent, as those which will be found at the base of my art teaching, and current through the entire body of my works.' And: 'The faith of Horace in the spirit of the Fountain of Brundisium, in the Faun of his hillside, and in the protection of the greater gods is constant, vital, and practical.' And: 'these St Mark's mosaics are as truly wrought in the power of Daedalus, with the Greek constructive instinct, and in the power of Athena, with the Greek religious soul, as ever chest of Cypselus or shaft of Erechtheum . . . these mosaics are not earlier than the thirteenth century. And yet they are still absolutely Greek in all the modes of thought, and forms of tradition. The fountains of fire and water are merely forms of the Chimera and the Peirene; and the maid dancing, though a princess of the thirteenth century in sleeves and ermine, is yet the phantom of some water-carrier from an Arcadian spring' (*ORR* 99, 79–82). Ruskin's earlier Christianity modulated into a religious sense at once more diffuse and inclusive, and less doctrinaire, perhaps a sense more like Pound's. Pound, certainly, would have responded to and approved such passages in Ruskin as much as Proust.)

The young Pound certainly associated Venice with important mysteries of return, or returning mysteries, as in 'San Vio June' and 'Almo sol Veneziae':

Old powers rise and do return to me
Grace to thy bounty, O Venetian sun.
Weary I came to thee, my romery
A cloth of day-strands raveled and ill-spun,
My soul a swimmer weary of the sea,
The shore a desert place with flowers none.

(*CEP* 233)

And:

Thou hast given me back
  Strength for the journey,
Thou hast given me back
  Heart for the Tourney.

O Sun venezian. . . .

Thou that hast called my soul
  From out the far crevices,
Yea, the far dark crevices
  And caves of ill-fearing
(*CEP* 246)

Whether the 'old powers' which return to him in Venice are his own or, more likely, older and deeper powers which he felt penetrating him in Venice, and which were unimaginable in America, may be said to be ambiguous, but clearly the city was a crucial site of a felt influx of extraordinarily vitalizing and energizing influences, nourishment, plenitude. Certainly, he was clearly apprehensive about what loss he might suffer when he left it. As in 'Partenza de Venezia':

Ne'er felt I parting from a woman loved
As feel I now my going forth from thee,
Yea, all the waters cry out 'Stay with me!'
And laugh reflected flames up luringly. . . .

As once, the twelve storm-tossed on Galilee
Put off their fear yet came not nigh
Unto the holier mystery.
So we bewildered, yet have trust in thee,
And thus thou, Venice,
show'st thy mastry.
(*CEP* 65–6)

Before leaving the young Pound and his inevitably young man's poetry about Venice, I must quote from one more of the poems in the 'San Trovaso Notebook' entitled 'In that Country'. It starts:

Looking upon my Venice and the stars
There stood one by me and his long cool hands
On mine were layed as in the times before

> Wherefor this question rose which I set forth.
> (*CEP* 248)

The question is, in brief, what kind of poetry should he try to write? Running through what he sees as the options, he concludes:

> Whether 'twere better, with one's own hand to fashion
> One lone man's mirroring on the sand
> Or were it better in the air to glide
> From heart to heart and fill each heart with passion
> To see, and make, and know what truths abide.
> (*CEP* 248–9)

The man with the long cool hands who is enacting the laying on of hands – in every sense – with the young poet, can only be Robert Browning (and the last three lines quoted must refer to his poetry), and what is of particular interest is that he should be doing it in Venice – 'my Venice': in the presence of the older poet, however hallucinated, Pound has felt a rush of territoriality. Why this might be so; and why Browning should, as it were, hand on the torch to Pound in Venice, are matters, I think, of real interest and import, and to suggest why will require something of a digression back to Browning in Venice, Browning's Venice.

Browning first visited Venice in 1838 when he was twenty-six. It was an immensely important visit. He was by then already engaged in writing *Sordello*, which he published two years later. This was a long and ambitious poem. It was not really, or certainly not principally, an attempt to re-create the life and times of the twelfth-century troubadour after whom it was named – such as a standard piece of Victorian medievalism might have done – but, in effect, a prolonged meditation on what kind of poet a modern poet should be, what kind of poetry he ought to – he could – write. In the course of the poem, some relatively obscure episodes from medieval and early Renaissance Italian history were made more obscure by an extremely elliptical, non-concessionary, semi-narrative treatment, in the course of which it is often difficult if not impossible to identify who might be 'speaking' or where the voice is coming from. From the moment of its publication the poem became a byword for obscurity and incomprehensibility, even a perversely private inaccessibility. Put thus summarily, it is possible to see Pound following rather uncannily exactly in Browning's footsteps – making *his* first really important visit to Venice when he was twenty-three, just seventy years after Browning, and starting, at least, to publish, not so many years later, a long poem which in part, and at an admittedly very basic level, meets the description I have just given of *Sordello*. The differences are enormous, of course. Not for nothing is *Sordello* one of the great unread poems of English literature (though understandable, this is a mistake – there are wonderful things in it), while the *Cantos* must be one of the most-read long poems of this century (even if the readings are sometimes hostile and castigatory). However we choose to assess their final achievement, my point here, simply, is that the *Cantos* start, not only effectively but literally, with Browning, and Browning in Venice.

Canto I was first published in 1917. It was subsequently dropped (with fragments rephrased and redeployed). But it was indubitably the start. Throughout this canto Pound is intermittently referring to, and responding to, Browning as he put himself forward – portrayed, revealed himself – in *Sordello*. This Browning most importantly does in 'Book the Third' when he breaks off from his story and seems to speak more directly ***in propria persona*** than elsewhere (we cannot always confidently identify the first-person narrator with Browning, compulsive ventriloquist that he is):

> I muse this on a ruined palace-step
> At Venice: why should I break off, nor sit
> Longer upon my step, exhaust the fit
> England gave birth to? Who's adorable
> Enough reclaim a – no Sordello's Will
> Alack! – be queen to me? That Bassanese
> Busied among her smoking fruit-boats? These
> Perhaps from our delicious Asolo
> Who twinkle, pigeons o'er the portico
> Not prettier, bind late leaves into sheaves
> To deck the bridge-side chapel, dropping leaves
> Soiled by their own loose gold-meal? Ah, beneath
> The cool arch stoops she, brownest cheek! Her wreath
> Endures a month – a half-month – if I make
> A queen of her, continue for her sake
> Sordello's story? Nay, that Paduan girl
> Splashes with barer legs where a live whirl
> In the dead black Giudecca proves sea-weed
> Drifting has sucked down three, four, all indeed
> Save one pale-red striped, pale-blue turbaned post
> For gondolas.
> You sad dishevelled ghost
> That pluck at me and point, are you advised
> I breathe? Let stay those girls. . . .
>
> Look they too happy, too tricked out? . . .

But in this magic weather one discards
Much old requirement. Venice seems a type
Of Life, 'twixt blue and blue extends, a stripe,
As Life, the somewhat, hangs 'twixt nought and nought:
'Tis Venice, and 'tis Life – as good you sought
To spare me the Piazza's slippery stone,
Or keep me to to the unchoked canals alone,
As hinder Life the evil with the good
Which make up Living rightly understood.

(A later version of those last two lines reads: 'As hinder Life what seems the single good / Sole purpose, one thing to be understood / Of Life',[31] which seems to me more explicit.) It is not entirely clear who the 'sad dishevelled ghost' is – perhaps the twelfth-century Italian character who wants him to get on with his story (at the very beginning he had boasted:

Confess now, poets know the dragnet's trick,
Catching the dead if Fate denies the quick
And shaming her. . . .

But there's a realm wherein she has no right
And I have many lovers: say but few
Friends fate accords me? Here they are; now view
The host I muster! . . .
                                        and they sit, each ghostly man
Striving to look as living as he can.[32]

Raising ghosts from the past for poetic purposes, and poetry's powers of exhumation, where alike crucial for Pound as well, of course.) But what the ghost is trying to pluck him from is quite unambiguous – busy girls among the fruit-boats; twinkling girls from Asolo; bare-legged girls in the canal . . . let stay those girls. And if that means ignoring and banishing the ghost – all the ghosts – so be it. What follows, though cryptic enough in all conscience (here the poem's obscurity may have served Browning well with his Victorian readers – those who reached book III), reads like nothing more or less than a pick-up of some Venetian Fifine figure.

Mistress of mine, there, there, as if I meant
You insult! Shall your friend (not slave) be shent
For speaking home? Beside care-bit erased
Broken-up beauties ever took my taste
Supremely, and I love you more, far more
Than her I looked should foot Life's temple-floor . . .

And hear
Me out before you say it is to sneer
I call you ravishing, for I regret
Little that she, whose early foot was set
Forth as she'd plant it on a pedestal,
Now i' the silent city, seems to fall
Towards me – no wreath, only a lip's unrest
To quiet, surcharged eyelids to be pressed
Dry of their tears upon my bosom: strange
Such sad chance should produce in thee such change,
My love! . . .

So sleep upon my shoulder, child, nor mind
Their foolish talk.[33]

It seems to me clear that, at this moment in the poem, Browning, sitting on the steps of the ruined Venetian palace, momentarily exhausted by his efforts to reawaken the past and to determine, through a kind of dialogue with ghosts, just what kind of poetry he should be trying to write, now and in England, focuses and fastens on one unquestionable value, 'the single good / Sole purpose, one thing to be understood / Of Life' (as the later version had it), and that, unambiguously, is sexual desire. Let stay those girls.

Pound responded – replied – directly to this part of the poem.

Your 'palace step'?
My stone seat was the Dogana's curb
And there were not 'those girls', there was one flare, one face.
'Twas all I ever saw, but it was real. . . .
And I can no more say what shape it was. . . .
But she was young, too young.
True, it was Venice,
And at Florian's and under the north arcade
I have seen other faces, and had my roles for breakfast, for that matter;
So, for what it's worth, I have the background.
And you had a background,
Watched 'the soul', Sordello's soul,
And saw it lap up life, and swell and burst –
'Into the empyrean?'
So you worked out new form, the meditative,
Semi-dramatic, semi-epic story,
And we will say 'What's left for me to do?
Whom shall I conjure up; who's my Sordello. . . .

Whom shall I hang my shimmering garment on;
Who wear my feather mantle, *hagoromo*;
Whom set to dazzle the serious future ages?' [34]

The similarities in the positions and stances of the poets are remarkable. Both, briefly expatriated, are sitting in Venice, striving to come to terms with their most influential predecessor – for in *Sordello* Browning was as surely trying to write himself out of the too overbearing power that Shelley then had over him, as Pound, who more than once referred to Browning as his 'father' ('Und überhaupt ich stamm aus Browning. . . . Pourquoi nier son père?'; *L*, 218), in his first canto was addressing himself to his own ghostly mentor. Not the anxiety of influence exactly; more a strenuous wrestling with their particular angels.

But Pound is stressing differences as well – even in where they were sitting. Browning could at least sit on the steps of a ruined palace; Pound has to make do with the city's customs house (in *Lustra* he made it 'the Dogana's vulgarest curb') – as though starting from a less privileged point and position than his ancestor. 'And there were not "those girls"' – only 'one face', and the girl was too young. But the face was also a 'flare', a Poundian word often used to refer to a visionary moment, and although he can no longer evoke her shape – 'it was real'. The young girl has variously been seen as alluding to Odysseus' Calypso, Dante's Beatrice (who was nine when he first saw her) and Browning's Pippa, who somehow enters everyone she 'passes'. All are plausible, if none is demonstrable; but whatever else, unlike Browning's girls, she is not depicted as an object of sexual desire. Her 'reality', whatever it was, however it might have been shaped, was surely something other, something higher, something older. Not, let stay those girls; more, bring back those gods. 'True, it was Venice' – but it is my 'background' just as much, or as little, as yours. After all, we are both visitors, and, anyway, anyone can go and have breakfast in St Mark's and look at the faces. Just because you sat on palace steps does not mean that you were, in some mystic way, more inward, more intimate, with the great city that is the past than I may be. In some such way the only half-articulated argument runs. Yes, indeed, Venice *is* 'a type of life' and in some important way one might even equate the two and say ''Tis Venice, and 'tis life'. But Pound would go on to make Venice an immeasurably richer 'type of life' than Browning did. Or if not richer – it depends perhaps on how you evaluate desire – then certainly more complicated. I think Ronald Bush, in his fine book on *The Genesis of Ezra Pound's Cantos* (a work to which I am happy to acknowledge my debt), is quite justified in suggesting that the poet-speaker of the first three cantos – all subsequently dropped or dispersed – is 'like Aeneas – sitting in a ruined city and about to set sail for another city that will be the spiritual completion of the first. . . . In

Three Cantos, Venice becomes E.P.'s vanished Troy and Pound's Ithaca to come.'[35]

But there is one other passage in *Sordello* which evokes Venice to quite different effect, and here I think Browning did point a way for Pound, even if by then he had sensed it was the way he would have to go. It occurs in 'Book the Fifth':

> How we attain to talk as brothers talk,
> In half-words, call things by half-names, nor balk
> From discontinuing old aids. To-day
> Takes in account the work of Yesterday:
> Has not the world a Past now, its adept
> Consults ere he dispense with or accept
> New aids? a single touch more may enhance,
> A touch less turn to insignificance
> Those structures' symmetry the past has strewed
> The world with, once so bare. Leave the mere rude
> Explicit details! 'tis but brother's speech
> We need, speech where an accent's change gives each
> The other's soul – no speech to understand
> By former audience: need was then to expand,
> Expatiate – hardly were we brothers! true –
> Nor I lament my small remove from you,
> Nor reconstruct what stands already. Ends
> Accomplished turn to means: my art intends
> New structure from the ancient: as they changed
> The spoils of every clime at Venice, ranged
> The horned and snouted Libyan god, upright
> As in his desert, by some simple bright
> Clay cinerary pitcher – Thebes as Rome,
> Athens as Byzant rifled, till their Dome
> From earth's reputed consummations razed
> A seal, the all-transmuting Triad blazed
> Above.[36]

We are familiar enough now with writers consciously using the writers and writings of the past – modifying, amplifying them; pillaging and displacing them; in every sense *building on* them. But I doubt if you could find a passage remotely resembling these lines from Browning in the literature which preceded him. In this sense, he really can be called a modern writer. And it is wonderfully apt that for the layering and splicing and importing of the past into the present he should choose the example and image of Venice (he had earlier described Dandalo deciding which of the marble pillars of 'vanquished Byzant' 'Twere fittest he transport to Venice' Square'[37]). In the short running-notes which he added to *Sordello* in the margins in 1863, next to the passages which precede the one just quoted Browning states that the poet-speaker is wondering whether his job was more properly that of an 'epoist' (writer of epics), or 'dramatist', or 'so to call him, analyst'. But by the beginning of the passage I have just quoted he simply says that the poet 'turns in due course synthetist'.[38] Whether the *Cantos* are to be regarded as a flawed triumph or a magnificent failure (and whether or not it matters), Pound has to be regarded as one of the great – indeed the greatest – 'synthetist' poet of this century. Certainly he was, in Browning's terms, trying to put together a Venice of a poem.

Proust uses exactly the same image as Browning – though I would be surprised indeed to learn that he had read *Sordello* – in describing Ruskin's writing: 'Ruskin, by way of quotation, but more often by way of allusion, incorporates into the structure of his sentences some biblical recollection, as the Venetians inserted in their monuments the sacred sculptures and precious stones they bought from the Orient' (*ORR* 7). Proust knew all about writing as citing – as quotation, allusion, incorporation. Proust *and* Pound incorporate, 'incrust', elements of Ruskin for their own ends. 'Ends achieved become means.' 'Incrusting' is a Ruskinian usage, and it occurs in a passage in his Venetian writing which could well have influenced both later writers:

> the school of incrusted architecture is *the only one in which perfect and permanent chromatic decoration is possible* . . . the ruling principle is the incrustation of brick with more precious materials . . . the system of decoration is founded on this duplicity . . . every slab of facial marble is fastened to the next by a confessed rivet and . . . the joints of the armour are . . . visibly and openly accommodated to the contours of the substance within. . . . It is at his choice either to lodge his few blocks of precious marble here and there among his masses of brick, and to cut out of the sculptured fragments such new forms as may be necessary for the observance of fixed proportions in the new building; or else to cut the coloured stone into thin strips, of extent sufficient to face the whole surface of the walls, and to adopt a method of construction irregular enough to admit the insertion of fragmentary sculptures; rather with a view to displaying their intrinsic beauty, than of setting them to any regular service in the support of the building.[39]

Taking 'brick' as the writing of the present, and the 'precious materials' available for 'incrustation' to be fragments of the writing and art of the past, one can see how powerfully relevant the passage is for writers working like Proust and Pound. Sometimes the 'rivets' are 'confessed' and the 'joints of armour' visible, as in Proust, and sometimes they are elided, as in Pound. But they are both 'incrusting'.

Thomas Hardy, a writer greatly admired by both Proust and Pound, did most of his thinking about aesthetic problems in architectural terms. In *The Laodicean*, much of the plot revolves around the matter of how to restore the fire-damaged Castle de Stancey. Without going into details of the plot, suffice it to say that there is a competition between architects, Havill only being able to think in terms of total restoration, an exact replica of the old building, and George Somerset offering a more imaginative plan, which is the successful one (he gets the girl, Paula, and the castle). This is Somerset's plan as seen through the envious eyes of Havill. 'It was original, and it was fascinating. Its originality lay partly in the fact that Somerset had not attempted to adapt an old building to the wants of the new civilization. He had placed his new erection beside it as a slightly attached structure, harmonizing with the old; heightening and beautifying, rather than subduing it. His work formed a palace, with a ruinous castle attached as a curiosity.'[40] This is not *exactly* 'incrustation', but it is certainly 'synthetism'. 'My art intends new structures from the ancient.' The moral that Hardy seems to be dramatizing would seem to be something like this. When the writer is faced with the problem of 'originality' (and just why this became such a problem for nineteenth-century writers is another story, perhaps connected to the increasing, too-engulfing availability of the literature of the past made possible by the mechanical mass production of books), the answer is neither to aim at *exact* imitation of the past – that is entirely inappropriate for a changed present age – nor to attempt a total replacement, building on an erased and forgotten past: complete originality is not possible, and anyway there is much of inestimable value and beauty in the fragments we have inherited. No – it is better, it is really the only way, to recontain, 'incorporate', what we have and wish to preserve from the past, in a new kind of structure. Make it new *really* means: make it old *in a new way.* It is Proust's way; it is Pound's way. It is perhaps the way of every serious modern writer.

To return to Pound's first ur-canto. Since Browning had covered so much of the ground, Pound had, as it were, to set about clearing it – which he does in the very first line.

> Hang it all, there can be but one *Sordello*!
> But say I want to, say I take your whole bag of tricks,
> Let in your quirks and tweeks, and say the thing's an art
> -form,
> Your *Sordello*, and that the world
> Needs such a rag-bag to stuff all its thought in.

Well, say he does, there are some problems. For one thing, Browning is pretty cavalier about historical accuracy and consistency:

And half your dates are out, you mix your eras;
For that great font Sordello sat beside –
'Tis an immortal passage, but the font?
Is some two centuries outside the picture.
Does it matter?
                    Not in the least.

(The font passage is indeed remarkable, and as I have not seen it quoted I will do so here:

                              Nay, stoop –
A dullish grey-streaked cumbrous font, a group
Round it, – each side of it, where'er one sees, –
Upholds it; shrinking Caryatids
Of just-tinged marble like Eve's lilied flesh
Beneath her maker's finger when the fresh
First pulse of life shot brightening the snow.
The font's edge burthens every shoulder, so
They muse upon the ground, eyelids half closed;
Some, with eek arms behind their backs disposed,
Some, crossed above their bosoms, some, to veil
Their eyes, some, propping chin and cheek so pale,
Some, hanging slack an utter helpless length
Dead as a buried vestal whose whole strength
Goes when the grate above shuts heavily.
So dwell these noiseless girls, patient to see,
Like priestesses because of sin impure
Penanced for ever, who resigned endure,
Having that once drunk sweetness to the dregs.[41]

Pound is right of course; it does not sound very twelfth century! More like an adumbration of the 1890s – and thus an interesting indication of the slight hangover thereof which still lingered in Pound's poetic taste.) Historical inaccuracy does not disqualify the poem as a model. Pound continues:

                    Ghosts move about me
Patched with histories. You had your business:
To set out so much thought, so much emotion;
To paint, more real than any dead Sordello,
The half or third of your intensest life
And call that *third* Sordello;
And you'll say, 'No, not your life,
He never showed himself.'

Is't worth the evasion, what were the use
Of setting figures up and breathing life upon them,
Were 't not *our* life, your life, my life, extended?
I walk Verona. (I am here in England.)
I can see Can Grande. (Can see whom you will.)
You had one whole man?
And I have many fragments, less worth? Less worth?
Ah, had you quite my age, quite such a beastly and cantankerous age?
You had some basis, had some set belief.
Am I let preach? Has it a place in music?

One of the ghosts 'patched with histories' was Browning himself of course – 'nor bid / Me rag by rag expose how patchwork hid / The youth' he says of Sordello/Browning[42] – and Pound is 'parleying' with him, as Browning did with his predecessors. And Pound is indeed learning how to raise the dead and make them speak. He is also learning from Browning to wander through space as well as in time. 'I walk Verona. (I am here in England.)' is an echo of, or allusion to, the magicianly invocation at the start of *Sordello* – 'Then, appear, Verona'.[43] (It also anticipates the, to me, very poignant line repeated twice in canto LXXVII, 465 and 473 – '"How is it far, if you think of it?"') Pound seems to feel that he is disadvantaged in comparison with Browning, in that his age is 'beastly' and thus unpropitious for poetry, that he lacks a 'basis' and 'set belief', and that Browning had 'one whole man' whereas he, Pound, has to work from 'many fragments'. I doubt that Browning felt he had certain access to any wholeness or unitariness, and, whatever his 'belief' was, it was anything but 'set', being endlessly worried at, dismantled and reformulated. But Pound is not giving up: rather, clearing the ground for his own particular singing (and, yes, preaching).

He moves immediately to *his* chosen locale and 'whole man' – Sirmio and Catullus. This sequence concludes:

And the place is full of spirits.
Not *lemures,* not dark and shadowy ghosts,
But the ancient living, wood-white,
Smooth as the inner bark, and firm of aspect,
And all agleam with colors – no, not agleam,
But colored like the lake and like the olive leaves,
Glaukopos, clothed like the poppies, wearing golden greaves,
Light on the air.
Are they Etruscan gods?
The air is solid sunlight, *apricus,*
Sun-fed we dwell there (we in England now);

It's your way of talk, we can be where we will be,
Sirmio serves my will better than your Asolo
Which I have never seen.

There it is again – 'It's your way of talk, we can be where we will be.' How is it far, if you think of it? Pound is establishing his own sacred places. And he insists on an important distinction. He is not raising 'shadowy ghosts' but summoning 'spirits' – 'the ancient living'. Bring back those gods. Of the details that follow, Guy Davenport writes: 'the physical details "wood-white" and "smooth as inner bark" align the visions with the groves where most congenially one could see them. *Glaukopos*, "grey-eyed" or "owl-faced" – Pallas Athene's epithet in Homer – gives them the eery presence of an owl in branches (and where an owl, there Athene).'[44] Gods not ghosts – gods you can still walk with or sense behind you – and light, not shades; 'solid sunlight, *apricus*' (which last word means 'drenched with sunlight').

Despite, or more likely because of, his closeness to Browning, Pound is determined to set out the terms for a different way of writing and – after the Venetian passage I have quoted in which he puts himself in a similar position to Browning – does so in a passage which starts in a very Browningesque manner, and then takes another direction. A turn to simplicity – leading back to splendour.

What a hodge-podge you have made there! –
Zanze and *swanzig*, of all opprobious rhymes!
And you turn off whenever it suits your fancy,
Now at Verona, now with the early Christians,
Or now a-gabbling of the 'Tyrrhene whelk'.
'The lyre should animate but not mislead the pen' –
That's Wordsworth, Mr Browning. . . .
That should have taught you avoid speech figurative
And set out your matter
As I do, in straight simple phrases:
Gods float in the azure air,
Bright gods, and Tuscan, back before dew was shed,
It is a world like Puvis?
Never so pale my friend,
'Tis the first light – not half light – Panisks
And oak-girls and the Maenads
Have all the wood.
Our olive Sirmio
Lies in its burnished mirror, and the Mounts Baldo and Riva
Are alive with song, and all the leaves are full of voices.
'Non è fuggito.'

'It is not gone.' Metastasio
Is right – we have that world about us.

There is a facile, prettified, ersatz sort of 'paganism' which seems to be inseparable from Decadence – Roman as well as Victorian – and Pound has to differentiate what he is doing from that. So it is not twilight (Celtic or otherwise) but 'first light' – a new dawn, so he hopes, in every sense. And he is seeing-painting-evoking, not the pale, dreamy figures of a Puvis de Chavannes, painter of etiolated mythological scenes of almost soporific pastoral sweetness or languid melancholy, but little Pans and oak-girls (hamadryads) and – since he changed 'Maenads' to 'Maelids' in *Lustra* – apple nymphs, and an almost fiercely beautiful landscape in bright light, 'full of song' and 'alive with voices'. Pound believes it is still possible to establish contact with ancient vital forces which have not died but somehow been relegated, forgotten, lost touch with. (Elsewhere he writes of 'our kinship to the vital universe; to the tree and the living rock. We have about us the universe of fluid force, and below us the germinal universe of wood alive, of stone alive' (*SP* 82). It is worth noting that belief in 'stone alive'.) Hence the reference to Metastasio, a Tuscan poet of the eighteenth century whose constant theme was Arcadia. 'Metastasio, and he should know if anyone, assures us that this age endures', wrote Pound in an essay in which he also stated: 'I would much rather lie on what is left of Catullus' parlour floor and speculate the azure beneath it and the hills off to Salo and Riva with their forgotten gods moving unhindered amongst them, than discuss any processes or theories of art whatsoever' (*LE* 8–9).

For the remainder of this first canto, Pound looks around and touches on many subjects from the past which he might use as the basis or departure point for his poetry. He concludes:

I have but smelt this life, a whiff of it –
The box of scented wood
Recalls cathedrals. And shall I claim;
Confuse my own phantastikon,
Or say the filmy sheel that circumscribes me
Contains the actual sun;
                                        confuse the thing I see
With actual gods behind me?
                                        Are they gods behind me?
How many worlds we have!
                                        If Botticelli
Brings her ashore on that great cockle-shell –
His Venus (Simonetta's?)
And Spring and Aufidus fill all the air

With their clear-outlined blossoms?
World enough
                    Behold, I say, she comes
'Apparelled like the spring, Graces her subjects,'
(That's from *Pericles*).
Oh, we have worlds enough, and brave décors,
And from these like we guess a soul for man
And build him full of aery populations.
Mantegna's sterner line, and the new world about us:
Barred lights, great flares, new form, Picasso or Lewis.
If for a year a man write to paint, and not to music –
O Casella!

How many worlds indeed. There is Pound's own world, or is it a 'phantastikon'? But he has seen things, whether or not they are gods. There is Browning's world, which also contained, or appropriated, Sordello's world. There is the world of cathedrals, and the more ancient world of pagan gods. There is, of course, the world of Shakespeare, and the smaller world of Marvell, who thought that, alas, there was *not* 'world enough'. But Botticelli's painting suggests that perhaps there *is* – and with that reference Venus sails into the *Cantos*, arguably never to leave. Bush's note on the line referring to this picture seems to me to have much to justify it. 'Simonetta was the bride of Juliano dei Medici and the reputed model for the figure of Venus in Botticelli's "Birth of Venus". As far back as this passage, Pound had decided to make Venus the reigning goddess of his poem. The goddesses of the *Cantos* are really one goddess seen in different lights, all related to Venus genetrix.'[45] And, I shall be suggesting, where Venus, there Venice. If Botticelli could bring Venus ashore, well – unspoken question – why shouldn't I? That will be world enough. But the outlines must be kept clear, and the lines stern, as in Mantegna – 'the most rigidly classical of Renaissance painters'.[46] As Davenport notes, there are some rather odd words in these lines. '*Décors*' suggests ornament rather than edifice; 'guessing a soul' does not sound altogether confident, and how valuable would a soul be that is filled with 'aery populations'? Perhaps that is what we would-be modern writers *have been* doing, and we had better make our 'lines' more ruthlessly incisive and excisive – clear as Botticelli, stern as Mantegna. The 'new world about us' means the need for 'new form'. Make it new. Look at Picasso and Wyndham Lewis.

This, I think, is the point of the final two lines. In the phrase 'write to paint' I think that 'to' means, not 'in order to', but more something like 'addressed to, in accompaniment with' – as in 'write to music'. The final apostrophe would be cryptic indeed to any reader not very well versed in Dante. But the Pound scholars can point us immediately to the relevant point near the end of canto II of *Purgatorio*, when Casella makes his appearance. Casella was a musician who once set Dante's poems to music and when Dante meets him in Purgatory he begs him to sing an old love song for the solace it will afford. Casella obliges:

> '*Amor che nella mente mi ragiona,*'
> cominciò egli allor si dolcemente,
> che la dolcezza ancor dentro mi suona.

('*Love that in my mind discourseth to me,*' began he then so sweetly, that the sweetness yet within me sounds.)

All the people nearby gather round, ravished and gladdened by the singing. Then the angry voice of Cato breaks in with reproach:

> Che è ciò, spiriti lenti?
>
> qual negligenza, quale stare è questo?
> Correte al monte a spogliarvi le scoglio
> ch'esser non lascia a voi Dio manifesto.

('What is this, ye laggard spirits? What negligence, what tarrying is this? Haste to the mount and strip you of the slough, that lets not God be manifest to you.')

And away they go:

> cosi vid' io quella masnada fresca
> lasciar lo canto, e gire in ver la costa,
> come uom che va, nè sa dove riesca

(so I saw that new company leave the singing, and go towards the hillside, like one who goes, but knoweth not where he may come forth)[47]

I have quoted the incident in some detail because it seems to illuminate a lot about Pound's position at this point in his writing career. He had always been drawn to *la dolcezza* in poetry, particularly in the Renaissance Italian poets but in writers such as Swinburne as well. Now, the implication is, he feels he must leave behind and go beyond the relatively simple, though undoubtedly exquisite, pleasures of the purely lyric poem. Since he did indeed, in his own way, want the gods to be 'manifesto' to him then he must set out and climb the mountain of the new long poem he was beginning to have in mind. And of no poet could it have ever been more truly and, as it was to turn out, more tragically aptly said, that at this point he was exactly 'come uom che va, né so dove riesca'. After completing these first three cantos, Pound was ready to set sail. 'And then went down to the ship.' O Casella!

After Odysseus (and Pound) have set sail for Circe, and the realm of the dead, canto I (in the final version) concludes:

> Venerandam,
> In the Cretan's phrase, with the golden crown, Aphrodite,
> Cypri munimenta sortita est, mirthful, orichalchi, with golden
> Girdles and breast bands, thou with dark eyelids
> Bearing the golden bough of Argicida. So that:
>
> (I, 5)

So that, whatever else, Venus-Aphrodite has immediately risen into the poem. She does so on numerous other occasions in the *Cantos*, of which I wish to cite three.

In the first of the Pisan Cantos when, in terrible conditions of deprivation and exposure, Pound writes to find ways of reasserting components of his earlier vision, Venus is born and borne again, not with serene ease – not surprising in the circumstances – but nevertheless she comes:

> but this air brought her ashore a la marina
> with the great shell borne on the seawaves
> nautilis biancastra
> By no means an orderly Dantescan rising
> but as the winds veer
>
> (LXXIV, 443)

She appears again in a later Pisan Canto – LXXIX:

> This Goddess was born of sea-foam
> She is lighter than air under Hesperus . . .
>
> terrible in resistance . . .
>
> a petal lighter than sea-foam
>
> (LXXIX, 492)

The 'Dantescan rising' occurs in 'Rock Drill', where it may be said that Pound was attempting to write paradise. These lines conclude canto XCI:

'Ghosts dip in the crystal,
adorned'
That the tone change from elegy
'Et Jehanne'
(the Lorraine girl)
A lost kind of experience?
scarcely,
O Queen Cytherea,
che 'l terzo ciel movete.
(XCI, 617)

Paradiso, canto VIII, opens:

Solea creder lo mondo in suo periclo
che la bella Ciprigna ill folle amore
raggiasse, volta nel terzo epiciclo

(The world was wont to think in its peril that the fair Cyprian rayed down mad love, rolled in the third epicycle.)[48]

The blessed spirits in Venus – which is the third heaven – sing to Dante, and one of them says to him:

'. . . tu del mondo già dicesti:

Voi che intendendo il terzo ciel movete;
e sem si pien d'amor che per piacerti
non fia men dolce un poco di quiete.'

('. . . thou from the word didst sometime say: *Ye who by understanding give the third heaven motion*; and so full of love are we that, to pleasure thee, a space of quiet shall be no less sweet to us.')[49]

Queen Cytherea – la bella Ciprigna, Venus – used to be responsible for 'il folle amore', mad love, or so the world thought; but she can be the moving source of a more radiant, beneficent, beatific love – *amor*: 'Beyond civic order, / l'AMOR' (XCIV, 634). Thus Pound in a later canto in 'Rock Drill'. But even that AMOR rises – like Venus, like Venice – originally from the sea. Venere – Venerandam.

That there are two kinds of love – let us say Venus and Circe, or a good and bad Venus – is clear throughout the *Cantos*, and adumbrated in Aphrodite's first appearance. This Aphrodite gave birth to Aeneas, founder of cities. And those 'golden Girdles and breast bands' she is wearing are important. Michael Bernstein has summarized exactly why, and I will quote his lucid words.

> Even in the Botticelli painting Pound so cherished, Venus emerges naked from the waters, but here her sexuality is simultaneously 'civilized' and restrained by the golden lines of the metalworker's craft. It [Pound's image] is a compelling image . . . it succeeds in linking the motifs of an ordered and order-building eros ['Eros, builder of cities'], of color (Aphrodite's flesh, as well as the gold itself) contained within the 'bands' that underline its perfect and stable form, and of a precious commodity that is used to serve an aesthetic rather than a mercenary end.[50]

Referring to Robert Hollander's *Boccaccio's Two Venuses*[51] Bernstein continues:

> The description of Aphrodite clothed in bands of gold is, moreover, a common Renaissance topos, traditionally intended to signify the dual nature of sexual desire. As Robert Hollander has shown, when Venus is represented without her *ceston*, or girdle, she embodies illicit and destructive lust with 'anti-social results', but when she is figured wearing the golden *ceston,* she stands for 'positive sexual love', present in matrimony and resulting in matrimony.

He then cites, as examples of incarnations of the destructive Venus, Helen of Troy in canto II, Eleanor of Aquitaine in canto VII and Circe in canto XXXIX. I think this dichotomizing is a little too tidy. Helen certainly emerges as another Venus:

> Seal sports in the spray-whited circles of cliff-wash,
> Sleek head, daughter of Lir,
>   eyes of Picasso
> Under black fur-hood, lithe daughter of Ocean;
> And the wave runs in the beach-groove:
>
> (II, 6)

True, Homer's old men are apprehensive and murmur against her:

> Moves, yes she moves like a goddess
> And had the face of a god
>   and the voice of Schoeney's daughters,
> And doom goes with her in walking
>
> (II, 6)

But that is just the point – they are *old* men. The theme of this canto is metamorphosis and it is a supreme demonstration that you abuse – try to divert or enslave – Dionysus at your peril. An undeflectable life and force flows through and from the 'lithe daughter of Ocean' which may build and destroy cities in turn. Canto VII is also full of 'old men's voices' but these are the hollow men, 'thin husks I had known as men / Dry casques of departed locusts', in a land and time (the present) of dry pods, empty shells, 'a petrifaction of air', 'dead dry talk' – and 'Eros drowned'. Against this, certainly, Eleanor – '(she spoiled in a British climate)' – and Helen (Nicea):

> The sea runs in the beach-groove, shaking the floated pebbles,
> Eleanor!
> The scarlet curtain throws a less scarlet shadow
> Lamplight at Buovilla, e quel remir,
> And all that day
> Nicea moved before me
> And the cold grey air troubled her not
> For all her naked beauty, bit not the tropic skin,
> And the long slender feet lit on the curb's marge
> And her moving height went before me,
> We alone having being.
>
> (VII, 25–6)

Buovilla and the phrase 'e quel remir' (and that I may look at her) both point to the troubadour poet, Arnaut Daniel, and there is no doubt what, in this canto, is being extolled and celebrated, and what deprecated and deplored. The closing lines hail 'Lorenzaccio / Being more live than they, more full of flames and voices' (VII, 27). Lorenzaccio Medici murdered his cousin, the tyrant Alessandro, in 1537. 'Murder most foul, as in the best it is', says Hamlet, quite rightly. But in this canto Alessandro is 'the tall indifference', a 'living shell'. What is important is who is 'more full of flames and voices'. What matters is 'having being'. 'The sea runs in the beach-groove' – the daughters of Ocean will walk no matter how cold the climate.

Bernstein's strongest case of a destructive Venus is of course Circe and the Circe canto, XXXIX:

> When I lay in the ingle of Circe
> I heard a song of that kind.
> Fat panther lay by me
> Girls talked there of fucking, beasts talked there of eating,
> All heavy with sleep, fucked girls and fat leopards,
> Lions loggy with Circe's tisane,
> Girls leery with Circe's tisane
>
> (XXXIX, 193)

This, certainly, is 'beastly' enough – appropriately one might think. We might move immediately to canto XLVII:

> Yet must thou sail after knowledge
> Knowing less than drugged beasts.
> (XLVII, 236)

This canto has to take the 'road to hell', to the bower of Proserpine, to the very source and root of fertility rituals and mysteries.

> Hast thou found a nest softer than cunnus
> Or hast thou found better rest
> Hast'ou a deeper planting, doth thy death year
> Bring swifter shoot?
> Hast thou entered more deeply the mountain?
>
> The light has entered the cave. Io! Io!
> The light has gone down into the cave,
> Splendour on splendour!
> By prong have I entered these hills:
> That the grass grow from my body,
> That I hear the roots speaking together,
> The air is new on my leaf,
> The forked boughs shake with the wind.
> (XLVII, 238)

'Paganism included a certain attitude toward; a certain understanding of, coitus, which is the mysterium' (*SP* 70). Or, even more succinctly, 'Sacrum, sacrum, inluminatio coitu' (canto XXXVI, 180). This, one may say, is where all mysteries start, at a deeper, lower level than even the beasts; but the irreducible mystery of sexual congress may lead on, or back, to splendour, to AMOR or even to *paradiso* – 'splendour on splendour'. It may, or it may not. Not all descents are fruitful. There are hells which house no Proserpine.

If the Circe canto starts in beast-liness and bestialization, it moves on to celebrate a mingling of resurgent spring and sexuality in a passage of astonishing beauty which contains these lines:

> with the Goddess' eyes to seaward
> By Circeo, by Terracina, with the stone eyes
> white toward the sea
> With one measure, unceasing:
> 'Fac deum!' 'Est factus.'

Ver novum!
            ver novum!
Thus made the spring
                                        (XXXIX, 195)

Monte Circeo near Terracina was thought to have been Circe's island before the sea receded. Pound, before the section of his *Selected Prose* which is entitled 'Religio', placed this statement as an epigraph: '*To replace the marble goddess on her pedestal at Terracina is worth more than any metaphysical argument. Aram nemus vult*' (*SP* 45). Again, later, under 'Credo': 'Given the material means I would replace the statue of Venus on the cliffs of Terracina' (*SP* 53). Such a statue – part of his religion and his creed – would, perforce, be literally in direct proximity to Circeo, and what I am suggesting is that, for Pound, Circe and Venus were a good deal closer to each other than some of his readers have thought. Even though Aphrodite triumphantly concludes canto I, the canto *starts* with Circe – 'Circe's this craft, the trim-coifed goddess'. They are perhaps, in some profound way, inseparable. ('Both jocundity and *gentilezza* are implicit in nature. There is plenty of propaganda for exuberance, plenty of support for Rabelais and Brantome. But that does not by any means exhaust the unquenchable splendour and indestructible delicacy of nature' (*GTK* 282). Nature – inclusive and seamless.)

The Circe canto concludes:

Beaten from flesh into light
Hath swallowed the fire-ball
A traverso le foglie
His rod hath made god in my belly
            Sic loquitur nupta
            Cantat sic nupta

Dark shoulders have stirred the lightning
A girl's arms have nested the fire,
Not I but the handmaid kindled
            Cantat sic nupta
I have eaten the flame.
                                        (XXXIX, 196)

Beaten *from* flesh (Circe) *into* light (the third heaven of Venus) – this surely is the movement of the canto, perhaps the *Cantos*. Light, lightning, fire, flame – anything that flares (a key word), flashes, gleams against the great dark, is welcomed, praised and venerated in Pound's work, and so here too. And notice 'Cantat sic *nupta*': thus sings the *bride*. Aphrodite is wearing her gold bands. So that:

So that – after a difficult interval (the gods, after all, are 'discontinuous') Aphrodite leads directly to Dionysus and *both* preside over the engendering, the emergence of Venice. 'So that' at the end of canto I is repeated at the start of canto XVII, which could, indeed, be called Pound's 'Birth of Venice'. True, Venice makes an earlier appearance – in canto III. The lines are a rigorously reduced version of some of the lines from the ur-canto I. Pound is in the Browning position, but Browning is no longer named.

I sat on the Dogana's steps
For the gondolas cost too much, that year,
And there were not 'those girls', there was one face,
And the Buccentero twenty yards off, howling 'Stretti',
And the lit cross beams, that year, in the Morosini,
And the peacocks in Koré's house, or there may have been.
Gods float in the azure air,
Bright gods and Tuscan, back before dew was shed.
Light: and the first light, before ever dew was fallen.
(III, 11)

The main point to notice here is that now Pound moves *immediately* from being in Venice to a vision of the 'bright gods' floating in the air. The city is no longer so splendid, perhaps – though there may still be peacocks in Persephone's house; but to be sited there is to be afforded a visionary sight of the earliest gods who presided over the first dawn. It is thus, in this wise, still a city of gods – if only in an imagination stirred to reverie.

Cantos I to XVI, published as a unit, move from Homer's Greece and its gods, through selected moments in history and other cultures, down to the hell of contemporary Europe enmired in the First World War and the Russian Revolution – a hell un-Proserpined. There is just a glimpse of what seems to be Elysium and the blessed dead:

and I through this, and into the earth,
patet terra,
entered the quiet air
the new sky,
the light as after a sun-set,
and by their fountains the heroes,
Sigismundo, and Malatesta Novello,
and founders, gazing at the mounts of their cities.
(XVI, 69)

But Pound falls asleep only to dream of contemporary wars – unheroic, godless, and fatal to cities. And then:

So that the vines burst from my fingers
And the bees weighted with pollen
Move heavily in the vine shoots: . . .

ZAGREUS! IO ZAGREUS!
With the first pale-clear of the heaven
And the cities set in their hills,
And the goddess of the fair knees
Moving there, with the oak-woods behind her,
The green slope, with white hounds
leaping about her;
And thence down to the creek's mouth, until evening,
Flat water before me,
and the trees growing in water,
Marble trunks out of stillness,
On past the palazzi,
in the stillness,
The light now, not of the sun.
Chrysophrase,
And the water green clear, and blue clear;
On, to the great cliffs of amber.
Between them,
Cave of Nerea,
she like a great shell curved,
And the boat drawn without sound,
Without odour of ship-work,
Nor bird-cry, nor any noise of wave moving,
Nor splash of porpoise, nor any noise of wave moving,
Within her cave, Nerea,
she like a great shell curved
In the suavity of the rock

(XVII, 76–7)

With the reappearance of the 'discontinuous' gods, Venice starts to emerge. The trees growing in water become 'marble trunks', become the columns of the unnamed Venice. The trunks and columns rise under the influence of Dionysus (Zagreus) and are phallic – let there be no doubt about that. 'Italy has lived more fully than other nations because she has kept up the habit of placing statues in gardens. The grove calls for the column. *Nemus aram vult*' (*SP* 302). Again, *Nemus aram vult* – exactly, the grove desires the altar. The female 'grove' is here and inevitably marine. Nerea is Nereid, daughter of Nereus, the old god of the sea, older than Poseidon. She is like the 'great shell curved' – the shell in which Venus was borne ashore. The shell is in the cave is in the 'suavity of the rock' – these are both sacred and sexual, sexually sacred, recesses and declivities. Venice and Venus are elided.

The way in which this inchoate and primordial Venice first appears is as in a dream – soundless, motionless, not a smell of work. It is there – not for the first time – as if by magic. And if the light is not (not directly) 'of the sun', it is because, in and out of the clear green-blue water, nature is being transformed – metamorphosing – into culture and art. The trees are turning to marble as the cliffs are turning to amber; and where was simple sunlight – 'Chrysophrase'. After this passage there is an Arcadian vision of fauns, panthers, nymphs and gods – Hermes and Athene as well as Dionysus; then we move out of myth and back into history and the actual making of the city, with, this time, lots of movement and work. This is not dream: this is how it was.

> A boat came,
> One man holding her sail,
> Guiding her with oar caught over gunwale, saying:
> ' There, in the forest of marble,
> ' the stone trees — out of water —
> ' the arbours of stone —
> ' marble leaf, over leaf,
> ' silver, steel over steel,
> ' silver beaks rising and crossing,
> ' prow set against prow,
> ' stone, ply over ply,
> ' the gilt beams flare of an evening'
> Borso, Carmagnola, the men of craft, *i vitrei*,
> Thither, at one time, time after time,
> And the waters richer than glass,
> Bronze gold, the blaze over the silver,
> Dye-pots in the torch-light,
> The flash of wave under prows,
> And the silver beaks rising and crossing.
> Stone trees, white and rose-white in the darkness,
> Cypress there by the towers,
> Drift under hulls in the night.
>
> 'In the gloom the gold
> Gathers the light about it.'
>
> (XVII, 78)

This is Renaissance Venice, the Venice of the time of Sigismundo Malatesta, as the last quotation indicates (I shall return to the Malatesta Cantos). The man in the boat who speaks is perhaps a sea-goer relating in wonder his sight of the miraculous city on the water. It is of course a place of stupendous and ceaseless artifice and artificing: wood, stone, marble, steel; bronze, silver, gold; glass, gilt and dye – flaring and flashing; rising and crossing. Thus, with that enormously suggestive compacted condensation of which he was such an uncanny master, Pound evokes Venice at its zenith. Venice *Venissima*.

At this point I have to address a matter which is central to any reading of Pound's Venice, and perhaps to this whole book. It concerns the notion of 'the forest of marble' and those 'stone trees'; not to mention gold *gathering* light, and waters *richer* than glass. (Ruskin saw Venice as a city composed of 'forest branches turned to marble' – see p. 100 above.) Davenport takes 'the forest of marble' to imply that the Venetian marble forest is 'petrified: a real forest that has suffered metamorphosis'. He goes on to speak of 'the eeriness of the stone forest . . . which makes one see Venice as the ominous, unworldly place *The Cantos* here begin to make of it.' In general, 'Venice is offered as an example of the unnatural, largely in terms of enigma, or in images that have the flavor of mystery and enigma.'[52] In much the same spirit, Hugh Kenner, commenting on this canto, makes the, to me astonishing, interpretative statement that 'Venice arose from the water a stone Aphrodite, splendidly dead'.[53] This line of thought, or reading, seems to me crucially wrong, and this is important, not just because of the distinction and authority of the two critics, but because it goes right to the heart of what we might conceive to be the distinction between nature and 'unnature' and the relation between nature and art in Pound's work.

At the very least Donald Davie was surely right to insist: 'The *Cantos* force us to dismiss from our minds most of the familiar connotations of "marmoreal" or "stony". Where "marble" appears, or "stone", it is a sign of resurgence and renewed hope.'[54] Remember that the 'marble goddess' at Terracina would be 'worth more than any metaphysical argument'. In Pound, marble is the material of art and piety; of civic beauty and of reverence for the generative (sometimes violent) something other, something greater, that flows through great creating Nature and sometimes creative Man alike. Talk of 'petrifaction' and dead Aphrodite could hardly be less to the point. More generally, the association of Venice, not only with marble, but with precious metals and stones, is used by these critics to associate Venice (pejoratively) not only with ominous enchantment and eerie magic, but more seriously with stagnation, corruption, negation – death. This is, of course, a not uncommon depiction of Venice (it occurs when she turns her Medusa face to the watcher); but in this case I think it is inapposite – perhaps not entirely, as I shall later suggest, but certainly in its major emphasis. In general, it can be said, the intimate conjunction of the organic with the inorganic or mineral is often radiantly positive in Pound.

Green veins in the turquoise,
Or, the gray steps up under the cedars
(III, 11)

the crystalline, as inverse of water,
clear over rock-bed

ac ferae familiares
the gemmed field *a destra* with fawn, with panther
(LXXVI, 457)

The roots go down to the river's edge
and the hidden city moves upward
white ivory under that bark
(LXXXIII, 530)

granite next sea wave
is for clarity
(CVI, 753)

But to hitch sensibility to efficiency?
grass versus granite
(CXIII, 788)

In mountain air the grass frozen emerald
(CXIII, 789)

The marble form in the pine wood,
The shrine seen and not seen
(CX, 781)

jasmine twines over capitols . . .

The columns gleam as if cloisonné,
The sky is leaded with elm boughs
(CVI, 755)

for the gold light of wheat surging upward
ungathered
Persephone in the cotton-field
(CVI, 753)

Forest thru ice into emerald
(CI, 723)

topaz against pallor of under-leaf
(CX, 778)

Grove hath its altar . . .

the stone taking form in the air
(XC, 607–8)

Turquoise and cedars; crystal the *in*verse of water, not *ob*verse; field *gemmed* with fauns and panthers; ivory *under* bark as Venice, the hidden city, 'moves upward'; granite next to sea waves, 'hitched' to grass; grass and forest iced to emerald; topaz against leaves; jasmine over the 'capitols' while the sky is *leaded* with elms; and the light of the wheat 'surging upward' is 'gold': in these and in many, many other instances we receive glimpses and intimations of the organic and the inorganic, of nature and art, working, moving, surging together; merging or metamorphosing into each other; including each other, inverting each other; felicitously and effortlessly juxtaposed – *not* 'yoked by violence together' (as Dr Johnson thought all such minglings in the Metaphysical poets) – for a maximum, if momentary, harmonious inclusiveness. (Davenport regards references to 'stone, metal, the inorganic' in the *Cantos* as indicative of Hades and the *opposite* – the obverse – of the organic associations of Persephone Stone. Again, I have to say that I think this piece of dichotomizing to be crucially out of tune with the *Cantos*. What about 'diamond clearness' (p. 449), 'eyes of turquoise' (p. 778), 'Topaz, God can sit on' (p. 745) and indeed 'the GREAT CRYSTAL' (p. 34) – are these infernal, because certainly 'inorganic'? I cannot believe it.) The stone takes form in the air like a tree, just as trees turn ivory to raise a Venice. The grove *should* have its altar – *nemus aram vult* – as much as female and male should work together. In this atmosphere, Venice – Venice at the height of its glory – is, and should be seen as, a *triumph* of nature; one of the finest, most magical products of whatever gods, or rather goddesses, there may – discontinuously – be. That there are other aspects to Pound's Venice will emerge; but this aspect is, I believe, central.

Talk of goddesses is very much to the point. The concluding part of canto XVII is thronged with them: Athene; an invented one named 'Zothar', associated with elephants, sistrums (jingling instruments used by ancient Egyptians, especially in the rites of Isis); another invented one, Greek this time, 'Aletha' (Unforgetting) –

with her eyes seaward,
and in her hands sea-wrack
Salt-bright with the foam.
(XVII, 78)

– and then Kore or Persephone 'through the bright meadow' (XVII, 78). In its compressed way, this manages to suggest all the goddesses – the most chaste and the most sexually ecstatic; the destructive and the regenerative. Trade and riches from every quarter, every culture, every clime, came to and through Venice, and just so all goddesses converge on and in her. Venice is a figure, one might say an avatar, of them all. Goddesses, in the world of the *Cantos*, crucially come from the sea – and look seaward.

with the Goddess' eyes to seaward
By Circeo, by Terracina, with the stone eyes
white toward the sea
(XXXIX, 195)

as by Terracina rose from the sea Zephyr behind her
and from her manner of walking
as had Anchises
till the shrine be again white with marble
till the stone eyes look again seaward
(LXXIV, 435)

Help me to neede
By Circeo, the stone eyes looking seaward
Nor could you enter her eyes by probing.
(CVI, 754)

Effectively, *all* goddesses come, rise from the sea – as did Venice – and ultimately they are inscrutable, un-probeable. Venus, or Circe? Artemis, or Zothar? Aletha, or Persephone? You cannot know. The eyes are stone; but they forget nothing.

After a complicated reference to an episode in the *Odyssey* (interestingly interpreted by Davenport), we seem to travel with travellers through tropics and deserts – 'Splendour, as the splendour of Hermes' – to conclude:

And shipped thence
to the stone place,
Pale white, over water,
known water,
And the white forest of marble, bent bough over bough,

The pleached arbour of stone,
Thither Borso, when they shot the barbed arrow at him,
And Carmagnola, between the two columns,
Sigismundo, after that wreck in Dalmatia.
        Sunset like the grasshopper flying.
(XVII, 79)

We are back in historical Venice. Incomprehensibly to me, Davenport thinks the phrase 'pleached arbour of stone' 'ominous'. 'Pleached', with its suggestions of both 'peach' and 'plash' and meaning 'interlaced', is a lovely word and Pound has elsewhere used it as such. And a 'pleached *arbour* of *stone*' (my italics) would, as I have tried to suggest, represent some sort of supremely restful and harmonious coming-together of the arts and the elements – not something of dark foreboding. (There is a 'pleached bower' in *Much Ado About Nothing* (III, i, 1:7) which is the reverse of ominous.)

Of the last line of the canto, Davenport writes: 'When the sun sets, its last direct light on the horizon in a green flash, like the green blur of the winged grasshopper flying. This haiku takes us back to the vine shoots and bees of the canto's beginning, decisively bounding off the natural from the dark moral entity of Venice.'[55] Characteristically sensitive in reading the line, he then pursues his relentless dichotomizing and we are left with good grasshoppers and bees, and bad Venice. Pound certainly did not like ambiguity, but I cannot think his vision of Venice was so simple – or so simplifying. However, Davenport is certainly justified in pointing out that the three men named in the penultimate three lines have one thing in common: their 'fortunes sank lowest in Venice'. Borso, a murdered would-be peace-maker; Carmagnola, a distinguished *condottiere* who had done the state some service and was treacherously executed for his pains; and Sigismundo . . . Sigismundo has now come up twice in connection with Venice and to understand his importance, and perhaps thence to come to a reading of the negative aspects of Venice as written in the *Cantos*, I want to look at the (earlier) Malatesta Cantos.

In canto CIV we find:

But in Venice more affirmations
                        of individual men
From Selvo to Franchetti, than any elsewhere.
(CIV, 743)

Nothing more is said about Selva (an eleventh-century Doge) or Franchetti (?), nor what these individual affirmations were. But the figure most celebrated for 'individual affirmation' in the *Cantos* is Sigismondo Malatesta, and he is closely associated with Venice in ways which I will try to outline. Sigismondo Malatesta (1417–68), Lord of Rimini, Fano and Cesena, was an Italian Renaissance *condottiere.* He fought more than once for Venice, but also for Florence, Milan and Siena. He made war against Pope Pius II and was excommunicated (and burnt in effigy). He won that battle but lost almost everything else, and finally died, broken and penniless. He was a violent, brave man in violent, chaotic times, and his opportunistic, dangerous, often ferocious life makes him something of a paradigm figure for that period of Italian history. But the most important thing about him, for Pound, was that he conceived and had built the Tempio Malatestiano, or the Malatesta Temple.

Next to the title-page of *Guide to Kulchur*, Pound reproduces a medal with a Malatesta head on it.

> I give the reproduction . . . to indicate the thoroughness of Rimini's civilization in 1460. If you consider the Malatesta and Sigismundo in particular, a failure, he was at least a failure worth all the successes of his age. He had in Rimini, Pisanello, Piero della Francesca. If the Tempio is a jumble and junk shop, it nevertheless registers a concept. There is no other man's effort equally registered.

In the same book, in the chapter entitled '24. Examples of Civilization', he wrote the following – when reading it, consider it as a (possibly unconscious) description of his own *Cantos* (this book was written after the publication of the first fifty-one) as well as of Malatesta's creation.

> The Tempio Malatestiano is both an apex and in verbal sense a monumental failure. It is perhaps the apex of what one man has embodied in the last 1000 years of the occident. A cultural 'high' is marked.
>
> . . . He registered a state of mind, of sensibility, of all-roundness and awareness.
>
> He had a little of the best there in Rimini. . . . The Tempio was stopped by a fluke? or Sigismundo had the flair when to stop it? . . . All that a single man could, Malatesta managed *against* the current of power.' (*GTK* 159)

Aspiration – 'an apex'? Foreboding – 'a monumental failure'? I will suggest later that the Tempio and the *Cantos* are homologous in an almost uncanny way. Fluke or flair, temple and poem were alike unfinished – perhaps unfinishable.

According to Ben D. Kimpel and T. C. Duncan Eaves, Pound took more pains with the research for the Malatesta Cantos (VIII–XI) than he did for any other part of the *Cantos*: 'The Malatesta cantos are the most complex, and probably the most convincing, accomplishment of Pound the historian; at least in this case, his history is as close to actual events as interpretive history is likely to be.'[56] (How historical Pound's 'history' is, I will comment on later.) His depiction of Sigismondo – in his very own way – is arguably the most fully articulated portrait of any historical figure in the *Cantos.* Drawing on original documents, letters, proclamations and various unidentified voices (sometimes, Sigismondo's own), Pound strives to take us back into the very moments when history was in the making – the letters in the reading, the battles in the fighting, the Temple in the building – with no discernible certainty of outcome. We have to work from (read from) the 'fragments' with which and in which and from which the actual protagonists worked and willed and wrought. Unlike *Sordello*, the *Cantos* do not have a single hero; but if there is, let us say, a *type* of hero that recurs, then Sigismondo must be counted the arche type.

The selected fragments which Pound 'tessellates' together in these cantos tend to focus on Sigismondo the Temple builder. 'He, Sigismundo, *templum aedificavit*' (VIII, 32). In canto VIII, in the midst of multiple alliances and battlings, he is revealed as more interested in 'arranging peace' (VIII, 28), and in keeping Piero della Francesca happy and, as it were, at it.

> But I want it to be quite clear, that until the chapels are ready
> I will arrange for him to paint something else
> So that both he and I shall
> Get as much enjoyment as possible from it . . .
>
> And for this I mean to make due provision,
> So that he can work as he likes,
> Or waste his time as he likes
>
> (VIII, 29)

This was a patron indeed!

In canto IX, 'he began building the TEMPIO' (IX, 35), and we are given a vivid, kinetic sense of the determined, rapacious, undivertible energy which went into the collection of materials for its erection.

> marble, porphyry, serpentine,
> Whose men, Sigismundo's, came with more than an hundred
> two wheeled ox carts and deported, for the beautifying
> of the *tempio* where was Santa Mario in Trivio
> Where the same are now on the walls. Four hundred
> ducats to be paid back to the *abbazia* by the said swindling
> Cardinal or his heirs.
> grnnh! rrnnh, pthg.
> wheels, plaustra, oxen under night-shield
>
> (IX, 36)

When the Sienese intercept Sigismondo's post-bag, suspecting him of double-dealing, they find notes and lists concerning marble, columns, derricks, beams, naves, walls, foremen, engineers. This man is *building*! And it takes a lot of effort:

> This to advise your
> 'M^{gt} Ld^{shp} how the second load of Veronese marble has
> 'finally got here, after being held up at Ferrara with no end
> 'of fuss and botheration, the whole of it having been there
> 'unloaded.
>
> (IX, 40)

Grnnh! rrnnh, pthg! But it gets done:

> 'and built a temple so full of pagan works'
> i.e. Sigismund
> and in the style 'Past ruin'd Latium'
> The filigree hiding the gothic,
> with a touch of rhetoric in the whole
>
> (IX, 41)

'Past ruin'd Latium' alludes to a poem by Landor:

> Past ruin'd Ilion Helen lives,
> Alcestis rises from the shades;
> Verse calls them forth; 'tis verse that gives
> Immortal youth to moral maids.

Since it was Davenport who pointed out the reference, I can hardly do better than quote his comment. 'The choice of Walter Savage Landor's lyric lends its own color to the passage, for . . . Sigismondo's passion was for a romantically conceived Roman past as much as it was for enduring fame.'[57] This, quite correct, observation contributes to Davenport's reading of a crucial line which stands on its own just before the end of canto XI and Sigismondo's total eclipse: 'In the gloom, the gold gathers the light against it' (XI, 51). For Davenport, the 'gloom' is 'the dark moral context' of treacherous Renaissance Italian politics; 'the "gold" is what stands out against it, the vision Sigismondo had of Roman chivalry and self-conduct, or the impulse in him that built the Tempio.'[58] This is valid enough in the context of the deepening dusk of Sigismondo's declining life. But it should not be carried over to the Venetian canto XVII when, after the lines describing Venice rising and flaring in the night, the line is quoted again, albeit with a small but significant difference. 'In the gloom the gold / Gathers the light about it' (XVII, 78). 'Against' is (or could be) adversarial, combative: 'about' is inclusive, cumulative. Both the Tempio and Venice are wondrous beautiful structures emerging from, built out of, the circumambient flux; 'crystallizations of chaos', in Davenport's words – light-gathering gold in the gloom around. Venice though – *Serenissima* – does not have to fight *against* the dark. But it is time to look more closely at Malatesta's Tempio.

The façade is the earliest Renaissance façade, and the architect, Leon Battista Alberti, thus faced an entirely new problem, for the temple was meant to glorify and perpetuate the power and the glory of the Malatesti as well as honouring God. Alberti turned away from Gothic and resolved to imitate the Romans in their solemn exaltation of man (there was, and still is, a magnificent Roman arch standing in Rimini – the Augustus Arch – which Alberti sought to imitate, thus likening Sigismondo to the great Roman emperor). He chose classical shapes and materials. Stones and marbles were bought, requisitioned, or stolen, from Istria and Verona, Savignano and Fano, Ravenna and Rimini itself. The façade is a complicated mixture of shapes and volumes. There are four Ionic columns, three Roman arches (of different sizes), and a deeply recessed porch and doorway, richly decorated with inset pieces of marble of different shapes and colours. These are all on different planes, so there is an effect of perspective relief. Above there are two more columns and an architrave with two sloping sides and a gap in the middle. The lines draw the eye to the dome, which was never built (but planned, according to a medal cast for Sigismondo) and which would have unified the whole. The sides, by contrast, are very plain. The south side contains sarcophagi of poets and scholars. One is particularly important – that of *Gemistus Pletho.* Gemisthus Plethon (1355?–1450?) was a neo-Platonic philosopher who found Italy ignorant and returned to his native Sparta to renew contact with ancient learning. Sigismondo brought his bones from Greece to bury them in his temple – which suggests he was, to say the least, sympathetic to his philosophy. Gemisthus wished to reconcile or synthesize Christianity and ancient Greek religion and did much to revive Greek mythology and learning. He was thus as important a figure for Pound as he was, seemingly, for Sigismondo, for he could also represent a link between the Greek mysteries (Eleusis) and medieval-Renaissance Europe.

> And with him Gemisthus Plethon
> Talking of the war about the temple at Delphos,
> And of POSEIDON, *concret Allgemeine*,
>   And telling of how Plato went to Dionysus of Syracuse
>
> (VIII, 31)

and

Gemisto stemmed all from Neptune
hence the Rimini bas reliefs
(LXXXIII, 528)

These bas reliefs were by Agostino di Duccio and refer us to the inside of the temple which seems to exist almost in a different world from the outside. Yet they *do* coexist, and produce something quite new in their coming together. The interior consists mainly of eight chapels, among them chapels for Sigismondo and the Malatesta family and for his lover Isotta degli Atti. (The letter 'S' entwining the letter 'I' is sculpted all over the temple. Perhaps it is a love knot, perhaps it represents the first two letters of 'Sigismondo' – some say this, some say that.) This latter is also called 'the Chapel of the Playing Angels' and contains a Crucifixion by Giotto. Two chapels, called respectively the 'Chapel of the Planets' and the 'Chapel of the Liberal Arts', contain bas-reliefs of the zodiacal cycle, and of the Trivium and the Quadrivium. There is a chapel of the 'Madonna of Water' which contains elephants bearing pillars, and a chapel of 'the Childish Games' with little angels playing in water. There is also a Cell of the Relics, which contained a magnificent Piero della Francesca of 'Sigismondo Pandolfo Malatesta Kneeling before St Sigismund, king of Burgundy' (and a fine pair of dogs who turn up in canto XI) – he may be kneeling but never did a figure exude more power and confidence and pride of life. It is one of the first depictions of what we now think of as 'Renaissance man'.

In all the chapels there are bas-reliefs by Duccio of magical beauty, the stone at times seeming to become air or turn into water – while on some of the banisters are little 'angels' bearing coats of arms, looking a good deal more like cheeky cupids. Elsewhere putti sport on dolphins. To what extent the whole interior was a great temple to humanism, to what extent the sculptural cycles contain obscure or occult philosophical secrets known only to the initiates at court, has been endlessly debated and can hardly be resolved. It is certainly packed with references to classical literature and learning, and the atmosphere is more pagan and playful than Christian and reverential. It certainly exalts Sigismondo more visibly than God – with decorations, writings, initials, heraldic symbols. It also contains many references to, and evidence of, his passion for Isotta, and some regarded the whole thing as a 'temple of love'. One can at least understand Pope Pius II declaring that the building was full of 'pagan works of art' which made it look like a temple for 'infidels' and 'worshippers of the devil'. No wonder he had Sigismondo burnt in effigy. He knew a rival when he saw one!

And what has this to do with Pound and Venice?

The whole eclectic, synthesizing drive of the temple, bringing together items and figures from different myths, religions, learnings, in an edifice which may celebrate and venerate various non-Christian and pre-Christian mysteries and values – including an AMOR both physical and Platonic – and which was perforce left unfinished: all this seems to me to make the temple and the *Cantos* astonishingly isomorphic. More than that, the temple itself, although in Rimini, has been seen as being, in some crucial ways, quintessentially Venetian. I must here bring in the work of Adrian Stokes, in particular his *Stones of Rimini* (1934).[59] Donald Davie was the first, to my knowledge, to write about the very real relevance of Stoke's work to Pound's,[60] and I simply want to quarry more from *The Stones of Rimini* than he did. Stokes met Pound a number of times in the later 1920s (after the Malatesta Cantos had been published). Avowedly, he felt influenced by Pound's poem-in-the-making: whether any influence went the other way must remain speculative, but *The Stones of Rimini* is very Poundian in spirit.

It opens with a paean to Venice in a chapter called, simply, 'Stone and Water'. 'In Venice the world is stone. There, in stone, to which each changing light is gloss, the human process shines clear and quasi permanent' (*SR* 16). It is effectively a sea-city, water turned stone: 'it is the sea that thus stands petrified, sharp and continuous till up near sky. For this Istrian stone seems compact of salt's bright yet shaggy crystals. Air eats into it, the brightness remains. Amid the sea Venice is built from the essence of the sea. . . . For the Venetian stones and waters are the Mediterranean essence' (*SR* 19–20). Further: 'if in fantasy the stones of Venice appear as the waves' petrifaction, then Venetian glass, compost of Venetian sand and water, expresses the taut curvature of the cold under-sea, the slow, oppressed yet brittle curves of dimly translucent water' (*SR* 20). Marble comes from limestone, and the forming of limestone is intimately associated with the sea ('Gemisto stemmed all from Neptune') – Stokes carefully and lyrically traces these origins and gradual metamorphoses. Venice is thus the ***ultimate*** expression of the stones and waters which compose it.

> Limestone, for the most part formed of organic deposits, is the link between the organic and inorganic worlds. Limestone exhibits in mummified state the life no longer found of the Silurian and other distant ages, just as the Istrian palaces of Venice present to us, in terms of space, the hoard of ancient Venetian enterprises. The very substance of limestone suggests concreted time. (*SR* 40)

This sense of the link between the organic and the inorganic, as though, over time, the one may shade into the other, is very important to Stokes, as I think it was to Pound. It enables Stokes more than once to refer to the 'fecund stone-blossom' (*SR* 41, 99) of quattrocento marble carving, and in connection with Duccio's sculptures. This, I think, is exactly the positive spirit of Pound's 'forest of marble'. Venice is blossomingly *continuous* with the elements that made it, as the marble palaces and columns are to be felt as miraculous extensions of the timber trunks which even now support them. And so: 'A Greek temple is an ideal quarry reconstructed on the hill. The Tempio Malatesta is an ideal quarry whose original organic substances were renewed by the hand of the carver to express the abundant sea collected into solid stone.' It 'stands as the emblem of all European art' (*SR* 43). Agostino's (as he refers to Duccio) 'reliefs glow, luminous in the rather dim light of the Tempio. Their vitality abounds. The life, the glow of marble has not elsewhere been dramatized thus. . . . These reliefs are the apotheosis, not only of Sigismondo who built the temple, and of Isotta his mistress, but of marble and limestone and all the civilizations dependent upon their cult' (*SR* 98). And the Tempio is, in a way, an apotheosis, or 'stone-blossom', of Venice.

> Before coming to Rimini, Agostino probably spent some time in Venice . . . the *fact* of Venice must, at any rate, have reinforced Agostino's imagination. And just as a writer can better visualize a place when he has left it, so Agostino turned the spell of Venice to better use at Rimini than he could have accomplished in Venice herself. . . . Venice is the witness of Mediterranean art. Here by themselves are the Mediterranean waters, and the Mediterranean stones each one of them shaped by man. (*SR* 99–100)

An amplifying evocation of the reliefs can speak for itself in this context:

> At the Tempio, the young Agostino evolved his style; under the influence of his patron, Sigismondo, who aroused choriambic visions, he created his masterpiece. The sea is vibrant with fish, boughs bend under the weight of birds, the active airs breed a flock of doves that descend to greet the new-born Venus from the sea to earth. The land undulates with vegetables and animal life just as the sea with fish. But his preoccupation with sea-movement – his garments, though ostensibly disturbed by wind, cling to and disclose naked forms like seaweed waving on submerged rocks, or they are like water falling clear as the bather rises to leave the pool – was undoubtedly stimulated by Venice. (*SR* 106)

Hugh Kenner has suggested that the lines in canto LXXX pertaining to a female figure 'in the moon barge' –

> with the veil of faint cloud before her
> Κύθηρα δεινὰ as a leaf borne in the current
> pale eyes as if without fire
>
> (LXXX, 511)

may well contain a memory of the carving of Diana (close enough to Deina) by Duccio in the temple (which is, in fact, mentioned by name earlier in the canto, LXXX, 497). This seems to me very plausible, and a characteristically imaginative and sensitive observation. But – there apart – Pound nowhere attempted any direct *description* of Duccio's reliefs, any more than he tried to re-create the temple as a whole. But, echoes, traces, memories, perhaps even emulations of Duccio's art – certainly as described by Stokes, an art of 'fecund moisture in stone, of glimmering forms seen under water' (*SR* 243) – seem periodically to pervade the *Cantos.* And here is Stokes again:

> Under the guise of planets we see here the first appearance, after the dark centuries, of real pagan gods and goddesses, Diana, Mercury, Venus, Mars, Jupiter, Saturn. Agostino's Quattro Cento technique causes their reappearing as planets to possess the quality of a materialization, an exorcism. A spell works that keeps the forms swimming about in the marble like goldfish in a tank. (*SR* 201)

And 'Such figures appear to float rather than stand.' See, they return, Gods float in the air . . . if Stokes is right, surely Pound's resolve and attempts to reinstate the discontinuous gods – and goddesses – is not so dissimilar. 'Marble statues of the gods are the gods themselves' (*SR* 18). That, presumably, is what Pound would have said if he could have afforded to replace the statue of Venus at Terracina.

As Stokes says, Venice 'is my constant theme . . . city of stone and water, the most stupendous, the most far-reaching of humanistic creation. After all, Venice is the one permanent miracle, and the presence of this miracle in the heart of Europe for fifteen hundred years is an historical factor whose influence is too vague and large for its conceiving by historians'. There follows a veritable humanistic hymn to Venice – calm yet lyrical – which works itself up, however, into what I can only call a strange teratological ecstasy as the 'permanent miracle' turns monstrous. It is an astonishing passage, worth quoting at length.

> Without conscious effort and without sacrifice of their humanity, the Venetians have come nearer to an element than have done all the races to another element, earth, with various mysteries and nature worship, especially spring and autumnal rite. Without loss of humanity, without dark ecstasy, without priests, they have done it. Such closeness of rational, supremely practical man to Nature is humanistic; and so pervasive is the closeness, that either man or sea animals may well find a home here. Even to-day in this the city of historical commerce created out of business enterprise, though the trappings of several civilizations are vaunted here, it would be little surprise if shading

> one's eyes when upon the piazzetta, scanning the lagoon that is only inches below the marble floor, one were to see framed between the two columns, twin heads and fast approaching coils, laocoon's serpents coming over from the horizon in the time that it takes to give a speech, and now breasting up the water-stair between the tattered gondolas. In spite of the ubiquity of their art here as nowhere else, human beings, with their staccato movement and perpendicular line, sometimes seem match-stick-like, superfluous. Then one would like the marine animals to take possession. Imagine rows and rows of serpents in horizontal glide, not stopping or turning at St Mark's, but rearing up their wet scales to coil them about the porphyry and serpentine pillars, to lay their eggs in the recesses of the massive foliage of the capitals, to leave their slime upon the porphyry head of Justinian and slither down the sheeted walls. . . . Along a narrow back canal an improbable monster is paddling, his head reared up on a level with the *piano nobile* so that he spews through windows either flank on to brocaded chairs. . . . Rank wash rushes up the water-stairs and refloats a flotilla of oozing toads. . . . A grampus with dripping paws has replaced St Theodore upon his column and cetacean roars reverberate in the porphyry dingles. Salmon jump a fondamenta, sea-snakes crawl up the sheer sides of every campanile, parti-coloured cuttle-fish staining the pavement black squirm to reach the shoals stranded upon Rialto. The tentacles of giant octopi, like so many hands raised in mysterious benediction, rise out of the lagoon over the façade of Palladian San Giorgio . . . (*SR* 100–2)

Stemmed all from Neptune indeed! Once again, Venice has turned her Medusa face upon one of her ravished admirers. My question now is, did she in any way ever do so to Pound?

Just as cantos I to XVI started with Homeric gods and concluded with the Russian Revolution, so, Hugh Kenner observed, do cantos XVII to XXVII. But, whereas the Venetian canto, XVII, was effectively preceded by three 'hell' cantos, canto XXVII, which annotates 'The last crumbs of civilization' (XXVII, 129) and records the destructive activities of 'tovarisch', the generic 'comrade' who 'lifted never stone above stone' (XXVII, 132) is preceded by two cantos which certainly seem concerned with aspects of the decline and fall of Venice. The sequence as a whole – that is up to canto XXX – is much concerned with deterioration and decline, decadence and degeneration, exhaustion and loss of direction, loss of civility – of civilization itself. It ends with the death of the bad Pope Allessandro Borgia in 1503, which also effectively terminates the major role played by the Italian Renaissance in the first thirty cantos. (It should be added that, as well as the death of the Pope, the end of canto XXX also celebrates the production, in the same year, of a book by Soncinus, the finest printer of the age, for his patron Caesare Borgia. The book was printed from a manuscript from the library of 'the Lords Malatesta', so the strong, creative period of the Renaissance is being perpetuated and transmitted, albeit in another medium. It is the first time in the *Cantos* that the beneficent power of the book, its indispensability for cultural transmission, is directly alluded to. Not everything need be lost. Not, certainly, if Pound can help it.)

Venice appears intermittently throughout the whole sequence, as well as crucially in cantos XXV and XXVI. In canto XX there is a reminder of the great work of 'Duccio, Agostino', whose lines had the supreme Poundian virtue of 'precision' –

> but a precise definition
> transmitted thus Sigismundo
> thus Duccio
> (LXXIV, 425)

– but, in keeping with other intimations of collapse and regression, there comes a passage when the jungle seems to be taking over, 'rising over the soul' (XX, 91). Though, even here, not all is loss:

> Wilderness of renewals, confusion
> Basis of renewals, subsistence,
> Glazed green of the jungle
> (XX, 92)

The canto moves on, famously, to a vision of the Lotus Eaters – those indolent and lethargic figures who gave up the Odyssean voyage and capitulated to Circe – and we hear their dreamy and drugged protestations of bliss. Whatever else, this leads to no civic building, no laying 'stone upon stone'. The canto concludes with some sort of procession of almost voluptuous splendour. The Renaissance is there (Isotta and Sigismondo's son), and so is the jungle (leopards and panthers); and so, one feels, is Venice, city of beautiful, seductive women, amorous dalliance – and two famous columns:

> le donne e i cavalieri
> smooth face under hennin
> The sleeves embroidered with flowers,
> Great thistle of gold, or an amaranth,
> Acorns of gold, or of scarlet,
> Cramoisi and diaspre
> slashed white into velvet;
> Crystal columns, acanthus, sirens in the pillar heads;

And at last, between gilded barocco,
Two columns coiled and fluted,
Vanoka, leaning half naked,
                waste hall there behind her.
'Peace!
                Borso . . . , Borso!'

(XX, 95)

'Vanoka' is Pound's own name, and whether it is meant to suggest a Venus gone awry I cannot say. But certainly the high-born ladies and exotic beasts, the sumptuous and beautiful costumes, materials, embroideries and colours of the Renaissance procession, end in – yield? hide? – a provocative semi-nakedness, a seemingly shameless lasciviousness which may indeed be a threshold to desolation, a prelude to, and premonition of, 'waste'. To the extent that this is a metonym for – or anamorphic glimpse of – an aspect or period of 'Venice', the city has indeed turned another face. 'Keep the peace, Borso' was what Niccolo d'Este, ruler of Ferrara (of whom more later), said to his son. Given Ferrara's precarious position, it was good advice. Borso indeed tried to heed it, attempting to reconcile Sigismondo Malatesta with Federigo d'Urbino. Blessed are the peace-makers – only he failed, and came to a violent end. In Venice. He was also a patron of the arts, and was responsible for the frescoes by Cosmè Tura and Francesco del Cossa in the Schifanoia Palace which, Pound maintained, served as a model for the *Cantos* – so the causes of *both* peace and art (Pound's most passsionate causes) suffered. 'Peace!' seems a forlorn hope – 'Borso . . . Borso' comes across as a lament. O Borso.

The next canto opens with a varied celebration of some powerful and creative individuals who with their energy and enterprise served to advance civilization in one field or another – finance and learning (the Medicis), courtly ceremony (Duke Sforza of Milan), arts and civil amenities (Jefferson), railroads (Pound's grandfather). Then a half-familiar line recurs: 'Gold fades in the gloom' (XXI, 98). The gold is 'fading' rather than 'gathering'. Perhaps this *is* a little ominous. Almost immediately Venice is summoned up again:

And the palazzo, baseless, hangs there in the dawn
With low mist over the tide-mark;
And floats there nel tramonto
With gold mist over the tide-mark.
The tesserae of the floor, and the patterns.

(XXI, 98)

The city is coming to seem 'baseless' and insubstantial as it 'hangs' in the mists of dawn, and 'floats' in the mists at sunset ('nel tramonto'). But we should remember that gods, too, 'float' in the air – and the mist is gold. Venice may be receding, fading ('Fades light from the sea-crest'; V, 17), but it is also perhaps becoming a vision – visionary. Seen *this* way – *as* a vision (think of 'the baseless fabric of this vision' and the 'gorgeous palaces' which are dissolving and fading in an 'unsubstantial pageant': we are surely not far from the twilight magic of *The Tempest*; see IV. i. 150–5) – it may be floating out of the shambles of history ('Fools making new shambles' is the line immediately following this passage) to join the gods in their air. For from the assorted shambles which do follow, there comes the cry 'Gignetei kalon' – a beautiful thing is born. And, shortly afterwards, there they are:

> In the crisp air,
>   the discontinuous gods;
> Pallas, young owl in the cup of her hand,
> And, by night, the stag runs, and the leopard,
> Owl-eye amid pine boughs.
>
> (XXI, 99)

And perhaps, too, 'discontinuous Venice' – discontinuous in that the historical Venice is entering decline (in the time-span of the *Cantos*) while another Venice is rising into the realm of myth to become an image of an earthly paradise, the City Beautiful. *There* indeed it may float – godlike.

Cantos XXV and XXVI, full of dated documents, are intimately concerned with historical Venice. They are preceded by a canto concerning nearby Ferrara and its ruler, Niccolo d'Este (1384–1441), who 'brought seduction in place of / Rape into government, ter pacis Italiae auctor' (XXIV, 112) – three times a peace-maker for Italy – married a Malatesta and, like Sigismondo, was a great patron of the arts. Canto XXIV is full of appropriate early Renaissance magnificence and luxury. But it goes wrong. In 1425 he has his wife and her stepson beheaded for adultery, and after this there is no more magnificence in the Ferrara of the poem. In Napoleon's time, the statues of Niccolo and Borso are melted down 'for cannon, bells, door-knobs' (XXIV, 114) – representative of more widespread dispersal and degradation – and the city is finally given over to idle, self-pleasuring 'cake-eaters' ('the consumers of icing'), and working servants. 'Ferrara, paradiso dei sarti, "feste stomagose"' (XXIV, 114). Paradise of tailors, disgusting festival – the great court culture of Ferrara has dwindled to iced cakes and clothes. The last two lines are a reminder of Ferrara's former glory and subsequent degradation: '"Albert made me, Tura painted my wall, / And Julia the Countess sold to a tannery . . ."' (XXIV, 114) – actually to a tobacco factory,[61] but in terms of vandalism and loss of dignity it is all one. For the 'me' that Albert made (Alberto d'Este, father of Niccolo) is the Schifanoia Palace – the stones are talking again – and the paintings on 'my wall' are the frescoes by Cosmè Tura and Francesco del Cossa which meant so much to Pound.[62]

Davenport sees canto XXIV as one-half of a diptych, forming an opposition and contrast with the canto to follow – Ferraran splendour as opposed to Venetian tyranny.[63] I doubt the opposition can be quite so stark, given that the canto ends with melted statues, gorging cake-eaters and the sold-off palace. 'Feste stomagose.' But there is one little detail which Davenport might have noticed which does seem to tell against Venice.

> And in '41 Polenta went up to Venice
> Against Niccolo's caution
> And was swallowed up in that city.
> (XXIV, 113)

Ostasia da Polenta was an ally of the Venetians in 1441, but they deprived him of Ravenna and he was exiled to Candia.[64] Historical Venice was becoming a less salubrious place – as the next two cantos intimate.

The dates of the documents cited in canto XXV range from 1255 to 1537 (dates are important, as I shall try to explain). The first deals with the banning of gambling – seemingly, peculiarly endemic to Venice – and the second with a supposed miracle involving a lioness, caged near the Doges' Palace, which gives birth to three cubs already 'vivos et pilosos' (living and hairy; XXV, 116). This portends the miraculous – or not so miraculous – lion of Venice, still to be seen in effigy in the cities of Veneto, and to be referred to again by Pound in a curious way. There then commences a series of references to the conversion of the Ducal Palace from what Ruskin called 'The Byzantine Palace' to 'The Gothic Palace' (in *The Stones of Venice*, volume II, chapter 8: canto XXV draws heavily on this chapter, albeit in characteristically abbreviated and succinctly stacatto form). In Ruskin's version, the Gothic Palace was created between 1301 and 1423, with a number of delays, procrastinations and interruptions. Pound's compressed references – sometimes almost quoting Ruskin – run from 1323 to 1415.

> Two columns (a.d. 1323) for the church of St Nicholas of the palace 12 lire gross.
> To the procurators of St Marc for entrance to the palace, for gilding the images and lion over the door
> (XXV, 116)

(Ruskin: '"1344, Nov 4. We have paid thirty-five golden ducats for making the gold leaf, to gild the lion which is over the door of the palace stairs."'[65])

1335.3 lire 15 groats to stone for making a lion.
1340. Council of the lords noble, Marc Erizio
Nic. Speranzo, Tomasso Gradonice:
                                        that the hall
be new built over the room of the night watch
and over the columns toward the canal where the walk is . . .
. . . because of the stink of the dungeons. 1344.
1409 . . . since the most serene Doge can scarce
stand upright in his bedroom . . .
                        vadit pars, two gross lire
stone stair, 1415, for pulchritude of the palace

(XXV, 117)

The Ducal Palace *is* – metonymically – Venice for Ruskin ('The history of the Ducal Palace, therefore, begins with the birth of Venice, and to what remains of it, at this day, is entrusted the last representation of her power'); the Ducal Palace is, then, 'the Parthenon of Venice'[66] – and so it is, in this canto, for Pound. But the shorthand references to its building are interrupted by an account of the treatment of Donna Sorantia Soranzo, who was exiled from Venice in 1320 and only permitted to return to attend her father, the Doge, when he was dying in 1328. Even then, strict conditions were imposed:

        not in that time leaving the palace, nor
descending the palace stair and when she descends it
that she return by night the boat in the like manner
being covered.

(XXV, 116)

Within the palace pulchritudinous, there was extreme and autocratic treatment of persons.

But – stone over stone, hall over columns – the palace was finally built:

Which is to say: they built out over the arches
and the palace hangs there in the dawn, the mist,
in that dimness,
or as one rows in from past the murazzi
the barge slow after moon-rise
and the voice sounding under the sail.

(XXV, 117)

We have seen this Venice, hanging in the dawn mist, before. But what follows is critical:

Mist gone.
    And Sulpicia
green shoot now, and the wood
white under new cortex
'as the sculptor sees the form in the air
    before he sets hand to mallet. . . .'
(XXV, 117)

Because of Pound's method of juxtaposing cleanly etched and sharply distinct items, without indicating the relationship between them, crucially, one cannot determine whether what is being suggested is a relationship of similarity or complementarity – this like this, this rhymes with this; or one of opposition and contrast – this unlike this, this the very opposite; or even a relationship of non-relationship – this unrelated to or incompatible with this, but there they both are. ('Any sort of understanding of civilization needs comprehension of incompatibles'; *GTK* 184). Or something else again – this associated with this in some imponderable, or to be pondered, way. This is important here because, when the mist suddenly clears and we are given Sulpicia and, or perhaps *as*, a 'green shoot', we also receive the suggestion of renewal and classic pastoral (Sulpicia was a Roman poetess (40 BC?) whose work is included in the work of Tibullus, who inscribed Cerinthe's love for her) that attends these references, and clear forms to be sculpted. Does all this 'replace', and contrast with, the misty Venice that preceded it? Critics like Hugh Kenner and Guy Davenport think it does, thus reinforcing their negative reading of Pound's 'forest of marble'. But the 'wood / white under new cortex' is very like the ivory under the bark of the growing city, and one could read the passages as being associated rather than opposed. I do not think it is possible to determine which, and perhaps it is not necessary – perhaps not even desirable. Let the images 'float in the air' together.

What is certain, however, is that following a paradisal passage we hear 'heavy voices' from the 'stone pits':

'Sero, sero . . .
'Nothing we made, we set nothing in order,
'Neither house nor the carving . . .'
(XXV, 118)

Sero, sero . . . too late, too late. The lines undoubtedly refer to the many procrastinations which interrupted the building of the Ducal Palace (123 years is a long time to take building even this palace), and the voices are the voices of the Venetian senate, responsible for the delays – all this well documented in Ruskin's chapter. A subsequent passage is unambiguously addressed to negation and sterility:

Noble forms, lacking life, that bolge, that valley
the dead words keeping form,
and the cry: Civis Romanus.
The clear air, dark, dark,
The dead concepts, never the solid, the blood rite
(XXV, 118)

That 'bolge' is a ditch in the *Inferno* and the darkness and death appertain to a 'Civis' – a civilization – that has somehow, at some time, gone wrong. 'Against this' – this clearly *is* by contrast – 'the flute', meaning Tibullus (and love), and:

Form, forms and renewal, gods held in the air,
Forms seen, and then clearness,
Bright void, without image, Napishtim,
Casting his gods back into the νους.
(XXV, 119)

Napishtim was the Sumerian equivalent of Noah, made immortal after he survived the flood. Renewal, clarity, immortality, and the gods back in nature, back in the air. This vision, whatever else, is devoutly to be desired.

The canto concludes with a series of documents. The first, a letter from Titian in 1513, undertaking some painting in the palace; the last two, senate documents concerning 'brokerage', recording the senatorial dissatisfaction at Titian's procrastination, annoyance that he has taken money and 'profited by it' (usury?), and attempts to get the money back (1522 and 1537). This patronage is clearly not going well, and the dereliction of the artist suggests that art and state are no longer working harmoniously together.

The Fall of (historical) Venice has begun. Ruskin, you will remember, dated the beginning of that Fall very exactly as April 1423 (in the Ducal Palace chapter), with the commencement of the 'Renaissance Palace'. Pound, with no less confident peremptory exactitude, dated the general decline in Renaissance art as starting some time later – he seems to have had more time for the whole of the quattrocento than Ruskin. 'Certainly the metamorphosis into carnal tissue becomes frequent and general about 1527. The people are corpus, corpuscular, but not in the strict sense "animate", it is no longer the body of air clothed in the body of fire; it no longer radiates, light no longer moves from the eye, there is a great deal of meat, shock absorbing, perhaps – at any rate absorbent.' (This is from the famous essay on Cavalcanti in which Pound laments: 'We appear to have lost the world where one thought cuts through another with clean edge' (*LE* 153–4). See also: '1527. Thereafter art thickened. Thereafter design went to hell' (canto XLVI, 234) and 'The appalling and nauseous decadence of architecture, stone cutting, art forms after 1500 etc., the loss of moral and terminological clarity' (*SP* 244). This is very much his master's voice!) This distaste for painterly 'meat' and 'thickness' (is it fleshiness, I wonder, that is incurring Pound's distaste, as female fleshiness certainly does in canto XXIX?) is taken up in canto LXXX:

> all that Sandro knew, and Jacopo
>   and that Velásquez never suspected
> lost in the brown meat of Rembrandt
>   and the raw meat of Rubens and Jordaens
>   (LXXX, 511)

We know that Pound admired the clean lines of Botticelli (1447–1510) and in the debate concerning line against colour he clearly preferred the stringency of line to what he sees as the 'meatiness' of painting which works primarily from colour – and Venice, of course, produced some of the supreme colourists, in whose work Ruskin gloried. (We need not defend Rembrandt and Velázquez against Pound – he could be quite as irrascibly eccentric and dismissively dogmatic as Ruskin himself.) The point about Titian, I think, is that his long life (1477–1576) spans both part of the great (for Pound) period of Venetian painting and the period of its decline into meatiness. That is what he is doing at end of canto XXV, looking both ways – at Venice the 'permanent miracle', and the Venice heading for historical decadence and decline.[67]

There is a sting in the tail, or rather in the margin, of canto XXV. Next to the lines detailing the rebuilding of the palace, Pound wrote in: 'Who fleed the lion's rump?' (There is a bit of a mystery about this marginal addition. It appears in the 1964 'New Collected Edition: I–CIX',[68] but does not appear in the 1987 Collected Edition of *The Cantos.* Was it overlooked, or deliberately cut? I have been unable to find out. As will be seen, it could be improtant.) The line is a nod – or wink – to T. S. Eliot, since it is a quotation (with, not uncharacteristically, a small spelling error) from the last stanza of 'Burbank with a Baedeker: Bleistein with a Cigar':

> Who clipped the lion's wings,
>   And flea'd his rump and pared his claws?
> Thought Burbank, meditating on
>   Time's ruins, and the seven laws.[69]

The clipped, flea'd and pared winged lion is of course the lion of Venice, once the symbol of its power, pride and strength, but now seen as tamed, domesticated and impotent – definitively wingless. This is Eliot's one Venetian poem and, given Pound's hint, should perhaps be read in conjunction with canto XXV.

The long, composite epigraph prefixed to the poem is, in the words of Giorgio Melchiori, 'a summary of what, borrowing a Jamesian expression, could be called "feelings about aspects" of Venice: it is a mosaic of quotations ranging from Gautier to the Latin motto on Mantegna's St Sebastian in the Ca' d'Oro, from Shakespeare's *Othello* (of course) to Browning's *Toccata of Galuppi's*; at the centre is a descriptive sentence from *The Aspern Papers*.'[70] Melchiori sees the poem as depicting the reactions to Venice of the two main types of American visitors – or tourists – at the time of Eliot's own first ventures to Europe. Burbank, rather like Eliot himself, meditative, impoverished, seeking out the artistic glories of the past with the aid of his guidebook; and Bleistein, notoriously, 'Chicago Semite Viennese'. Burbank 'falls' – perhaps for the whole city, certainly *with* Princess Volupine. Two clear echoes from *Antony and Cleopatra* are probably there for the usual mock-heroic purpose – to indicate what a falling-off, as well as a falling, there is in this etiolated little Venetian affair. No Antony he: no Cleopatra she. But deflationary and perhaps slightly self-mocking references to *Antony and Cleopatra* are one thing. Allusions to *The Merchant of Venice* are, in the context of a 'Bleistein' already described in terms which make him seem repellent, quite another. For Bleistein occasions two now infamous stanzas:

A lustreless protrusive eye
  Stares from the protozoic slime
At a perspective of Canaletto.
  The smoky candle end of time

Declines. On the Rialto once.
  The rats are underneath the piles.
The Jew is underneath the lot.

There is no way you can keep Shylock out of the poem at this point, perhaps even his voice.

What if my house be troubled with a rat,
And I be pleas'd to give ten thousand ducats
To have it ban'd?

(*Merchant of Venice*, IV. i. 45–7)

In the event *he* turns out to be the rat troubling the house, who has to be 'baned' in one way and another. The play raises uncomfortable problems – Eliot's lines even more so. Guy Davenport maintains that the lines about the rat and the Jew are not, as it were, directly Eliot's but are an example of how the generic 'blank modern mind' with its 'lustreless eye' looks at history and 'explains' the decline of Venice.[71] I really do think this is a case of special pleading which will not hold (the first three verses are clearly Burbank: it is hard not to read the next three, just as clearly, as Bleistein). Most readers react like Melchiori, who thinks Eliot in these lines is indulging 'a rabid and irrational form of antisemitism' in an excessively defensive attempt to distance and differentiate himself from the Bleistein type of tourist.[72] I fear this is a piece of pre-Holocaust anti-Semitism which cannot be blinked away.

And this, I think, is behind Pound's little shorthand acknowledgement of the Eliot poem. He could be suggesting: you have seen what I can see in Venice; to get some idea of the abysmal and benighted myopia of modern visitors to Venice, see Eliot's poem. Or: things indeed started to go wrong in Titian's time, but, my God, you should see the pathetic and repugnant American types who visit that poor enfeebled city now – consult Eliot's poem. Or he could be intimating: you are right, Tom – it is the Shylocks of this world who have contributed to the undermining of our civilization, as exemplified in the decline of Venice ('the rats are underneath the piles'). *The Merchant of Venice* was an important play for Pound.

> Lombard law behind Venetian penalties against mayhem. The ethical barrage versus usura. The undercurrents in the *Merchant of Venice*, glossed over in Victorian treatment, in the low and vile era 'of usury' the century of Victoria and Franz-Josef reaching its maximum squalor in such administrations as that of U. S. Grant, Herbert Hoover and Baldwin. For we are not yet out of this filthiness by a long chalk.
>
> 'Is your gold rams and ewes?'
>
> (*GTK* 149)

That last quotation, often invoked by Pound, is, characteristically, a slight misquotation from the play in question. Antonio is questioning Shylock about his obsession with money: 'Or is your gold and silver ewes and rams?' To which Shylock replies: 'I cannot tell, I make it breed as fast' (I. iii. 94–5). For Pound it is a quick and vivid way of referring to the perversion of values by which non-nature, or indeed anti-nature, is preferred to nature and threatens to displace it – gold for ewes. The unnaturalness is greatly compounded by allowing money, impossibly, to 'breed'. This of course is 'usury'. Neither the metaphor nor the revulsion is new. Compare, for example, Pope's lines:

> While with the silent growth of ten per cent
> In dirt and darkness hundreds stink content.[73]

I am not going to consider Pound's economics, nor address the matter of his indisputable anti-semitism, in this context. Despite the fact that usury was practised in his preferred period of European history – Giotto was a famous, and apparently quite ruthless, usurer, and also one of Pound's favoured artists, a possible difficulty for his theories he never examined or confronted; and despite the hopelessness of trying to find and assert *one* reason for the decline in art, cities, quality of life, Pound seems to have thought that in the 'undercurrents' of *The Merchant of Venice* could be found and traced an awareness and indication of what threatens, increasingly, to undermine civilization from, well, nearly a century before the writing of the play (1597?) up to the present day. Thus, in some indirect way, the figure who clipped the wings and flea'd the rump of the Venetian lion would be – Shylock–Bleistein. It is hardly a thesis which would bear much scrutiny, and it is perhaps just as well that Pound abandoned Venetian history at the point he did.

The next canto continues Pound's selective excursus into early Venetian history. It opens with a picture of Pound himself, lying in St Mark's day after day, changing his position as he looks at Venice from different angles, effectively engaged in a patient 360-degree survey of the city. It is perhaps a spatial image for what he is engaged in temporally, peering into this and that corner of Venetian history. The canto concludes (almost) with a letter from Carpaccio written at about the same date as Titian's letter in the previous canto – 1511. This time, however, it reveals, not a defrauding, but a dedraud*ed* Venetian artist. The beginning of bad times all round for the relationship between art and patronage, art and state. The final letter of all jumps, seemingly incongruously, to Mozart and a letter from him abusively denouncing, in good plain terms, his patron the Archbishop of Salzburg, because 'your exalted pustulence is too stingy' (XXVI, 128). Since he is receiving no support, Mozart simply asks for permission to leave. It is a far cry from the immensely imaginative and creative patronage of Sigismondo Malatesta, with whom the first four documentary fragments in the canto are, in one way or another, indirectly involved.

The first concerns the release of the Veronese sculptor and medalist, Matteo de Pasti, who had been sent by Sigismondo to make a portrait of the Turkish emperor, Mohammed II. The Venetians suspected him of being in league with the Turks because he was also carrying a famous work on explosives and fortifications – 'Valturio's "Re Militari"' – sent by Sigismondo to the emperor. He is set free with the warning 'caveat ire ad Turchum' (XXVI, 121): beware of going to the Turks – a cry with special resonance for Venice, coming under the growing threat of Islam and the East. (Davenport says the date of this document should be 1481, not 1461 – which is the date of the following documents.[74]) The next document charges Nicolo Sagundino, the Venetian ambassador in Rome, to arrange a peace between Sigismondo and Pope Pius II – 'Give peace to the Malatesta'. References to two pages protesting that 'Faithful sons (we are) of the church' are followed by brusque, ungilded 'fix-it' language: 'in any case get the job done' (XXVI, 121). Given that Venice was secretly aiding Sigismondo, there is more than a touch of hypocrisy in the peace-seeking initiative. It is there again in the next fragment – 'Our galleys were strictly neutral' (XXVI, 121) – for, in the struggle over Fano, the Venetians were again secretly helping Sigismondo while declaring neutrality. And again, in the following fragment, when Annibale de Malatesta ('Hanibal'), an agent from Sigismondo, asks Venice whether it will provide open armed help under the leadership of the Venetian *condottiere* Carlo Fortebraccio, the reply is: 'They cd. not . . . but on the quiet, secretissime' (XXVI, 122), they will lend money for the hiring of soldiers. All this may be seen as evidence of Venetian duplicity and deviousness, of unprincipled double-dealing and general Machiavelliansim. In terms of the *Cantos*, one might think that Sigismondo was a figure worthy of help; but the 'help' was not sufficient and the 'peace' was disastrous for him – we have already seen his decline and know in what penurious conditions he died. *Serenissima* is indeed 'secretissime' in its workings and manipulations. Venice helps Venice. One can hardly think it was alone in such behaviour at that time (or, indeed, any other time), but Pound is undoubtedly 'moralizing' history.

The next section of the canto refers to three earlier occasions in Venetian history. From the period of Doge Selva (1071–81) we are reminded of the notorious introduction of forks to eat with – 'Bringing in thus, the vice of luxuria' (XXVI, 122). That is what some moralists of the time certainly said, regarding use of the gold-pronged instrument as the utmost in sybaritic behaviour,[75] and some modern critics have followed them, reading this section as a damning indictment of Venetian luxury. But as Pound notes, Selva was responsible for the mosaics in St Mark's. If *that* is luxury then we would surely do better to take the forks with the mosaics and leave the moralists to fulminate among themselves. (Forks, in any case, are simply a continuation of culture, freeing the hand from the need to touch the food. Writing in the twentieth century, Pound himself cannot possibly have regarded them as a sign of decadence. The unoriginated comment on 'luxuria' must therefore be a contemporary one.) The remainder of this section alludes to the festivities at the installation of Doge Lorenzo Tiepolo (1268–75), and the celebrations at the marriage of Niccolo d'Este's son Leonello to Margherita Gonzaga in 1435. The lines ring with venetian magnificence and 'fine work': barbers, beads, furriers, 'Master pelters for fine work', silver cups, wine flasks, wool cloth, glass-makers, jewellers in scarlet, horses in jewels – these are the signs and trappings of a rich and confident city, tending perhaps towards excessive self-indulgence in matters of adornment and display. The next section gives details of the gathering of the delegates for the Council of Trent-Ferrara in 1438, an attempt to resolve the differences between the Eastern and Western churches (where Gemisthus Plethon's reconciling attempts failed). The failure of the council and, in the canto, the xenophobic mockery of the Greek clothes and appearance may indicate that religious feeling is ebbing while a more vulgar spirit of secular triumphalism and superiority is on the increase. 'And the guild spirit was declining' (XXVI, 124). The sentence comes from nowhere, but we seem to be shifting towards a new phase of the Renaissance. More opulence and finery follow: furs lined with scarlet, horses clothed in silk, yellow kerchiefs for the young ladies. But meanwhile:

> And to our general Pandolfo, three legates,
> With silk and with silver,
> And with velvet, wine and confections, to keep him –
> Per animarla – in mood to go on with the fighting.
> (XXVI, 124)

Pandolfo is Sigismondo. While Venice dresses up, he fights on. And the confections and riches of the city are sent to 'animate him' ('per animarla') – bribery? encouragement? Whatever, so long as he stays in the mood 'to go on with the fighting'. This sumptuous and luxurious civilization depends, ultimately, on the commitment and prowess of its *condottieri* – as perhaps, *mutatis mutandis*, all civilizations do. Sigismondo did the Venetian state much service, so it is perhaps a small adumbrating of his final abandonmment and fall that this sequence ends, cryptically: 'That Sigismundo left Mantua / Ill contented' (XXVI, 125). There follow short references to the break between the Albizzi family and the Medici Bank (a bad sign, since, for Pound, the Medici Bank was the *good* bank); and a treaty between Venice and Constantinople, signed in 1454, which would not of course last. 'Wind on the lagoon, the south wind breaking roses' (XXVI, 125). In Venetian history, there are storms ahead. 'And they are dead and have left a few pictures' (XXVI, 125). Is that all that there might, one day, be left to say?

The five documents, or parts of documents, that conclude the canto, run as follows: a letter from Pisanello of 1453 which makes it clear that he is being employed to inspect and purchase horses and hacks for Duke Alessandro Sforza. Since he was, among other things, a fine drawer of animals and, more important, involved in the building of the Tempio Malatesta, this can certainly be seen as indicating an improper use of an artist and the degradation of his art. The second document records the importing of the silvered head of St George at about the same time as Pasti was arrested for having in his possession Valturio's up-to-the- minute work on military matters – piety is safer than politics, perhaps; but I am sure Davenport is correct in saying that this juxtaposition is making the point that 'the Dogana simultaneously admitted saints' relics and confiscated scientific manuscripts'.[76] Third is a letter dated 1548 from an ambassador in Venice to a cardinal in Mantua urging that the murderers of Lorenzo de' Medici be helped to escape – Lorenzo, you may remember, was the Medici 'more full of life . . . more full of flames and voices'. Fourth comes the letter from Carpaccio seeking justice from Gonzaga of Mantua, one of whose painters has stolen a work from Carpaccio's workshop. And the fifth, from Mozart, marks a kind of terminal break between artist and patron. These letters hardly involve Venice or Venetians in any culpable way, or even reflect adversely on them. But they make their contribution to a general atmosphere in which the relations between the realm of the civic – diplomacy, politics, economics; pageantry, adornment and display – and of the artist and the artistic, are going, or have gone awry.

It is quite a jump to the next canto and 'the last crumbs of civilization', and the connections and inferences are left to the reader. There are two dominant pictures or images in canto XXVII, contrasted yet strangely connected. The building of the cathedral of San Giorgio in Ferrara – peace-loving Borso d'Este's city – is conceived of as having been built by popular will in a sudden rush:

> All rushed out and built the duomo,
> Went as one man without leaders
> And the perfect measure took form.
> (XXVII, 130)

This soon shades into rather different manifestations of the popular will:

> Brumaire, Fructidor, Petrograd.
> And Tovarisch lay in the wind

– French Revolution, Russian revolution: these people rush out and wreck. Generic comrade Tovarisch,

> Carved stone upon stone.
> But in sleep . . .

Awake:

> These are the labours of tovarisch,
> That tovarisch wrecked the houses of the tyrants,
> And rose, and talked folly on folly,
> And walked forth and lay on the earth
> (XXVII, 131)

That the houses of tyrants should be destroyed is not, self-evidently, any bad thing (though 'the crumbling of a fine house / profits no one' – Pound quotes Yeats; (LXXX, 507). The poetry here is not all unsympathetic by any means. The trouble with the hapless and benighted Tovarisch is, as he proclaims:

> 'I neither build nor reap. . . .
>
> I sleep, I sleep not, I rot
> And I build no wall. . . .
>
> I sailed never with Cadmus,
> lifted never stone above stone. . . .
>
> Laid never stone upon stone.'
> (XXXVII, 132)

Lifting stone above stone, and laying stone upon stone – these are the very founding gestures and acts of civilization. Stone upon stone – 'stone, ply over ply' (XVII) – is originally associated with the emergence and raising of Venice. Once again, there is the suggestion that whatever it was of 'civic order', art, even 'AMOR', that emerged as, started in, developed from Venice, was – effectively – finally destroyed or came to an end in the wars and revolutions of the twentieth century.

The last invocation of Venice in the first thirty cantos occurs at the end of canto XXIX, a particularly complicated canto concerning the metaphysics of love, sexuality and the feminine which seems to suggest that there is, at present, a 'love of death' abroad. Then the concluding lines:

> nondum orto jubare;
> The tower, ivory, the clear sky
> Ivory rigid in sunlight
> And the pale clear of the heaven
> Phoibos of narrow thighs,
> The cut cool of the air,
> Blossom cut on the wind, by Helios
> Lord of the Lights' edge, and April
> Blown round the feet of the God,
> Beauty on an ass-cart
> Sitting on five sacks of laundry
> That wd. have been the road by Perugia
> That leads out to San Piero. Eyes brown topaz,
> Brookwater over brown sand,
> The white hounds on the slope,
> Glide of water, lights and the prore,

Silver beaks out of night,
Stone, bough over bough,
                    lamps fluid in water,
Pine by the black trunk of its shadow
And on the hill black trunks of the shadow
The trees melted in air.
(XXIX, 145–6)

No dawn or sunrise yet – 'nondum orto jubare'. So then: images – images to hold on to, to bear in mind, to take consolation and resolve from. Images of clarity, purity, beauty; of Apollo and Helios (the Sun); of blossoms and edges; of Light and spring. Image of Nausicaa, helper of Odysseus, and exemplary woman of selflessness, courage, modesty and generosity. Athena sent her a dream to go down to the river, so in the morning she took the washing to the water (hence the 'sacks of laundry'), and, having found Odysseus and helped him to the palace, herself returned in the servants' cart (hence 'Beauty on an ass-cart'). Image of (perhaps) Diana's hounds in an Arcadian landscape, gliding without pause or sentence-break into a final images of Venice – water, lights, silver beaks, Stone, 'bough over bough'. After the images, the canto sinks downward to darkness – black shadows on the hill – until all, *Tempest*-like, melts into air. It is appropriate that, as Pound prepares to move away from the Italian Renaissance on to other points of departure, Venice should be glimpsed one final time with gods and goddesses, the company that attended her rise. Venice as vision, as 'Venice', belongs in and is part of that divine and paradisal landscape. The permanent miracle.

(Reading the canto this way, I must thus take issue with Davenport one final time when he comments on the conclusion that it fades 'into a canal scene that become the sinister forest of marble in Venice, the poem's symbol of great energy gone stagnant, and of great achievement allowed to drift into decay.'[77] Things certainly seem to be going wrong in historical Venice when Pound abandons it in, say, the early sixteenth century. But to read back from this a Venice which is stagnant and dead – dead from the start, Kenner would say – inorganic and infernal, seems to me to involve a radical, and rather programmatic, misreading of an essential, constituent element of the *Cantos*. For one thing, it makes them even more polemical and tendentious than at times, God knows, they are.)

Venice thereafter figures only fleetingly in the *Cantos* – a cryptic reference here, a glimpse or allusion there, the intermittent surfacing of a scattering of memories somewhere else. But one thing is indisputable: all the references or allusions have a positive discharge or resonance or affect – even in small, rather inscrutable details. There is, for instance, at the end of canto XLVIII, following the description of a flying ant or wasp, this unexplained cameo:

> at the Lido, Venezia
> an old man with a basket of stones,
> that was, said the elderly lady, when the beach costumes
> were longer,
> and if the wind was, the old man placed a stone.
> (XLVIII, 243)

Is this a gallant old man placing a stone to alert the ladies to the wind so that they might take care that their costumes would not blow up? Whatever it is, it somehow suggests the more considerate manners of an older age. Again, the lions of St Mark's turn up again – not flea'd and clipped, but somehow diminutive and benevolent rather than imperial and proud:

> & from the nature the sign,
> as the small lions beside San Marco. Out of ling
> the benevolence
> (XCVII, 675)

they come back to him again, in the same form and positively, well, frisky:

> and from the nature, the sign.
> Small lions are there in benevolence
> to the left of San Marco
> AISSOUSIN,
> the spirits,
> Berenice, a late constellation.
> (CII, 730)

'AISSOUSIN' – rushing or flying: the word was applied to Berenice in canto XCVII. (Berenice, wife of Ptolemy II, had left a lock of her hair in a shrine when her husband went to campaign against Syria. The lock disappeared and was 'discovered' as a new constellation.) The lions of Venice have joined her, all of them late for their 'constellation', but hurrying now. (Pound himself, in these years, was moving towards writing 'My *paradiso*', and perhaps he sensed he was moving towards a release from St Elizabeth's and was – stretching his wings?)

But a more profound series of references and repetitions brings Venice to another, a different, late and important flowering. In canto XXVI, among the fine materials used in Venice was this:

A silk cloth called cendato
That they still use for the shawls
(XXVI, 124)

The shawls? Which shawls? We probably do not notice this at the time. We might not put anything together when, in canto XCVIII we read:

But the lot of 'em, Yeats, Possum and Wyndham
had no ground beneath 'em.

Orage had.
Per ragione vale
Black shawls for Demeter
(XCVIII, 685)

(He repeats that last line three lines later.) But we might register the suggestion that respect for, veneration of, Demeter might provide a sort of 'grounding' lacking in the great modern writers (I am not here concerned with the kind of 'grounding' Orage's economic theories might have given him – though of course it was important to Pound). Since Demeter is goddess of the harvest, and thus of wheat, and thus of bread, we might remember her, and the shawls, when we read in the next canto, 'Food is the root. / Feed the people' (XCIX, 695), and we *might*, though we certainly might not, recall an uncontextualized assertion in canto LXXXIX: 'In Venice the bread price was stable' (LXXXIX, 602). Pound does not say *when* the price of bread was stable, nor for how long: the line is phrased in the non-historical for-everness of myth, where it may join Demeter, as, indeed, the city, in due course, does:

不 But the lot of 'em, Yeats, Possum, Old Wyndham
had no ground to stand on
Black shawls still worn for Demeter
in Venice,
in my time,
my young time
OIOS TELESAI ERGO . . . EROS TE
(CII, 728)

The last line means: 'such as to complete the task ... and love', a slight twist on a Homeric line.[78] Perhaps Demeter and Venice, and the piety betokened by the black shawls, will provide a true 'grounding' for a young poet who still had his task – and his love (EROS/AMOR) – to 'complete'; if, that is, there ever can be, or ever could be, any finishing of either. It all comes together at the start of canto CVI:

> And was her daughter like that;
> Black as Demeter's gown,
>   eyes, hair?
> Dis' bride, Queen over Phlegethon
>   girls faint as mist about her?
>
> The strength of men is in grain. . . .  *Kuan*
>
> A match flares in the eyes' hearth,
>   then darkness
> 'Venice shawls from Demeter's gown'
>   (CVI, 752)

There is no need to stress the absolutely central importance for Pound, and the *Cantos*, of the figure of Persephone.[79] The 'girls faint as mist about her' suggests Botticelli's *Primavera* – Persephone is becoming art, or art is becoming religion. Gown and grain; hair and hearth; girls and eyes; mist and men; Persephone and Demeter – all, incandescently, there: 'faint', yet *flaring*. And all somehow brought together and remembered in, perhaps perpetuated by – the shawls of Venice.

This Venice merges into myth. But there is another, historical, indeed autobiographical, Venice which recurs, particularly in the Pisan Cantos. In these cantos, Pound can clearly be seen seeking consolation (and doubtless trying to hold on to his sanity) by remembering some of his cherished, if not sacred, places – 'how is it far, if you think of it?' (LXXVII, 465). Sometimes it is just that – a gladness that beautiful places (sometimes) endure:

> and the Canal Grande has lasted at least until our time
>   even if Florian's has been refurbished
> and shops in the Piazza kept up by
>   artificial respiration
>   (LXXVI, 456)

Even just to write about the places, even just to name them, is presumably to be partly back there – 'Trovaso, Gregorio, Vio', three churches in Venice he knew particularly well. And indeed he returns to his earliest days in the city – for instance, when he met the Reverend Alexander Robertson at 'the Scotch Kirrrk in Venice' (LXXVI, 461); where he lived

well, my window
looked out on the Squero where Ogni Santi
meets San Trovaso
things have ends and beginnings
(LXXVI, 462)

So they do, and few poets can have had less inkling of what the 'end' might turn out to be than Pound, cramped in his cage outside Pisa. Beginnings were, in this case, more certain, and Pound returns to the start of his poetic career, and his first book which he nearly threw away:

by the soap-smooth stone posts where San Vio
meets with il Canal Grande
between Salviati and the house that was of Don Carlos
shd/ I chuck the lot into the tide-water?
le bozze 'A Lume Spento'/
and by the column of Todero
shd/ I shift to the other side
or wait 24 hours,

free then, therein the difference
in the great ghetto, left standing
with the new bridge of the Era where was the old eyesore
(LXXVI, 460)

The 'Era' is, unfortunately, the Era Fascista: Pound is still thinking resolutely in Mussolinian time. As a – long-distance – result of which he is, indeed, no longer free. How poignant, then, to tell the beads of the names of the places he frequented and loved when he was young – and free.

Will I ever see the Giudecca again?
or the lights against it, Ca' Foscari, Ca' Giustinian
or the Ca', as they say, of Desdemona
or the two towers where are the cypress no more
or the boats moored off le Zattere
or the north quai of the Sensaria DAKRUŌN ΔΑΚΡΥΩΝ
(LXXXIII, 532)

'DAKRUŌN' – tears, and no wonder 'tears'. Though, even here, we should note that, even though *in extremis* and at times seemingly reduced to the barest lists and iterations, Pound is working, surviving; striving to stabilize, if not renew himself, on and through the riches of the past – his own, and then the world's. He will not remain passively confined in a space where he has mainly an ant for company. So – not weeping, but writing.

One church in Venice meant more to Pound than all the others – Santa Maria dei Miracoli. As early as 1913, he sent Dorothy Shakespear a postcard of the interior as 'a reminder of the precise meaning of the term "Quattro cento"' (*EPVA* 41), and it is recalled three times in the Pisan Cantos:

> stone knowing the form which the carver imparts it
> the stone knows the form
> sia Cythera, sia Ixotta, sia in Santa Maria dei Miracoli
> where Pietro Romano has fashioned the bases
> (LXXIV, 430)

Either Venus (Cythera), or Isotta, lover of Sigismondo Malatesta and one of the animating and shaping forces of the Tempio Malatesta – or Santa Maria dei Miracoli. As it were, a heavenly and an earthly Venus linked with a church (thus in turn associated with the Rimini reliefs) where, supremely, 'the stone knows the form'. It was a 'knowledge' which Venice, the Venus city, supremely engendered.

At the end of a list of memories in canto LXXVI, this:

> Vendramin, Contrarini, Fonda, Fondecho
> and Tullio Romano carved the sirenes
> as the old custode says: so that since
> then no one has been able to carve them
> for the jewel box, Santa Maria Dei Miracoli,
> Dei Greci, San Girogio, the place of skulls
> in the Carpaccio
> and in the font to the right as you enter
> are all the gold domes of San Marco
> (LXXVI, 460–1)

The sculptures of Pietro and Tullio Lombardo make of Santa Maria dei Miracoli a 'jewel box' much as those of Duccio had done the Tempio Malatesta. Clean lines, stern lines – Botticelli and Mantegna in stone: it was what Pound wanted to remember; it was how he wanted to write. This is relevant when the church appears again in canto LXXXIII:

> Le Paradis n'est pas artificiel
> and Uncle William dawdling around Notre Dame
> in search of whatever
> paused o admire the symbol
> with Notre Dame standing inside it
> Whereas in St Etienne

or why not Dei Miracoli:
mermaids, that carving
(LXXXIII, 529)

Paradise is not artificial, something made, something fabricated:

I don't know how humanity stands it
with a painted paradise at the end of it
without a painted paradise at the end of it
(LXXIV, 436)

It is not to be apprehended, or sought, in any kind of symbolism. Pound is referring here to the period when he took against Yeats's work as being the vague, blurred, misty (etc. – all the things he was coming to dislike in writing) work of a *symboliste*, interested more in associations and 'whatever' an ancient site might suggest, than the thing itself. It was the latter that Pound, incipient imagist, was becoming more interested in. Whatever paradise there might be, for Pound it was not over-and-above, 'at the end', supplementary, superadded to the real. It had to be, and could be, *there* – perceptible, tangible, ad-mirable: absolutely clear, perfectly outlined – the stone rising from the water and, miraculously, knowing the form to take. The gods are still there if you know where to look, *how* to look. Paradise may be '*spezzato*' (broken) and may exist 'only in fragments' (LXXIV, 438); it may even be 'jagged' (CXII, 620) and seen and felt only in flashes and flares. But it is not artificial – not simply a dream of art. It could still be seen, glimpsed, perhaps supremely for Pound, in Santa Maria dei Miracoli in Venice – Church of the Miracles in the city which was, itself, the 'permanent miracle'.

The very last reference to Venice by name in the *Cantos* might seem a little strange:

and he, John Law, died in Venice in poverty.
We are far from recognizing indebtedness.
(CXIV, 791)

John Law (1671–1729) was a Scottish financier who set up the Royal Bank in France. He had many ideas concerning state credit which were ahead of his time. After one of his schemes failed, 'presumably because of the avarice of speculators', in 1720 he fled to Venice, where he died in poverty nine years later.[80] Pound's reproachful and regretful remark concerning the non-recognition of 'indebtedness' has, of course, particular aptness in relation to a well-intentioned banker ruined by an ungrateful and rapacious clientele. But the reproach involves all of us, and the regret is for a general failure. This is part of the intensely moving atmsphere of these last fragments, full of paradisal aspirations and intimations, yet streaked with pain and remorse and shadowed with a sense of sadness and a sense of failure, leading to a new recognition of mutual *inter*-indebtedness – 'And that the truth is in kindness', as he concludes the same canto (CXIV, 793).

Of his attempts to 'write paradise' over which he so movingly meditates in these last pieces, one can only say that he did and he did not – perhaps no man could do more. Certainly, if there is any 'paradisal' poetry written in the twentieth century, it is by Pound, and perhaps precisely because both poetry and poet had been so deeply involved with the 'hells' created by this century.

> Many errors,
>   a little rightness,
> to excuse his hell
>   and my paradiso.
> And as to why they go wrong
>   (CXVI, 797)

Why *do* they; why did *he*, as he undoubtedly did? It is the paradox of 'man seeking good, / doing evil' (CXV, 794). It is perhaps the oldest and most imponderable of paradoxes – a basic concern of Greek tragedy. What else is Oedipus? Does that blink the problem of evil? Perhaps Proust's point, in another context, must be taken. 'Now a desire for goodness, followed by a bad act, cannot be sufficient to establish the goodness of the human being, for then the bad act is caused by something bad that is in us' (*ORR* 159). But – 'Fear, father or cruelty, / are we to write a genealogy of the demons?' (CXIV, 793). Perhaps there comes a time for a looking-beyond – beyond the undoubted demonic, the unblinkable infernal, written all over history. Towards whatever paradise can still be written. Which was what the aged, and in some ways shattered, Pound was trying to do.

> Thy quiet house
> The crozier's curve runs in the wall,
> The harl, feather-white, as a dolphin on sea-brink . . .
> Hast' ou seen boat's wake on sea-wall,
>   how crests it?
> What panache?
>   paw-flap, wave-tap,
>   that is gaiety
>   (CX, 777)

The 'quiet house' is the Byzantine basilica in Torcello, but that is the Venetian lagoon, and again we are effectively back in Venice – as Pound himself was soon to be for his last years. In his beginning was his end, and his poetry, like its author, returns to where, effectively, it started out – went down to the ship and set sail. He seems to have found some sort of point of rest.

A nice quiet paradise,
                    Orage held the basic was pity
                                compassione,
                                        Amor
Cold mermaid up from black water –
        Night against sea-cliffs
                        the low reef of coral –
And the sand grey against undertow
        as Geryon – lured here but in splendour,
Veritas, by anthesis, from the sea depth
    come burchiello in su la riva
The eyes holding trouble –
        no light
                ex profundis –
naught from feigning.
Soul melts into air,
                anima into aura,
                        Serenitas.
                                (CXI, 783)

Geryon is the monster of Fraud in Dante's *Inferno* who 'pollutes the whole world' ('colei che tutto il mondo appuzza',[81]) and he was an obvious figure for Pound to invoke, particularly as Geryon associates with usurers. 'The usurers are there against nature, against the natural increase of agriculture or of any productive work. Deep hell is reached via Geryon (fraud) of the marvellous patterned hide, and for ten cantos thereafter the damned are all of them damned for money' (LE 211). 'Splendour' is what Pound asks to be led back to ('A little light, like a rushlight / to lead back to splendour'; CXVI, 797), and it is strange to see it attributed to, or associated with, Geryon. Perhaps it is his 'marvellous patterned hide':

con piu color, somesse e soprapposte
  non fer mai drappo Tartari nè Turchi,
  ne fur tele per Aragne imposte.

(never did Tartars or Turks make cloth with more colours, groundwork and broidery; nor by Arachne were such webs laid on her loom.)[82]

It sounds like a sumptuous work of art, but, since it is used to clothe Fraud, we may see it as art used to conceal, dazzle, misrepresent and deceive. Pound wants a different kind of beauty, a different kind of art – 'naught from feigning'. In the *Inferno*, Geryon is 'lured up' by Virgil:

> ch'io vidi per quell' aer grosso e scuro
> venir nuotando un figura in suso,
> meravigliosa ad ogni cor sicuro.

(that I saw, through that air gross and dark, come swimming upwards, a figure marvellous to every steadfast heart.)[83]

Pound, I think, wants Truth also to swim up from whatever depths, but 'Veritas, by anthesis' – not lured up, but by coming into 'full bloom', as if by a process of nature rather than the devices of art; and not swimming up in misleading Geryonous 'splendour', but cold from the sea, honest eyes bringing 'trouble' rather than 'light' from the depths. 'Naught from feigning.' But art *is* feigning: as his project 'gathers to a head', Pound seems ready to break his staff and drown his book, preferring simply to acknowledge and point to the supreme, and supremely *un*adorned, values of – *compassione*, Amor, Veritas. After that, the *Tempest*-conclusion, soul melting into air and spirit into golden light. Pound seems on the verge of abjuring his 'rough magic', looking, perhaps with pardonably troubled eyes, to 'Serenitas'. Serenitas in *Serenissima*. Let us hope he found it.

> but about that terzo
> third heaven,
> that Venere
> again is all 'paradiso'
> a nice quiet paradise
> over the shambles
> (CXVI, 796)

'The difference between a gun and a tree is a difference of tempo. The tree explodes every spring' (*SP* 424). That sounds like a good, hard, futuristic or vorticist no-pastoral-nonsense pronouncement. One feels it could have appeared in *BLAST* (in fact, in *The Criterion*, July 1937). It is a striking formulation and wrong only by one letter, yet I believe that slight error gives us an insight into a problem with the *Cantos*. For maximum accuracy, Pound should have written 'temp*i*'. Trees 'explode' every spring (albeit with fresh blossoms) – and that is recurrence. A gun never shoots the same shell twice – and that is history. Guns can be fired from behind trees, but when it comes to exploding and blossoming they inhabit different time schemes. Pound knew this well enough of course, and it is clear that in some way he is trying to relate, or at least incorporate, the eternal (gods and myths), the seasonal (recurrence and renewal) and the contingent (the one-offness of history). But because of his theory of 'Luninous Detail' or 'interpreting detail. A few dozen facts of this nature give us intelligence of a period' (*SP* 22–3), he developed no theory of history nor saw any need to – he thought he had, as it were, 'cracked' it, which is a different and more dangerous thing. Truly speaking, despite his assiduous reading, he had no *sense* of history – history in the making or the marring, history slowly, continuously, and multi-causally on the move (in this, too, curiously like Ruskin). Having selected what, *to him*, were the luminous, interpreting details – of Italian, American, Chinese history or that of his own life and epoch – he felt it enough to juxtapose them like discrete bits in a mosaic – 'mosaic? any mosaic. You cannot leave these things out' (CV, 750). But, seemingly, you do not have to relate, articulate, the things you put in. The result is that, appropriately enough for a mosaic, history is petrified. It moves, often furiously, within each monadic fragment, but is frozen and static in the whole. By the same token there is little or no indication of how the three time schemes are related, or indeed what relates them. There are glimpses of the beauty of the gods; and items from the shambles of events: but juxtaposition is not mediation or, indeed, dialectic – and the realms tend to remain separate. Michael Bernstein is right, I think, to maintain that in the *Cantos* mythos and history split apart.[84]

Proust's work is also a kind of mosaic, and what he wrote about Ruskin's manner of composition and his way of writing might, indeed, be extended to apply to the work not only of Proust himself but of Pound as well. In Ruskin's works, says Proust,

> there may be links he does not show, which he hardly lets appear for an instant. . . . The multiple but constant preoccupations of [his] thought, that is what assures these books of a unity more real than the unity of composition, generally absent, it must be said. . . . In reality Ruskin arranges side by side, mingles, manoeuvres, and makes shine together all the main ideas – or images – which appeared with some disorder in the course of his lecture. This is his method. He goes from one idea to another without apparent order. But in reality the fancy that leads him follows his profound affinities which in spite of himself impose on him a superior logic. So that in the end he happens to have obeyed a kind of secret plan which, unveiled at the end, imposes retrospectively on the whole a sort of order and makes it appear magnificently arranged up to this final apotheosis. (*ORR* 145–6)

Proust can discern and appreciate this way of composing so sensitively because it was, or became, his own method. Pound too had a secret, or not so secret, 'plan' for this massive side-by-side arrangings, minglings and manoeuvrings. The debatable point is whether it is enough to 'impose retrospectively on the whole a sort of order'. And instead of a 'final apotheosis', which makes everything that preceded it come to seem 'magnificently arranged', the paradisal moments and intimations at the end of the *Cantos* – which are real enough – are sometimes shadowed with glimpses of despair: 'my errors and wrecks lie about me . . . I cannot make it cohere' (CXVI, 796).

Both men had certainly read, and deeply registered, Ruskin's praise of mosaics.

> But the great mosaics of the twelfth and thirteenth centuries covered the walls and roofs of the churches with inevitable lustre; they could not be ignored or escaped from; their size rendered them majestic, their distance mysterious, their colour attractive. They did not pass into confused or inferior decorations; neither were they adorned with any evidence of skill or science, such as might withdraw the attention from their subjects. They were before the eyes of the devotee at every interval of his worship; vast shadowings forth of scenes to whose realisation he looked forward, or of spirits whose presence he invoked. And the man must be little capable of receiving a religious impression of any kind, who, to this day, does not acknowledge some feeling of awe, as he looks up to the pale countenances and ghostly forms which haunt the dark roofs of the Baptisteries of Parma and Florence, or remains altogether untouched by the colossal images of apostles, and of Him who sent the apostles, that look down from the darkening gold of the domes of Venice and Pisa.[85]

If we can generalize a mosaic as a strategic resiting of selected fragments in the interests of a larger picture, a greater vision, then we may fairly say that, in addition to Ruskin himself, Proust and Pound were great mosaicists, incrusting, embedding, arranging and rearranging fragments the whole time (fragments of time past, of people loved, of books read, art seen, stories heard, cities visited – fragments of absolutely anything at all which seem to the purpose.[86]) Proust draws special attention to the 'Sanctus, Sanctus, Sanctus' chapter in *St Mark's Rest* describing the mosaics in the Baptistery of St Marks, which he very accurately characterizes as 'a kind of Ruskinian Holy of Holies' (*ORR* 91). It was a Proustian one, too, and, given his admiration for such mosaics and desire to emulate them, very likely a Poundian one as well. Fittingly in more than one sense, since both writers aspired, in their different ways, to create works of art which would finally open on eternity.

Yet, while we may say both men worked as mosaicists, there is a crucial difference between them which a quotation from near the end (or cessation) of Proust's novel can serve to bring into focus. The writer, he maintains, 'can describe a scene by describing one after another the innumerable objects which at a given moment were present at a particular place, but truth will be attained by him only when he takes two different objects, *states the connexion between them* – a connexion analagous in the work of art to the unique connection which in the world of science is provided by the law of causality.'[87] They are both great writers of memory – recapturing, salvaging, reclaiming, reconstituting, reinstalling personal and cultural treasures. But Pound, quite deliberately, suppressed or left throbbingly silent the connections between the fragments he is shoring. It is as if he believed that, if you chose just the right fragments and put them next to each other, they would release a power, a kind of compacted and compressed cultural energy, the distillation of the best of our past – like beneficent radioactivity – a power which was actually latent or nascent within the images and fragments; this power would, as it were, burn its way into the reader's mind, whether or not that reader fully comprehended the reason for the selection, the logic of the juxtaposition. Sometimes, the effects can be electrifying – to shift the metaphor of power a little; sometimes it seems not to work and the fragments lie there inert, cut off as well as cut out; keeping their secrets, not yielding their power.

But perhaps it is pointless, or fruitless, to concentrate on what the *Cantos* fail to do. Like Proust's work, they can be said to constitute, in Blanchot's words, 'une oeuvre achevée-inachevée' (*ORR* lii). Sometimes they communicate, and sometimes they do not – though the more you work at the reading, Ruskin-style, the more they communicate. 'Truth is not untrue'd by reason of our failing to fix it on paper. Certain objects are communicable to a man or woman only "with proper lighting", they are perceptible in our own minds only with proper "lighting", fitfully and by instants' (*GTK* 295). His main concern, I think, was 'the preservation of verities' (*SP* 302) – as he saw them – in the most vivid and arresting way he knew how. Hence his attempts to resurrect the old gods and goddesses, to make them feel and seem real. He was bitterly against the religion currently – or notionally – practised in the Western world – 'an alleged religion which has taught the supreme lie that the splendour of the world is not a true splendour, that it is not the garment of the gods' (*GTK* 401). *That* is the 'splendour' he wanted to lead back to. 'Remove the mythologies before they establish clean values' (LXXXVII, 570). That is what he imagines the usurious officialdom of the West to be collectively saying. We need not accede to the simplistic generalities of his indictment to appreciate his efforts to revive a sense of the values he felt to be latent in the figures of the older gods. In this, he was trying to emulate the attempts of Gemisthus Plethon, 500 years earlier, to bring the Greek gods back into European awareness and respect.

> But Gemisto: 'Are Gods by hilaritas';
> and their speed in communication. . . .
>
> a fanned flame in their moving
>
> (XCVIII, 685)

His attempts to 'figure' and 'image' the gods was very far from being an escapist indulgence in nostalgic Arcadianism (as it can be). 'Tradition *inheres* ("*inerisce*") in the images of the gods, and gets lost in dogmatic definitions' (*SP* 293). The restoration, perpetuation, transmission of clean values – his images are at important work. 'Suspect anyone who destroys an image' (*SP* 287). For Pound, tremendous forces of erasure had been at work throughout what we think of as modern history. If they can 'wipe out' Ruskin, what can they *not* delete from common consciousness? 'Who has wiped the consciousness of the greatest mystery out of the mind of Europe – to arrive at an atheism proclaimed by Bolshevism, in Russia but not of Russia?' (*SP* 287). Or – why *is* 'a modern Eleusis . . . possible in the wilds of a man's mind only'? It would be impossible, or if possible, factitious and undesirable, to force a 'religious revival'. We know what happens in those. But one can work for preservation. 'We find two forces in history: one that divides, shatters, and kills, and one that contemplates the unity of the mystery. . . . There is the force that falsifies, the force that destroys every clearly delineated symbol. . . . But the images of the gods, or Byzantine mosaics, move the soul to contemplation and preserve the tradition of the undivided light' (*SP* 276–7). This almost Manichaean dichotomizing of the forces driving history is expressive rather than analytic. He deeply abhorred 'destruction' (think of the last line in the *Cantos*), and he wanted his images of the gods to preserve – like 'Mantegna's frescoes. Something to be there and STAY there on the wall' (*GTK* 95). Pound's images of the gods are indeed *there* – and 'STAY there', if only on the page. Images of gods and goddesses, and I want to add images of Venice, the city where the paradisal, the sacred work, was still – vestigially, discontinuously, fitfully and only by instants – palpably and perceptibly present. On the page and, as they were for Pound in Pisa, 'now in the mind' (LXXIV, 442), 'now in the heart – indestructible' (LXXVII, 465).

8

Conclusion: A Shore of Farewells

VENICE is not just another European city. It especially raises, as we have seen, questions concerning the relations between culture and nature, art and life, writing and desire. By way of conclusion I want, briefly, to consider works by a poet, a novelist and a philosopher-essayist – Rainer Maria Rilke, Thomas Mann and Jean-Paul Sartre. Rilke, that most peripatetic and itinerant of poets, first visited Venice in 1897 when he was twenty-two. 'This most singular of all historical settlements', as he termed it, struck him as a 'stone fairy-tale'. He came to love and know Venice better than any other city, Paris possibly excepted.[1] On a visit to the city in 1903 he described it as 'this dreamlike town which, in essence, resembles a scene in a mirror'.[2] Given Rilke's particular kind of lyricism, a city of dreamings and mirrorings would clearly have a special attraction – though for a time he became interested in historical Venice and in particular the fourteenth-century Venetian admiral, Carlo Zeno. This from Donald Prater:

> The history of Venice held a fascination for him, and he had a vague notion of writing the life of this saviour of the Republic at the battle of Chioggia against the Genoese. Introductions from Marie Taxis opened every facility to him: but he soon had to admit himself defeated, as he had been in earlier years, by his total incompetence in handling the materials of book-learning. 'They treat me like a scholar, lay out everything for me, but I just crouch over the folios as a cat might, concealing what is in them and at most taking a pleasure in the novelty of its situation. And when the lagoon down below laps and laps again at the old marble foundations my attention concentrates completely on the noise, as if there were more to be learned from that than from the old prints.'[3]

Rilke is not the first writer whom the waters of Venice have lapped into historical inattention – and reverie. More poet than historian; more cat than scholar.

Rilke wrote three poems directly about Venice in Paris, during the summer of 1908. 'Venetian Morning' feminizes the city. It is both 'pampered' and 'troubling'. It is a city which, whenever the sky feels a touch of the sea, perpetually 'will start becoming without ever being'. The German, 'sich bildet', suggests, rather, a city which is perpetually forming itself without ever arriving at final and definitive fixity. This fluid-fluent water-woman of a city has to be tempted – seduced – into 'rising' again for another day.

> Each morning must be showing her the selection
> of opals she wore yesterday and freeing
> from the canals reflection on reflection
> and bringing past times to her recollection:
> then only she'll comply and be agreeing
>
> as any nymph that gave Zeus welcoming.
> Her ear-rings tinkling at her ears, she raises
> San Giorgio Maggiore up and gazes with
> lazy smile into that lovely thing.[4]

'Some exquisite sea-thing will surely rise to save': Browning's Venice shades into Rilke's 'lovely thing' – the city raising its own wondrous structures from the water, just as the canals give up reflections and recollections; the past surfacing each morning as the amorous and satisfied city bejewels itself for another day. This is Venice as the city voluptuous, not to say narcissistic – more than half in love with its own lovely things.

'San Marco' registers a more ambivalent sense of the city's atmosphere. Rilke imagines the great church's interior as a place in which:

> this city's darkness was accommodated
>
> and secretly heaped up to balance out
> that overplus of brightness, so pervading
> all her possessions they were almost fading. –
> And 'Aren't – they fading?' comes the sudden doubt:

'Overplus of brightness' is perhaps an over-enthusiastic translation of, simply, 'des Lichtes', a light which indeed multiplies itself in all her (lovely) things ('Dingen' again). It is as if Rilke feels the city has need of this central edifice as a place to hold its 'darkness' ('Dunkelheit') – a city so shining must perforce have much darkness somewhere, is only to maintain some kind of equilibrium. There must be another side, or dimension, to the luminous city. And there is a further consideration: the city seems so saturated in brightness that you can have the sudden feeling that perhaps it is beginning to pass or fade away, melting and dissolving into light. It is a vision familiar to any student of Turner's Venetian paintings and watercolours.

A sense, then, that Venice may be tiring of its own aftermath, wearying a little of its own too-longness in time:

> you hail the unimpaired illumination
>
> of that wide view; yet somehow mournfully
> measuring its fatigued continuation
> with that of the adjacent four-horse team.[5]

The 'heile Helle' – the intact brightness or clearness; but also the 'müde Weile' – the tired lingering. Rilke touches a chord of mournfulness or melancholy ('wehmütig') which is certainly inseparable from the city in some of its moods. Almost as if it has somehow outstayed its own history. Venice – the city that outlasted itself.

There is something of this sense of weariness in 'Late Autumn in Venice': the word 'müde' recurs, the 'glassy palaces' have turned 'brittle' to the gaze, and the city no longer 'drifts like a bait' or lure ('Köder'), catching the days as they emerge. However, there is life in the underside of Venice:

> Out of the ground, though, from dead forest tangles
> volition mounts: as though before next day
>
> the sea-commander must have rigged and ready
> the galleys in the sleepless Arsenal,
> and earliest morning air be tarred already
>
> by an armada, oaringly outpressing,
> and suddenly, with flare of flags, possessing
> the great wind, radiant and invincible.[6]

Perhaps his desultory 'research' on the fourteenth-century Venetian admiral, Carlo Zeno – so triumphant at sea – has fired a part of Rilke's imagination. The 'volition', or will, or determination ('Willen') – and no city had more than Venice in its prime – is conceived of as rising from the very timbers and tree-trunks which literally support Venice in the water. Venice itself as a colossal act of will, perched precariously on, literally, skeletons of the woods ('Waldskeletten'), sending forth its very unskeletal armadas to dominate the seas, 'radiant and invincible'. The German is 'strahlend und fatal', and, while 'radiant' is exactly right for 'strahlend', 'invincible' for 'fatal' is perhaps a leap of translator's licence which misses a point. The word more ordinarily means 'unfortunate' and, indeed, 'fatal'. This seems to me to introduce a note of appropriate doubleness. If Venice is supported by the skeletons of trees, there is a sense in which you could say it is built on death. At the height of its powers it was indeed fatal to its enemies, but perhaps it also carries a fatality within it. Venice – radiant *and* fatal. That there is 'death in Venice' is, of course, what Thomas Mann was to explore in one of his most famous stories – a work which I shall consider next.

Rilke continued to visit Venice periodically, and on one of his later visits, in a letter written on 26 June 1920, he perhaps came as close as he ever did to distilling what the city meant to him. He is talking about one of the gardens on the Giudecca and his appreciation of the very special relation between brick, garden and the sea:

> I have always admired the great tact of the 18th century which decreed that the bright profusion of the garden should not be carried forward to the edge of the sea water; nothing is more affecting than this strip of world between, whose purpose is seemingly to wean you away from the pluralities of the garden and prepare you for the simplicities of the eternal. . . . At certain seasons of the year this ribband of seaboard, pathless and turfy and quite silent underfoot, is like a Shore of Farewells, – never have I known the feeling of farewell undergoing such a sea-change, such a spatial transformation; now, under the gathering rays of summer, a sense of easement also reigns there – the lagoon dazzles you and involuntarily you turn back to the garden and dwell in the consciousness of its undisturbed joy. The lovely old trees in the background shape themselves aloft against the pellucid sky, and over them, in pale shades of rose and grey, the walls and domes of the Redentore! I know, dear Countess, that this is not a description – no more than a face, a view, a feeling can the Giardino Eaden be described, only experienced, – indeed in the end this is true of Venice as a whole, there is nothing you can take up with vessels or hands, only as though with mirrors – it is all beyond your grasp and you are merely made the confidant of its evanescence. All day long you brim over with pictures, but you would be hard put to it to point to any one of them – Venice is an act of faith.[7]

> But of course! When one wanted to arrive overnight at the incomparable, the fabulous, the like-nothing-else-in-the-world, where was it one went? Why, obviously; he had intended to go there, whatever was he doing here? A blunder. He made all haste to correct it, announcing

> his departure at once. Ten days after his arrival on the island a swift motor-boat bore him and his luggage in the misty dawning back across the water to the naval station, where he landed only to pass over the landing-stage and on to the wet decks of a ship lying there with steam up for the passage to Venice.[8]

Gustave Aschenbach, Thomas Mann's quintessential German, North European, classical artist, has now truly started his – last – vacation. A believer in form, discipline, strictness, asceticism – his forebears 'had all been officers, judges, departmental functionaries – men who lived their strict, decent, sparing lives in the service of king and state' (p. 11) – Aschenbach has hitherto scarcely permitted himself any intermission from work. Austere, fastidious, detached, his writing has become 'fixed and exemplary, conservative, formal, even formulated' (p. 17). With high moral contempt he despises and castigates all romantic notions of the extra-sociality of the artist. 'With rage the author here rejects the rejected, casts out the outcast – and the measure of his fury is the measure of his condemnation of all moral shilly-shallying. Explicitly he renounces sympathy with the abyss, explicitly he refutes the flabby humanitarianism of the phrase: "*Tout comprendre c'est tout pardonner*"' (p. 16). An acquaintance says that '"Aschenbach has always lived like this" – here the speaker closed the fingers of his left hand to a fist – "never like this" – and he let his open hand hang relaxed from the back of his chair' (p. 12). Such a figure – almost a caricature of the repressed, all-taut, uptight Germanic writer (and, given the description of his published works to date, something of a self-portrait of the author himself) – is clearly ripe for cracking. And indeed the first fissure occurs while he is taking a walk in Munich, where he lives. Tired, and as 'a storm was brewing', he stops to wait for a tram by the North Cemetery.

> He found the neighbourhood quite empty. . . . Nothing stirred behind the hedge in the stonemason's yard, where crosses, monuments, and commemorative tablets made a supernumerary and untenanted graveyard opposite the real one. The mortuary chapel, a structure in Byzantine style, stood facing it, silent in the gleam of the ebbing day. Its façade was adorned with Greek crosses and tinted hieratic designs, and displayed a symmetrically arranged selection of scriptural texts in gilded letters, all of them with a bearing on the future life, such as: 'They are entering into the House of the Lord' and 'May the Light Everlasting shine upon them'. Aschenbach beguiled some minutes of his waiting with these formulas and letting his mind's eye lose itself in their mystical meaning. He was brought back to reality by the sight of a man standing in the portico, above the two apocalyptic beasts that guarded the staircase, and something not quite usual in the man's appearance gave his thoughts a fresh turn. (p. 8)

Byzantine structures, Greek façades, hieratic designs, scriptural texts in gilded letters, apocalyptic beasts – Aschenbach is already 'in' Venice, even if he does not yet know it. The unusual-looking man – exotic, grimacing, curled lips, bared teeth, a ruthlesss air – is the first of a number of harbingers of Death he is destined to meet – though he does not know that yet, either. And 'a storm was brewing' over Europe too, at that time – Mann was writing the novella from 1911 to 1913 – as a whole bourgeois order entered an omen-ridden twilight from which there would be no new dawning.

The turn Aschenbach's thoughts take as, unbeknownst to him, he regards the two premonitory figures of Venice and Death, starts the cracking of his Teutonic carapace. 'Yet whether the pilgrim air the stranger wore kindled his fantasy or whether some other physical or psychical influence came in play, he could not tell; but he felt the most surprising consciousness of a widening of inward barriers, a kind of vaulting unrest, a youthfully ardent thirst for distant scenes' (p. 9).

> Desire projected itself visually: his fancy . . . imaged the marvels and terrors of the manifold earth. He saw. He beheld a landscape, a tropical marshland, beneath a reeking sky, steaming, monstrous, rank – a kind of primeval wilderness-world of islands, morasses, and alluvial channels. Hairy palm-trunks rose near and far out of lush brakes of fern, out of bottoms of crass vegetation, fat, swollen, thick with incredible bloom. There were trees, mis-shapen as a dream, that dropped their naked roots straight through the air into the ground or into water that was stagnant and shadowy and glassy-green, where mammoth milk-white blossoms floated, and strange high-shouldered birds with curious bills stood gazing sidewise without sound or stir. Among the knotted joints of a bamboo thicket the eyes of a crouching tiger gleamed – and he felt his heart throb with terror, yet with a longing inexplicable. Then the vision vanished. (p. 9)

The vision, one feels, is itself extremely literary, or painterly. The landscape could be by Henri Douanier Rousseau, while the crouching tiger could come from Blake, with perhaps an echo of Henry James's 'Beast in the Jungle'. But it is a disease from a real 'primeval island-jungle' (p. 61) – Asiatic cholera – which he will contract in Venice, and the city itself, with its stagnant lagoon and sultry, mephitic atmosphere, becomes something of a 'primeval island-jungle' (or labyrinth) itself. From the Aschenbach-Munich point of view, Venice is an oriental city where the East more than meets the West – rather, penetrates, suffuses, contaminates and undermines it.

On the boat to Venice, there is an 'elderly coxcomb', cosmeticized as a youth, cavorting around in an embarrassing and undignified manner – shades of things to come; while the brutish-looking gondolier (with, again, bared teeth) who insists on rowing him across the lagoon to the Lido is a straightforward avatar of Charon. There is little doubt, even at this stage, of Aschenbach's final destination. He steps with a secret thrill into the gondola. 'That singular conveyance, come down unchanged from ballad times, black as nothing else on earth except a coffin – what pictures it calls up of lawless, silent adventures in the plashing night; or even more, what visions of death itself, the bier and solemn rites and last soundless voyage!' He finds lying in the gondola relaxing, even enervating, and he 'gave himself to the yielding element . . . in an indolence as unaccustomed as sweet' (p. 23). Thus begins the entire demoralizing, dismantling, of all his Apollonian-Germanic principles of discipline and control. I use these words advisedly, since Mann tends to work by and with fairly stark, even schematic, oppositions, and – following Nietzsche's famous opposition – Aschenbach is about to capitulate or succumb to Dionysus, the East, and the southern seas. It would be quite in line with Nietzsche's use of the terms to infer that perhaps an extreme Apollonianism always contains a secret Dionysianism only seeking or waiting the occasion of its irruption into the open.

The main agent, or occasion, of Aschenbach's dissolution is of course the beautiful boy with whom he becomes infatuated, Tadzio, with his 'tender and soft' features, Greek perfection of body, 'head of Eros', and 'soft and blurry tongue'. This last is important, for the polyglot Venetian hotel is the site of the dissolution of language as well. Aschenbach's austere, august, classical German cannot hold out against the various tongues from eastern Europe and the Balkans which here debouch into a babble. But it is Tadzio's voice and name which are the principle unravelling agent. At first he cannot catch the name – 'could make out nothing more exact than two musical syllables, something like Adgio – or, oftener still, Adjiu, with a long-drawn-out *u* at the end. He liked the melodious sound, and found it fitting' (p. 33). The name and the voice blur into music. This small hint of the musicalization of language is important, and that long-drawn-out *u* sound adumbrates a more total and terrible invasion of Aschenbach's consciousness by a music which is wild, bestial and irresistible. The music – pre-language, anti-language – of Dionysus.[9] Aschenbach has various encounters with kinds of music and musicians while in Venice – both usually disturbing and often distasteful, particularly for the fastidious man which, however, he is ceasing to be, as he gives into increasingly unashamed love and desire for Tadzio.

The name, the desire and the music all come together in a terrible dream which he has a few days before his death. The dream starts with howls ending in a long-drawn *u* sound and 'flute-notes of the cruellest sweetness'. Then comes a 'whirling rout' of men, women and animals and a cry of '"The stranger god!"' Tadzio's blurred name has become the maenadic cry of a Dionysian mob.

> And one and all the mad rout yelled that cry, composed of soft consonants with a long-drawn *u*-sound at the end, so sweet and wild it was together, and like nothing ever heard before! . . . But the deep, beguiling notes of the flute wove in and out and over all. Beguiling too it was to him who struggled in the grip of these sights and sounds, shamelessly awaiting the coming feast and the uttermost surrender. He trembled, he shrank, his will was steadfast to preserve and uphold his own god against this stranger who was sworn enemy to dignity and self-control. (p. 65)

But Apollo will of course give way to Dionysus: indeed, as we have seen, Venice is notoriously a site where opposites begin to blur and distinctions fade – it is no longer certain that there *are* two gods. Soon – dreaming on – 'His heart throbbed to the drums, his brain reeled, a blind rage seized him, a whirling lust, he craved with all his soul to join the ring that formed about the obscene symbol of the godhead, which they were unveiling and elevating, monstrous and wooden, while from full throats they yelled their rallying-cry' (p. 65). The Venice dreamed by Browning's Don Juan finally resolved itself into a primitive phallic column and, here again, under very different circumstances a dream in, if not *of*, Venice has climaxed with a recovered vision of the primeval phallic symbol. But what was epiphany for Don Juan portends annihilation for Aschenbach. For he joins the dance and shares the feast.

> But now the dreamer was in them and of them, the stranger god was his own. Yes, it was he who was flinging himself upon animals, who bit and tore and swallowed smoking gobbets of flesh – while on the trampled moss there now began rites in honour of the god, an orgy of promiscuous embraces – and in his very soul he tasted the bestial degradation of his fall. (p. 65)

At the start of his infatuation with Tadzio, watching him, as he does every day, playing on the beach, Aschenbach feels a 'desire to write'. He has a vaguely Platonic belief, or hope – Phaedrus is mentioned – that the boy's beauty can act as an elevating inspiration.

> This lad should be in a sense his model, his style should follow the lines of this figure that seemed to him divine; he would snatch up this beauty into the realms of the mind, as once the eagle bore the Trojan shepherd aloft. Never had the pride of the word been so sweet to him, never had he known so well that Eros is in the word, as in those perilous and precious hours when he sat at his rude table, within the shade of his awning, his idol full in his view and the music of his voice in his ears, and fashioned his little essay after the model Tadzio's

> beauty set: that page and a half of choicest prose, so chaste, so lofty, so poignant with feeling, which would shortly be the wonder and admiration of the multitude. (p. 46)

Eros in the word – Eros builder of cities, Eros writer of books. Only not quite. For if Eros is in the word it is, effectively, to end the word. Those one and a half pages – one and a half pages from this seriously productive writer! – are Aschenbach's last. The chaste and lofty language can no longer withstand the disintegrative, illiteratizing allure of *that* music. Aschenbach is another writer for whom Venice is the place where the writing had to stop. (Thomas Mann too, in a more limited and indirect way: after 'Death in Venice' he wrote no more fiction for over ten years.)

Because of Tadzio, and Aschenbach's aroused desire, the gods – and goddesses – start returning to Venice, though not in any Poundian way. The sight of him coming from the sea 'conjured up mythologies, it was like a primeval legend, handed down from the beginning of time, of the birth of form, of the origin of the gods' (p. 34). Venus transformed, and we may say, with no censorious intent, Venus perverted. There are days, for Aschenbach, 'gilded with mythical significance' when the clouds look like 'grazing herds of gods' (p. 48). But which gods? As well as Eros, 'Eos was rising' – Eos, personification of the dawn and mother of the winds; a Titan envied by the Olympians; ravisher of Orion and, by legend, punished by Aphrodite by being turned into a nymphomaniac (one of the odder punishments, one might think, for a sexually insatiable woman – or goddess!). Her legendary life was a series of sexual intrigues. Her winds bring 'Poseidon's horses' up from the sea, and it becomes 'a world possessed, peopled by Pan'. Tadzio becomes Hyacinthus, loved and accidentally killed by Apollo when jealous Zephyr deflects the discus thrown by Apollo on to Hyacinth's head. Apollo, then, is there, though unnamed – but in his most helpless, hapless role. Then Tadzio becomes Narcissus – apt enough in this 'water-city of mirrorings and reflections'. Apt enough too, perhaps, for the writer – for where are the other people in Aschenbach's life? Wife dead, daughter distant, no mention of family or friends – he is man alone, and his writing is based on that aloneness. 'Solitude gives birth to the original in us, to beauty unfamiliar and perilous – to poetry. But also, it gives birth to the opposite: to the perverse, the illicit, the absurd' (p. 26). Most of Mann's work involves, in one way another, an exploration of the ambiguities involved in the relationship between art and life (the opposition is at times almost embarrassingly simplistic, as in 'Tonio Kröger'), and nowhere more than here is there a stronger sense that writing writes out living, so that one effect of the novella is, morally or even existentially speaking, to write out *writing*. It is perhaps not so surprising that Mann wrote no more – as an *artist* (there are of course political writings) – for ten years. A writerly contempt for 'the abyss' (the perverse, the transgressive, the bestial, whatever) will, it seems, lead you unerringly right into it. All gods turn out to be, or revert to, one god – as in Aschenbach's dream. An Apollonian is only a Dionysiac, temporarily self-deceived.

All this takes place in a Venice – 'this most improbable of cities' (p. 22) – which already carries a deathly sickness within it. The cholera which has insinuated itself into the heart of the city, and which the authorities are trying to conceal or deny,[10] strikes Aschenbach as being comparable to the diseased passion which has fastened on him and which he is, unsuccessfully, trying to refuse or repress. 'These things that were going on in the unclean alleys of Venice, under cover of an official hushing-up policy – they gave Aschenbach a dark satisfaction. The city's evil secret mingled with the one in the depths of his heart – and he would have staked all he possessed to keep it, since in his infatuation he cared for nothing but to keep Tadzio here' (p. 52). He has learned the city's guilty secret from an honest English travel agent who tells him how the disease has spread across Europe, finally reaching northern Italy, so that now the fruit and vegetables and meat in the city are probably infected (Aschenbach would seem to have contracted the disease from some overripe strawberries on which, in his new mood of ever more relaxing sensuousness, he gorges himself): 'death unseen and unacknowledged was devouring and laying waste in the narrow streets, while a brooding, unseasonable heat warmed the waters of the canals and encouraged the spread of the pestilence' (p. 61). In the event, Aschenbach keeps both secrets – never actually declaring his love, nor warning the boy's family of the danger of staying in Venice. Instead, he simply follows Tadzio everywhere, ever more shamelessly. One day, he follows him in a gondola and, passing gardens, Moorish lattices, a beggar on the marble steps of a church, an antiques shop with a fraudulent-looking owner trying to entice people in, he thinks:

> Yes, this was Venice, this the fair frailty that fawned and that betrayed, half fairy-tale, half snare; the city in whose stagnating air the art of painting once put forth so lusty a growth, and where musicians were moved to accords so weirdly lulling and lascivious. Our adventurer felt his senses wooed by this voluptuousness of sight and sound, tasted his secret knowledge that the city sickened and hid its sickness for love of gain, and bent an ever more unbridled leer on the gondola that glided on before him. (p. 54)

The City of Art is sick, the classical writer is sick – is art itself a form of sickness, so that it is not so much a matter of death in Venice as that death which *is* Venice? This increasingly becomes the mood of the story as this itself seems to sink into the malodorous mephitic stagnation it has itself evoked. No winds of resistance blow.

> The knowledge that he shared the city's secret, the city's guilt – it put him beside himself, intoxicated him as a small quantity of wine will a man suffering from brain- fag. His thoughts dwelt on the image of the desolate and calamitous city, and he was giddy with fugitive, mad, unreasoning hopes and visions of a monstrous sweetness. . . . His art, his moral sense, what were they in the balance beside the boons that chaos might confer? (p. 63)

Aschenbach is now settling ever more contentedly into 'the abyss' he once so loftily scorned, and the gondola's ultimate destination comes closer by the moment.

Almost his last act is to have himself tailored and barbered and cosmeticized into a garish simulacrum of youthfulness – thus re-enacting the spectacle of the obscene and embarrassing young-old man which he had found so loathsome on the voyage into Venice. He has become exactly that which he most abhorred. Mann is not subtle, but it is a powerful image of a thing turning into its seeming opposite in the city most tolerant, pehaps productive, of inversions and reversibilities. In his new guise, he renews his quest for Tadzio, and by now the air in the city is 'heavy and turbid and smelt of decay'. It is effectively his last expedition and it brings home to him as never before that chasing is losing.

> One afternoon he pursued his charmer deep into the stricken city's huddled heart. The labyrinthine little streets, squares, canals, and bridges, each one so like the next, at length quite made him lose his bearings. He did not even know the points of the compass. . . . he stole upon the footsteps of his unseemly hope – and at the end found himself cheated. The Polish family crossed a small vaulted bridge, the height of whose archway hid them from sight, and when he climbed it himself they were nowhere to be seen. He hunted in three directions – straight ahead and on both sides of the narrow, dirty quay – in vain. (p. 67)

As in Hofmannsthal, Venice has become a place of major disorientations and inexplicable disappearances. After this, Aschenbach gluts himself on the overripe strawberries and then simply sinks down and rests his head on the rim of a well. 'It was quiet here. Grass grew between the stones, and rubbish lay about.' It seems that nature is reclaiming the city, and that he is becoming part of the accumulating detritus and gathering litter. The end is inevitable, and inevitably takes place on the beach of the Lido as Aschenbach watches Tadzio taking a final bathe before the family's departure. He fancies the boy-god is summoning him to the water and indeed he has reached the term of his dissolution – the oceanic can reclaim him. He has found that death in Venice which he first glimpsed in Munich and set out, initially all-unknowingly, to seek.

In 1957 Jean-Paul Sartre published part of a work in progress now translated as 'The Prisoner of Venice'.[11] It was a study of the life and times of Tintoretto, and in the fragment we can recognize familiar Sartrean themes, not least that of the figure of the artist as being misunderstood, alienated, suspected.

> This artist's fate was to be the incarnation of bourgeois puritanism in an aristocratic republic during its decline. . . . The ill-will shown towards Tintoretto by official and bureaucratic Venice was the same kind which the patricians bore toward the Venetian bourgeoisie. These rebellious merchants and their painter posed a threat to the Order of the Most Serene Republic; they would have to be watched.[12]

Sartre portrays a wretched and maligned artist who was unappreciated by his own city – which preferred Titian: 'Perverse Venetians! Fickle bourgeois! Tintoretto was their painter. . . . First and foremost, Tintoretto's painting is the passionate love affair between a man and a city.'[13] In fact, the artist, the art and his city are one.

> Tintoretto was the chief mourner for Venice and its world. But when he died unlamented, silence fell and hands of pious hypocrisy hung veils of crepe over his pictures. But if we tear away this black veil, we find one portrait, painted a hundred times. Was it a portrait of Jacob or the Queen of the seas? Whichever you prefer; the city and her painter have but one and the same face.[14]

For Sartre an artist either celebrates, reflects or contests the dominant values of his society, and clearly Tintoretto was going to be a celebrator, albeit without honour in his own country, or city. Sartre wanted to produce a study of an artist who was at once a product and an excoriator of the bourgeois class, and Tintoretto was hardly the most suitable figure. Flaubert and his bourgeois class proved more fertile. He never finished the piece.

But in 1953 Sartre had written an essay on Venice in the first person, 'Venise de ma fenêtre',[15] which is remarkable – not least for being absolutely non-political. It is also remarkable in its account of an encounter with the Other. The essay, for some inexplicable reason, was not translated when the English version of *Situations IV*, in which it appeared in France, came out; so I have to offer my own unprofessional renderings of certain key passages. From the start he experiences Venice as a place of inversions, mixings, reversals. He looks over a bridge and finds that the sky has fallen into the water. 'It's like that here: air, fire and stone never stop mingling with each other or inverting each other, never stop changing their natures or their natural places.' The capriciously inter-metamorphosing elements, he says, are still playing antiquated games which are far from innocent. Venice is an 'unstable compound' which holds many surprises. In Venice, 'nothing is simple':

> Because this is not a city, no: it is an archipelago. From your small island you look enviously at the island facing you: over there is . . . what? a solitude, a purity, a silence which is not to be found, you would swear, on this side. Wherever you may be, the true Venice, you will find, is always elsewhere. For me, at least, it is like that. Usually, I tend rather to content myself with what I have; but in Venice I am the prey of a kind of mad jealousy; if I didn't restrain myself, I would be on bridges and in gondolas the whole time, desperately looking for the secret Venice of the other side [*la Venise secrète de l'autre bord*]. Of course, as soon as I get there, everything fades; I come back: the tranquil mystery has re-formed itself on the other side. There are good times when I simply resign myself: Venice is just exactly the place where I am not [*Venise, c'est là où je ne suis pas*]. Those princely chalets, opposite me, surely they come up out of the water. Impossible to believe that they float: a house, that doesn't float. Nor do they lie heavily on the lagoon: it would sink under their weight. Nor are they imponderable: you can see quite clearly they are made of bricks, stone and wood. What then? You really have to feel them emerging: you look at the palaces of the Grand Canal from top to bottom and that is enough for you to sense in them a sort of frozen momentum [*élan figé*] which is, if you like, their density turned upside-down, the inversion of their mass. A splash of petrified water, perhaps: you would say that they had only just appeared and that there had been nothing before these little stubborn erections. In short, they are always slightly apparitional. An apparition – now, you can guess what that would be like: it would take place in an instant and it would make it easier to grasp the following paradox – pure Nothingness would remain and yet Being would already be there [*le pur néant subsisterait encore et pourtant déjà l'être serait là*]. When I look at the Palazzo Dario . . . I always have the feeling that, yes, it is certainly there, but at the same time that there is nothing there. So much so that sometimes it seems as if the whole city had disappeared. One evening, coming back from Murano, my boat found itself alone and out of sight: no more Venice. Somewhere to the left the water rose in clouds under the gold of the sky. Just for a moment all is clear and precise. . . . And then – what is

> that opposite me? The Other foot-path of a 'residential' avenue, or the Other bank of a river? At any rate, it is the Other [*de toute façon, c'est* l'Autre]. Come to that, the left and the right of the Canal are hardly distinguishable. To be sure, the Fondouque des Turcs is on one side, the Ca' d'Oro is on the other. But, finally, it's always the same caskets, the same marquetry work, interrupted here and there by the billowings of large town halls of white marble, gnawed away by tears of filth. Sometimes, when my gondola has been gliding between these two funfairs, I have asked myself which was the reflection of the other. In short, it's not their differences which distinguish them: on the contrary. Imagine that you are approaching a mirror: an image starts to form there – there is your nose, your eyes, your mouth, your clothes. It's you, it should be you. And yet, there is something about the reflection – something which is neither the green of the eyes, nor the line of the lips, nor the cut of the clothes; something which makes you suddenly say – they have put an other in the mirror in place of my reflection. That is pretty nearly the impression which the presence of Venice [*Venise d'en face*] always makes. Nothing today prevents me from thinking that it's our funfair which is the real one [*la vraie*], and the other only an image, very gently blown eastward by the Adriatic wind.

Sartre goes on to explore his sense of the difference in this feeling from the one he has when he looks out of his window in Paris and sees a crowd on the terrace of Deux Magots. Since he shares the same land as those people, he feels that he does not look *at* them; rather, he *regards* them, effectively touching them. The *Others* are always across the seas ('les *Autres* sont au-delà des mers'). And so, he continues, 'the other Venice is across the sea'. The other Venice, or perhaps the Venice of the Other. He describes seeing two women in black across the canal, by Santa Maria della Salute. They seem as far away ('lointaines' – a word I will come back to) as the Arab women he had seen prostrating themselves on Arab soil. 'Strange' – and 'untouchable'. And there is another 'untouchable'. Horrors! It is 'mon semblable, mon frère' – a tourist with his Blue Guide and his Rolleyflex camera:

> Now what is more stripped of mystery than a tourist? Well, this one, fixed in his suspicious immobility, is as alarming as those savages in horror films who push apart the marsh reeds, following the beautiful heroine – and then disappear. This is a tourist of the Other Venice and I will never see what he sees. Opposite me, these walls of brick and marble preserve the fleeting strangeness of those lonely towns perched up on hills which you see from a train.

All this is the fault of the canal, because instead of honestly proclaiming that it separates people – so that you could say that over there is a certain town, different from ours but, by the same token, similar – it pretends to *reunite* ('ce Canal prétend *réunir*'). It looks like something that joins, like a highway. Indeed:

> everything prompts me to run across this causeway to assure myself that the tourist over there is actually the same species as myself, and that he doesn't see anything which I can't see. But the temptation disappears even before it has properly arisen; it has had no other effect than to activate my imagination. Already I feel the sun opening out – feel that the Canal is only an old branch, rotten under its moss, under the black and drying shells with which it is covered and which crack if you step on them. I sink in, I am swallowed up while raising my arms, and my last sight will be of the indecipherable face of the Unknown of the Other side [*le visage indéchiffrable de l'Inconnu de l'Autre bord*], just now turned towards me, agonizing over his helplessness or delighting to see me fall into the trap. In short, this false unifying feature (the Canal) only pretends to bring things together, the better to disunite them. It circumvents me without difficulty and gives me to believe that communication with my own kind is impossible; even the proximity of this tourist is an illusion. . . . The water of Venice gives to the whole city a delicate, nightmarish quality; for it is in nightmares that tools let us down – the revolver aimed at the mad murderer that doesn't fire; it's in nightmares that we are desperately running away, closely pursued by a mortal enemy, and suddenly the road goes all soft, just when we want to go down it. The tourist has gone. Mysterious. He climbs up the little bridge – then he disappears, and I am alone above the motionless Canal.

Another disappearance in Venice of a sought or pursued quarry. Mysterious. Separation and disjunction are much in Sartre's mind as he experiences Venice, that and more ontologically disturbing intimations of nothingness. As he looks at the two quays – 'il n'y a *rien*'; just 'a transparent scarf thrown hastily over the void'. Those dwellings 'are separated from ours by a crack which runs through the whole world'. He feels that 'the two halves of Europe are in the process of coming apart; they are drifting away, the one from the other. Already there are *two* human species which have already started to go their different ways for ever, though nobody realizes it yet.' (Given the time of writing, I suppose that could be construed as an implicitly political comment on the state of Europe and East–West relations.) Venice, he says, is 'always in the process of dislocating (or disassembling) itself' –

'toujours en train de se disloquer'. And clearly Sartre himself feels dislocated in this Venice which always remains inaccessible, always holds itself off, never communicates. 'In Venice, silence watches itself – it is the taciturn defiance of the Other Bank' ('A Venise, le silence se voit, c'est le défi taciturne de l'Autre Rive').

Sartre makes Venice, or finds there, a site of his deepest phenomenological, psychological, even metaphysical preoccupations. Because it seems to be that impossible thing, a city floating on water rather than surging up out of it, Venice becomes that 'unstable compound' which serves to destabilize other conceptual and existential standpoints to the point of nightmare. For the visiting philosopher, it calls into question the location of the true – 'le vrai'; it renders uncertain what is real and what is image or reflection; it offers apparitional glimpses of the paradoxical co-presence of Being and Nothingness. Venice is also the 'always elsewhere' ('toujours d'ailleurs'); whatever it is, it is always where he is not and can never be – provocative and elusive, definitively unreachable. This serves to awaken desire – desire in the form of jealousy and a desperate seeking for what he knows he will never find and can never have; this leads to a sense of the uncanny and a nightmare of being swallowed up in the treacherous 'softness' of streets made of water (another feminization of the city, given what Sartre associated with what was neither absolutely hard nor absolutely liquid but softly, moistly, viscously – and, to him, disgustingly – in between). And at the centre of this experience of hopeless pursuit and fatal flight is his experience of being in the presence of the Other – the other side, the other bank, whatever; it is the Other – 'de toute façon, c'est l'Autre'. That is, a sense of generic otherness or alterity. The theme of the Other echoes throughout the essay and recurs in his description of the various sensations he experiences when confronted by Venice. It is like approaching a mirror and finding an other looking back at you. The tourist he sees – 'mon semblable, mon frère' – becomes the Unknown of the Other Bank whom he imagines looking at him with an inscrutable gaze as he sinks in that Canal which seems to promise connection and communication but which serves only to dramatize our separation and inability to communicate.

There is no point here in tracing out Sartre's evolving notions of the Other. His most sustained account is to be found in part 3 of *Being and Nothingness* (1943) in the section entitled 'The Look' (the one piece of Sartre which Lacan insisted his pupils must read – so I am told). His contestatory, even gladiatorial, conception of the relationship to the Other was certainly influenced by the adversarial, master–slave relationship outlined in Alexander Kojeve's famous lectures on Hegel given in Paris between 1933 and 1939 (published as *Introduction to the Reading of Hegel*).

But there is another line of thinking about the Other which can be discerned in twentieth-century (particularly French) thought, and which I will trace back to Victor Segalen, a ship's doctor who had considerable experience in China and Tahiti, and who worked continuously on an unfinished project called 'Essai sur l'exotisme', subtitled 'Une aesthétique du divers' (written between 1904 and 1918, the year of his death). For Segalen, 'l'exotisme' was above all 'le pouvoir de *concevoir autre*' – that is, the ability to conceive of otherness, to think the other. Everything which is 'en dehors' of our customary way of thinking has this potential value of the exotic, the diverse, the different ('la nation de Différence'). What it is *not* is the 'état kaléidoscopique du touriste'. Tourists he calls 'les Proxénètes de la Sensation du Divers' – *procurers* of the sensation of variety, with perhaps a sense of a merely distracting something-elseness. The exotic may be the elsewhere and other times – 'les ailleurs et les autrefois'; but it is primarily and constitutively what is other. 'C'est par la Différence, et dans le Divers, que s'exalte l'existence'. The true exotic or other is a 'source d'énergie', and Segalen was saddened or appalled at the way in which so-called Progress was eating away at the diminishing exoticity in the world. 'Où est le mystère? – Où sont les distances?' Hence the importance, earlier alluded to, of *le loin* – the far, far-awayness: for Sartre, for Segalen, for Proust, for Baudelaire too, of course. There is no need at this stage to stress the intimate connection between farness and desire. In a summarizing way, Segalen writes: 'Je conviens de nommer "Divers" tout ce qui jusqu'aujourd'hui fut appelé étrange, insolite, inattendu, surprenant, mystérieux, amoureux, surhumain, héroïque et divin même, tout ce qui est *Autre*.' It is an inclusive list: the strange, the unusual, the unexpected, the surprising, the mysterious, the amorous, the more-than-human, the heroic, even the divine; comprehensively, all that is *Other*. Interestingly, he notes that 'Le "colonial" est exotique, mais l'exotique dépasse puissamment le colonial' – the colonial is exotic, but the exotic far exceeds the colonial. Segalen was writing in the early years of the century when, you might say, colonialism was in its heyday or, in retrospect, entering its twilight.

It would seem that one of the products of the declining years of European colonialism was just this conception of the Other as a site of value, to be respected and cherished in, and because of, its alterity. In general, Western thought has tended to regard the Other as representing what we *were* and what we *aren't*; as either a threat to be reduced, or a potential for conversion into the Same – what the Swiss writer Bernard Schlurick nicely calls the compulsion or drive to effect 'le verrouillage de l'Autre dans le Même' (the locking-up of the Other in the Same). But there has developed a counter-tradition which would include the names of Bataille, Leiris, Blanchot, Derrida, Levinas – this last arguing that it is the Other who constitutes our ethical being, since the unknowable Other not only demonstrates the limits to our mode of knowing, but also confronts us with the responsibility of responding and communicating non-manipulatively, non-appropriatingly, noncoercively. Michel de Certau continued to develop this line of thought in his work and his (sadly) last book was called *Heterologies: Discourses on the Other*. The seeds for this line of thinking seem to me to be found in Segalen (though de Certau might have wanted to say Montaigne). It is a line to set alongside that of Sartre.

In Sartre's Venetian essay, the alterity of the city itself – in a way the whole city is the Other – disturbs and displaces him, goading him to desperation by its elusiveness, its self-withholdingness, its always-else-whereness. And when he sees the Other, it is – a tourist (and perhaps we are all 'tourists' now), hostile, or indifferent or helpless, and definitively indecipherable and unreachable. The experience quickly turns to nightmare, with the fantasy of being sucked down as the city goes soft under him as he runs from a mortal enemy. Sartre loved Venice and often visited it, but this is the Venice he 'wrote'. With his adversarial sense of the Other, Sartre finds what he most dreads in Venice and at the end of the essay, rather than being nourished by Venice, he feels empty – 'vide'. His last words are 'Je sors' – I go out, but also, more abruptly, I go, I leave. The reaction to his imagined Venice is – as it was for Melville, to go back to the beginning – flight. Venice was the last point of departure for merchants, pilgrims and Crusaders travelling to the East, and since then, in many different ways, the city has proved to be, has provided, a 'shore of farewells'.

Not for the first time, the epiphanies occasioned by Venice have turned negative. For Melville, it was a triumph of the art of Pan, which proved to have a Basilisk glance; for Byron, the greenest island of his imagination turned into a sea-Sodom; for Ruskin it was the Hesperid Ægle with a Medusa face; for James, it was brilliantly Veronesean but also darkly venereal; for Hofmannsthal it offered ecstasy and effected dissolution; for Proust, the promise of an all but unbearable beauty turned into a vacancy; for Pound, it always retained some miraculous beauty, but somehow, at some time, fraud and corruption had entered the city; for Rilke, it was voluptuous but weary, radiant and fatal; for Mann, this most supreme of cities disclosed the sickness of art – perhaps the sickness which *is* art – and for Sartre, was it the place of 'le vrai' or 'le vide'? Venice is indeed a site of 'absolute ambiguity'. I take the phrase from a remarkable essay by Georg Simmel, written in 1922 and simply called 'Venedig' – 'Venice'. I will afford myself one last, long quotation which I think fittingly draws this book to a conclusion.

> As one is propelled along the Grand Canal . . . one becomes aware that, whatever life may be like, it cannot at any rate be thus. Here, standing in St Mark's Square, in the Piazza, one feels the presence of a force, of an iron will, of a gloomy passion which stands behind the serene façade like the *Ding an sich*, the essential object, independent of the subject who perceives it. The appearance, however, exists as if

deliberately independent of the reality, the external receives from its internal aspect no form of direction or sustenance, it does not obey the law of a comprehensive spiritual reality but rather that of an art form, which seems to be expressly formulated to deny the latter. However, where the sense of a meaning of life behind the work of art has either vanished or is flowing in the opposite direction, the result is of artificiality, no matter how perfect the work may be in itself. . . . Venice . . . is an artificial city. Florence will never become a mere mask, because it manifests itself as the genuine language of a real existence; but here, where all the serenity and brightness, the ease and freedom, served only as a façade for the dark and violent, remorselessly purposeful life, the demise of that existence has left behind only a soulless theatrical set, the false beauty of the mask. . . . all action seems to represent a foreground which has no background, one half of an equation whose other portion has been obliterated. . . . It is as if everything had collected on its surface all the beauty which it could for itself, and then withdrawn from it, so that it is left as if fossilized, protecting that beauty which is no longer involved with the animation and development of real existence. . . . The nature of all Venetian rhythms denies us the shakings and batterings which we require for a sense of complete reality, bringing us closer to the dreams where we are surrounded by the appearance of things without the things themselves . . . this is the tragedy of Venice, whereby it becomes the symbol of a quite unique order of our formal world order; the tragedy of a surface which has been left by its foundation, the appearance in which no being persists, and which still presents itself as something which is complete and substantial, as the content of a life which can still be experienced. . . . The character of the squares is ambiguous, devoid of vehicles, their narrow symmetrical enclosed nature gives them the appearance of rooms. . . . Ambiguous, too, is the double-life of the city, at once a maze of alleyways and a maze of canals, so that the city belongs to neither land nor water – rather each appears like the protean garment, with the other concealed behind it, tempting as the true body. Ambiguous too are the dark little canals whose waters move and flow so unquietly without revealing the direction in which they flow, constantly moving, without going anywhere. The fact that our life represents merely the foreground, with death standing behind it as the only certainty – this is the final reason, as Schopenhauer says, for the 'absolute ambiguity' of life; for if an appearance does not grow from a root, whose sap will hold it in one direction, it is left at the mercy of every interpretation. It is permitted to art alone, in its most favoured moments, to take up an existence within an appearance and to proffer it along with itself. For this reason art is not complete and

> beyond artificiality until it is more than art. Florence is like this, a city which gives the wonderful, unambiguous security of a home. Venice, however, has the ambiguous beauty of an adventure, which floats, rootless amidst life, like a torn-off blossom in the sea. The fact that it was and remained the classical city of the adventurers represents only the realization of the eventual fate of its overall image – that it will never be able to be a home, but only ever an adventure for our souls.[16]

A Western city saturated with the East; a city of land and stone everywhere penetrated by water; a city of great piety and ruthless mercantilism; a city where enlightenment and licentiousness, reason and desire, indeed art and nature flow and flower together – Venice is indeed the surpassing-all-other embodiment of that 'absolute ambiguity' which is radiant life containing certain death. On 3 September 1873 Ruskin wrote to his friend, the American art historian Charles Eliot Norton,[17] as follows: 'I am *so* glad you are at work on Venice. You can't have any subject so fine. She's too big for me, now.'

But if she's too big for Ruskin . . .

Notes

Preface

1 Henry James, *European Writers and the Prefaces*, ed. Leon Edel, Library of America (New York, 1984), p. 1070.

Chapter 1 Introduction

1 W. H. Auden, *Collected Shorter Poems 1927–57* (London, 1966), p. 170.
2 Sigmund Freud, *Civilization and its Discontents* (London, 1930), p. 102.
3 Ibid., p. 80.
4 Ibid., p. 72.
5 *Plutarch's Life of Theseus*, trans. Ian Scott Kilvert (London, 1967), 24, 1–4; quoted in Gerald Bruns, 'The metaphorical construction of cities', *Salmagundi*, 74–5 (Spring–Summer 1987), pp. 70–85.
6 Leo Strauss, *The City and Man* (Chicago, 1964), pp. 110–11.
7 Bruns, 'The metaphorical construction of cities', p. 79.
8 Ibid., p. 74.
9 Paul Ginsborg, *Daniel Manin and the Venetian Revolution of 1848–9* (Cambridge, 1979).
10 *The Heart of Emerson's Journals*, ed. Bliss Perry (New York, 1958), p. 72.
11 William Dean Howells, *Venetian Life* (London, 1891), Vol. II, pp. 282–3.
12 Herman Melville, *Journal of a Visit to Europe and the Levant*, ed. Howard C. Horsford (Princeton, NJ, 1955), pp. 233–5.
13 *Selected Poems of Herman Melville*, ed. Hennig Cohen (New York, 1964), p. 144.
14 Ibid., p. 150.
15 Ibid.
16 Quotations are taken from *Robert Browning: The Poems*, vol. II, ed. John Pettigrew (Harmondsworth, 1981), pp. 3–74.
17 Joseph Conrad, *Lord Jim* (1900; London, 1961), p. 214.

CHAPTER 2 LORD BYRON

1 Mrs Piozzi, *Glimpses of Italian Society* (London, 1852), pp. 111–20.
2 Ibid., p. 135.
3 Ibid.
4 Milton Wilson, 'Traveller's Venice: some images from Byron and Shelley', *University of Toronto Quarterly*, 43, 2 (Winter 1974), pp. 93–120.
5 Ann Radcliffe, *The Mysteries of Udolpho* (Harmondsworth, 1966), p. 174.
6 *The Complete Works of John Ruskin*, ed. Edward T. Cook and Alexander Wedderburn (London, 1903–12), vol. 35, p. 293.
7 *Byron's Letters and Journals*, ed. Leslie A. Marchand (London, 1976–8), vol. 5, p. 13 (hereafter abbreviated as *L*, with volume and page numbers); 5 December 1816.
8 *L* 5, 165; 28 January 1817.
9 *L* 6, 5; 8 January 1818.
10 *L* 5, 134; 27 November 1816.
11 *L* 5, 177; 28 February 1817.
12 *L* 5, 187; 25 March 1817.
13 *L* 5, 146; 24 December 1816.
14 Ibid.
15 *L* 6, 66; 19 September 1818.
16 *L* 6, 66; 18 September 1818.
17 *L* 6, 220; 29 August 1819.
18 *L* 6, 232; 26 October 1819.
19 *L* 6, 231; 15 October 1819.
20 *L* 6, 9; 27 January 1818.
21 *L* 5, 136; 27 November 1816.
22 *L* 6, 192–8.
23 *L* 6, 232; 26 October 1819.
24 *L* 6, 226; 3 October 1819.
25 *L* 5, 146; 19 December 1816.
26 *L* 6, 217; 3 October 1819.
27 *L* 5, 176; 28 February 1817.
28 Quoted in John Buxton, *Byron and Shelley* (London, 1968), p. 95.
29 Ibid., p. 82.
30 *L* 5, 129.
31 *L* 6, 237; 29 October 1819.
32 *L* 6, 262; 31 December 1819.
33 *L* 6, 236; 29 October 1819.
34 *L* 5, 138; 4 December 1816.
35 *L* 5, 130; 5 December 1816.
36 *L* 5, 137; 5 December 1816.
37 *L* 5, 142; 19 December 1816.
38 *L* 5, 203; 2 April 1817.
39 *L* 5, 244; 1 July 1817.
40 Wilson, 'Traveller's Venice?', p. 99.

41 Charles Dickens, *Little Dorrit* (London, 1954), p. 479.
42 *L* 5, 129; 17 November 1816.
43 *L* 5, 132; 25 November 1816.
44 Geoffrey Ward, in *Byron and the Limits of Fiction*, ed. Bernard Beatty and Vincent Newey (Liverpool, 1988), p. 194.
45 *Georg Simmel 1858–1918*, (1911) 'Die Ruine' trans David Kettler, (Ohio, 1959), pp. 259–68.
46 Lord Byron, *The Complete Poetical Works*, ed. Jerome McGann, vol. II (Oxford, 1980), p. 228, note to line 134.
47 Jerome McGann, *Fiery Dust* (Chicago, 1968), pp. 133, 159.
48 Vincent Newey, in *Byron and the Limits of Fiction*, p. 148.
49 Byron, *Complete Poetical Works*, vol. II, p. 236.
50 *L* 6, 9; 27 January 1818.
51 *L* 6, 207; 12 August 1819.
52 Terry Castle, *Masquerade and Civilization* (London, 1986), p. 76.
53 Mikhail Bakhtin, *Rabelais and his World*, trans. Helene Iswolsky (Cambridge, Mass., 1968), p. 119.
54 Castle, *Masquerade and Civilization*, p. 25.
55 Ibid., p. 84.
56 *L* 6, 67; 19 September 1818.
57 *L* 5, 125; 6 November 1816.
58 Quotations from *Beppo* are taken from Byron, *The Complete Poetical Works*, ed. Jerome McGann, vol. IV (Oxford, 1986).
59 *L* 6, 11; 20 February 1818.
60 Wilson, 'Traveller's Venice'.
61 Drummond Bone, in *Byron and the Limits of Fiction*, pp. 97–125.
62 Ibid., p. 105.
63 *L* 5, 203; 2 April 1817.
64 *Marino Faliero*, V. i. 502–5 (hereafter abbreviated as *MF*, with act, scene and line numbers); in Byron, *Complete Poetical Works*, vol. IV, pp. 244–446.
65 *The Two Foscari*, III. i. 15–21, 25–9, 118–22 (hereafter abbreviated as *TF*, with act, scene and line numbers); in *The Poetical Works of Lord Byron* (Oxford, 1964), pp. 492–520.
66 *L* 8, 153; 14 July 1821.
67 *L* 7, 37; 22 July 1820.
68 *L* 7, 190; 1 October 1820.
69 *L* 7, 237; 23 November 1820.
70 *L* 7, 184; 29 September 1820.
71 *L* 7, 194; 8 October 1820.
72 *L* 7, 195; 8 October 1820.
73 *L* 8, 187; 23 August 1821.
74 Malcolm Kensall, *Byron's Politics* (Harvester, 1987), pp. 91, 117.

CHAPTER 3 JOHN RUSKIN

1 *The Complete Works of John Ruskin*, ed. Edward T. Cook and Alexander Wedderburn (London, 1903–12), vol. 11, p. 233. Unless otherwise noted, all

references are to this edition, hereafter abbreviated as *CW*, with volume and page numbers.

2 Denis Cosgrove, 'The myth and the stones of Venice', *Journal of Historical Geography*, 8, 2 (1987), pp. 145–169.

3 See, for example, John Gage, 'Turner in Venice', in *Projecting the Landscape*, Anu, HRC Monograph no. 4 (1987), pp. 72–7.

4 Quoted in Jeanne Clegg, *Ruskin and Venice* (London, 1981). This is the absolutely seminal work on Ruskin and Venice and my debt to it will be clear throughout this chapter.

5 Cosgrove, 'The myth and the stones of Venice', pp. 86, 147, 148.

6 Clegg, *Ruskin and Venice*, p. 110.

7 Dante, *Inferno*, Temple Classics (London, 1964), vol. I. pp. 93–5.

8 She came for him again, this time in the form of a cloud, drawn and described in *Modern Painters*, vol. V – 'the serpents about her head are the fringes of the hail, the idea of coldness being connected by the Greeks with the bite of the serpent, as with hemlock' (*CW* 7, 184). The accompanying illustration was entitled 'Venga Medusa'.

9 I note, and only note (since it would be hard to imagine a more petty activity than the attempt to catch this majestic and tragic mind out in contradictions), that in a strange chapter entitled 'Castel-Franco' added to the Travellers' Edition of 1877 Ruskin asserts: 'Never in the moral or material universe does the great art of man acknowledge guilt, grief, change, or fear' (*CW* 11, 241). By this time Ruskin no longer cared to see the 'horrors and phantasms' rising in art, perhaps because too many of them had started to rise in his own life.

10 This was the incident as reconstructed in *Fors*, letter 76: 'in 1858, it was with me, Protestantism or nothing: the crisis of the whole turn of my thoughts being one Sunday morning, at Turin, when, from being before Paul Veronese's Queen of Sheba, and under quite overwhelmed sense of his God-given power, I went away to a Waldensian chapel, where a little squeaking idiot was preaching to an audience of seventeen old women and three louts, that they were the only children of God in Turin; and that all the people in Turin outside the chapel, and all the people in the world out of sight of Monte Viso, would be damned. I came out of the chapel, in sum of twenty years of thought, a conclusively *un*-converted man' (*CW* 29, 29).

11 Francis Haskell, 'The Old Masters in nineteenth-century French painting', *The Arts Quarterly*, 24, 1 (1973), p. 73.

12 Geryon and fraud were to be crucial for Ezra Pound.

13 Dante, *Inferno*, canto VI, pp. 66–7.

14 Ruskin would have understood, and approved of, a comment made by Henry James recalling some cardinals he had seen in procession in Rome: 'as they advance the lifted black petticoat reveals a flash of scarlet stockings and makes you groan at the victory of civilization over colour'; *Italian Hours* (New York, 1958), p. 147.

15 Quoted in T. Pignatti, *Giorgione* (Oxford, 1971), p. 73.

16 Henry James, *A Small Boy and Others* (London, 1956), p. 3.

17 Gerard Manley Hopkins, *Collected Poems* (Oxford, 1952), pp. 103–4.

18 There is nothing new under the sun. When I wrote this I thought it was an original observation. But there it is in John Davenport's fine essay, 'The house that Jack built', in *Geography of the Imagination* (London, 1984). His development of the comparison is different from mine, but characteristically brilliant.

19 Ezra Pound, *The Cantos* (London, 1986), canto XLV; all quotations are taken from this edition.

20 See, in particular, Peter Nicholls, *Ezra Pound: Politics, Economics and Writing* (London, 1984).

21 Ruskin's father quite early on complained that his son was producing 'a mass of Hieroglyphics – all true – Truth itself – but Truth in mosaic' (*CW* 8, xxiii).

CHAPTER 4 HENRY JAMES

1 *Letters of Henry James*, ed. Leon Edel, 4 vols (London, 1974–84), vol. I, p. 134; hereafter abbreviated as *L*, with volume and page numbers.

2 *Complete Tales of Henry James*, ed. Leon Edel, 12 vols (London, 1962), vol. II; hereafter abbreviated as *T*, with volume and page numbers.

3 'Other Tuscan Cities', in *Italian Hours* (New York, 1958), p. 319; hereafter abbreviated as *IH*, with page numbers.

4 'Siena Early and Late', *IH* 259.

5 Henry James, *The Princess Casamassima* (New York, 1959), p. 276.

6 Ibid., p. 334.

7 Barbara Melchiori, in Sergio Perasa (ed.), *Henry James e Venezia* (Florence, 1985), p. 131.

8 *The Complete Notebooks of Henry James*, ed. Leon Edel (Oxford, 1987), p. 23; hereafter abbreviated as *N*, with page numbers.

9 Henry James, *European Writers and the Prefaces*, ed. Leon Edel, Library of America (New York, 1984), pp. 1173–4.

10 Ibid., pp. 1177–9.

11 Robert Browning, *Poetical Works 1833–1864*, ed. Ian Jack (Oxford, 1970), p. 580.

12 *The Aspern Papers and Other Stories*, ed. Adrian Poole, World's Classics (Oxford, 1983), p. 202.

13 Ibid., p. 201.

14 Henry James, *Essays, American and English Writers*, ed. Leon Edel, Library of America (New York, 1984), pp. 107–8.

15 James, *European Writers*, p. 739.

16 Ibid., p. 776.

17 Ibid., p. 777.

18 Ibid., p. 740.

19 Ibid., p. 740.

20 Ibid., pp. 742–3.

21 Perosa (ed.), *Henry James e Venezia*, p. 54, in a very interesting essay by Alide Cagiddemetrio.

22 D. C. Woodcox, 'The travel essays of Henry James and Edith Wharton', D. Phil, thesis (Oxford, 1990), p. 299.

23 Henry James, *The Wings of the Dove* (Harmondsworth, 1966), p. 99; hereafter abbreviated as *W*, with page numbers.
24 *The Complete Works of John Ruskin*, ed. Edward T. Cook and Alexander Wedderburn (London, 1903–12), vol. 10, p. 84.
25 Ibid., vol. 10, pp. 141–2.

CHAPTER 5 HUGO VON HOFMANNSTHAL

1 Hermann Broch, *Hugo von Hofmannsthal and his Time* (1947–50; trans. Chicago, 1984), esp. pp. 117–25.
2 *The Selected Prose of Hugo von Hofmannsthal*, trans. Mary Holtinger and Tania and James Stern, intro. Hermann Broch (London, 1952), p. 130; hereafter abbreviated as *H*, with page numbers.
3 Carl Schorske, *Fin de Siècle Vienna* (Cambridge, 1981), p. 317.
4 Broch, *Hugo von Hofmannsthal and his Time*, pp. 138–9.
5 Ibid., p. 130.

CHAPTER 6 MARCEL PROUST

1 Marcel Proust, *Contre Sainte-Beuve*, ed. Pierra Clarac (Paris, 1971), pp. 520–1 (my translation).
2 Marcel Proust, *On Reading Ruskin*, trans. and ed. Jean Autret, William Burford and Phillip J. Wolfe (New Haven, Conn., 1987), p. 81; hereafter abbreviated as *ORR*, with page numbers.
3 Marcel Proust, *Remembrance of Things Past*, trans. C. K. S. Moncrieff and T. Kilmartin, 3 vols (Harmondsworth, 1984), vol. III, p. 926; hereafter referenced in the text with volume and page numbers only.
4 Marcel Proust, *Selected Letters*, ed. Philip L. Kolb, trans. T. Kilmartin (London, 1989), vol. II, p. 210; hereafter abbreviated as *L*, with volume and page numbers.
5 The bibliographical details are something of a nightmare. For my purposes, suffice it to say that in 1954 Gallimard published a collection of some of these essays and fragments, together with the material on Sainte-Beuve, edited by Bernard de Fallois, and simply entitled *Contre Sainte-Beuve* (Paris, 1954); this edition is hereafter abbreviated as *CSB*. A new collection, also entitled *Contre-Sainte Beuve*, was published by Gallimard in 1971 (see note 1 above). The following quotations are taken from the English edition, *By Way of Sainte-Beuve*, trans. Sylvia Townsend Warner (London, 1958); hereafter abbreviated as *BWSB*, with page numbers.
6 Peter Collier, *Proust and Venice* (Cambridge, 1989), p. 21. I greatly admire this book, and learned from it. Inevitably some of our material overlaps – but we have different ends in view.
7 Ibid., pp. 79 ff.
8 *The Complete Works of John Ruskin*, ed. Edward T. Cook and Alexander Wedderburn (London, 1903–12), vol. 10. pp. 141–2.

9 *Sésame et les lys*, Editions Complexes (Paris, 1987), p. 159.
10 The words are, of course, Yeats's, from 'The Song of the Happy Shepherd', *Collected Poems* (London, 1955), p. 7:

> But O, sick children of the world,
> Of all the many changing things
> In dreary dancing past us whirled,
> To the cracked tune that Chronos sings,
> Words alone are certain good.

CHAPTER 7 EZRA POUND

1 Marcel Proust, *On Reading Ruskin*, trans. and ed. Jean Autret, William Burford and Phillip J. Wolfe (New Haven, Conn., 1987), p. 27; hereafter abbreviated as *ORR*, with page numbers.
2 *The Correspondence of John Ruskin and Charles Eliot Norton*, ed. John Bradley and Ian Ousby (Cambridge, 1987), p. 297.
3 *The Selected Letters of Ezra Pound*, ed. Forrest Read (New York, 1968), p. 212; hereafter abbreviated as *L*, with page numbers.
4 *Selected Prose of Ezra Pound*, ed. William Cookson (London, 1973), p. 194; hereafter abbreviated as *SP*, with page numbers.
5 There is only one acknowledgement of Ruskin's importance in the *Cantos*, and that an indirect one: '"What he meant to *us* in those days" / said old Image (Selwyn) referring to Ruskin.' Ezra Pound, *The Cantos* (London, 1987), canto LXXXIX, p. 601.
6 See *Ezra Pound and the Visual Arts*, ed. Harriet Zinnes (New York, 1980); hereafter abbreviated as *EPVA*.
7 Lee Bartlett and Hugh Witemeyer, 'Ezra Pound and James Dickey: a correspondence and a kinship', *Paideuma*, 11, 2 (1982), pp. 292–3.
8 *Pavannes and Divagations* (London, 1960), pp. 3, 5.
9 Ibid., pp. 5–6.
10 Ibid., pp. 3–4.
11 John Gould Fletcher, *Life is my Song* (New York and Toronto, 1937), p. 60.
12 *The Cantos* (London, 1987), canto XLV, p, 230; hereafter references to this edition of the *Cantos* appear with canto and page number only.
13 *The Complete Works of John Ruskin*, ed. Edward T. Cook and Alexander Wedderburn (London, 1903–12), vol. 9, pp. 130–2.
14 Ibid., vol. 9, pp. 377–9.
15 Hugh Witemeyer, 'Ruskin and the signed capital in canto 45', *Paideuma*, 4, 1 (1975), p. 87.
16 Ezra Pound, *Personae* (London, 1952), p. 201; hereafter abbreviated as *P*, with page numbers.
17 Witemeyer, 'Ruskin and the signed capital', p. 24.
18 Ruskin, *Complete Works*, vol. 17, p. 54.
19 Ibid., vol. 17, pp. 61–2.
20 Ibid., vol. 17, pp. 63–4. On this passage – and it is a nice coincidence that he

should have translated 'Of Kings' Treasuries'; – Proust commented: 'this sort of obscurity which envelops the splendor of beautiful books like that of beautiful mornings, is a natural obscurity, the breath in some way of genius, that it gives forth without knowing it, and not an artificial veil with which he willfully surrounded his work in order to hide it from the common people.' And he talks of a great work's 'noble atmosphere of silence, that marvelous varnish which shines with the sacrifice of all that has not been said' (*ORR* 152–3). We might fairly apply that to the *Cantos.*

21 *Literary Essays of Ezra Pound*, ed. T. S. Eliot (London, 1985), p. 269; hereafter abbreviated as *LE*, with page numbers.
22 Ruskin, *Complete Works*, vol. 17, p. 66.
23 Ezra Pound, *Guide to Kulchur* (London, 1978), p. 16; hereafter abbreviated as *GTK*, with page numbers.
24 Ruskin, *Complete Works*, vol. 17, p. 65.
25 Ibid., vol. 17, pp. 68–9.
26 Ibid., vol. 17, p. 84.
27 Ibid., vol. 17, p. 103.
28 Ibid., vol. 17, p. 103, note 1.
29 'Und Drang', in *Collected Early Poems of Ezra Pound*, ed. Michael John King (London, 1977), p. 167; hereafter abbreviated as *CEP*, with page numbers.
30 Robert Browning, *Sordello*, book III, ll. 610–14, in *Browning: Poetical Works 1833–1864*, ed. Ian Jack (London, 1970), p. 224; subsequent book, line and page numbers refer to this edition, unless otherwise stated.
31 Ibid., III, ll. 676–730; pp. 226–7. (The later version appears in *Robert Browning's Poems and Plays*, ed. John Bryson, Everyman Library (London, 1956), vol. I, p. 272.)
32 Browning, *Sordello*, I, ll. 35–50; p. 158.
33 Ibid., III, ll. 745–85; pp. 228–9.
34 From ur-canto I, first published in *Poetry*, 10, 3 (January 1917); repr. in Ronald Bush, *The Genesis of Ezra Pound's Cantos* (Princeton, NJ, 1976), pp. 54–60.
35 Bush, *The Genesis of Ezra Pound's Cantos*, pp. 86, 117.
36 Browning, *Sordello*, V, ll. 625–51; pp. 278–9.
37 Ibid., III, l. 137.
38 Ibid., V, ll. 580, 598, 626; pp. 276–7.
39 Quoted in Peter Collier, *Proust and Venice* (Cambridge, 1989), pp. 40–1.
40 Thomas Hardy, *The Laodicean* (London, 1958), p. 164.
41 Browning, *Sordello*, I, ll. 409–27; pp. 167–8.
42 Ibid., I, ll. 897–9; p. 180.
43 Ibid., I, ll. 59–60; p. 158.
44 Guy Davenport, *Cities on Hills* (Ann Arbor, Mich., 1983), p. 36. Of the many good writers on Pound, Davenport seems to me the best and I have learned a lot from his fine work.
45 Bush, *The Genesis of Ezra Pound's Cantos*, pp. 140–1.
46 Davenport, *Cities on Hills*, p. 50.
47 Dante, *Purgatorio*, Temple Classics (London, 1962), vol. II, pp. 22–3.
48 Dante, *Paradiso*, Temple Classics (London, 1962), vol. III, pp. 90–1.
49 Ibid., pp. 92–3.

50 Michael Bernstein, 'Image, word, and sign: the visual arts as evidence in Ezra Pound's *Cantos*', *Critical Inquiry*, 12 (Winter 1986), p. 360.
51 Robert Hollander, *Boccaccio's Two Venuses* (New York, 1969).
52 Davenport, *Cities on Hills*, p. 197.
53 Hugh Kenner, *The Pound Era* (Berkeley, Cal., 1971), p. 422.
54 Donald Davie, *The Poet as Sculptor* (London, 1965), p. 129.
55 Davenport, *Cities on Hills*, p. 199.
56 Ben D. Kimpel and T. C. Duncan Eaves, *Paideuma*, 11, 3 (Winter 1982), p. 419.
57 Davenport, *Cities on Hills*, p. 171.
58 Ibid., p. 178.
59 Adrian Stokes, *The Stones of Rimini* (London, 1934; New York, 1969); hereafter abbreviated as *SR*, with page numbers referring to the 1969 edition.
60 Davie, *The Poet as Sculptor*, esp. pp. 127–31, 155–6.
61 See John Hamilton Edwards and William W. Vasse, *Annotated Index to the Cantos of Ezra Pound* (Berkeley, Cal., 1957), p. 106. This work is indispensable.
62 This is a subject in itself, but two quotations may serve here. First, from W. B. Yeats: 'He has shown me upon the wall a photograph of a Cosimo Tura decoration in three compartments, in the upper the Triumph of Love and the Triumph of Chastity, in the middle Zodiacal signs, and in the lower certain events in Cosimo Tura's day. The Descent and the Metamorphosis . . . his fixed elements, took the place of the Zodiac, the archetypal persons . . . that of the Triumphs, and certain modern events . . . that of those events in Cosimo Tura's day': *A Vision* (London, 1937), p. 5. And from Pound himself in interview: 'The Schifanoia does give – and there is an analogy there. That is to say, you've got the contemporary life, you've got the seasons, you've got the Zodiac and you have the *Triumphs* of Petrarch in different belts': William Cookson, *A Guide to the Cantos of Ezra Pound* (London, 1985), p. 33. That Pound was trying to combine, or juxtapose, the contemporary, the seasonal and the fixed – elemental, archetypal, divine – in some similar sort of way seems clear enough. See Davenport, *Cities on Hills*, pp. 81–9.
63 Davenport, *Cities on Hills*, pp. 223–4.
64 Edwards and Vasse, *Annotated Index*, p. 175.
65 Ruskin, *Complete Works*, vol. 10, p. 343.
66 Ibid., vol. 10, pp. 337, 340.
67 I know of only one other reference to Titian in Pound's writing, and here again he seems to stand somewhere between the art Pound esteemed and the art he deprecated. 'At the age of twelve I found what I thought was a good painting in some Roman or Neapolitan gallery. I liked it because it was a prettier lady than I cd. find in any other frame. (Titian's *La Vanita, the outlines are fairly clear.*)' (*EPVA* 305; my italics). He continues: 'At 21 I entered the Velasquez room of the Prado and wondered what all the fuss was about. . . . I still really prefer Carpaccio, and the Bellini in Rimini, and Piero Francesco and in general paintings with clearly defined outlines to any with muzzy edges' (ibid.). This was writted in 1929, and thus around the time of the composing of the Venetian cantos, XXV and XXVI.

68 *The Cantos*, New Collected Edition I–CIX (London, 1984), p. 122.
69 T. S. Eliot, *Collected Poems* (London, 1954), p. 40.
70 Giorgio Melchiori, in Sergio Perosa (ed.), *Henry James e Venezia* (Florence, 1985), p. 118.
71 Davenport, *Cities on Hills*, p. 228.
72 In Perosa (ed.), *Henry James e Venezia*, p. 118.
73 Alexander Pope, *Imitation of Horace*, book l, epistle I, ll. 132–3.
74 Davenport, *Cities on Hills*, p. 231.
75 See John Julius Norwich, *History of Venice* (Harmondsworth, 1983), p. 60.
76 Davenport, *Cities on Hills*, p. 233.
77 Ibid., p. 24.
78 See Cookson, *A Guide to the Cantos*, p. 142.
79 But see Guy Davenport's essay 'Persephone's Ezra', in *Geography of the Imagination* (London, 1984), pp. 141–64.
80 Cookson, *A Guide to the Cantos*, p. 138. This is another indispensable work.
81 Dante, *Inferno*, Temple Classics (London, 1964), vol. I, p. 180.
82 Ibid., pp. 180–1.
83 Ibid., pp. 176–7.
84 Michael Bernstein, *Tale of the Tribe* (Princeton, NJ, 1980); see in particular pp. 127–61 of this excellent book.
85 Ruskin, *Complete Works*, vol. 10, p. 132.
86 Collier sees the whole of Proust's novel as 'one enormous, three-dimensional mosaic': *Proust and Venice*, p. 41.
87 Marcel Proust, *Remembrance of Things Past*, trans. C. K. S. Moncrieff and T. Kilmartin, 3 vols (London, 1986), vol. III, pp. 924–5; my italics.

CHAPTER 8 CONCLUSION

1 See the excellent biography of Rilke, *A Ringing Glass*, by Donald Prater (Oxford, 1986), pp. 32–3.
2 Rainer Maria Rilke, *Selected Letters 1902–1926* (London, 1988), p. 39.
3 Prater, *A Ringing Glass*, pp. 176–7.
4 Rainer Maria Rilke, *New Poems*, trans. J. B. Leishman (London, 1964), pp. 244–5.
5 Ibid., p. 247.
6 Ibid., p. 245.
7 Rilke, *Selected Letters*, pp. 303–4.
8 Thomas Mann, 'Death in Venice', in *Stories of a Lifetime*, vol. II, trans. H. T. Lowe-Porter (London, 1961), p. 18; hereafter referred to in the text by page number only.
9 Erich Heller makes this point in his excellent section on the novella in *The Ironic German* (London, 1958), pp. 98–115.
10 Mann perhaps had in mind the last great outbreak of cholera in Europe that occurred in 1895 in Hamburg, where the authorities behaved in a similar way. See Richard Evans, *Death in Hamburg* (Oxford, 1987).

11 Jean-Paul Sartre, 'Le Séquestré de Venise', *Situations IV* (Paris, 1964), pp. 291–346.
12 *Situations IV*, trans. Benita Eisler (London, 1965), p. 1.
13 Ibid., p. 38.
14 Ibid., p. 60.
15 Jean-Paul Sartre, 'Venise de ma fenêtre', *Situations IV* (Paris, 1964), pp. 444–59.
16 Georg Simmel, 'Venedig', *Zur Philosophie der Kunst* (Potsdam, 1922). No English translation of this essay has been published. This translation is by Jayne Barret, to whom I am most grateful.
17 *The Correspondence of John Ruskin and Charles Eliot Norton* (Cambridge, 1987), p. 297.

INDEX

Index

Index